Eucharist *and* Globalization

Eucharist *and* Globalization

Redrawing the Borders of Eucharistic Hospitality

CLÁUDIO CARVALHAES

PICKWICK *Publications* · Eugene, Oregon

EUCHARIST AND GLOBALIZATION
Redrawing the Borders of Eucharistic Hospitality

Pickwick Publications
An Imprint of Wipf and Stock Publishers
199 W. 8th Ave., Suite 3
Eugene, OR 97401

www.wipfandstock.com

ISBN 13: 978-1-61097-346-5

Cataloguing-in-Publication data:

Carvalhaes, Cláudio.

    Eucharist and globalization : redrawing the borders of eucharistic hospitality /
Cláudio Carvalhaes.

    x + 330 pp. ; 23 cm. Includes bibliographical references and index.

    ISBN 13: 978-1-61097-346-5

    1. Liturgics. 2. Globalization—Religious aspects—Christianity. 3. Close and
open communion. I. Title.

BV873.L6 .C38 2013

To my *Mother*, Esther Carvalhaes,
who studied up to the second grade,

and to my *Father*, Waldemar Carvalhaes,
who studied up to the fourth grade.

Contents

Acknowledgments   *ix*

Introduction   1

1   Borders, Globalization, and Eucharistic Hospitality   15

2   Eucharist and Hospitality and the Early
      Christian Meals   35

3   Reformed Eucharist and Hospitality   78

4   Feminist Liturgies, Borders, and Hospitality   141

5   Latin American Hospitality and Sacraments   166

6   Christians and Yorubá People Eating Together
      —Eucharist and Food Offerings   203

7   Performing Hospitable Eucharistic
      Borderless Borders   242

      Conclusion: *Onkotô?*   294

      Bibliography   307

      Index   321

Acknowledgments

THIS WHOLE PROCESS OF writing needed the help and support of so many people and I must start this book with gratitude, since this book is about Eucharist, thanksgiving! Two very special people shaped me in deep ways: my advisers Professors Jaci C. Maraschin and Janet R. Walton. Without their love, wisdom, care, endless patience, and continued *real presence*, I would not have come this far. They taught me to love liturgy. Also, Professors Delores S. Williams, Randall Styers, Roger Haight, Hal Taussig, Rosemary Ruether Radford, David Jensen, Martha Moore-Keish, Siobhán Garrigan, Nancy Cardoso Pereira, and Christopher Elwood offered their wisdom and critical analysis of my work. Professors John C. W. Webster and Paul Galbreath read the manuscript very closely several times and helped me put this book in shape. Obrigado to Zé Neves, my precious Brazilian friend, non-documented immigrant, member of our little church in Massachusetts, and illustrator of the book, who is now celebrating the real meal with Jesus. My thanks to Gene LeCouteur who did a wonderful job proofreading and formatting the book, and to Emily A. Everett who carefully read one of the versions. Many thanks to Charlie Collier, my editor, to Dave Belcher, Patrick Harrison, and to Wipf and Stock Publishers for publishing the book. I am grateful to Union Theological Seminary for the wonderful teaching I received there. I am grateful to Louisville Presbyterian Theological Seminary for giving me the conditions to work on this book and now to Lutheran Theological Seminary at Philadelphia for welcoming me as their new professor of liturgy and worship. To all of my students who stretched me and taught me more than I knew. To Drs. Sheila Erlich and Bill Stanley for being with me through difficult times. To Paul Galbreath, Penny Webster, Pam Garner, Dean Thompson, Ann Deibert, Brad J. Wigger, Christopher Elwood, Amy Plantinga Pauw, Carol Cook, Dianne Reistroffer, Loren Townsend, Johanna W. H. Bos, Clifton Kirkpatrick, Scott C. Williamson, David R Sawyer, David Gambrell, Robina Wimbush, Esther F. S. Carvalhaes, Miriam Rosa dos Santos, Marcos Oliveira dos Santos Datdtv, Jorge Sayago-Gonzalez, and also to

Acknowledgments

Rebecca Barnes, Josh Robinson, and Rev. Jeanette Cooper Hicks' families, all of them very special friends who helped me in ways that they only know. To my father and mother, my sisters Mércia and Ana Maria, my brother José, my in-laws Lola and Reginaldo, and my nephews and nieces in Brazil, who have always been a powerful, real, and loving presence to me. Especially Rebeca Carvalhaes Ortiz, my adorable niece.

To each one of these amazing people, my honor and my deepest thanksgiving.

Introduction

The constancy of God in my life is called by other names.
—Jacques Derrida

Óscar Romero, archbishop of El Salvador, died at the Eucharistic altar while celebrating Mass. His work against oppression and violence and his fight for justice and for the poor in his country were not separate from what he did and said at the Eucharistic altar. As a way to fight governmental repression and corruption and to engage *campesinos* in the struggle against oppression, Archbishop Romero once cancelled masses throughout the country on a Sunday morning except at the cathedral in San Salvador. He intended to call attention to the rampant violence in his country and to organize people to fight against the regime that was supported by the U.S. government. Around the table, a new world was called for, rehearsed, and organized. Through gathering at the altar, the ground of God's holy, just, and communal food was to be spread around the country to transform structures of injustice, unchain the ties of misery, and turn lives and land into a holy, just, and communal ground. There, around bread and wine, the life and death of a people were at stake, the pulsing of life for many and God's option for the poor over and against the threatening powers that sustained oppressive governance, abuse, and exploitation. Around singing and the passing of the peace, a time of justice and solidarity with the poor was to gain new meaning. Around bread and wine came an unwavering call issued by God for all to live together in solidarity and love. Through the Bible reading, homilies, prayers, and singing, there was a staunch affirmation that the common good was indeed for all and not just for a few! Signs and actions of resistance saying yes to God's life and no to the powers of death!

Christian masses became a scary place for the powers that be, a continuous in-and-out movement of people empowered by the Holy Spirit, invigorated by the struggles on the street, and a celebration of God's love enacting the dangerous memories of Jesus Christ to bring about a revolution: freedom, justice, solidarity, dignity, and life for all!

Romero's life, words,[1] ministry, and liturgies created enemies and he died while celebrating a Mass. Around the table were power dynamics, economic interests, and class struggles. Popular imagination would say that Archbishop Romero was even holding the host while he was shot dead. His death is emblematic of a fundamental connection between the Gospel of Jesus Christ and the struggle for a world of justice, between the liturgical work of the church of Christ and the social and political life of communities and countries.[2]

Archbishop Romero's death at the Eucharistic altar served as a witness to the death of Christ, as the death of the poor announces/ have announced/ will always announce the many injustices that shape and try to define our world. However, the death of Archbishop Romero at the altar of Christ also announces/ has announced/ will always announce that the gospel of Jesus Christ carries this kernel of unsettlement, of uneasiness, of critique, and unrest, this always annoying and revolutionary challenge of love, justice, egalitarianism, peace, and hospitality for the time we call now, and for any power that is. The breaking of the bread and the pouring of the wine promise a new time, now and always, a new earth and new heaven, where justice will roll down like a river, as we rest assured by the promises of God that our tears will be wiped away and we all will be freely welcomed at the altar/table/feast of Christ.

1. "In our preaching to rich and poor, it is not that we pander to the sins of the poor and ignore the virtues of the rich. Both have sins and both need conversion. But the poor, in their condition of need, are disposed to conversion. They are more conscious of their need of God. All of us, if we really want to know the meaning of conversion and of faith and confidence in another, must become poor, or at least make the cause of the poor our own inner motivation. That is when one begins to experience faith and conversion: when one has the heart of the poor, when one knows that financial capital, political influence, and power are worthless, and that without God we are nothing. To feel that need of God is faith and conversion" (Romero, *Church Is All of You*, 61).

2. Throughout Latin America the relation between the sacraments, liturgical practices, and social-political practices is deeply marked especially in the Roman Catholic Church. In Brazil, the work of people like Dom Helder Camara, Paulo Evaristo Arns, and Pedro Casaldáliga leading the church against the military government was fundamental to leading the church in resistance. In Argentina the resistance work of Carlos Mujica, Enrique Angelelli had them killed. In Chile, the work of the church against the rule of Augusto Pinochet can be seen in the work of Cavanaugh, *Torture and Eucharist*. However, more than the work of single individuals, these priests represent the work of the church as a whole against exploitation and oppression.

The sacrament of the Eucharist is one of the most powerful rituals in the Western world. It has been practiced in different ways for two thousand years and has defined the ways of living the faith and being Christian around the world. As we shall see, the Eucharist is not a thing in itself, a self-enclosed ritual that has nothing to do with the world "outside" of the borders of the ritual and the church itself. Instead, this Christian practice crosses boundaries as it affects laws, shapes behaviors, forms politics and counter-politics, issues ethical demands, and creates worldviews. Whatever we do at, in, or around the Communion altar/table is fundamentally connected to the very practical ways we live. The Eucharistic table gives us a framework that guides us in our decision-making as we are constantly re-creating this world of God. As we re-create the world, how do eucharistic tables deal with our time and offer hospitality to our disastrous world, so as to create a "new world"?

Our world is in such distress. The processes of globalization are daily shaping a new world order, deeply affecting the ways we live. The mobility of people around the globe has become a huge, complex, and divisive issue in our time. The borders of countries have been pressed by political, economic, military influences more than ever; the idea of the nation-state is up for redefinition. The United Nations has published a long study guide to understand this global transformation where they state that two hundred million people are moving around the globe.[3]

International migration has been both a cause and an effect of the globalization process. The world's neo-liberal "unregulated" free market economy is expanding its economic controlled, exclusionist boundaries against poor countries, making thousands of people move from their homes to places where the money is located. As an extension of the unregulated market is the paradoxical regulated agreements between rich nations to protect their economies. The NAFTA agreements for example, show how the United States are subsidizing their farmers making it impossible for countries like Mexico and its farmers to compete in the market.

3. "According to the UN's Population Division, there are now almost 200 million international migrants, a number equivalent to the fifth most populous country on earth, Brazil. It is more than double the figure recorded in 1980, only 25 years previously. Migrants are now to be found in every part of the globe, some of them moving within their own region and others traveling from one part of the world to another. Almost half of all immigrants are women, a growing proportion of who are migrating independently" (Global Commission on International Migration, "Migration in an Interconnected World: New Directions for Action," Report of Global Commission on International Migration, United Nations, October 2005: http://www.queensu.ca/samp/migrationresources/reports/gcim-complete-report-2005.pdf).

Moreover, big agribusiness corporations are buying lands in poorer countries, overusing their natural resources, dumping garbage in their front and backyards and pushing for uncontrollable desires/consumerism[4] without any notion of the limits of the earth. Such "unruled" economic movements have disastrous consequences for the world such as: unemployment, floods, draughts, and excruciating economic inequalities that widen the gap between richer and poorer countries.[5] Even more, it has produced millions of destitute people whose living conditions are minimal, where survival is the only mode of life. For those who can afford to move, they search for a better life elsewhere,[6] redrawing the once known limits of religious, political, social, economic, class, ethnic, and sexual borders.

In the midst of this chaos, there are movements of resistance rising and growing everywhere. *Via Campesina*, Landless Movement in Brazil, the Arab Spring, and the Occupy Movement are but a few of these movements of resistance and transformation around the globe proposing new ways of engaging with capital, of producing, of sharing resources and of establishing communal ways of living.

These demanding global issues have a profound effect upon the ways in which Christian believers live and profess their faith in Jesus Christ, as indeed they should. In this book, I want to join and engage these movements by bringing to the forefront of our faith beliefs and practices, the celebration of the Eucharist and its powerful message/practice for a world of equal access to production, wealth, land, God, and to the whole world. At the table, we hold the belief that earth, soil, water, seeds, animals, living creatures, and all of the natural resources belong first and foremost to God and thus, to all of the communities of the earth as we belong to them in a web of sustainable, deeply connected living.

Local Christian congregations everywhere must be aware of the complexities of living in our world and engage it in their songs, prayers,

---

4. "The United States comprises 6 per cent of the world's population but it consumes 30–40 per cent of our planet's natural resources" (Steger, *Globalization*, 86).

5. Inclusion and exclusion not only concern individuals but also entire nations from the world economic scenario. The top one hundred richest individuals have more money than dozens of countries in Africa together. The IMF and the World Bank are still neo-colonizing forces that secure the power of the United States empire over many countries.

6. E.g., areas in Rio de Janeiro, Iraq, Mexico, Colombia, Syria, etc., and the destruction of a growing number of less fortunate communities are increasing poverty and thus migration everywhere.

sermons, sacraments and creeds. Christian churches can be powerful social agents in changing unequal and unfair aspects of globalization and can offer a sustainable model for a new world, a more just and humane network of local, national, and international relations. Christian churches are interpreters of the world and can be a place for survival, struggle, imagination, and utopia; Christian churches can be strongholds of hope and sustenance; Christian churches can be ethical markers of the limits of possessions, socializers of the common good, holders of the earth's health and keepers of each other's dignity; Christian churches are movements of disorder and breakers of the law when the order is oppressive and the laws are unjust; Christian churches are symbolic places of sustenance when life is stretched beyond its ability to cope; Christian churches must be like base communities, holders of dreams that rehearse a world of a peace and equality that is yet to come; Christian churches must be holders of a gospel that says that the world of God in Jesus Christ can be just for all.

Through the eucharistic table, Christian churches hold very high that the *oikos* of God is a house where we all can live together, grounded in a *servant economy,* where we become stewards of God's house and God's people. The eco-nomos of the Eucharist is thus deeply related to what Wendell Berry said recently in his lecture at the 41st Jefferson Lecture in the Humanities:

> . . . so I'm nominating economy for an equal standing among the arts and humanities. I mean not economics, but eco-nomos, the making of the human household upon the earth. The arts of adapting kindly the many human households to the earth's many ecosystems and human neighborhoods. This is the economy that the most public and influential economists never talk about. The economy that is the primary vocation and responsibility of every one of us . . . Under the rule of industrial economics, the land, our country, has been pillaged for the enrichment supposedly of those humans who have claimed the right to own and exploit it without limit. Of the land community, much has been consumed. Much has been wasted. Almost nothing has flourished. But this has not been inevitable. We do not have to live as if we are alone.[7]

Eucharist is a constant reminder of this sense of *eco-oiko-nomos,* of our deep relation with the earth as stewards, of our necessary agreement that some people cannot have more than others, because the earth is our

7. Berry, "It All Turns on Affection."

common ground and we need to live together. From this common *oikos* we must always offer a radical hospitality to one another.

In many ways, this work of hospitality grew out of my relationship with poor people in Brazil and non-documented immigrants in the United States. As an officially "alien" resident to this country, working and living with these communities for a long time, I came to realize that the sacrament of the eucharist stands at the heart of our liturgical life. Now, even as I become a citizen, I am still a foreigner in many ways. Notions of multiple belonging, citizenship, authenticity, cultural rubrics, (i.e., the expectation of the performance of foreign cultures and proper ways of behaving) and access are always hovering around the Eucharistic tables. One thing is certain: as bread never comes alone, the Eucharistic table also never comes alone. Around the sacramental table, poor people and undocumented people's lives cross a whole array of boundaries—ecclesiological, theological, liturgical, social, sexual, political, and economic which are fences where their lives are always negotiated. Within and around the table, the poor also have to wrestle with a world that despises them, sees them as failures, a threat, igniters of violence, and deprives them of the benefits of rights, food, health care, jobs, just salaries, and citizenship.

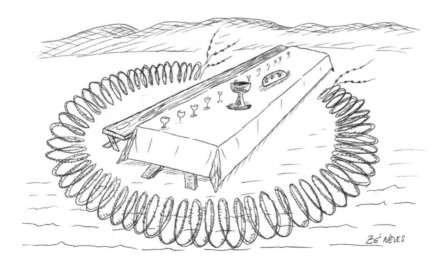

ZÉ NEVES

As a pastor in Presbyterian churches both in Brazil and in the United States, I realized that this table also divides or keeps the division between those who are poor and those who are not. The table clearly has the in- and the outside of itself, and many other sides in between, where there are people celebrating the Eucharist with and without the privilege of accessing life in a fuller way. The access to the table entails more than an inner spiritual exercise since it includes the crossing of the many borders mentioned above. However, on every side of the fence, people participate in the eucharistic meal as if this altar/table is unmarked by any borders. Nonetheless, the table/altar is deeply marked, even tainted by many things. The spiritual (theological, ecclesiological, liturgical) frame one gives to the eucharistic table involves political, economic, and social commitments as well. One does not eat the bread alone, without either implicitly or explicitly making political or identity claims. Bread and wine always come along with political views and markers of exploitation.[8]

This book is an attempt to clarify the presence of these complex borders and to break, expand, and make bridges to impossible places, an exercise of incarnation between order and dis-order, safety and violence, placement and dis-placement and everything in between that marks the location of our liturgical spaces and what goes on in and outside of it. This book crosses many fences, unsafe theological regions, economic injustices, desolate human situations, liturgical deserts, and social classes to locate the political and social markings on the borders of the eucharistic table along with its practices. In the same way that there is no theology that is not also political, so there is no eucharistic sacrament that does not, passively or actively, support or resist, in one way or another, political views and ideological programs.

The Eucharistic rites have overloaded historical relevances to our planet and many possibilities for our communities and personal lives. My hope is both to examine some of these relevances and possibilities and to expand Eucharistic practices and emotions and social actions. As Don Saliers says, "How we pray and worship is linked to how we live—to our desires, emotions, attitudes, beliefs and actions."[9]

In this book I intend to address this connection between church and society, the theological and the political through the Eucharist/Lord's Supper/Communion. Christian practices around the altar/table are deeply related to the ways in which we understand and shape the world around

8. Crossan, *Historical Jesus*.

9. Saliers, "Liturgy and Ethics," 16.

us. This book is about the sacrament of the Eucharist and the endless re-creation of a new and desperately needed world. This book is about the sacrament of the eucharist, its connections and borders, and how these borders mark not only the very relations between God and God's people but also the ways in which we live together in the world. Finally, this book is about how the issue of *hospitality* is configured around church and society through the Eucharistic table/altar.[10]

This feast of hospitality, justice and solidarity for the poor is constantly re-enacted around the Eucharist. There, always at a certain time and in a certain space, in a neighborhood somewhere in the world, we are connected to God, each other and the larger world by the mysterious presence of the Christ through the Holy Spirit. There, at the table/altar, which always points us to elsewhere, under the powerful message of the life, death, and resurrection of Jesus Christ, we experience past, present, and future united in hopes for the fulfillment of history, announcing the new *parousia* of Christ in our midst, creating and realizing a new world order. At this table we say to each other and to the world: Lift up your hearts! Glory be to God! Christ has died, Christ is risen, Christ will come again. We sing Gloria, Alleluia, Christe Eleison, and we pray Come Holy Spirit, come! While we do it, our checking accounts, endowments, credit cards, and possessions will be challenged and we will have to be accountable to the concrete ways we relate to the singing, praying and remembering this mystery.

The questions that guide this research can be summarized as follows: How can we share God's table, the feast prepared by God, with all peoples? In what ways can the Christian church live this *oikos* of equality and offer hospitality through the eucharistic sacrament? How can the borders of the Eucharist be negotiated so that unexpected guests might participate in it? If the problem here is related to borders, what borders are we talking about? In what ways do the borders of the outside world mark the borders of the liturgical space? How do we connect the proposed new global order of justice and solidarity present in the Eucharistic sacrament to a terribly disordered, brutal, violent world? And, is it possible to think and practice the eucharistic rite as a *borderless border* sacrament? In order to answer these questions, I will develop the notion of hospitality through

10. The words *altar* and *table* entail a variety of theologies that clearly divide the Christian churches. Catholics, Episcopalians, Lutherans, and Methodists would call it an altar with very different sacramental theologies, while Presbyterians, Baptists, and Pentecostals would call it a table, also with very different understandings of what this sacrament means.

understandings and practices of the sacrament of the Eucharist in various thinkers and communities from the past.

I am writing as a pastor to local churches, to pastors, deacons, elders, lay people, community leaders, theology students, and social activists, even professors, all of those who are going to wrestle with these concrete situations at their local parishes, streets, work, home, communities, etc. where life is happening in its fullness. They are the ones who are already keeping and undoing borders, making bridges or isolating their communities between social classes, ethnic groups, and religions.

I am focusing *only* on the sacrament of the eucharist and placing this work within the intertwined fields of liturgical and sacramental theologies.[11] I do not want to make any universal claim about how to approach hospitality, or propose universal forms of hospitality, but rather, suggest ways in which local communities can develop forms of hospitality in Eucharists that engage the borders of hospitality in a global sense.

I use the word "Eucharist" instead of "Lord's Supper" or "Communion" to describe the church's sacrament with bread and wine. The word Eucharist means thanksgiving and encompasses a broad Christian tradition. Also, I am choosing the word Eucharist according to the argument I develop within this book, which points to a more accurate understanding of the historical origins of Eucharist/thanksgiving.

Moreover, throughout the book, I use the word "Eucharist" in various ways, even against grammatical rules. In English, one finds the word "Eucharist" with a capital letter as a noun, and the word "eucharistic" either capitalized or not, as an adjective. The fact that this word "cannot" be used without a capital letter is relevant. One can affirm that words are not detached linguistic signs but rather, they carry a load of different meanings according to its cultural usages. In the case of the word Eucharist, it carries heavy western theological meanings.

The capitalized word "Eucharist" conveys the historical order of the sacrament within Christian denominations. The meaning of the word "Eucharist" has to do with the complying with the official ritual rules and theological guidelines defined by each Christian denomination. Thus, the grammatical use of the word Eucharist is directly related to the theological meanings and ritual approvals attached to the word. It is the theological borders that institute the grammatical rules and the limits of the vocabulary usage of the word Eucharist.

---

11. For a contemporary review of the field of sacramental theology and liturgical studies, see Garrigan, *Beyond Ritual*.

In the early Christian churches, the Eucharist never had a fixed practice grounded on a univocal theological meaning. Moreover, throughout history there have been huge debates over its practices and theological understandings. In recent history of the sacrament, feminist and liberation theological inputs, for instance, have expanded the theological notion of the word Eucharist and weighted life aspects and different liturgical celebrations with *Eucharistic* meaning. However, in spite of the expansion of theological qualifications of the adjective "eucharistic," they could not hold the same weight and meaning as the official word/noun "Eucharist" does. The very word Eucharist as one finds in ecclesiological and theological traditions, as well as in the English dictionary, has rarely been theologically and grammatically challenged. Thus, one has to shift the borders of both theological and grammatical rules in order to use the word without a capital letter.

Also, since in this book I am proposing a *borderless border* sacrament, it must also deal with grammatical borders of the sacrament. It is my intention to challenge the sovereignty of meaning of the word Eucharist and de-essentialize the sacrament in its theological, ecclesiastical, and liturgical aspects. This process entails an array of grammatical uses that are inconsistent with the use of the article, singular or plural formats, and the uncertain capitalizing of the word E/eucharist. The probable lack of "clarity" that this inconsistent use of word might bring, aims to remind the reader that the sacrament of the Eucharist might not be as clear as one might think. Besides, that *small* change can spur various ways of thinking and practicing eucharist(s).

If the maintenance of the existent grammar means the keeping with one given meaning, then the incorrect use of grammar will serve as a reminder to the reader that what defines "the Eucharist" might be within the traditional use of the word, but also, it might be beyond the official borders of the grammar/theology/ritual of the (S)acrament. This uneven use of the word intends to point to the fact that the definitions of an/the E/eucharistic(s) sacrament are movable, open, and at the end, very difficult to be defined, be it with our without a capital letter. Nonetheless, it does not mean that it cannot be defined. The intertwined use of Eucharist and eucharist will hopefully confuse the meaning of the sacrament as it will continue to ask the question: what is it that makes eucharist, a eucharist/Eucharist?

The film-documentary called "Romántico" shows the life of a Mexican man, Carmelo, who crosses the borders to find a better life in California.[12] After a few years he goes back to his hometown to meet his family. After a while, he cannot make ends meet and decides to go back to the United States. This time, however, he does not want to cross the desert, he does not think it is right and besides, his bad health makes it difficult. He then proceeds to ask for proper documents to get a visa. The man who helps him says that he has to have a checking account, savings, credit cards, and that it would not be difficult to get the visa. Carmelo barely has money in his pockets. These prerequisites are unthinkable for him. He quits. On the Mexican side of the fence he is not worth much, but has citizenship and a house in which to live. On the other side of the fence he is just another immigrant who needs to be prevented from crossing to the other side. These political and economic borders become enmeshed in the borders of the Eucharist table when he goes to participate at the local Roman Catholic Church. There he participates with full citizenship, and prays for access to the other side. In the United States, the eucharistic table disappears for him. Carmelo belongs to a social class that does not make it possible to go beyond his location. His search for diaspora is denied.

Throughout the book I have included stories, vignettes as the one above, woven throughout the text with a different font and space that serve as signposts to remind the reader that we are constantly talking about excluded people and that the practice of expanded Eucharistic hospitalities is urgent. The more positive stories you will read are grounded in hopeful possibilities. Some of them are based on true stories that I have heard, read, or lived. Since I cannot recollect precisely where they come from, I do not cite a source for most of them. However, these vignettes are central to my argument and have deeply shaped my thought and aligned my social, economic, theological, and liturgical commitments.

Thus, they are placed here to call our attention to and guide everything else that is written here. They are often very difficult to hear, and they beg for ways to be engaged with and within our theological writings and liturgical actions. I do not intend them to be coherent to the issue at stake nor with the chapter in which they are placed. Rather, they are dispersed unevenly as a way to transgress the academic writing and serve as reminders about a world that is often not considered in liturgical practices.

12. *Romántico*, directed by Mark Becker, Meteor Films, 2005.

In addition there are also drawings spread throughout the book that show relations between borders and notions of eucharistic sacraments. These drawings were created by José Neves especially for this book. Neves is a Roman Catholic man who was a temporary member of the Presbyterian church where I was a minister for almost five years in Fall River, Massachusetts. He was the artistic creator of our Sunday bulletin covers. The creation of these drawings follows the same pattern that we used while working together in Fall River. I would tell him what I was thinking about doing during each Sunday service and he would draw whatever he felt was appropriate for the bulletin. Sometimes he would create the sermon with his drawings. For this book, I told him what I was thinking about and "Zé Neves" created these drawings. They convey the vision of a former non-documented immigrant in this country and his perceptions of world borders and eucharistic celebrations.

Throughout the book, I will wrestle with the idea of *borderless borders,* which is both a theological theme and a liturgical perception of the world. These perceptual borders are located around eucharistic tables which encompass theological understandings of incarnation and the *ordo* of the Christian liturgy, regulations of the global market, and the stories and practices of local communities. In other words, *liturgical borderless borders* serve as maps to help Christian communities move within, around, and beyond the known borders of liturgical practices and redraw the lines of eucharistic hospitality in an ongoing negotiation.

These maps might help to deconstruct, resist, or at least confuse the global, political, and economic borders that keep poor people outside of the borders that offer access to a decent life, to full citizenship. These maps will take us to a place, a very important place where we should ask continuously: "Where am I? Where are we?" as we continue our journey towards a new heaven and new earth, continuously forming the body of Christ amidst our differences in a multireligious world.

As Henri de Lubac says, "The Eucharist makes the Church."[13] If the Eucharist is to give shape to who we as church and society might continuously become, socially, culturally, economically, etc., we are to become a multiple people by multiple ways of celebrating the sacrament. The body of Christ will be reenacted in its multiplicity every time we gather to celebrate the sacrament of the multiple ways of God's love. Crossing many borders, by the power of the Holy Spirit, bonds of affection will be created, the poor will be poor no more, we will honor each other fully and Christ

13. Lubac, *Corpus Mysticum,* 103.

will receive all the glory so that we can become the society/church/the body of Christ. The relation between the multiple relations and singularities among the people of God will create multiple eucharistic rituals thus forming a polidoxy body of Christ as the eucharist might also be multiple in its theologies and practices by different communities.

By experiencing more consciously these multiple blurred borders, depending on each other to find our way around the world, eating at somebody else's eucharistic tables, we can redraw together the lines of our liturgical worlds. *Borderless borders* are thus negotiations between unconditional hospitality, i.e., hospitality without borders, without conditions, and the necessary borders of conditional hospitality. This is the unending work of Christian communities as they offer hospitality and position themselves in the world.

Methodologically, I will position myself within what Don Saliers calls the "liberationist moral and political critiques of Christian liturgy," and the "ambiguity of liturgical formation" and continue to press what he affirmed when he said that "liturgical theology suffers when it fails to acknowledge 'hidden' power issues and the malformative histories of practice."[14] Following Don Saliers, I am affirming that the world can be interpreted through liturgical lenses, or using his own words, to "interpret human life liturgically."[15]

Recapping the hopes for this book my goal here is to do the following: *first*, to show how the borders of the eucharistic table are marked by theological, biblical, political, social, ethnic and economic considerations, which mark the faith of the believer/participant of the sacrament; *second*, to dismantle present theological and biblical presuppositions that sustain understandings and practices of the Eucharist within some Christian churches and as a consequence, *third*, to indicate how the borders of hospitality within and around the eucharistic tables of Christian churches can be expanded.

To do this, I will divide the book as follows. In the first chapter I will set the theoretical approach of the book dealing mainly with the notion of hospitality and consequently borders. In chapter 2 I focus on how the early Christian churches developed their own senses of hospitality around the practices of meals within the Greco-Roman world. I will then examine how eucharistic tables might and might not be related to these early texts and practices. Then, in chapter 3 I analyze the relationship between

14. Saliers, "Afterword," 214.

15. Ibid., 208.

hospitality and the Eucharist from the writings/location of John Calvin. I will trace the political, theological, biblical, liturgical, and ecclesiological ways in which the understandings and practices of this sacrament were developed and how this reasoning created borders around the table. This analysis provides a starting point from which I can relate other practices of eucharistic hospitality. The fourth chapter will focus on North American feminist perspectives and practices of the Eucharist to show how they challenge and indeed change both theological and liturgical understandings of the Eucharist. The fifth chapter does the same thing by analyzing the understandings and practices of eucharistic hospitality within Latin America Liberation theology, especially in the thought of Leonardo Boff and the practices within Ecclesial Base Communities. In chapter 6 I venture into an inter-religious dialogical-praxis, hoping to find hospitality between Christianity and an African-Brazilian religion called *Candomblé* around issues of Eucharist and food offering, inventing an inter-religious dialogical-praxis for these two traditions to live together. In the seventh and last chapter I offer my proposal of the eucharist with *borderless borders*. The conclusion ends with a question "*Onkotô?*" (Portuguese slang for "Where am I?") which issues a call, a challenge, and a demand for eucharistic tables to become un/conditional hospitable places around a space for foreigners. By the end of the book, I hope to have explored possibilities of hospitable practices within and around the eucharistic meal.

I believe that the eucharistic table can hold the entire world around its borders and issue a call for justice and solidarity, salvation and liberation. As we open ourselves to our own and other's prayers, gestures, songs, movements, words and stories, and practices, we can and must create new worlds. And as the "World Social Forum" often proclaims: another world is possible. This "another world" of justice can only be possible if structures of power and meanings are challenged. As the French philosopher Jean-Luc Nancy says, "The only task of justice is thus to create a world tirelessly, the space of an unappeasable and always unsettled sovereignty of meaning."[16]

---

16. Nancy, *Creation of the World or Globalization*, 112.

1

Borders, Globalization, and Eucharistic Hospitality

> One can take it as a certain experience of hospitality, as the crossing
> of the threshold by the guest who must be at once called, desired and
> specified, but also always free to come or not to come.
>
> —Jacques Derrida

In this chapter, I will begin by developing a correlation between hospitality, liturgy and globalization. Then, I show how borders are always permeable. Next I deal with Jacques Derrida's notion of "unlimited hospitality" that informs the main argument of this book. Finally, I relate "unlimited hospitality" to the liturgical idea of *borderless borders*.

Sacramental Hospitality, Borders, and Globalization

During my childhood, my family was surprised by the arrival of unexpected guests. Members of my mother's extended family, who were all very poor, would usually arrive just before lunch time and we were always unprepared. The bell would ring and at the gates of the house there would be from one to seven people saying "Hi, we were around and decided to stop by to visit." Sometimes my mother would send me to the supermarket right away to buy food and when we did not have money, she would improvise with whatever we had at home.

In my Christian home, I learned that we should love our neighbors, be mindful of those who had less than we, and be ready to welcome the stranger. However, whenever my mother's extended family disturbed the order of my personal life, my home, my school work, and even our limited food supply, I could not always follow the necessary practices that these teachings of love and hospitality entailed. Because my mother would never tell them to leave or even let them go without feeding them, I often hated them. Since I had no other choice but to be disrupted and surrender to the situation, I learned at home that hospitality was a hard thing to practice.

Later, when I became a pastor of a small church in Santa Fe, a shanty-town in the outskirts of São Paulo and then a pastor of a non-documented immigrant community in Fall River, Massachusetts, I had to revisit constantly the hospitality I learned during my childhood. As a pastor, hospitality had become a more complicated matter since it was extended to a broader perspective of issues that needed to be observed.

In my mother's house, I had her protection and knew our guests were family. But in these religious places/liturgical spaces—whether at the door of the church or even in the middle of the worship service—I was constantly asked to offer hospitality to people with whom I had neither connections nor anything in common. I had no idea who they were or where they came from. I could not tell if they were Christians, a part of the larger community, robbers, fugitives from the police, people searching for comfort, *illegal immigrants* who had just crossed the Mexican border, or immigration police in disguise.

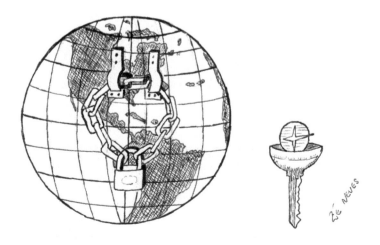

Presented by a harsh reality of my people, and trying to serve them conscientiously, I had to decide many times whether I would offer sacramental hospitality to those who were waiting at the door. It was at the doors of these two small churches, Santa Fe and Fall River, that poor and illegal immigrants were confronting the symbolic borders and orders of ecclesiastical spaces, liturgical practices, theological beliefs, eucharistic rules and political laws, both ecclesiastical and nationwide.

It is within these blurred, complicated, and interconnected borders that liturgical practices and spaces must engage and be engaged. The messy, nervous, and uneasy interrelations of these borders are a challenge to every Christian believer and privileged place for the field of worship. They require entire communities to figure out ways to incarnate the gospel of Jesus and enact hospitality especially to "the least of these," those who are on the "other side" of the borders.

The Eucharist can help us with ways to understand these borders and the ways Christian hospitality might be (un)framed. At the eucharistic table, one is able to describe the ways in which Christian hospitality is understood, presented, and performed. At the same place, one also sees *ecclesiastical borders* which delimit the ways a community defines who is in and who is out and determines the norms and standards of its identity; *theological borders* which give content to the ecclesiastical borders and ensure that liturgical procedures are correctly done and expressed in obedience and faith to God; *liturgical borders* which limit and locate the liminal space, giving contours (and content in their own way) to the theological and ecclesiastical borders, depicting a proper language, bodily gestures and ritual actions to make the rite right and familiar; *social/economic borders* which define the sacred spaces where social classes attest how God acts and who belongs there; *political borders* which show that the limits of eucharistic hospitality have to do with political choices and allegiances, economic commitments and social engagements.

The borders that mark the eucharistic sacrament also delineate ways in which the country should/could/must develop its own borders, its political commitments and degrees of order. Within the liturgical space, the "inner" life of the gospel is always already connected with the "outer" side of the world. Both are inside and outside of themselves and within and around the liturgical borders, where hospitality and identities are endlessly negotiated. In fact, when one looks at the "outside" part of the liturgical world border, one sees that one of the major challenges for our time, and consequently to the liturgical field, is the problem of globalization and the problem of the exclusion of millions of people from a life with a minimum of dignity.

One of the pointed problems related to globalization is human mobility. The movement of approximately 200 billion people around the globe raises questions of human access/excess, displacement, exclusion, citizenship, borders, and hospitality. Within the United States, immigration, especially the non-documented community, is increasingly gaining national political attention.[1] In June of 2006, a group of scholars wrote a letter to President Bush:

> Legitimate concerns about the impact of immigration on the poorest Americans should not be addressed by penalizing even poorer immigrants. Instead, we should promote policies, such as improving our education system, that enable Americans to be more productive with high-wage skills. We must not forget that the gains to immigrants coming to the United States are immense. Immigration is the greatest antipoverty program ever devised.[2]

Massive human migration around the globe has a deep impact on the ways we understand hospitality, on the ways we relate and connect to the Christian faith and celebrate the table of Jesus Christ in our bordered liturgies.

What does the border of the eucharistic table have to do with immigration, the bill that created a wall of separation at the borders, signed by President Bush, and the excluded people around the world? This question has to do with the idea of hospitality vis-à-vis the understanding of the incarnation of Christ and how the Christian church performs it.

Hence, hospitality, or sacramental hospitality, is about much more than welcoming people at the church door or distributing name tags to guests or saving the best spots in the parking lot. It has to do with the transformation of ourselves through theological, ecclesiological, and liturgical demands. Thus, in order to think about hospitality, one has to find its ways within and around the liturgical, sacramental, theological, ecclesiastical, and political borders. These borders are porous and permeable.

1. There is estimated that there are 11 to 12 million illegal immigrants in this country. Former President George W. Bush saw the borders as the best way to keep unwanted people away. "On the way to his ranch in Texas, President George W. Bush stopped along the Rio Grande for a 'look-see.' He touted new prisons like Raymondville's and said '*I understand this border*'" (Matt Taibbi, "Jailhouse Nation," *Rolling Stone Magazine*, August 24, 2006, 40; emphasis mine).

2. Alexander T. Tabarrok and David J. Theroux, "Open Letter on Immigration," *The Independent Institute*, June 19, 2006, www.independet.org/new/article.asp?id=1727.

PERMEABLE BORDERS

Borders are everywhere. Every border regulates and contains and excludes. Borders are controlling apparatus, concrete and symbolic, real and imaginary, paradoxical and de-termined, entangling space and power within various other areas such as knowledge, identities, politics, economics. Borders also mark spaces: margins, frontiers, hinges, lines and thresholds in constant relation with something else, separating, and marking space and differing positions. Borders, controlled from the inside, keep out everything that cannot be accepted, invited, and lived. The various degrees of invitation entail categories of participation according to some chosen criteria. Some will be invited as short term guests, others as distinguished guests, others as a long term guests, and so on. Borders also serve as signs of protection, safety, and order. They convey stability, permanence and duration. On the other hand, this protection and stability demand that those who are inside do not challenge the authenticity of the borders. Gloria Anzaldua says that the borders of "culture take away our ability to act—shackle us in the name of protection."[3]

However, in spite of the idea of protection and separation that borders convey, they are often made of a porous structure with unattended spaces. Borderlands are nervous spaces filled with anxiety.[4] They are

3. Anzaldúa, *Borderlands/La Frontera*, 21.

4. Ibid. Anzaldúa develops this border's anxiety and nervousness from a woman's perspective.

permeable to that which they do not yet know. Algerian-French Jewish philosopher Jacques Derrida says that "[i]t is clear that concepts of stability, permanence and duration . . . are too lax and open to every uncritical investiture."[5] Border control and protection are threatened and unguarded by the arrival of the unpredictable, which make the idea of borders frail spaces where different crossings can occur.

He wanted to study Spanish and went to a restaurant-coffee shop downtown in that Mexican city. He order coffee and opened his grammar books. It was a beautiful afternoon. Soon after he opened his books a girl, perhaps nine years old, approached him and offered gum and sweets. He said no but then offered her something else. She said "una Coca-Cola." He bought her a Coke and she left. "Gracias!" she said. Not after two minutes another boy around the same age came to him offering him gum and sweets. "No, muchas gracias. ¿Quieres algo?" "Una Coca-Cola," he said. He got his Coke and left. In ten minutes this same scene was repeated five more times. He started to talk to them and some could not understand. Three boys and four girls, from two to ten years old. He thought his Spanish was really bad but soon realized that three of the children only spoke their own indigenous language. They started to play and the owner of the coffee shop wanted to send the kids away. He said, "They are with me," and the owner couldn't do anything. The mother also came because they were not working. They begged their mother to stay they spent three hours together. Then he left. The next day he went to the coffee shop hoping to study but as soon as he sat down all of the children came to him again. They played together and when it was about 5 p.m. he asked the kids if they had eaten. They said, "No." He was hungry and he had eaten around lunch time. When was the last time you ate? "Por la mañana," they said. They then got a big table and ordered all the food the kids wanted. Very soon they were having a banquet and the kids were eating fast. One of the girls opened a big tortilla and filled it with beans, chicken, and salsa. She folded carefully and tried to stick it in her pocket. He asked, "¿Porque estas ponendo comida en tu pocket?" And she said, "Para mi mama e irmanito." He promised her she would have a bag with food for them later. However, she kept the tortilla in her pocket just in case. The next day the same playing together and meal happened with a difference. An artist trying to sell his

5. Derrida, *Of Grammatology*, 42.

> *art also stopped by to offer his art and once asked if they had eaten he said, "No Señor." And then the waiter was also invited and they all filled a large table. Strangers, with nothing in common, not much to share besides laughter and silliness and stories. None of the kids go to school, they work on the streets everyday. All of them from Oxaca. The next day another meal and all were there without making any plans. The children were already at the door of the restaurant and the artist seated at the entrance as well. At this time, they all went to wash their hands and they all said the Lord's Prayer before eating. The following day the kids were taken to buy shoes. The owner hated to see these dirty kids running around the store and ushered them out. The man said they were with him and the manager couldn't say anything, they were granted access. Dirty feet trying brand new shoes made the manager sweat. They all left with new shoes. They all took a picture together with the burrito at the corner and they said goodbye. The kids asked him fifty times, "Are you coming tomorrow?" The realm of God is made of food and shoes. The meal gained new boundaries and a Eucharist was celebrated with those who didn't have access to almost anything.*

Border walls have holes and empty spaces that allow crossing paths and open conditions and possibilities of relation between the inside and the outside. The inside and outside of borders are always playing within each other. Outside and inside are already blurred, contaminated, and it is this confluence of blurred lines that spurs the possibilities of changes. Moreover, that which borders repress and try to keep away is what conditions the possibility and the constitution of its existence. Borders would not exist if it was not for that which it must avoid and deter.

Border crossings produce and sustain meaning, create and maintain power. Derrida discusses three types of borders: borders that separate territories of nations as well as languages and cultures, borders that separate domains of discourses and what they can share, and borders of conceptual determinations.[6]

These three border limits, even though clearly distinct, are intrinsically connected. Borders of territories have to do with borders of concepts, of knowledge, of language, of culture, of language, of beliefs. These concepts/borders try to keep their demarcations of purity safeguarded against

---

6. Derrida, *Aporias*, 23.

"opposition of all contamination, of all participatory sharing, of all parasitism, and of all infection."[7]

Through a game of rational authentication, conceptual borders are supposed to keep their own logical self-referentiated spaces, with clarity and an "uncontaminated" sense of self-understanding, i.e., of identity. That means that the given logic that undergirds the rationality of certain concepts expels the possibilities of other rationalities different from that one already given and even banishes other concepts that are named stranger, or intrusive to the borders of the recognizable and authenticated.

In a way, I am, like Roxanne L. Doty, examining the "interconnected boundary-producing practices."[8] However, in order to get to these "boundary-producing practices," one has to get inside of these interconnected boundaries to see how these practices settle and the ways that they can be either/or, both/and, neither/nor changed, severed, expanded. In Derrida's *deconstruction*, one must start by understanding "the necessity of lodging oneself within the traditional conceptuality in order to destroy it."[9] However, destruction here does not mean annihilation but rather, ways to find the fissures and wounds of this tradition,[10] and then challenge the very order of it in order to move to a new time, an unexpected thing and a different place, a way of severing and at the same time maintaining and expanding the line of the tradition.[11] Tradition is not to be kept as unchanged but to be reworked so that we can pass it on to other people.

As a start, one has to search for the porous parts of the liturgical-theological-ecclesiological borders. There have been a number of theologians, liturgists and artists breaking down these borders and creating other spaces with expanded boundaries. They have taken "a certain step" (see below) into the tradition and into the crossing lines of these borders, expanding possibilities for hospitality to be enacted and understood.

Guillermo Gómez-Peña has taken a certain step and challenged the borders of art, identity and ethnicity; Saint Francis took this certain step and crossed the lines of a known and expected life with God,

---

7. Ibid., 41.

8. Doty, Review of *Challenging Boundaries*, 511.

9. Derrida, *Writing and Difference*, 111.

10. "brisure [*joint, break*] '—*broken, cracked part. Cf. breach, crack, fracture, fault, split, fragment,* [brèche, cassure, fracture, faille, fente, fragment.]—*Hinged articulation of two parts of wood- or metal-work. The hinge, the brisure [folding-joint] of a shutter. Cf. joint.*'—*Roger Laporte (*letter*),*" cited in Derrida, *Of Grammatology*, 65; brackets and emphases original.

11. Derrida, in Caputo, ed., *Deconstruction in a Nutshell*, 6.

of a spirituality engaged with lepers and a deep connection with nature; Brother Roger took a certain step and created an liturgical ecumenical community that gathers Christians from all walks of faith; John Calvin took a certain step and provided hospitality to the immigrants in Geneva; Dorothy Day also took this certain step and expanded the ecclesiology of the Christian church to beyond the realm of Christians; Leonardo Boff took this certain step and said that the church is made of the poor and the church should give away its hierarchical structure; the Landless Movement in Brazil continuous to take a certain step by challenging the private properties and pressing for agrarian reform.

These steps cannot anticipate for sure what is necessarily about to come, even though they must be taken with an affirmation and hope for what is yet to arrive, "awaiting at the ending line" which has no end. Derrida says, "The crossing of borders always announces itself according to the movement of a certain step [*pas*] . . ."[12]

These permeable border-crossings, this trembling trespassing of "interconnected boundary-producing practices" render the indivisible line both divisive and visible. There, at the waiting line of customs and passenger identification with police looking over our trembling shoulders or at the edges of the eucharist table while holding the bread and the cup, not knowing for sure if we could take it or not, the injunctions of all these borders-crossing moments, entail a call for justice, for border-producing practices that issues a duty of ethical hospitality.

HOSPITALITY

Jacques Derrida develops the historical concept of hospitality in the three Abrahamic religions (Judaism, Christianity and Islam) and expands it in various ways. For my purposes I will concentrate on his idea of conditional and unconditional hospitality.

Derrida starts his analysis from the etymological meaning of the word hospitality both in Latin and in French, identifying in the roots of the word the dual meanings of host and hostile.

That is the root of the neologism *hospitality* that Derrida coins to describe both sides of hospitality: hospitality and hostility. The *hôte* as the guest or enemy, guest or parasite, entails the crux of the distinction between the conditionality and unconditionality of hospitality.

---

12. Derrida, *Aporias*, 11.

To be hospitable is also to be hostile or to be taken hostage of by your guest. Since one never fully knows one's guest, we are always dealing with measures of hospitality, with conditions and/or no conditions depending on the situation, on the guest, on the place. Thus, in order to know whether the *arrivant*, the one who arrives at our door, at the borders of the country or at the table/altar, is a guest or an enemy/parasite, there must be a set of structures and distinctions that must turn this *arrivant* into a knowable other as a way of distinguishing those who are not the same and keeping the space of arrival on this side of the border safe. For the *arrivant* to be considered an honorable guest or a parasite lies a very thin line made of set conditions. But can the *arrivant* as a parasite be a blessing to me? Can this honorable guest take away my place at the table? Derrida develops the idea of the parasite between conditional and unconditional hospitality as follows:

> How can we distinguish between a guest and a parasite? In principle, the difference is straightforward, but for that you need a law; hospitality, reception, the welcome offered has to be submitted to a basic and limiting jurisdiction. Not all new arrivals are received as guests if they don't have the benefit of the right of hospitality or the right of asylum, etc. Without this right, a new arrival can only be introduced "in my home," in the host's "at home," as a parasite, a guest who is wrong, illegitimate, clandestine, liable to expulsion or arrest.[13]

How are new arrivals received in the church, "the house of God?" This house has to deal with its own members, guests and parasites. The house of God has borders and has to establish the limits of its hospitality.

The first "Sanctuary Movement" in United States shows the expansion of the church's borders and how the task of distinguishing the guest from the parasite entails a difficult differentiation.[14] With church buildings turned into "homes" for immigrants, refugees and asylum seekers, all new arrivals were guests, even if some of them were, perhaps, parasites. Where are the lines of hospitality within these borders crossing?

In the sanctuary movement and in many churches across the country, the "house" of God swings its doors open, offering a true sanctuary for the living, offering incarnational hospitality, protection and refuge

---

13. Derrida, *Of Hospitality*, 59, 61.

14. See Tomsho, *American Sanctuary Movement;* Lorentzen, *Women in the Sanctuary Movement.*

unconditionally to those who need shelter. In this case, hospitality challenged the very law, and even offered "immunity" from the law.

> *She loved to go to school. She could see other girls and boys and play with them. But she could go only a few days during the week, when her mother could stay home. He mother was a cleaner and when she could find a job, she had to take care of her brothers and sisters while her mother worked. During the week her mother used to go to the Universal Church of the Kingdom of God waiting for some miracle. They could barely eat. The five of them lived in a small room covered with cardboard in a shantytown. One day, when the girl was preparing herself to go to school, her mother said that she couldn't go that day and that she was supposed to put her things in a plastic bag because she was going to travel to another state. She asked why and her mother said that she would have to go with a man that was coming to pick her up. She asked who this man was and where she was going to but her mother didn't say anything. She kept asking but her mother would not say a word. Confused, she didn't know what to do. Soon after a man came to the door and when the mother saw him she said, "This is the girl, she is my daughter. Are you going to take care of her?" The man replied with sounding assurance, as he looked at her daughter's body patiently. The man approached the girl and said that she was going to be all right. The girl got desperate, started to cry and tried to escape. As the man held her thin arm, she begged her mother to stay. Her mother said that it was going to be better for her. Dragging her out of the house, the man placed $500,00 in the mother's hand and left. The girl kept screaming to her mother. Her mother took the other kids and walked to the supermarket. The girl was thirteen years old.*

Nonetheless, in order to offer hospitality, every house has to make a judgment, a distinction in regards to its sovereignty. The welcoming of the stranger is scanned through the legislation at work within the personal/familial, civic, ecclesial, institutional, and nation-state grounds. Derrida notes that:

> No hospitality, in the classic sense, without sovereignty of oneself over one's home, but since there is also no hospitality without finitude, sovereignty can only be exercised by filtering,

choosing, and thus by excluding and doing violence. Injustice, a certain injustice, and even a certain perjury, begins right away, from the very threshold of the right to hospitality.[15]

Between the conditional and the unconditional, we are to make decisions. We thread our way through conditional hospitality, the hospitable offering of gifts, food and shelter, as prepared for those who are expected or for those who are able to pass the screening process. That aspect of hospitality is under the horizon of the expected, of the imagined, of the circumscribed law. The site where the welcome is issued is under control; it is guarded, safe, defined and power is kept. The guest is received and is taken under the banner and conditions of accorded hospitality.

However, if these conditions are dissolved, the hospitable event would entail a process in which the welcoming space is opened and can be taken by anyone, even by the enemy. Without legislation, hospitality entails the loss of boundaries/identities and allows the coming of the unexpected, prior and beyond any invitation, with the host unprepared for the reception of an unknowable guest, and somewhat conditioning the possibilities of the impossibility of hospitality.

Thus, if unlimited hospitality is to be experienced, one has to lose something: space, money, identity, language, etc. or everything altogether and become whatever the guest wants, begs and/or demands. The *stranger at home* entails endless possibilities including the guest becoming the host and the host becoming the target of the guest's hospitality.[16]

In an effort to secure oneself, a host may establish a set of restrictions that serve to control and define the guest. How does one offer hospitality without restriction, or absolute hospitality? Derrida talks about absolute hospitality:

> Absolute hospitality requires that I open my home and that I give not only to the foreigner ([one who is] provided with a family name, with the social status of being a foreigner, etc.), but to the absolute, unknown, anonymous other, and that I *give place* to them, that I let them come, let them arrive, and take place in the place I offer them, without asking of them either reciprocity (entering into a pact) or even their names.[17]

15. Derrida, *Of Hospitality*, 55.
16. Derrida, *Aporias*, 10–11.
17. Derrida, *Of Hospitality*, 25.

An *absolute* hospitality entails the hosting of any guest, any stranger, any foreigner without conditions, to give a place without questions asked, previous knowledge required, names in advance, historical background or proper documents. More than that, it is to wait for the *arrivant* who is coming from beyond the horizon. In fact, it is to be caught by surprise, unprepared, in unexpected ways and yet, be ready to offer hospitality without complaining. Derrida says that that "radical hospitality consists, would have to consist, in receiving without invitation, beyond or before the invitation . . . to be hospitable is to let oneself be overtaken [*surprendre*], to be ready not to be ready."[18]

That is very hard! If conditional hospitality always entails certain presuppositions, a certain horizon to look at, to think about, unconditional hospitality is to think beyond the laws that make hospitality possible, to imagine beyond any horizon or condition.

To make things more complicated, let us think about the verb to give. The very use of the verb to give, to offer, to invite, entails a certain power since only the host, the one who has power to control something, i.e., space, food or shelter, documents, etc, can give, offer and invite those who do not have.

Unconditional hospitality then is a way of giving oneself entirely, even to the point of giving the food one is eating, of having one's space taken by the guest and the house destroyed by the enemy. In other words, hospitality would have to lose its sovereignty, its power and be at the will of the *arrivant*, the stranger.

This is a very difficult place to be but one we cannot escape! There is a certain *indeterminacy* here that does not preclude decision as one might imagine but rather, it conditions the possibilities of the unconditional, of the not yet imagined or thought and that is what keeps calling any decision of hospitality.

In a sense, one cannot offer unconditional hospitality. Derrida finishes his book, *Of Hospitality* by asking, "Are we the heirs to this tradition of hospitality? Up to what point? Where should we place the invariant, if there is one, across this logic and these narratives? They testify without end in our memory."[19] Borders are not only necessary, they are vital to our safety, survival and development.

Thus, between the limits of conditioned hospitality and the unconditional hospitality we must act. Instead of being paralyzed by the

18. Derrida, *Acts of Religion,* 361.

19. Derrida, *Of Hospitality,* 155.

aporia of unconditional hospitality, one is invited into an unending double movement: on the one hand, the unconditionality of hospitality should be always kept as it presses the borders and limits of the conditions that hospitality must create. Every act of hospitality should be challenged and checked against the unconditionality that holds the event of hospitality or the right of hospitality. On the other hand, the conditionality of hospitality is that which structures the possibilities of the unconditional to happen. This tension holds irreducibly both the *conditionals* accountable to their impermanence, limitedness and historical constraints and the *unconditional* from its *mere* impossibility and lack of historical and ethical actions and claims.

Thus, the undecidability of this paradox does not preclude one from moving or making ethical judgments of decisions.[20] On the contrary, what cannot be decided begs for decision. Derrida is clear when he holds this tension and the work that it beseeches:

> . . . far from paralyzing this desire or destroying the require-
> ments of hospitality, this distinction requires us to determine
> what could be called, in Kantian language . . . intermediate *sche-
> mas*. Between an unconditional law or an absolute desire for
> hospitality on the one hand and, on the other, a law, a politics,
> a conditional ethics, there is a distinction, radical heterogeneity,
> but also an indissociability. One calls forth, involves, or pre-
> scribes the other.[21]

These *schemas* laid between these poles and their heterogeneity will always insist on its indissociability, will always be irreducible to their own structures, impeding us from homogenizing difference. By ways of differ-ing that which conditional hospitality tries to regulate, i.e., turning the other into the same, the other, the other of myself will always appear with its imprecise, indeterminate, strange and aporetic impossibilities trou-bling the waters of conditional hospitality. Then, we try other formats of hospitality with the hope that these very appearances, unexpected as they are, will surprise us again and again with its impossibilities.

We must work within this *aporia* and improve the laws we have in our world. Derrida himself does not want to live in this ethical suspension either. He will hold this tension continuously and without end but from it he will make decisions. He said in an interview:

---

20. See Kearney, *Strangers, Gods, and Monsters*, 73.

21. Derrida, *Of Hospitality*, 147.

> I am for the Enlightenment, I'm for progress, I'm a "progressist."
> I think the law is perfectible and we can improve the law. We
> have to improve the conditions of conditional hospitality, we
> can change, we should change the laws on immigration, as far as
> possible, given a certain number of constraints.[22]

In between conditions and unconditionals of hospitality, I am looking for moments where this tension might be solved temporarily in our
liturgies, where the unconditionality of hospitality might become possible for "an instant."[1] How can we prepare the way of Christ as John
the Baptist did and experience Christ in our midst, in the midst of our
chaos and see an unconditional hospitality happening among the people
of God, even if for an instant. Even though the occurrence of the event of
hospitality might be fleeting, as an instant, we might be able to measure,
very poorly, God's epiphany by ways of God's traces in and through us. I
do believe that the eucharistic moments can spur these instants, the pre-
cipitation of various forms of hospitalities led by the Holy Spirit. Thus,
well aware of its impossibility, and pressed by the desperate need of some
kind of possibilities, I wonder how the constant redrawing of eucharistic
hospitable practices, i.e., its conditions, can bring about the possibility of
the impossible to happen.

BORDERLESS BORDERS—THEOLOGICAL AND LITURGICAL HOSPITALITY

Borderless borders are about wrestling with the excesses of life's thinkable
and unthinkable possibilities and the permanent confusion of its signs.
Borderless borders are about a certain desperation about the life of the
world. They are about bodies going hungry, bodies being excluded from a
proper living, about battered women and sexually abused children. Borderless borders create order in places where anything goes, systems of justice where there are no ethical demands, sustenance to those afflicted by
struggles and forms of resistance to powers that rule for private benefits.
Borderless borders are about remembering those who are forgotten, about
those brutally marked by violence, about money and private property and
about the place and value and use of money.

There, right there at that very place, at the juncture of life's horizons
and lack thereof, around the blurring of several con-texts and manifolds

---

22. Derrida, "Deconstruction Engaged," 313.

of questions, at the brink of anxiety and desperation, at the risk of losing ourselves, at the eye of the storm, at the top of the abyss, we, the churches of Christ are to continue to try to figure out what life is all about without the chance to give up or to look away. There, with the dejected, those who are made garbage of the world, we, Christians who believe and hope to believe, have to try to figure out the complexity of life, of these woven possibilities and impossibilities through calls to worship, prayers, songs, sacramental practices and liturgical actions, knowing that our responses to God and to the world will always already be limited and impermanent.

Borderless borders is an event that Christian believers and those who hope to believe cannot prepare or be prepared for properly but we prepare it anyways, hoping that Christ will come, an *arrivant* and that will visit us and change our lives forever, until we do it again next time. Jesus' arrival is never certain but we hope and pray that he will come. That is why border-less borders is about the endless preparation of a celebration of a feast, a meal where we share all we have as we receive from God Jesus Christ! A meal with shared food that feeds those who are there and promises to feed those who are not gathered there. Thus, borderless borders liturgies are about preparing a meal for all who will arrive for the festivity, never letting the doors of our gatherings be closed but always open, even to the point of being brutally assaulted by the cold winds or by the heat, or by scavengers and the poor of this earth. We are reminded of Óscar Romero again.

This endless preparation with those who are there and those who are yet to come is made of connections with what we know, what we have and what we find around us. In this sense, to constantly create a border-less border hospitable liturgy is a theological Sisyphean task of creating, relocating, connecting and dismantling borders.

Weaving the life of the world, the life of our neighbors and life of the Christian churches, we see how the borders of the eucharistic table are tainted by political, theological, class, gender, social and economic in-terests and then try to wrestle with the ethical demand issued by the love of God for an unconditional hospitality to all and the needed conditions for the community to continue to live. In this process I am guided by the words, "with," "preparing," and "connecting." The celebration of the Chris-tian worship and consequently the sacrament is done with one another, with different communities, with a composition of different eyes, hands, perceptions and histories. The very core of the Christian community is "life together" which is the blessing and the curse of these communities since it issues demands of comprehension, different ways of living, under-standings and worldviews and saves us from self-enclosed communities, individualisms, arrogance and self-righteousness. The Christian worship is not about saving our identities but rather, about the loss of de-termined demarcations. "Being with"[23] around the table is to learn to be plural.

As we gather "with" one another we must prepare the tables and al-tars as we "prepare the way" for our neighbors and for the world. Hearts, spaces, food, minds and bodies ready for communion with somebody else. There we share what cannot be shared and commune with those who might have nothing in common with us. There, the Christian worship might be festive and challenging, offensive and healing, stretching and transformative. Together, with little or nothing in common, we pray and sing and walk and talk and believe and lose our beliefs, we understand and have no idea, and practice with one another what we have received from traditions and that which we invent and add to the traditions.

As we prepare we rehearse our lives in our liturgies and do there what we say there! As Louis-Marie Chauvet said, "the basic law of liturgy is 'do not say what you are doing; do what you are saying.'"[24] By saying and doing and showing, the borders we are constantly and necessarily setting around us must be checked, challenged and redistributed by that we do and say and show.

23. Nancy, *Being Singular Plural*, 3.

24. Chauvet, *Symbol and Sacrament*, 328.

"Being-with" is also a way of criticizing and challenging global systems of oppression around us, a way of setting boundaries against exploitation, exclusion, greed, and of dealing with our fears and our continuous movements of seclusion and self protection. "Being-with" sets the table with an intentional task of searching for justice through the search of the other, thereby issuing a constant invitation to those who do not belong to our communities to come into our midst with the consequential unsettling of our assurances and levels of comfort. Our commonality is attained by our differences. It will certainly entail offenses, difficulties and misunderstandings and, in this sense, it is an impossible task. However, and as Christians, that is what we receive from God, to love one another as we love God.[25]

Borderless borders entails that eucharistic borders are troubled by the movement of the Spirit through different gestures, words, connections and associations in order to find different ways to think, practice and understand the eucharistic sacrament in its un/thinkable hospitable demands. By "being with" one another, preparing for our meetings as if we are going to meet in the New Jerusalem, negotiating and expanding the borders of our faith in Christ, Christian believers can practice a just and hospitable borderless border eucharistic meal/life.

Borderless border is a way of finding "intermediate schemas," negotiating hospitality, giving political and ethical tones to it, expanding the possibilities toward the unconditional without losing the concern for the conditional, aligning oneself to "forms of solidarity yet to be invented,"[26] loving and preparing a place for the other, *as an instant*, "*as if* the stranger or foreigner held the keys . . . It's *as if* (and an *as if* always lays down the law here) the stranger . . . was going to save the city or promise it salvation,"[27] as if the stranger held the keys of my happiness, as if "prolong[ing] the moment of the open door."[28]

In order to do that, we provide Eucharist under *borderless borders* as a way of improving the laws of hospitality, as if we were taking a certain step, ". . . once again, of progression, aggression, transgression, digression."[29]

Borderless borders perform a continuing exercise of losing and finding our faith, ourselves, our identities, each other. The gospel calls us to

25. 1 John 4:19–21.

26. Derrida, *On Cosmopolitanism and Forgiveness*, 4.

27. Derrida, *Of Hospitality*, 123.

28. Ibid., 129.

29. Ibid., 89.

create eucharistic tables that concentrate on "being with" the poor, preparing meals for and with communities that are forgotten and unheard. We do it by being together, being-with one another, checking our porous borders endlessly, preparing each other's tables, and connecting what we have at hand. If we all get lost, we will find ourselves together in God and God will become our permanent home through the impermanence of contingent eucharistic tables and sacramental encounters along the way around the world as we experience a vast array of experiences of life with one another.

The theological idea of *borderless borders* entails neither a denial of borders nor a ritual solution to the problem of border exclusion. It does not intend to resolve the circulating fact that the welcoming of one often entails the exclusion of another. It is rather, a way to become aware of these borders, deconstructing them as each community engages with both indigenous and foreign ways to expand their hospitality and attempts, liturgically, to materialize open borders that might provide eucharistic practices that are open to all. This idea serves as a theological and liturgical reminder that there are borders all around us that continue to exclude people.

Borderless borders are not a universal mode of ritual but rather a perceptual one, a paradoxical and multilayered pressing theme, heterogeneous practices of resistance, a challenge to autonomous, pure, and precise *unblurred* rituals, a search for gestures and tools that will help liturgical performances to access and dismantle the actual bordered global designs of exclusion. Again, it is a Sisyphean task of preparing and being prepared to God and each other. This perception of the world is a search for connections made here and elsewhere, a way of mapping our world through gestures and movements around the table of the eucharist. As Catherine Bell states, rituals should be more

> concerned with mapping the orchestration of complex relationships of power—especially how the power at stake is deemed to be of nonhuman or nonimmediate (god, tradition, virtue, and so on) and is amenable to some degree of individual and communal appropriation.[30]

This mapping of human encounters and living *with* each other was what explodes borders of exclusion, fear and hatred, building flexible borders of hospitality. By exposing ourselves to one another around eucharistic

---

30. Bell, *Ritual, Perspectives and Dimensions*, 83.

tables, we find ways to negotiate and cope with ourselves, with the other and with the world at large. My hope, then, is that Christian communities, if they want to live a radical hospitality, will dare to move away from their rigidity of place, sacrament, understanding and liturgical practice and venture into a world that is yet to be created. We must remember that we are on a journey together, a journey towards the New Jerusalem and on this journey, we pass by Emmaus and break bread together as we invite Christ to stay with us because it is dark and we are afraid . . .

By eating together, we see each other's hands and engage into each other's stories. By creating a variety of eucharistic liturgies we might be able to open up gestures, movements, practices and various performances that they might help us expand the borders of our own comprehension of the sacrament and perhaps, only perhaps, foster a radical theology of hospitality that might take the stranger and the poor into greater consideration, even at the risk of losing one's own place at the table.

"Onkotô?" ask the people from Minas Gerais in Brazil. "Where am I?" To be around any eucharistic table is to be lost and found in many ways: liturgically, theologically and personally. From time to time we will have our hearts burning, as we prepare and walk the path to see Jesus. To keep asking "Onkotô?" "Where am I?" is to know that eucharistic tables are places that do not belong to anybody but to God. Had I known that when I was a boy, then the lunch table at home could have been a eucharistic table to my visiting relatives. Without knowing it at that time, they were already bringing the sacrament to me, showing me their hands, taking me to the path to Emmaus and teaching me what I would only be able to learn more than thirty years later.

2

Eucharist and Hospitality
and the Early Christian Meals

We must . . . keep together flesh and spirit, body and soul, religion and
politics, theology and economics. God's law always embraces those
dichotomies together; for example, food is about justice and justice
is about God. The Kingdom of God is about food and drink—that is,
about divine justice for material bodies here on material earth. We do
not live by bread alone. But bread is never alone.[1]

—JOHN DOMINIC CROSSAN

IN THIS CHAPTER I provide an understanding of the eucharist and hospitality in early Christianity through the social institution of *meals/banquets*
within the Greco-Roman world. Much of the recent scholarship on this
subject[2] shows wonderful possibilities for us to reconsider our theological

---

1. Crossan, *Birth of Christianity*, 422.

2. The scholarship that interprets early Christianity through the social event of
meals practices and the diversity of Christian origins is fairly new. An important book
that frames this field was written by H. Taussig, *In The Beginning Was the Meal*. Some
of other references are: Bauer, *Orthodoxy and Heresy in Earlier Christianity*; Robinson
and Koester, eds., *Trajectories through Early Christianity*; Mack, *Who Wrote the New
Testament?*; Bradshaw and Hoffman, eds., *Making of Jewish and Christian Worship*;
Bradshaw, *The Search of the Origins of Christian Worship*; McGowan, *Ascetic Eucharist*.
For this chapter I am relying mostly on Smith, *From Symposium to Eucharist*; Smith
and Taussig, *Many Tables*; H. Taussig, "Dealing Under the Table"; Klinghardt, *Gemeinschaftsmahl und Mahlgemeinschaft*; Lee, *Paul and the Politics of Difference*; Crossan,

and cultural thinking as well as our practices. Unfortunately, most of the denominational worship books do not pay attention to it. To look at the early Christian church's practices through the lens of the Greco-Roman banquet is to open an immense variety of understandings of early Christian communities, their social settings, their community social habits, and their ways of developing their theologies and liturgical practices. Undeniably, this material challenges most of the ways in which Christian churches today celebrate the sacrament of the eucharist, while creating a whole set of tools that help to foster various forms of hospitality today.

In this chapter I present the Greco-Roman banquet material to show that this material can undo, redo, and keep open many notions/practices of sacraments/eucharists which is also a way of helping us rethink our own world today. The deconstruction of the theological and liturgical grounds of eucharistic understandings of Reformed traditions can be powerfully enhanced into new comprehensions and practices as it can open many possibilities for a *borderless borders* eucharistic hospitality.

I begin by describing the Greco-Roman banquets. Then I analyze the dynamics of hospitality played out within these meals and go on to show how this data can be applied to the study of how early Christian communities practiced the gospel and understood hospitality. Next I demonstrate how New Testament scholarship can affect the understandings of contemporary worship practices. Finally, I relate some aspects of the banquet and of recent New Testament scholarship to some of the most crucial aspects of the eucharistic sacrament as understood in the Reformed tradition.

SYMPOSIUM: GRECO-ROMAN MEALS

This new scholarship shows that common meals, i.e., *banquets*, in all their diversity, were not marginal or private social events; they were a central element within the cultural structure of the Greco-Roman period, which extended from 300 BCE to 300 CE. The Greco-Roman societies, including Jewish and later Christian groups, were patterned on banquets. Gathering to eat together was an element in the structuring of a very diverse society by providing a sense of cohesion, belonging, and social obligation. Following the anthropological work of Mary Douglas,[3] Dennis Smith and Hal

---

Historical Jesus; Crossan, *Birth of Christianity*; Corley, *Private Women, Public Meals*.

3. "If food is treated as a code, the messages it encodes will be found in the pattern of social relations being expressed. The message is about different degrees of hierarchy, inclusion and exclusion, boundaries and transactions across the boundaries"

Taussig, we see the use of food as a social code within a culture. When they read the banquet data, Smith and Taussig find that the meals were free associations of groups within the general population in search of social placement, identity and order. Banquets provided social bonding, implicit or explicit social obligations and social boundaries within different social strata. Dennis Smith calls the banquet a social institution, certain aspects of which need to be highlighted here.[4]

Social Values. The banquet as a social institution was responsible for keeping the dominant society's main social threads. As Matthias Klinghardt says, *koinonia* was the central value, a main element of the society and of community meals. In fact, *koinonia* meant primarily "meal community" (*mahlgemeinschaft*).[5] Due to political and social changes in the third and fourth centuries BCE, it was no longer possible to actively practice *koinonia* within the larger society. Instead, it was practiced and developed in the small community meals, performed in the clubs (*vereinswesen*), social and religious groups.[6] Within the meal communities the values of society were upheld, developed and expanded (e.g., mutuality, joy, modesty, order, peace, etc.) which were values of the *charis*. The banquets were schools that spread social values, teaching the individual how to behave in society and be an active citizen in the polis. The meals enforced justice, equality and friendship: *koinonia*, *isonomia* and *philia*.[7] These values were the matrix of the social values of society, from which all the other values were to be practiced in society.

   Koinonia was the guiding principle. If *koinonia* was not in place, the *koinon*, the common good of society, would be in danger and the society could lose its social order. To have a stable meal community was to preserve the social order of society. *Koinonia* was preserved by two kinds of *isonomia*: *absolute distributive isonomia*, which affirms that everybody has the right to get the same treatment in society; and *proportional isonomia*, which allows that somebody might have the right to receive more according to a higher level of status or virtue.[8] It was between these two social instruments of *isonomia* that the balance of society was kept. In

---

(Douglas, "Deciphering a Meal," 249).

4. See Smith, *From Symposium to Eucharist*, 1–12.
5. Klinghardt, *Gemeinschaftsmahl und Mahlgemeinschaf*, 156.
6. Ibid.
7. Ibid., 158.
8. Ibid., 160.

this way, the symposium illustrates the complex structure of society that the individual experienced in the meals, both in a practical knowledge of the division, social rank, and differences in society and state, and in the highest utopian ideas of *homonoia*,[9] i.e., harmony, unity and peace. In this sense, community meals were enacting a utopian community held in eschatological expectations, while embracing the present experience of social reality (status quo). *Philia*, or friendship, was a fundamental means by which *isonomia* could work towards *koinonia*. *Philia* was the reason people met. It was already there in the threads of the community meal and, by being part of it, participants preserved it. Klinghardt says that the utopian content within the banquets came under the rubrics of *charis* which had broad meanings: joy, festivity, modesty, order, peace, wealth, mutual giving and receiving.[10]

Secular and Sacred. Banquets did not separate the secular and the sacred. In almost every banquet there was a prayer, a song or a libation to a god. What distinguished the religious banquets from other banquets was the emphasis on the purpose and themes developed by each social group. The sacrificial banquets, for instance, were overtly religious because the meat sacrificed and eaten at the banquet (the main diet) involved libations; it was a "gift of the god."[11]

The custom of reclining. The Jews already practiced this custom but when the Greeks adopted it, it became a universal sign of social status, which was than used by other social groups. It was mostly men who could recline during a banquet even though the presence of women reclining was an increasing reality. They reclined on pillows in the couch: they also reclined on each other's backs or laps.

Women. The women participated in the banquets in different ways. They served the meals, and as flute girls, they entertained the guests after the first course of the meal with music or with sex, since they were also prostitutes. On the other hand, in some of the Greco-Roman/early Christian meals, women could sit on the floor at the feet of their husband, or even participate fully which meant that they could also recline, a gesture of power.

9. Ibid., 96.

10. Ibid., 173.

11. Ibid., 84.

Host, location and Invitation. A host would invite his friends to the meal, usually at his home. The architecture of the house was built around the dinning room, which was the room most decorated and closest to the main door. However, these meals could also be held in temples and other buildings.[12] There were many reasons why hosts had meals: the festive joy of eating with friends, philosophical discussions, celebrating someone's birthday, a public honor received, weddings, somebody's death, a gathering of a specific group or a sacrifice to the gods. Written and oral invitations were usually given a few days in advance or even the day before the event.

Guests and Ranking. Usually, banquets were social events where people of the same social status gathered to eat together. In spite of different themes developed within these banquets, they were occasions to draw together people from the same social group. The sharing of place, food and time created a strong social bond. However, there was always social ranking at every banquet; the most important guests would sit to the right of the host and the less important to the left. Nonetheless, the permeable boundaries of this ranking were often trespassed. It is not uncommon to find in the literature uninvited guests or latecomers who would lose their seat/rank to a lower ranked guest, or even guests who would come unexpectedly and take over the place of the host.

Space, Welcoming, Eating. The banquets were usually held in the dining room of the host's house, which usually seated nine guests on couches spread around a square room. Hosts would have their guests' hands and feet washed before their placement at the couches. Food was served either on small tables or passed around by the guests. There were no napkins, as bread was used to clean the hands and mouth. These pieces of bread along with leftover food were thrown on the floor for dogs to eat. After the first course of the meal (*deipnon*), the floor would be cleaned so that the guests could enjoy the second course of the meal (*symposion*) where an extended drinking party (wine mixed with water) would be offered; guests would be entertained by either music or pleasant discussion a pre-determined theme. The symposium could last from two to almost four hours.

---

12. "[B]anquet facilities were provided for general use (by citizens only, of course) in various public buildings in the normal Greek city, including temple complexes" (Smith and Taussig, *Many Tables*, 23).

Social Predicaments. The banquet not only concerned eating etiquette, it had a strong ethical component attached to it. According to Smith, there were three main "theoretical bases for the meal ethics," which were *koinonia, friendship* and *pleasure* or *festive joy*.[13] These elements were not fortuitous or random components within the social institution of the banquet, but were ethical principles that served to structure not only the meal itself but also the core of society at large. With these ethical standards, the banquets became a *cultural symbol* that nurtured values of "celebration, community, equality,"[14] and strengthened society's bonding structures.

These elements were customs, instructions, limits and central features of the "proper meal." Moreover, these elements were present in some way in every meal and varied according to the emphasis and specificities of different social groups. Smith and Taussig take on the diversity of these banquets and the variations of meals as a way to interpret the Christian eucharist; they debunk the eucharistic meal as a unique and isolated historical meal that shaped Christianity. This is a representation of how meals functioned in the Greco-Roman world, where common meals were a broader social value adapted to various places and divided into various social groups:[15]

Common	→	Adapted	→	= family gatherings
				= funerary banquets
meal	→	to various	→	= sacrificial banquets
				= philosophical society meetings
tradition	→	settings	→	= trade guild meetings
				= religious society meetings
				= Jewish festival meals
				= Christian meals

These different meals were adapted to various locations and group definitions and formed the structure of the cultural life. Since meals were created by voluntary associations, each group, or *club,* would create its own rules of entertainment, admission, identity, etc. It is within this scenario of diversity and plurality, where food and eating were key elements

13. Ibid., 54–65.
14. Ibid., 85.
15. Ibid., 21.

of socialization, that the Christian community created its own dynamics and identity and where the eucharistic meal was crafted.

HOSPITALITY DYNAMICS WITHIN THE GRECO-ROMAN MEALS

If food is interpreted as a "social code," then banquets, their etiquettes, customs and structure enable us to understand both how society functions and how that functioning was affected by these meals. Kathleen Corley says that meal customs "reflect and symbolize a culture's social and political relationships."[16] Thus, the patterns that existed within these social eating events constituted some of the social threads woven within society, which can reveal how the Greco-Roman society looked. Smith and Taussig call these patterns the "ideology of the banquet,"[17] and Smith later called it "banquet ideology," "to refer to ways in which banquets communicated social values, including discussions of the ethical foundations for banquet customs found in various types of ancient literature."[18]

This ideology not only weaves the common cultural threads and created a bond within diverse groups of people but also created boundaries. As Smith affirms:

> Whom one dines with defines one's placement in a larger set of social networks. Because of the clear boundary-defining symbolism of table fellowship in the ancient world, banquets became a significant feature of various identifiable social groups. The social code of the banquet represents a confirmation and ritualization of the boundaries that exist in a social situation.[19]

The fact that these banquets were an exercise in sharing community, a socialization and a social bonding reinforced and challenged larger social threads in society. One could follow Clifford Geertz by saying that a banquet was a *thick place* that provided a *thick description* of the ways individuals and small groups influenced society at large and created new cultural elements. This socialization included practices of hospitality. There are several aspects of the "banquet ideology" that show the development of powerful local hospitable practices which contribute to a dynamic and expanded understanding of hospitality.

16. Corley, *Private Women, Public Meals*, xvi.
17. Smith and Taussig, *Many Tables*, 31.
18. Smith, *From Symposium to Eucharist*, 25.
19. Ibid., 9.

Social bonding. Meals were a social practice around which people organized themselves. Klinghardt shows that there was an analogy between the symposium and politics and the idea of polis.[20] The loss of *koinonia* in the banquet puts the *koinonia* within the polis in danger, and threatens the vitality of the polis. The symposium provided an education in political values, especially with moderation as a way to get to the ideal of isonomy. Even though, as Klinghardt says, the banquets mirrored both society and the differences within it through seating, positions, ranking, better portions of food, etc.), it also shows how the rhetoric of *egalitarianism* (*isonomia*) searches for a sense of cohesion and a sense of social connection between the participants of the banquets. The symposium represents a utopia of a peaceful, harmonic and egalitarian society based on Plato's sense of isonomy. In many ways these meals gave to each social group a sense of identity by creating a sense of belonging and social bonding through the *convivia* of the banquet. Christians called their community meals and meetings agape which included a wider range of social constituencies. Also, the size of the Christian gatherings was larger than the symposium. The idealization of meals as places for absolute isonomy was foundational for theories about how to form and organize a state. In that sense, Klinghardt says that whether isonomy was a relative or absolute practice is not important because it was the presence of the ideal of harmony and peace that made its participants search for this higher goal in society and for their own togetherness.[21]

Social Obligation. Another aspect of banquet hospitality was the *ethical* elements within the symposium. Smith mentions *koinonia, friendship* and *pleasure/festive joy* [22] as key elements developed by the symposium that extended to the larger society as a whole. They were signs of *social obligation.* The ethical aspect brought and measured by friendship, *koinonia* and pleasure demanded that the participants of the banquets extend their hospitality, i.e., friendship, communion and pleasure to the other guests. From a society made up of so many diverse groups. Smith says, "both 'entertainment' and 'hospitality'" were of exceptional social importance and were experienced primarily on the occasion of a banquet. The banquet provided an opportunity for social intercourse in a large variety of settings and contexts."[23] *Koinonia* was the common sharing of the food, table, wine

20. Klinghardt, *Gemeinschaftsmahl und Mahlgemeinschaft,* 158–59.

21. Ibid., 162–63.

22. Smith, *From Symposium to Eucharist,* 55–56.

23. Ibid., 13.

and conversation. When people gathered, they were supposed to share with one another and never to take more than their neighbors. In ideal meals, everybody shared accordingly so that none would be left empty or disconnected at the banquet. *Friendship* was also an ethical concern, a social obligation. The bond of friendship was political because friendly relations governed the interests of both parties, and reduced greed and the desire to take advantage of one's neighbor. The banquets were supposed to foster friendship as well as justice in social relationships. Smith also developed the theme of *pleasure* from an Epicurean perspective. Pleasure is deeply related to the body and the need to be fed and have one's thirst quenched. After the resolution of these basic needs, joy was a key component of pleasure which was intensely related with laughter. The banquet was intended to entertain its participants so that they would enjoy their time together. For Smith, these three ethical elements were fundamental aspects of community bonding, hospitality and ritualization of boundaries.

Reclining.[24] All of the guests had a place within the structure of the banquet and this place was defined by their social class. Smith describes a ranking of the guests at the banquet which defined both the posture/reclining and the distribution of food. However, the growing participation of women in the social institution of the banquet also showed social changes. Reclining was a gesture that became a powerful social posture which could be done by almost everybody. Reclining was intrinsically associated with ethics and social relations. With this gesture, social bonds were enhanced as well as the social obligations that were expected from each participant in relation not only to other guests but also to society at large.

Guests, Servants and Hosts. Meals were centered on the idea of *hosts* and *guests*. These terms indicate that hospitality was a central and evolving theme within this society. There were tensions in the ranking of the participants in these meals, namely: hosts, general guests, guest of honor, late guests, paid guests, uninvited guests, party crashers, lower-class guests, and some women. Even deities were treated as hosts and guests.[25] Certain types are especially described in the literature on the *philosophical banquet.* Smith says: "The stock characters included the host, the jester, the uninvited guest, the physician, the late-arriving guest, the heavy drinker,

24. Ibid., 14–18, 40–42.

25. Smith, *From Symposium to Eucharist*, 77–78.

and the pair of lovers."[26] Matthias Klinghardt examined the significance of the presence of certain characters or participants within the banquet. He criticized the accepted idea that the banquets were based on homogeneous social ranking and attests to its diverse participants. Based on Plutarch's literature, Klinghardt identified three types of guests: the *uninvited guest*, the *belated guest,* and the *secondary guest.*[27] The uninvited guest was not unexpected, but was undesired. His place at the banquet was very ambiguous. He was the inconvenient party-crasher, who could help entertain the other guests, but was usually seen as unwanted. The uninvited guest unbalanced the event, challenging the host's plans and interrupting the flow of interaction between the guests. For example, he intruded into their conversation, insulted the host and the authorities by criticizing them vehemently. The uninvited guest was also called a *parasite.* The classic type of parasite was a jester, a clown, the one who entertained and amused the guests. They were related to the Cynics, poor people living on the streets, masturbating in public without care for sanity's rules.[28] One other interesting feature of the meals was that in most of the common invitations, "those invited are never named," so that, "the same invitation could be used by a messenger who would read it to the various individuals whom the host would designate."[29] In the banquet literature, the uninvited guest was sometimes not named as well. They could always get an invitation on the spot and sometimes even take over the host's dinner party. Smith mentions one of Plato's discussions of the uninvited guest:

> later, another group of less disciplined uninvited "revelers" (*komastai*) arrive, having secured an entrance when the door is opened for a departing guest. They are allowed to take over the symposium and impose their own drinking rules, leading to the gradual dissolution of the entire occasion. The uninvited guest became a standard literary figure, but how common this practice was at actual meals is less clear.[30]

Still within the structures of welcoming, there was a certain expectation, even if not eagerly anticipated, for the arrival of the uninvited guest which may have made him inconvenient but never unexpected. The belated guest was usually not a disturbance because he was late and had to accept

26. Ibid., 49.

27. Klinghardt, *Gemeinschaftsmahl und Mahlgemeinschaf,* 84–98.

28. Ibid., 84–85.

29. Smith, *From Symposium to Eucharist,* 23.

30. Ibid.

the subordinate position left of the host. However, he could cause the host trouble if his position at the table had already been given to somebody else whose social ranking was lower than the expected guest. The secondary guest was the guest invited not by the host but by one of the official guests. His awkward presence could cause complications around issues of ranking and seating order, social class, membership, differed interests, etc, that could reveal that the banquet's goal of cohesion, unity, inclusion and harmony was but an ideal. Klinghardt says that the secondary guest was related to the status of women, slaves, freedmen, and children, as well as to the way that Christian missionaries got inside people's houses.[31] Most interestingly, the secondary guest was also named *shadow*, a name that implies, in the words of Lee, that "they were often put into a very odd situation at meals."[32] These guests were to keep their shadows carefully around the banquet, i.e., behave according to the norms of the meal. To have a guest named a shadow was to have him out of the main light, of clarity and focus; it drew a certain obscurity, an opacity, over that guest. This created a relationship with a space in between, a half way rejection, a suspicious and deliberately distant aspect.

Loose Behavior and the Loosening of Social Structures. The presence of these characters at the meals and the many regulations around them show not only the heterogeneity of the banquets but also how little social equality led to unity among the participants of a meal.[33] It also shows the dynamics of hospitality and the constant negotiations around the meals. The literature shows there were *laws of hospitality*, social codes to prepare hosts and guests to deal with late comers, the uninvited, the lower class, drunkards, as well as guests whose behaviors were excessive. In some cases, actual laws were passed concerning the amount of money to be spent on banquet meals or the amount of wine to be drunk. Even within the proper boundaries set up by the symposium, its borders were always permeable because of the uncontrollable, the excessive and the unexpected behaviors of human participants. The borders of hospitality expanded accordingly to accommodate such behavior and laws were created to limit breaches of hospitality.

The banquet was also both a *literary genre* and a *cultural symbol*. As a literary genre, the banquet allowed storytelling about the society, playing

---

31. Klinghardt, *Gemeinschaftsmahl und Mahlgemeinschaft*, 90.
32. Won Lee, *Paul and the Politics of Difference*, 112.
33. Klinghardt, *Gemeinschaftsmahl und Mahlgemeinschaft*, 94.

with stock characters and motifs, excess, irony, etc. These elements serve to show aspects of the banquet that general descriptions omit, i.e., behavioral excesses, the lack of cohesion, unethical aspects, and the lack of proper manners. In Smith's words, "[i]n satire, the banquet was seen as a symbol for the excesses of luxurious living or, in Lucian specifically, as a symbol for the pretensions of cultured living."[34] The storytelling showed both the real and the ideal ways that the banquet was experienced by its own participants. As a cultural symbol, the banquet was able to hold itself as a matrix for the problems and solutions of society:

> as a symbol, it was widely utilized in ethical discussions, for it indicated what the cultured life should not be, in the case of satire, or what the life should be, in the case of philosophical studies. Thus, the banquet as cultural symbol transcended genre and literary context. It carried such a symbolic force in itself that it could function as a paradigm for comments on social ethics in a variety of contexts.[35]

Thus, the banquets were places of engagement with society's ideals as well as with its abnormal behaviors. They helped foster an ideology that society wanted to spread and enhance: ethical values of cohesion, friendship, community and joy.

Poor People. Poor people could also participate in banquets. Since the banquets were social spaces where people organized themselves, there were clubs, funeral or religious groups that held their own banquets according to specific beliefs and/or interests, so that even the poorest could have a place at the banquet. Smith says: "[c]lubs came to be organized for a variety of reasons, as 'trade guilds,' burial societies, religious societies, ethnic organizations, and so on. But their primary purpose was to provide social intercourse and cohesion for their members, and the central activity for meeting those goals was the banquet."[36] Within these banquet organizations, poor people could pay their duties according to their financial means and have the opportunity to celebrate a birthday, a wedding, a birth and even a meal after his/her death. The quantity of wine dispensed at each banquet depended on how much each individual contributed to the social group. These social groups, which were marked by such shared characteristics as beliefs, ethnic bonds, social access to a good meal or a

34. Ibid., 64.
35. Ibid.
36. Smith, *From Symposium to Eucharist,* 88.

proper burial, helped foster identity and social bonds as well and. Thus, the poor could also have a place within the social structure of the banquet. The very variety of banquets opened access to poor people and maintained *isonomia*, egalitarian rhetoric, and the social bonds of *koinonia*, friendship and pleasure.

Xenia and Women. One can see that even within the constraints imposed by these meals, people could still move beyond their social strata. Smith has pointed out that:

> One example is the Greek tradition of xenia, or the extending of hospitality to a stranger or foreigner, which usually meant inviting the stranger to one's table. Even in this case, however, there was an assumed social network to which one was usually responding in offering such hospitality; that is to say, one would tend to extend it or expect it in a situation of social connection or social parity.[37]

Xenia included and involved women. One of the reasons for that was the Empire's desire for control. Wanting to expand its power, it intended to include those who were excluded, including women. The economic factor was another reason. Corley affirms:

> The controversy over the inclusivity of many Christian groups is rather a result of an empire-wide social innovation beginning in the Late Republican era, whereby women began to have increased access to the "public" sphere and took public roles previously denied to them. This social innovation was the result of larger economic changes and fluctuations in the market economy which placed economic and social power in the hands of women.[38]

In the Hellenistic era, women began to participate actively in banquets, not only reclining but also becoming hosts. The porous borders of existing social strata could be negotiated and, if hospitality was not offered, excluded people such as women would negotiate and conquer their spaces within the social ideology of the banquet.

Private and public boundaries. Banquets also blurred the public and private spaces. Banquets were used for social, religious and/or civic events:

37. Ibid., 10.
38. Corley, *Private Women, Public Meals*, xv.

Dining rooms were designed so that couches could be arranged around a central axis and diners could share tables and communicate easily with one another. The same form was used for domestic, public and religious settings, supporting the argument that the same meal customs were followed for banquets regardless of the setting of the context.[39]

Along with porous boundaries regarding public and private spaces, there was little distinction between the sacred and the secular dimensions of the banquet. Smith had this to say about the sacrifice banquet:

. . . if the religious event that was the sacrifice tended always to include a feast, then the feast must relate in some sense to the overall religious meaning. Defining the banquet as the secular part of the total event does not do justice to its importance. Rather, the feast should be seen as an event partaking of both sacred and secular meanings.[40]

This blurring between secular and sacred helped to create a social bond that existed prior to any religious commitments. People could move and participate in civil/religious banquets without necessarily having to be members. This helped to broaden the borders of banquet hospitality by marking the meals as a social place that accepted strangers and guests who might not shared the religion of the banquet's hosts. Greco-Roman meals were more likely to be more open than exclusive religious spaces.

The banquet literature seems to idealize the proper meal, but it also reveals larger problems of social class divisions, exclusion, and inappropriate moral behaviors, exploitation of some women and the problems of the scarcity of food. Within the banquet, there were conflicts related to reclining and seating privileges, unequal distribution of food to guests, excessive drinking, the exclusion of those who worked at the banquet, etc. Jae Won Lee makes this point that

there was a tendency to avoid mixing together people of different class, rank, and status. In such a tendency, the same status of homogeneity of the participants at a meal was privileged over differences which were assumed as disturbing the homogeneity

39. Smith, *From Symposium to Eucharist,* 25.

40. Ibid., 69. Or, when Smith quotes Michael Jameson imagining "the use of the dining room in a private house for such purposes such as 'farm and business deals, marriage negotiations, politics on the local level and relating to the numerous cult organizations to which Greek men belonged'" (M. Jameson, "Private Space and the Greek City," 92–113).

or unity of table fellowship. It becomes clear that the question of difference, depending on whose perspective is viewed, is closely linked to the perception of superiority/inferiority or exclusion/inclusion.[41]

It seems that cohesion, commonality, control, order, decency, and refinement were highest ideals of the banquet ideology within a society that had only *ranking* attributions rather than social class conflicts. Smith's use of "social ranking" avoids the fact that the banquet perpetuated the exclusion of the poor. The fact that the servants had their own societies and clubs, and thus access to banquets does not prevent the social structure from being unjust and exclusionary. The servants mentioned in descriptions of the meals are sometimes understood as mere parts of the banquet scenario, never as a social class entitled to richer meals, i.e., better food and wine. Such description of the servants renders the socially excluded invisible.

The women as prostitutes, known as flute girls were similarly invisible. Smith describes the presence of these prostitutes as follows: "[A]lso, in the center of the room is a flute girl, who is providing the entertainment for the evening."[42] *Public women* at banquets were seen as prostitutes because private (proper) women would not call attention to themselves or appear in male company without their husbands. Kathleen E. Corley says that "[p]ublic meals or large banquets held in private homes were also reserved for men, except for those woman classified as prostitutes or hetaerae, women present to enhance the entertainment of the men." Won Lee adds that "[t]hese prostitutes in antiquity, just like prostitutes today, were actually forced to enjoy freedom to get access to public space. Like slaves, their freedom to be public, that is, 'available for all' was not their choice, but the consequence of their birth as well as a product of hierarchical economy."[43] The sexual aspect of the banquets, both heterosexual and homosexual, which seems to be a very common theme in the literature, is also invisible in these idealized accounts. For instance, the vase paintings seem to commonly express the element of sexuality, at the symposium. As Corley affirms, "[t]he most characteristic feature of vase painting from Ancient Greek is the banquet context as a setting for erotic scenes."[44] It seems that Smith lacks an *economic eye* to see the power of the Roman

41. Ibid., 111.
42. Smith and Taussig, *Many Tables*, 16.
43. Won Lee, *Paul and the Politics of Difference*, 109.
44. Corley, *Private Women, Public Meals*, 25–28.

Empire maintaining extreme poverty and class differences, in spite of the access to the banquets, and a *queer eye* to see sexual activities and women's exploitations, and the interconnectedness of these elements, which points to the exploitation of lower classes in society.

In that orphanage, more than one hundred children waited for somebody to arrive at any moment and take them home. Each child was a bearer of a painful story of abandonment, mistakes, drug addicted parents, sexual abuse, and other troubles. One day a pastor went to the orphanage to pay a visit and learn about the work that has been done there. It was his first visit and as soon as he arrived at the gate, all of those who could walk tried desperately to hold his legs while screaming with festive welcome. Many of the children thought they could make a good impression and be "chosen" to go "home." Some others had apparently given up. After some time, it was time for the children to take a nap. The pastor lingered there talking to the workers. After some more time, he entered one of the rooms to watch the kids sleep and pray for them. As soon as he opened the door, a four year old girl said: "dad?" He could not move. He was not there to adopt anybody. She said again: "dad?" He walked in and looked at her on the bed. She then offered him her small second hand, torn stuffed bear. He did not know what to say. He said something to her and left the room. He remembered Calvin, "the church is a mother." But a mother of whom? Before he left the orphanage, one of the social workers said that most of these children will never be adopted.

Notwithstanding, and in spite of all these problems, the structure of hospitality within the banquet is a powerful thread that helps us see how social location is permeable, how social spaces can be negotiated, how the arrival of an unexpected guest is always radically welcome even at the risk of having the meal destroyed, how the egalitarian rhetoric is continuously present, how women negotiate their spaces, how loose behavior can change the social structure, and so on. In all of that, hospitality was played out in between the porousness of the social codes of the banquets. All of these aspects reflect a meal that is much broader in its scope and closer to movements around what I am calling borderless borders hospitality than most of our Eucharistic services today.

SYMPOSIUM AND NEW TESTAMENT SCHOLARSHIP

When I took a class on "Ritual and Early Christian Meals" at Union Theological Seminary, Professor Hal Taussig had us read the biblical passages about the Last Supper. He asked the class: "What do you make of all the differences in the Last Supper accounts in the gospels, Corinthians and other early church documents?" Until that point, even as a pastor, I had never paid attention to those differences. Moreover, to be told that the actual Last Supper of Jesus could not be considered a historical event was theologically and personally discombobulating. Over time I learned that New Testament scholarship on the Eucharist was a way of both nurturing faith and for re-thinking Christian worship practices.

This scholarship uses the Greco-Roman banquet to understand worship and eucharist. As we saw, the structures of the symposium entailed a voluntary association and a social event that created cohesion between social groups. The new Christians started to use these associations in order to meet other people and create their own clubs, their own social bonding, affection and belonging under. The general social circumstances of the Mediterranean world and the social institution of the banquet gave shape to the new Christian movement and its spiritual practices.

Gathered around a meal, people used to tell stories. This storytelling showed the disjunctions between the Christian and Roman worlds. Storytelling combined the participants own stories, popular morality, ethical judgments, and the ways that society worked. In this manner, the ways that the meals were circumscribed by so many stories added to the description of the meals itself. For example, there was the confusion between Jewish and Gentile "Christian" meals; there were stories created about the Christians, their meal practices, their new social identity, the consequences of their faith, the miracles and sayings of Jesus were recounted and the letters they received from leaders of the church about *ways* to live the Christian life and the developments in other Christian communities were read aloud. At first, these communities were creating a sense of identity as Christians more than a theological corpus. Notwithstanding, these group identities attest to the fact that a variety of meal practices fostered different spiritual practices as well as the development of a variety of theologies. In a sense, the banquets were the first experimentation on how to be or to become a Christian. As Smith affirms ". . . the primary ways in which boundary divisions and community identity were indicated, was through the banquet. Certainly, a primary way in which disciples are identified is as those who 'follow' Jesus."[45]

Within these contexts, Christian meals were also a counter cultural formation within the Roman Empire. They enforced themes of equality and commensality, within a clearly stratified Empire. The first liturgical actions started and were developed within those meals, where prayers and libations to the gods were already an intrinsic part of the Greco-Roman meal. A plurality of worship rites were developed until in the beginning of the process of homogenization in the fourth century.

A central element to the understanding of the movement from ritual plurality to the unification of rites within the early Christian churches has to do with the absorption of Christianity by the Roman Empire. This change influenced the barebones of this nascent religious movement. The geographical move from house meetings to large gatherings in Basilicas for instance, from house tables to altar tables, was fundamental to defining the limits of theological understandings, liturgical practices, ecclesiological borders and social power relations/structure. Christianity changed its role from being a counter agency within the Roman Empire to becoming a key partner.

Prior to that change in the fourth century, social gatherings around the banquet were the privileged space for Christians to gather together and worship. One can find meal practices all over the New Testament, other extra-canonical gospels, letters, and other early Christian documents. It was the intersection between religious imagination, different group contingencies and sociocultural forms that shaped the plurality of the early Christian church. This powerful combination was helpful in challenging the social order and opening possibilities for change. For instance, some women moved from the back room of the house to become active participants in the banquets, even to become hosts.

To illustrate how New Testament scholarship on the Greco-Roman banquet affects our understanding of the Eucharist and hospitality in the early church, I will explore the relation of the meal practices to the Gospel of Mark.[46]

The early Jesus movements and the "Q" document clearly describe community meals, even though interpretations vary. As the early churches

---

45. Smith and Taussig, *Many Tables*, 242.

46. As already mentioned, the New Testament scholarship related to the banquets is vast. I decided to concentrate on the notion of hospitality in the Gospel of Mark for the reasons I present in the text.

began to develop its theological understandings of Jesus and its liturgical practices, it started to create images, apply correlations, and develop pat-terns of actions, social bonding and social obligations that helped define each group's understanding of what it meant to live the Christian faith(s). Each group was composing its own configuration/understanding (beliefs) concerning Jesus and developing its own ritual actions regarding the memory of Jesus.

Prior to the Gospel of Mark, there was a written collection of mir-acles. This miracle chain contained, for instance, the multiplication of loaves of bread and the resurrection of a woman's daughter. This "miracle chain" was trying to present Jesus as a new Elijah, Elias or Moses. The pre-Markan community made Jesus a miracle worker related to marginalized, poor people. The idea of miracle workers was not new to them: it was a common role for healers in a society of destitute people who lacked proper health care.

In the Gospel of Mark, Jesus is always portrayed as the host at meals. Smith says: "[w]hen Jesus attends a meal in Mark, He is always the host, except in one instance when he is guest of honor at the home of Simon the Leper in Bethany (14:3–9). Jesus' actions at the meals were always contrasted to those of his opponents, thus establishing the difference be-tween Jesus' meals and other group meals, usually those of the Pharisees. Compared to them, Jesus is always pushing the boundaries, eating with improper guests, eating and healing on the Sabbath, etc. This portrait of Jesus around meals also had an apocalyptic perspective, challenging the prevalent Jewish Sabbath rules and dietary laws surrounding banquet meals. Mark is fond of the community banquet and often utilizes this motif to portray Jesus within this new community. Jesus' banquets were the idealization of a new era and the establishment of new rules. Smith affirms that "[t]he idea of a new age is symbolized by the connection of the banquet of Jesus with the abolition of dietary laws and the invitation of 'the nations' and the unclean to the messianic banquet."[47]

Since Jesus is always portrayed as a host, he is always serving "at the table." Even when people follow him to the desert, he "sets a table be-fore them" and nourishes them instead of sending them back home. The apostles here do the work of servants. Smith describes the significance of hospitality:

> To the ancients "hospitality," which was represented as provid-ing a meal to guests or strangers, was seen as a primary form

47. Smith, *From Symposium to Eucharist*, 243.

of honoring one's neighbors. To provide hospitality was, in the social code of the banquet, to offer to them a place in one's social world, whether it be in one's family or one's community or one's polis. In Mark's story the offering of hospitality refers to the offering of community membership to the other.[48]

Honoring is central to the notion of hospitality. The other is not only received but honored. The guest receives a place, a social location, a value within the structure of the house. The house is offered to the guest, whoever s/he might be, and the life of the hosting family or community is planned accordingly. The house/community becomes what it offers and ends up depending on the hospitality it devotes, "[h]ospitality is also the mode whereby the community is established. When Jesus invites tax collectors and sinners to his table, he is thereby extending hospitality to them (2:25–27)."[49]

There is no hospitality without a guest and no guest without a host. One depends on the other to exist. Itinerant preachers/teachers/healers were always on the go, stopping at houses to get food and develop their ministries among the hospitality embedded within the banquets. Crossan calls Jesus' sending of his disciples to travel as a *missionary movement* with an ideology that targeted the negotiations of hospitality with the host

48. Ibid., 245.
49. Ibid.

house. For Crossan, Jesus' ministry was based on the social-economic ideology of commensality.

> Commensality was, rather, a strategy for building or rebuilding peasant community on radically different principles from those of honor and shame, patronage and clientage. It was based on an egalitarian sharing of spiritual and material power at the most grass-roots level. For that reason, dress and equipment appearance was just as important as house and table response.[50]

The disciples become guests in other houses with specifications about what to take and how to negotiate the variable conditions of hospitality.

How would the Christian communities handle the coming of teachers to their community banquets as unexpected guests? Who was to be included in the meal and what were they suppose to eat? The *Didache* suggests that hosts should keep guests for three days, and if they ask for money they should not be invited. The communities are being formed and dangerous visits could lead them astray from the Christian faith. Jesus and Paul were in the same situation. They were travelers and party crashers. As we can see, within the Christian community, hosts were turned into guests and guests into hosts. In the Gospel of John, in what was supposed to be a narration of the Last Supper, Jesus is portrayed as being the servant, the invisible presence in the banquet structure. Thus, one can see that the fact that there was a movement between Jesus' table and society, a social "revamp," and a connection through the expansion of Jesus' promises of a new era where people would finally have a place in the final banquet with Jesus.

This aspect of hospitality as expanded, prevented or negotiated, is a strong element in the Gospel of Mark. With the use of the figure of bread, for instance, Mark describes the story of the encounter between a Syrophoenician woman and Jesus as an example of wrestling with power and place in society (Mark 7:24). Hal Taussig says:

> It is the only first century text where Jesus is corrected and instructed by someone else. It is the only first century text where Jesus is portrayed as acting with prejudice. And it is the only Markan text where Jesus associates with a Gentile. The narrative is quite clumsy and seems to work against itself, showing Jesus as both the sovereign leader and the mindless bigot, without seeming to notice the contradiction.[51]

50. Crossan, *Historical Jesus*, 344.
51. H. Taussig, "Dealing Under the Table," 264.

In this passage, Mark is working with the structure of the Cynics, a popular movement at that time which taught that one had to be clever, attuned to nature and have the courage to challenge society. Women were included as Cynic philosophers, challenging the gender roles of society. For the rest of society, a Cynic meant a "dog." This Syrophoenician woman is marked by two problems: she is a Gentile and a public (hence promiscuous) woman.[52] Working inside and outside of early Christian meals, Taussig is able to show that this story is neither an example of an "egalitarian meal" between men and women within the Jesus movement, nor Jesus' own advocacy for a community of equals ("discipleship of equals").[53] Instead he affirms that, "[m]uch more likely is that at a time when gender roles were being hotly debated in Hellenistic cultures, the flexibility and openness of these new 'Christian' groups made their meals especially easy loci for the signification of the power of women in their communities."[54] Underlying his analysis is the methodological conviction that

> [e]ach of the stages of textual development corresponds dramatically to a particular first century community or moment of social formation. The unfolding of this contextual trajectory elucidates a complex set of negotiations concerning women in particular "early Christian communities especially at the community meals."[55]

Even though hospitality seems to be a central theme in Mark, it has to be fought for, claimed and taken. There is a place for everybody around the apocalyptic eucharist table with Jesus the Messiah. There is also a place around the table of Jesus, the *table servant* in his historical life. However within this same table of the historical Jesus, where he offered an expanded sense of hospitality, there were also borders, prejudices, barriers and social conflicts that could not be avoided. Jesus' ideal of *commensality*, as proposed by Crossan, encounters a series of problems within the boundaries of Jesus' own ministry.

Mark gets his story of the Last Supper from Paul, who was his primary source. First Corinthians 11 was the first narrative of Jesus' Last Supper. Until the late 60s and early 70s, the Corinthian Christians' meals might have not been in connection to the Last Supper of Jesus. The story could have been developed to fit the community's needs Paul saw in Corinth;

52. Corley, *Private Women, Public Meals*, 102.
53. H. Taussig, "Dealing Under the Table," 275–76.
54. Ibid., 275.
55. Ibid., 266.

alternatively, the Last Supper might have been an historical event, an account of which was passed around and Paul heard it from somebody from Palestine. Paul allowed almost no interest in the historical life of Jesus, but offers this one time the exact words spoken by Jesus at the meal. Mark dismisses those words and links Jesus' last words with the anointing of Jesus feet by a nameless woman. The social conditions in which the Markan community lived must have been tense and difficult. As they were threatened by persecution and the possibility of death, Mark associates Jesus' last supper with their reality. They were disciples of Jesus, who gave his life for them, and now they were giving their lives to martyrdom. As Smith affirms,

> The meals of the Markan community as promoted by this Gospel would have given special emphasis to the sharing of bread and wine on the model of Jesus' Last Supper . . . The liturgy at the meal can therefore be seen to represent a ritual response to their specific social situation.[56]

There is another layer of complication in understanding hospitality in Mark, which is, the negotiation of the space offered as a community and how that correlation with the spaces the community was trying to find for themselves within a larger society that was not hospitable towards them.

The meals in the New Testament show us not only what people eat but also how they eat which has enormous consequences. The way they eat deeply influences the stories they tell. Therefore, the plurality of meal gatherings within the early Christian church evokes a plurality of worship practices as well. This plurality infers a whole set of gestures and symbols and theological discourses patterned by the institution of the banquet. Stories which describe Jesus at meals around "many tables" also reflect the plurality of approaches concerning rituals and conceptions of hospitality in connection to the social structures.

The fact that a place in society had to be claimed and disputed "under the table" as we saw in the story of the Syrophoenician woman is pivotal for the understanding of hospitality. As the story shows, a place at table (in society) must be claimed, negotiated and carved out from the steep borders of social privilege. Negotiations under and around the table are always difficult. They require the excluded to be courageous and determined. Since the negotiation for a place at Jesus' table is also a claim for

---

56. Smith and Taussig, *Many Tables*, 253.

a place in society, these performances are always surrounded by noise.[57] Moreover, since hospitality entails a sense of intimacy, I wonder how and in what ways hospitality is negotiated in the story of that woman. After Jesus dismisses her and establishes a border and a safe distance between them, the woman brings Jesus closer to her by engaging his arguments. She manages to cross his border, show him his prejudices and ends up entangling him in a net of negotiations that forces him into a sort of cultural intimacy. Already and irrevocably close to her, Jesus expands his table towards this woman and offers her a place to sit.

Jesus' meals help us to infer different perceptions of negotiation and intimacy between hosts and guests. The noise that comes out of it depends on our capacity to hear it. The Last Supper and the many meals within the early Christian church can help us find some clues to discern the noise and perform negotiations around the borders of hospitality.

CHRISTIAN ORIGINS, EUCHARIST MEALS, AND RE-VALUING THE AUTHORITY OF TRADITION

Food has always been a central part of the cultural aspects of society. In Mediterranean society at that time, it was a key element to understanding the divisions and structures of society. As we saw, Smith described the banquet as a social institution. This institution however, was not enough to make justice happen. The paucity of food for the poor made life a continuous struggle for survival, and not all poor people could pay their fees to be members of a club. As Peter Brown describes in a stronger economic aspect, the access to food was the access to a better life and not everyone could afford it.[58] It is not without reason that the gospels have miracles, etiquette and social formation around meals, parables, negotiation to ac-

---

57. *Noise* is everything that goes on between the guest and the host: space, gestures, tradition, understandings, values, culture, world views and so on. It makes communication an arduous event, complicates conversation, confuses signs and disturbs negotiations.

58. "The first . . . there is a direct and unveiled link between wealth and the power to draw to oneself, with varying degrees of unabashed brutality, a share of the limited good of others . . . The second aspect is . . . the pervasive linking of status and diet. Power was the power to eat. The divisions of society coincided transparently with gradations of access to foodstuffs: more food, more varied and better prepared at the top; less food and less varied towards the bottom . . . This is an age where thought about eating was, inevitably, a form of second thought about society and its blatant divisions" (Brown, "Response," 419).

cess at the table, promises of future banquets, etc. that are related to food. Food was a social symbol that meant status, honor, access or exclusion from society. For Christian communities, the eucharistic meal became an eschatological symbol of inclusion. It was both a challenge to the social divisions in society, an apocalyptic promise that functioned as a social critique and a way of dealing with the frailty of life lacking access to better food/life. The eucharistic meal could be a social critique of society. Peter Brown declares:

> It may be that one of the deepest changes of mentality associated with the rise of Christianity in the Mediterranean world is the rise to prominence of one single meal (the Eucharist), which, though heavy with associations of interpersonal bonding in a single human society, was carefully shorn, from an early time, of any overtones of organic, non-human abundance.[59]

In spite of the central place of food as a determinant social and economic element, and its spreading network throughout the Greco-Roman culture, liturgical studies in general have never paid much attention to food, much less tried to trace the origins of worship within the context of meals as Smith and Taussig do. Food has never been a developed theme in the liturgical data. Usually, liturgical studies' emphasis on the origins of worship relies on a single line of tradition that traces the beginning of liturgical actions back to the gospel scenes of Jesus with the disciples; then projects from the gospels forward as it progresses uniformly through the apostolic lineage into to the future. The historical homogenization of one liturgical *ordo* derived from a "single apostolic model"[60] has always been accepted within the field of the liturgical studies.

As Paul Bradshaw argues, there has always been a sense that the eucharistic rite within the Christian church was always based on the same *archetype*, same shape/structure, that was handed over to following generations and that is what we have today. To use an influential example, Gregory Dix in *The Shape of Liturgy* held that the liturgy had a common origin with a proper structure/shape and that later changes happened only in regard to the change of words or length of the rite according to its uses in various places. Dix believed that the single origin of the eucharistic rite was found in the gospels, passed on by the apostolic tradition, and kept by the church. For him, the uniqueness of a single *rite* was the core element that structured Christian eucharistic worship. He conceded though that

59. Crossan, *Birth of Christianity*, 419.

60. Bradshaw, *Search for the Origins of Christian Worship*, 1; emphasis added.

this rite had a variety of meanings as it was celebrated in various places and occasions. The eucharist is understood by its *sameness* and not by its diversity. He also took for granted that the bread and the wine were the only elements of the eucharist:

> One remarkable feature of the N.T. allusions to the Eucharist is the rich variety of meanings they already find within the single rite of the broken Bread and the blessed Cup . . . But because the Eucharistic action was everywhere the same, the prayer which expressed the meaning of that action had necessarily certain fixed characteristics, though these were phrased and expressed in a great variety of ways by different churches.[61]

Thus, since the eucharistic rite was always considered the same, this sameness could be traced back to the apostolic origin:

> The outline of the rite—the Shape of the Liturgy—is everywhere most remarkably the same, after 300 years of independent existence in the widely scattered churches . . . The outline—the Shape—of the Liturgy is still everywhere the same in all our sources, right back into the earliest period of which we can as yet speak with certainty, the earlier half of the second century. There is even good reason to think that this outline—the Shape—of the Liturgy is of genuinely apostolic tradition.[62]

However, this single and uniform shape/archetype of the liturgy does not hold in the most recent studies in New Testament scholarship. As said before, Bradshaw seems to be one of the few liturgical scholars who attest to the plurality of worship origins and practices in the New Testament world. In two of his books, Bradshaw makes the same criticism of the symposium approach. For him, there is evidence that other Christian meals were developed beyond the context of the symposium, which for him somewhat invalidates the study of the Christian eucharist through the lens of the symposium.[63] Thus, he confines the eucharistic meal mostly to bread and wine and relies on New Testament narratives to explore the plurality of the relations between these two elements in various early Christian eucharistic practices. However, he cannot go as far as Smith and Taussig and locate the eucharist practices within larger cultural expressions and propose that the eucharistic meals had a plethora

---

61. Dix, *Shape of the Liturgy*, 4.

62. Ibid., 5.

63. Ibid., 71, and Bradshaw, *Eucharistic Origins*, 43.

of shapes, formats, practices, foods, themes and motifs, which could present current challenges to theological perspectives, liturgical practices and ecclesiological boundaries. What might annoy Bradshaw about Smith and Taussig's scholarship is the openness that they propose for the eucharistic meals to a vast array of food, meal/ritual practices and performances, so that the eucharistic meal might eventually lose its *sacramentality*, be distanced from the church setting (altar), the doctrine of transubstantiation and priestly control, and even perhaps, be severed from its links with the historical Jesus. Moreover, since Bradshaw's interpretation of the eucharist reduces the eucharistic meal to the two main symbolic elements of the wine and the bread, a whole meal becomes *only* bread and wine. John Dominic Crossan challenges the reduction of what was before both a real and symbolic meal to only a symbolic meal by distinguishing between the two eucharistic descriptions in the Didache 9 and 10:

> all Christians get too little Eucharistic food . . . Why symbolize divinity through a medium of food that is non-food? Maybe non-food symbolizes a non-Jesus and a non-God? . . . My suspicion is that just as the Eucharistic prayers get shorter as you move from Didache 9 to Didache 10, so does the Eucharistic menu . . . The point in all of this is not whether ritualizations are done before, during, or after the meal but whether the meal itself is an intrinsic part of the Eucharistic symbolism. Bread and wine should summarize, not substitute for, the Eucharist; otherwise, it is no longer the Lord's Supper . . .[64]

When one acknowledges the breadth of possibilities the approach to the ritual practices through the hermeneutical tool of the symposium opens up, the study of the eucharist as only bread and the wine seems to weaken both the symbolism and the reality of the eucharistic event, thus reducing the sacramental aspect of the rite and its many relations. The study of the eucharist through the notion of *a whole meal* has the power to bring back to the fore not only food elements, but a whole array of social relations and interactions, including bodily/performative gestures, global perspectives, and so on.

In *Many Tables, The Eucharist in the New Testament and Liturgy Today*, Dennis Smith and Hal Taussig challenge current scholarship on the origins of the eucharist and develop a relation between the most recent research on New Testament scholarship and liturgical and ritual studies. Their proposals are both theoretical and practical, aiming to help the

---

64. Crossan, *Birth of Christianity*, 424, 438.

academy and church to engage in new practices of eucharistic celebration. The definition of their project can be described as follows:

> On the one hand, liturgy must respond to the recognized foundations of the tradition. That tradition is to be found especially in the New Testament and other documents of the early church. On the other hand, liturgy must also respond to the "social and cultural circumstances of our time."[65]

As they search for the links between liturgy and the New Testament, they re-examine the tradition and point to different ways to approach and understand it. While the tradition affirms Jesus' Last Supper with the disciples as an historical event, they say that the Last Supper can hardly be thought of as historical, "[i]n the New Testament scholarship, however, it is widely acknowledged that we cannot reconstruct one version of that event, nor even establish with certainty that there was such an event."[66] The tradition also affirms one meal practice or one eucharistic rite with different orders regarding its elements. Smith and Taussig affirm instead, that there was a plurality of eucharistic practices within the Christian communities in the first centuries.

> . . . what we do find in the New Testament is the significant variety in the "eucharistic" practices of the New Testament communities . . . Rather than singularity, the New Testament witness to a multiplicity of liturgical practices. That multiplicity reflects the fact that for these churches liturgy was not seen as a means to preserve a relic from the past but rather a dynamic way to address the church of the present.[67]

They are undoing centuries of unchallenged scholarship. Their work questions the power structure and the very elements that hold the central ritual practices of the churches in place. However, they do not intend to create a new tradition or to break with its historical underpinnings but rather, to re-position its authority. They say that "this interpretation results not in devaluing but in a 're-valuing' of the authority of tradition, for it provides a model that allows us to value the multiplicity in current liturgical practice and empowers us to extend liturgical renewal in more creative directions."[68]

---

65. Smith and Taussig, *Many Tables*, 15.

66. Ibid.

67. Ibid., 15, 16.

68. Ibid., 16.

This shift opens up a whole range of practical and theoretical perspectives. Some of them include: 1) Local churches are free to create their own eucharistic meals within their communities without following the eating of the bread and the drinking of the wine and still remain faithful to the early church tradition and to the historical Jesus movement. 2) "Word and action"[69] within worship rites are to be used according to social and cultural norms, and the ways that local communities might want to use them accordingly in the context of their religious gathering.[70] 3) The sacramental perspective of the eucharist does not *depend on* recognized gestures around the table or the reading of New Testament texts.[71] The criteria for a eucharistic meal are the nourishment of the community, commonality, sharing, and togetherness of a Christian community partaking in a meal. 4) The eucharistic place is dislocated. People can celebrate the eucharist anywhere, in the basement, on the streets, at the park. The

69. Ibid., 18.

70. This definition of worship encourages local assessment of a eucharistic rite as well as opening many perspectives regarding the use of language, body movements, and playing with the borders around the eucharistic table.

71. It is important to mention that even thought eucharistic meal does not *necessarily* need to have the presence of the bread and the wine or the proper sayings of Jesus to be a eucharistic meal, they do not give up the biblical language in their descriptions of the eucharistic meals. From their research, they show that eucharist has many definitions since the beginning and what they do is to encourage new definitions of eucharist by different communities.

only criterion is the gathering of a community of solidarity, a community that has social bonds. Moreover, the ecclesiology proposed by Smith and Taussig is also dislocated. The ritual practices are bound to the needs and challenges of the local community, and do not need to follow a universal practice. 5) Eucharistic celebrations are able to engage a broader range of issues in different contexts. In the liturgies provided at the end of the book, themes like racism, ecology and women's rights are woven into the eucharistic gathering. Since their proposal depends on one social location, their examples are located in specific communities celebrating particular events. Moreover, they are well aware that they are dealing with a meal, a very conservative social institution, which in the Christian tradition is conflated with religious dogmas and rigid practices.

These main points have the power to push eucharistic practices into renewal and openness. A main theological challenge will be to understand the real meal as eucharistic and, consequently, as sacramental. Such a vision of the sacrament (*sacramentum, mysterion*) is more akin to the sacramental perspectives of feminist and Latin American liberation theologies in which power is not concentrated in one person but dispersed through the hands of its participants. The sacramentality of that proposal empties the bread and the wine from any *a priori* meaning, so they lose their ecclesial obligatory presence within the liturgical rites and open space for other elements of a meal to be filled with sacramentality.

Smith and Taussig's theological view changes the liturgical community into a place where sacramentality, revelation, ethical and political instances are all correlated. The focus of the context of the gathering turns the eucharist into a concern with whatever goes on around the community: unemployment, violence, festivity and that expanded version of the table can also be expanded to world issues. Moreover, the table as real meal enforces questions of hospitality: who from our community is not here? Who is not being fed? How can we feed them?

With an expanded table, the sacramentality of the eucharistic meal will be placed on the liturgical gathering as a whole. For them, "God in the body of Christ is encountered primarily in the community of the faithful. Therefore, if liturgy from the point of view of ritual theory nourishes and maintains the community, it can be seen as a primary means to God."[72] Thus, God's presence is not only in the elements of the eucharist but already there within the relations between the participants. Smith and Taussig's re-valuing of the tradition comes with the proposal to expand the

72. Ibid., 109.

table to others and to other performative movements at table with a clear sense of hospitality and inclusion.

The work of John D. Crossan can also help us to insist on the idea of hospitality through the ideological notion of commensality in the Jesus movement, even if it was not fully accomplished. Even if, as pointed out by Smith, Crossan's ideas were not historically based, his insistence on the idea of commensality has a powerful impact in our search for a more *material* reading of the eucharist, a more political perspective around the meals. Moreover, it might help us to deal with radical hospitality where everybody is invited into the negotiations around the table. Crossan affirms:

> If you actively insist that open commensality is the kingdom of God, that food and drink, the material bases of human life, must be equally available to all by God's command, you should be ready for some form of social elimination. Because open commensality and official execution are concomitants. The Lord's Supper is both about God's justice and the price for attempting that justice here below.[73]

This *material* reading can help the reading of the structural patterns of the symposium by exploring the barebones of injustice in society as seen in the meal structure, if one takes into account a more sociopolitical reference of reality. One might avoid the mistake of affirming *social cohesion* when social class differences are still drastically maintained.

It was another brutally cold winter night in New York City, and a dozen homeless people were lined up in front of the church door of the Presbyterian church in order to sleep on the church steps. The church was serving the homeless by offering them the steps of the church to sleep on. Then, in the morning the church had somebody cleaning up after them in order to keep the street clean and in proper order. But this evening, they heard something else. They heard that the coyote would pass by and on that night they could sleep inside the church where the church pews enjoyed, every night, the warmth of the inside of the church. But then, and very unfortunately, the coyote didn't show up and the homeless people were not allowed to sleep inside. Christian hospitality must go to a certain point. There must be boundaries and the church cannot have homeless sleeping inside of the sanctuary and disturb its order.[74]

73. Crossan, *Birth of Christianity*, 434.

74. The case of the Fifth Avenue Presbyterian Church, Presbyterian Church (U.S.A.), against the City Council of New York became famous because the church

One needs to think about the eucharist from the situation of poor people who would fit the characterization of the parasite and the shadow guests over our own eucharistic tables. A material reading on the eucharist, one that blurs poor people, eu-*charis*-tic sacrament (liturgical, theological, ecclesiological), and economy in the polis, can help us blur the difference between the symbolic and the real borders of the eucharistic food. In Smith and Taussig, the table is the sacramental presence of God who is already there for those who are coming to eat. The ritual and the meal are the same and one cannot separate the meal from the eucharistic definition. The same is true in Crossan:

> There is, in other words, no way to separate meal from ritual. The Lord's Supper is both fully meal and fully ritual . . . Paul was absolutely correct to insist that symbolism *and* reality should go together, that the Eucharist should involve a *full* but communal share-meal, and that anything else was not the Lord's Supper but business as usual . . . But they symbolized a reality whose material manifestations were on the table before them.[75]

The juncture of the many aspects of this New Testament scholarship strikes a powerful liturgical, theological and ecclesiastical cord, especially to what refer to the possibilities of incarnation, of bodies well nurtured and bodies suffering from malnutrition, of bulimic bodies, bodies of children starving, bodies of pregnant women without access to drinking water or heath care. These meals avoid sheer symbolism and beg for real food and real meals where God's presence, be it through transubstantiation, consubstantiation and/or real presence, will always be at stake, and will always be enacting different modulations of incarnational sacraments. If we consider the whole meal as central to the sacrament of the eucharist, new questions about the "do this" of Jesus mentioned by Paul can be developed, and the incarnation of Christ in all these bodies might take on unforeseen possibilities.

---

allowed homeless people to sleep at its doors steps while the city wanted them removed to a homeless shelter. The debate was intense and a long legal process was going back and forth between the church and the city. My point here is that the church showed its Christian love only as far as these people would not disturb things inside of the building. Even though the church provided some assistance to the homeless and "cleaned" after them every morning, they could not offer them the warmth of the church. Pews, as it has always been for most churches everywhere, sleep better than benches for homeless people. See Vitullo-Martin, "Fatal Kindness."

75. Crossan, *Birth of Christianity,* 436, 439.

Moreover, if we approach the eucharistic meal from the framework of the symposium, we might expand the range of gestures, words and movements around the eucharist and consequently the practices of hospitality. The social elements of *community (koinonia), friendship* and *pleasure* (joy, laughter), seen as ethical postulates can contribute to the convolution of the eucharistic borders and open a space perhaps not yet developed by liturgical reformed communities.

Banquets were also a *literary genre*. Banquets and storytelling went together. The satire was a common literary form that used popular morality, stock characters (jester, host, uninvited guest, whiner, heavy drinker, pair of lovers), and stock motifs which often mentioned excesses, faults, lack of manners, unethical behavior, and etc. Early Christian preachers used this literary genre to tell their own stories. They used the *chreia* which Vernon K. Robbins defines as "a saying or act that is well-aimed or apt, expressed concisely, attributed to a person, and regarded as useful for living,"[76] to tell stories about Jesus and create their own identity. Using stock motifs usually connecting Jesus to the figure of a hero eating with the despised people from society, they also wanted to foster and spread their theological identity, their ideological drive and their own beliefs around the table.[77] These ways of describing the meals and Jesus are helpful in expanding the real and the symbolic aspects of the eucharistic table today and in exploring the ways that it prevents hospitality. To think about borderless border hospitality today is to think about the elements that foster its possibilities and prevent its actuality.

Moreover, as we saw, the banquets were also a *cultural symbol* that can help us to see the eucharistic table as a social and political space, an interconnected performance, a device that helps us to think and to practice hospitality, both the hospitality that we usually offer and the one we cannot afford. This idea of a cultural symbol cannot be disassociated from the use of the space. Religious spaces help define economic, social and sexual structures. The movement from house meetings to gatherings in basilicas is also central to understanding the ways in which the Last Supper was turned into one unmovable rite. Eucharistic meals taken from the altar to become real meals gathered at any other space, as Smith and Taussig propose, also entail an ecclesiological and political move. Issues connected to power relations are always at stake here. Food and drink are essential aspects of life, and life is organized around these elements. The

---

76. Robbins, "The Chreia," quoted in Smith, *From Symposium to Eucharist*, 228.

77. Smith, *From Symposium to Eucharist*, 235.

very constitution of the eucharist is made on bread, wine, water and God, as if holding the basic and most important aspects of life on the table. As Crossan says, "the Lord's Supper is political criticism and economic challenge as well as sacred rite and liturgical worship."[78]

Having a critical vision of society and feeding the imagination/reality with symbols, images, horizons, movements and practices, one can find ways of social transformation, which includes social bonding, moving borders, gender, class, sexual and political negotiations, and space designing as ways to redraw the lines of the liturgy as well as the lines of a society towards a more egalitarian life.

BANQUETS, NEW TESTAMENT, REFORMED CHURCHES, HOSPITALITY AND EUCHARISTIC SACRAMENTS

The scholarship around the banquets, or symposia, developed in this chapter brings a full range of possibilities that can be related to new understandings of eucharist/sacrament, borders and hospitality. The ways in which Klinghardt, Smith, Taussig, and Corley approach the early Christian meals have enormous consequences for the ways that the Christian church in general and the Reformed church in particular, have generally understood the sacrament. These authors provide an ample re-assessment of the early Christian sources that force a re-evaluation of the tradition. One could say that they *explode the center* that has always guided the understandings of the eucharistic meal and, consequently, the meanings and practices of the sacrament. I will conclude by showing how this scholarship challenges two main premises aspects that structure the ways Reformed churches understand and practice the sacrament of Eucharist.

Whole Meal

As already shown, "the early Christian meals were variations of the Greco-Roman banquet."[79] This relation between the early Christian churches and the social institution of the banquet demonstrates how early Christian communities used the form of the banquet for their liturgical actions. The variety of meal practices to which they were accustomed suggests that there could not have been one strict meal practice, one liturgical action.

78. Crossan, *Birth of Christianity*, 434.
79. Smith and Taussig, *Many Tables*, 36.

Such plurality of local liturgical practices and theologies make impossible any theological or liturgical suggestion that there is a univocal meaning or pattern developed in their eucharistic meals.

Since the early Christian communities based their "worship services" in the social institution of the symposia, they followed very precise procedures about creating, conducting and experiencing a meal. The table was prepared with a variety of codes regarding gestures (washing of hands and feet before sitting in the couches), words (oblations, discussion of a variety of themes, etc) and behavior (proper manners around the table that would enhance the idea of friendship, *koinonia*, pleasure). Moreover, the meal was a long event, usually more than two hours with two courses. The second part would become a drinking party with abundance of wine, sometimes music, sexual activities and philosophical and religious discussions where life, social values and the gods were discussed. Due to the often excessive consumption of wine, excessive behavior was a constant mark of these meals. They could be messy, disrupted and transgressed, with inappropriate manners and heated discussions.

Hence, the codified liturgical actions registered in the early data cannot be interpreted as a liturgical pattern that fixed its forms and contents based on a handful of gestures or a few food elements on the table such as bread and wine, or honey and milk as the entire meal. The liturgical experiences of the early Christian communities were, in fact, done around a real meal within its cultural limits. They were based on a social event composed from a variety of elements that could blur and move many collective borders: it was diverse, messy, fun, often "with a festive air,"[80] an educational event that served to educate the individual in citizenship duties, a space with few formalities and many informal aspects, loud, excessive, sensual, also sexual, sometimes out of control, filled with "inappropriate" behaviors, but open for unexpected guests.

If we take the liturgical patterns that Reformed churches follow today we will see that there is very little similarity to the ways that the early church celebrated the eucharist meal. In most Reformed churches today its food and drink are a meager and minimal caricature of the meals in the early church. The atmosphere is often somber, conversations are not allowed, actions constrained, random participation avoided, and for the most part, guests can only sit at the table if they are baptized. Around the table, there is not much drinking or eating, not much bodily movement, much less any bodily "excess," no fun, no jokes, no "improper" behavior, and no space for any kind of spontaneity whatsoever. Order and decency seems to mean minimal bodily gestures. The pressing rigidity of the order and the formality of the liturgical actions end up constraining the liturgical space not only to unexpected actions, but also to any form of hospitality offered to someone else. The primary liturgical structure is created with the intention of not allowing any unexpected event to happen and the result is that any guest cannot move freely or comfortably. In other words, the formality of the ritual and the liturgical space entails a loss of space for the other to move around and feel welcomed.

This is almost antagonistic to the ways the guests felt at the banquets. The meals offered a more open space for the guest to arrive late and behave unexpectedly. The hospitality of the banquet was marked by a variety of guests. The structure of the meals allowed strangers, unknown guests or even not proper guests to join the occasion. The unexpected guest could act in the way he wanted and wouldn't be expelled out of the meal. Moreover, the guest could even take the role of the host and lead the banquet as he wished, defining the limits for the drinking of the wine and even choosing the topic to be discussed. As Smith and Taussig affirm about early Christian meals and Jesus movement, "[t]heir meals are also characterized as being slanderously open to outsiders."[81]

Around Reformed eucharistic tables however, when the authorized leader is standing at the eucharistic table, the fences are highly set: the

80. Ibid., 49.
81. Ibid., 50.

space is formally established, only the ordained minister of the word and the sacrament can speak, and only those who belong to the group can come and eat. In the same way that the meals in the early Christian church followed the social pattern of the Greco-Roman society, the eucharistic tables within the Reformed churches in United States follow the same social pattern found in the North American culture, where fences of individualism and safety surround these tables with high borders, leaving the stranger *as* stranger unless the stranger becomes "known," i.e., adapted to the demands of the table.

Historicity and Words of Institution

There is another aspect that radically differentiates the Reformed eucharistic table and the early Christian meals. Calvin believed that the sacrament of the eucharist was commanded by Christ himself. For Calvin, the New Testament story of the Last Supper, when Jesus gathered with his disciples, was a historical event and the words of institution pronounced in the Upper Room were truly Jesus' words.

What recent scholarship about meals shows is that neither the historical event of the Last Supper in the Upper Room nor Jesus' words of institution can be proved as historical facts. Instead, these events were interpreted later on as ways to relate Jesus to Passover and confer historical validity to the orthodox approach of the early Christian sources. However, if Jesus' last gathering with his disciples did not occur in the way described in the gospels and Jesus did not say the words of institution the historical basis for Reformed church eucharistic practices collapses. These possibilities diffuse theological reasoning about the sacrament, destabilize fixed eucharistic practices, and make eucharist a more open event, since they cannot with certainty be directly attributed to Jesus himself.

The warrants of the known sacramental words and practices enacted within Reformed church today cannot be *fixed* as dogma anymore as Jesus' own words and practices, and cannot serve as the only model for the celebration of the Eucharist. Moreover, the use of the Last Supper and Jesus' words as a sole tradition within the early Christian communities cannot be held because these early communities had to adapt their meals according to their needs and local situations. These adaptations entailed different sets of practices that were not based on the Last Supper or Jesus' words of institution. Thus, what is understood as one tradition, or one eucharistic table, has to be understood as many traditions, or many eucharistic tables within the early church.

5.3. Sacraments/Eucharists

Shifting from one table to many tables entails several movements in the understandings and practices of the sacrament. First, from gathering around the table at the altar at the center of the sanctuary to the gathering around any table (or even no table), the sacrament can be placed anywhere that is consistent and important to a local community. Second, from relying on the leadership, organization and supervision of a national church or one single person, now eucharistic tables are open to different forms and configurations of leadership. Thus, the sacraments of the eucharistic tables break a top-down power relation into a horizontal structure of relationships where God is to be met. Third, instead of high doctrinal fences around the table, the invitation to eat the food that the community prepares can be an open invitation to the larger community since the notion of the sacrament gains an open-ended quality with each community deciding, what an encounter with God around the table might mean to them.

The cohesion of the table is now marked by its multicentric structure and intrinsic plurality rather than one dogmatic set of beliefs, actions and words to be strictly followed, even though those need not to be dismissed completely. Thus, what happens to the eucharist is that it becomes plural, i.e., eucharists and sacraments.[82] What determines the expansion of the table is not the proper elements of bread and wine, but instead, with whom people gather and how they eat.[83] Thus, eating together, either in the morning or in the evening, inside of the sanctuary or around a kitchen table, during a trip or in a picnic, in all of these places, sacrament(s), i.e., the presence of God can happen.

All of these aspects of these many tables open a vast myriad of possibilities for hospitality. What is on the table and what we do around the table is more prone to sharing, to friendship and pleasure rather than safeguarding the table with theological and practical warranties. If to eat together is communion, a *koinonia* sacrament, then the table is open for anyone who comes to eat. Moreover, the issues around the table would also be open to a myriad of stories, brought either by the community leader,

82. This notion is also developed in the following chapters.

83. On this matter, see Mitchell, *Eucharist as Sacrament of Initiation.*

community members, or by unexpected guests. At my mother's table there was always a place for anybody who arrived at lunch time, even if I had to give up my own place at the table. Moreover, it was up to our guests to decide what we were to talk about around the table.

Thus, the many tables within Reformed churches gain the power to expand its borders to a variety of guests. When a Reformed church in Providence, for instance, invites the Portuguese speaking communities from Africa to a meal together, the table expands beyond normal ecclesiastical limits and social, economic and class divisions. If Reformed churches are to invite excluded communities to eat together, spontaneous spaces will be created and no food will be eaten in silence, no gestures will be necessarily constrained, and no private prayers limited to inward feelings will be said.

> At a local dumpster, people try to collect food, cardboard and other things to sell. Three local churches decide to form a group of people to go listen to their voices, strengths and needs. After they get to know each other, the church people ask if they can have an ecumenical worship service at their work place. They all agree to get together. The people from the dumpster prepare the space and the churches bring the bread and the wine. They sit together, they tell their stories and the stories of Jesus. They say they belong to each other and they continue to meet. Next time they meet at the church, and they share their space and have a whole meal at the table. They feed each other, they learn how it is that each other live, and they decide to create a food pantry for all. Now everybody's food is shared. No one has its own food. Life is to be shared and they think how they can create a cooperative. They give thanks to God at the table and ask for God's guidance.

To eat together and with strangers is to live up to the ways that the early Christian churches did, acknowledging the pressing possibility of the arrival of unexpected guests. Moreover, to share a meal with somebody else does not need to rely on proper religious beliefs about how the presence of Jesus might occur at eucharistics tables. Many words can become words of institution, said by Jesus through the other. Beliefs and meaning might come later, as we go, as we practice the sacrament, as it become useful[84] to each community, and as we meditate on many scriptures in order

84. For Wittgenstein, meaning was determined by use. See Galbreath, *Doxology and Theology.*

to find ways to offer hospitality within and beyond our constructed and necessary borders.

This practice entails not only an expansion of hospitality but also an enlargement of the limits of ecclesiology. If sacraments of eucharists become a community gesture of eating together a regular meal, communion becomes an open-ended ecclesiastical *fold*, unfolding itself to anyone who comes to the table. Then, homeless people do not need to use the soup kitchen to eat while the official congregation celebrates the proper Eucharist upstairs. The soup kitchen becomes the sacrament and the eucharistic meal upstairs becomes the soup kitchen. In both places, we all celebrate the sacraments of the eucharists.

Moreover, the openness to other practices around the table can foster new understandings of what a sacrament might be or look like. God's *real presence* can be seen in a variety of gestures that might be called a sacrament. The "do this" of Jesus' words in Paul can be translated in many "doings" around many tables. And hospitality can be considered along with the sacrament as plural: many types of hospitalities issuing many sacraments of many eucharists.

Social Reimagination

These meals around the first centuries represented a fight against the empire, a way of criticizing and undoing the social structures and a form of reimagining a new world. Prof. Taussig says that "it is possible to explore ambitious, fanciful, and cosmic imaginations of early Christians and set them firmly within the meal. How appropriate was the meal for Christians to generate magnificent visions of alternate worlds fueled by some cosmic imaginations from the Israelite and Greco-Roman legacies."[85]

This social reimagination can be marked by, among others, three aspects strongly mentioned by Taussig: the vocabulary of the rituals, the mixed public/private aspects of the meals, and the identity recreation. The vocabulary of the rituals around meals created possibilities to engage in reimaginations and made people able to engage

> how men and women related, who was in charge, how wealth
> was distributed, what ethnicity did and did not mean, how work
> and leisure fit together, who belonged to society, what roles

---

85. H. Taussig, *In The Beginning Was the Meal,* 103.

families and tribes could play, and what to make of the complex social mix of the Hellenistic society.[86]

Rituals offer vocabularies beyond the creation of discourses but the practices and movements of the body are also uttered words from which we posit ourselves to engage the inner theaters of our lives and the outer plays of our societies. Also, the mixed aspects of these meals as semi private and semi public blurred the limits of both worlds and created a liminal space that served to spill over into each self defined structures and open possibilities of change and transformation. Taussig says:

> The mix of private and public encouraged the imagination of alternate worlds. The opening of the larger society forced the presentational consciousness, while the security of the closed walls and intimacy of reclining together invited a kind of longing not allowed in blatantly public settings. The meals invited participants to live in an imagined world constituted by the meal's formal stability, a certain longing for something different occasioned by the meal's intimacy, and a vague awareness of the world perking into the room.

Rehearsing what life should be about, the meals were a moment of practicing what society also should be about. Also, the society would always rush in as a way to not let this ritual be self-enclosed and enough for itself. The social reimagination entailed both the reimagination of the meals and society and its constant practice, a testimony of resistance against the structures of exclusion and injustice.

The Greco-Roman meals were a space to engage, struggle, resist, dismantle, organize, negotiate and perform various identities, be it social, ethnic, religious, sexual or cultural. When we think about the search for the Christian identities, Judith Lieu calls for "a grammar of practice,"[87] where the variety of practices attest to the contradiction, instability, ambivalent and fluid aspects of identity. The search for an essential Christian identity is grounded on a belief that there is such a thing and from that imaginary one beginning, one can call for a proper order of practices, organized theological thinking and boundaried organization. What we see at those meals from what our authors show is that this search is not only impossible but the search of Christian early beginnings show a variety of practices with many beginnings, many beliefs, and a constant shuffling of

86. Ibid., 102.

87. Lieu, *Christian Identity in the Jewish and Graeco-Roman World*, cited in H. Taussig, *In The Beginning Was the Meal*, 182.

identities that were always disputed, adjusted, imagined, negotiated. As Taussig tells us,

> meals became a place where the almost endless mix of national and ethnic identities in the Mediterranean was contested, expanded, rethought, and improvised on . . . Pressure from and resistance to Rome's attempt to impose identities of citizens, barbarian and client were negotiated at meals. The meal's relatively stable form, however, did provide a safe space in which the contradictions, pressures, and possibilities of identity could be held. Its openness for disagreement, social experimentation, and expressiveness invited provisional reworking of identity . . . participants consistently came back for more risk taking, confirmation and negotiation of identity.[88]

Liturgical spaces are places where social reimaginations are always at stake. If Reformed churches could expand the vocabularies of their liturgies, see more clearly ritual practices as the negotiation of liminal spaces between the private and the public systems, where worlds are constructed through beliefs and practices, and let our worship and ritualizing be a performance of our identities, our beliefs and possibilities for a new world, we will be able to expand the hospitality around our eucharistic tables and think, dream, pray and practice the possibilities of a new world of justice.

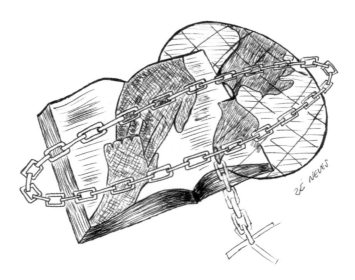

88. H. Taussig, *In the Beginning Was the Meal*, 182–83.

The structure of the symposia and the variety of meals within the early Christian world can inspire Reformed Christian churches to continue examining the hospitality offered at their eu*charist*ic celebrations, and expand them by celebrating it in varied spaces, with different gestures, alternative sources, varied meals formats, fostering ways to think and practice wider forms of hospitality. With an open-ended notion of the sacraments, liturgical practices around plural eucharists can issue a series of challenges to the constraints, search for essences and borders of several eucharistic tables today that impede people from being part of the larger communion table of Christ. In these ways, as local churches re-negotiate the spaces and understandings of eucharistic meals, they might be able to aim at borderless borders liturgical practices, signaling a new society along the way.

3

Reformed Eucharist
and Hospitality

[The sacrament] is an external sign ... a testimony of the divine favor
toward us, confirmed by an external sign, with a corresponding attestation of our faith towards Him ... "a visible form of an invisible grace."[1]

—JOHN CALVIN

IN THIS DISSERTATION I am exploring the notion of the sacrament of the
eucharist in its relations to hospitality, within the Reformed Tradition.[2]
Here I want to analyze the ways in which John Calvin developed his
theological, liturgical, and ecclesiastical understandings of the eucharistic sacrament as well as how that shaped his own context and the tradition that followed. Calvin's comprehension of the eucharistic table had a
deep impact on the construction of the notion of power at that time and
changed the ways in which the relation between God and the world was
understood. Calvin's heritage was taken up in many different ways by different groups. My intention is not to follow these differences, but instead

1. Calvin, *Calvin's Institutes*, 4.14.1. The quotes used will be taken from this translation unless stated otherwise.

2. What I mean by Reformed Tradition encompasses a great variety of churches
that locate their theological influence on the work of John Calvin. Wandel names some
of the churches that are influenced by the Calvinist tradition : "A plethora of modern
churches situate their 'origin' more or less in the thought and work of John Calvin: from
the Huguenot, Presbyterian, Dutch Reformed, Arminian (sic), to Anglican, American
Congregationalist and Presbyterian" (Wandel, *The Eucharist in the Reformation*, 173).

to analyze the ways in which the Presbyterian Church (U.S.A.) assumes this tradition and establishes its own borders around the eucharistic table.

In this task, I first introduce some aspects of the historical/liturgical antecedents to the Reformation. I then analyze the political and theological aspects of Calvin's interpretation of the eucharist. Thirdly, I describe some of the elements in the Presbyterian Church (U.S.A.)'s current understanding of the Eucharist. I then focus upon the rigidity of movements around the table and propose an expansion of eucharistic movements. I finish the chapter by returning to Calvin's perspectives on liturgy, the Eucharist and hospitality.

THE EUCHARIST IN JOHN CALVIN'S CONTEXT— HISTORICAL ANTECEDENTS

The congregation got together that morning for eucharist. Before the service started she said: I have a story: "This 14-year-old girl lost her mother, father, uncles, aunties, cousins, and her whole family with the Tsunami. She was alone with her younger six-year-old sister. Without a house or anywhere to go, she wandered aimlessly on the streets of this destroyed city. A man approached her and asked her if she needed help. She nodded, yes. In his room, she lost her virginity to this man. He kicked her out after the rape. Bleeding, she ran, crying with her sister. She sat on the floor and cried until she and her sister slept. The person who told me this story says that she was taken to another house but nobody knows if this house was a place for displaced people or for prostitution. How can we eat this meal with this story on the table?" After a long silence, a woman said, "Let us give them a name: Jennifer and Lidia." A man said, "Let me go to the computer of the church and search for some facts about the Tsunami." A women who had been a dancer many years before, offered a dance around the table and started to practice. A couple other women decided to choose the hymns. The pianist started to play an old song she had learned with her mother and rehearse for the liturgy. Another couple went home and brought some of their daughters' dresses and their daughters brought some of their dolls to put on the table while they ate and send afterwards to some of the places affected by the disaster. The pastor prepared a small homily, and two women were in charge of creating the prayers of confession. While other members were writing letters to these two girls, other members prepared the food

> *for the table. Some other people stayed in the pews. After thirty minutes they had their liturgical order ready. Their eucharist was in memory of these girls, Jennifer and Lidia. After their worship service, they decided to learn more about people that had lost families in the Tsunami and see how they could help. They decided that the Tsunami was going to be the theme of the month in their liturgies and that, somehow, Jennifer and Lidia were going to be present.*

Unlike Luther, who had always had a close link with the peasants and the land, Calvin was involved with middle-class people who also wanted to create a new world.[3] This difference should be noticed. The twenty-five years of birth difference between Luther and Calvin was enough to have both worlds already completely changed.[4] The whole political and geographical map of the world was shifting and the newly conquered/discovered/invaded continent of the Americas was already in communication with the European countries of Spain and Portugal. In addition, it is important to say that Calvin lived a life in exile and this affected his theological production. [5] In 1541, just few years after Calvin published his *Institutes* in 1535, there was an increase in persecution against Protestants. Calvin was among those Protestants who had fled the persecution in France. As a consequence, Calvin developed most of his theological thought as a foreigner, a refugee, a man between worlds, writing to pastors and communities that were being persecuted as well, communities which were minorities in their own countries. He was careful in advising these communities to wait to institute the eucharist until they had learned the "true gospel," for a lack of proper knowledge could lead to grave theological misunderstandings and spiritual mistakes. Calvin's theological production came from that experience of being exiled, divided and scattered. Calvin's itinerant life, while limited, included the use of a foreign language

---

3. M. C. Taylor, *After God*, 98.

4. Wandel, *Eucharist in the Reformation*, 140.

5. "Calvin's was a life of exile. If Luther lived and died within a day's journey of the town in which he was born, Calvin left his native city, Noyon, at fourteen, first to Paris, then Basel, Geneva, and Strasbourg, before settling in Geneva, where he lived from 1541 to his death in 1564, but where he only became a 'bourgeois,' with some but not all the rights of citizenship in 1559. Calvin lived his adult life not native to communities to which he ministered . . . and the communities to which he preached were all, like him, refugees—linked by a language, French, which was more or less foreign to the places in which they lived" (ibid., 142–43).

and an estranged relationship with Christian believers, was central to the formation and development of his thought.

Calvin also construed a dual perspective in relation to his own thought and the emphasis to word and deed. His biographer, William Bouwsma, describes two Calvins:

> One of the Calvins was a philosopher, a rationalist and a school-man in the high Scholastic tradition represented by Thomas Aquinas, a man of fixed principles, and a conservative. For this Calvin, Christianity tended toward static orthodoxy, a Christian was a person endowed with certain *status*. This philosophical Calvin, peculiarly sensitive to the two contradictions and dilemmas of an eclectic culture and singularly intolerant of what we now call "cognitive dissonance," craved desperately for intelligibility, order, certainty . . . The other Calvin was a rhetoretician and humanist, a skeptical fideist in the manner of the followers of William of Ockham, flexible to the point of opportunism, and a revolutionary in spite of himself. This Calvin did not seek, because he neither trusted nor needed, what passes on earth for intelligibility and order; instead, he was inclined to celebrate the paradoxes and mystery at the heart of existence.[6]

Later, each of these "two Calvins" was to become a theoretical ground for extreme scholastic thinkers who either imprisoned Calvin in doctrinal shackles or interpreted him as a spiritual guide to the most intense spiritual yearnings within Pietism. Calvin's rigorous thought was developed to encompass the whole of human nature, as well as relations between people and God. This search made him a moralist, a man who had strong views of how people should behave morally and spiritually within society. His anthropological theology was deeply rooted in a very somber sense that humanity was decayed and estranged from God, which ended up making Calvin's God not only fearsome and distant, as is shown in his doctrine of predestination, but also exceedingly loving and gracious, as in his doctrine of providence.

Even though his humanism was based on deeply rooted negative images of the human predicament, his theological humanism carried the possibility of the construction of a better society through the regeneration of the individual in the context of the covenant community. Thus, Calvin was intensely severe about personal human tendencies towards errors regarding God's will and grace; his theological perspective was also overtly

6. Bouwsma, *John Calvin: A Sixteenth-Century Portrait*, 230–31, cited in Taylor, *After God*, 68.

open to the reconstruction of human life and social threads through God's grace. That double perspective provided a strong theoretical ground for the ethical development of the growing Protestant world.

Calvin's thought cannot be viewed as focusing on the individual's relation to God in isolation from the relation of persons in church and society. The concern with the health of society, its holiness and transformation was a duty of the Christian church and requires that human laws be created in relation with God's laws. Consequently, between proper human laws and God's law lies the measure of a healthy human life. The entanglement between divine and human laws is thus mirrored in personal salvation and social accomplishments. Moreover, the rationalization of faith within political laws, the calculation and control of social morality, along with the spiritualization of economic ability, played a powerful role in Calvin's theology, one that was well received in various European countries at the end of the sixteenth century.

In all of Calvin's theological and practical works, the eucharistic table served as a privileged place. As will be seen, the table of the Eucharist was a place where theological, liturgical, ecclesiastical, social, and political definitions were at stake, borders were raised, erased, blurred, and undone. The analyses of some of his theological and political positions, seen through the controversies he experienced in Geneva, show how all of these aspects define and are defined by the centrality of the eucharist in Calvin's mind.

CALVIN'S EUCHARIST

Political Dimensions

One might make a bold affirmation by saying that the sacrament of the Eucharist *hosted* a privileged place in the political battles in Europe. Over the meaning of the bread and the wine and the presence of Christ, people determined their own place in their world. As Christopher Elwood states:

> In the cities and towns of France, people rioted, fought, killed, and died over the theological definitions of the eucharist. But this symbol was not simply the site upon which political struggles were concentrated. To a larger extent, it served as the catalyst for those struggles. The eucharist and the meanings attached to it created particular habits of thought and action that shaped the political understanding and commitments of men

and women in the sixteenth century. In its Calvinistic interpretation, the eucharist created the environment that made social and political revolution possible . . . the eucharist was the central symbol defining power in the late medieval and early modern periods.[7]

One cannot understand the eucharistic theology of Calvin without the political and social underpinnings of this doctrine. As mentioned before, no theological work is apolitical, and in the case of Calvin's theology, what was at stake was not only a doctrinal dispute between theologians or preachers regarding the proper spiritual formation through Christian sacraments, but also, the seed of a whole range of power disputes including the French and American Revolutions, the transformation of the European political landscape with the re-formation of nation states, and the development of what was later to be known as capitalism.[8]

One could say that theological positions structure certain ways of thinking and limit their practical effects. However, one could also say that practices create ways of thinking that influence and even form theological positions. In this relation needs and feeds the other in an unending (un) folding into each other as part of the constant convolution of the theological and social threads. The corruption of one is also the corruption of the other. That is why, for Calvin, theological positions entailed not only a proper life of faith but carefully designed social boundaries. For him, ways of living influence the ways of believing.

Calvin had a very important role in the city of Geneva. It is in this city that one can see the correlation of these issues fully at play. The strength of his theological and liturgical positions had to match the convoluted situation of Geneva, which William Naphy describes as, "smaller, less secure, and decidedly isolated. It was a locale facing the constant threat of armed assault. It was over-crowded and stuffed with refugees. And it was poor."[9] When Geneva decided to follow the Reformation in 1536, Calvin was persuaded by Guillaume Farel to come to Geneva, Calvin started with a series of writings that were supposed to give shape to the church.[10] There

---

7. Elwood, *Body Broken*, 4.

8. For the correlations between these topics, see M. C. Taylor, *Confidence Games*; and M. C. Taylor, *After God*.

9. Naphy, "Calvin's Geneva," 25.

10. Some of Calvin's writings regarding the structuring of the church were: *Articles concernant l'organisation de l'église et du culte à Genève*, 1537; *Instruction et confession de foy en l'église de Genève*, 1537 which was changed and became the Catechism of Geneva; *Le Catechisme de l'église de Genève* in 1542; *La Manière d'interroguer les enfants*,

was little cohesion in the city in which many groups with different theologies and liturgical and eucharistic practices were floating around preaching their own beliefs. Calvin had to control the theological and liturgical spaces from threats these groups posed to the nascent Reformed church in Geneva. He attacked these groups and wrote extensively against theologies that put the Reformed faith in danger.[11] In doing so, he was also giving shape to a proper direction that the city would follow.

Calvin had to work closely with the city council of Geneva. Calvin and Farel wanted the church not to have controlling power in the city, but they did believe that the church needed to have a degree of power in relation to church affairs, notably over discipline. They were not content to have the church be a subsidiary association of the civil government. The struggle in these early years related to whether the church should be controlled by the civil government, or whether it should be a kind of partner of government, with a degree of limited autonomy (as Calvin wished). Calvin did accept a kind of governmental power over church.

Calvin wanted the church there to go back to the apostolic time and celebrate eucharist every Sunday. However, the city council of Geneva turned down Calvin's recommendation and approved the Eucharist to be celebrated only four times a year. While Calvin did not protest in any sustained way since the government had the power to approve or disapprove this, Calvin called this decision a "defect" because "it failed to follow 'the apostles' example."[12] It was only later, when Calvin was invited back to Geneva a second time, that he became a stronger theological authority in the city and was asked to exercise a role that was both religious and civil. "Calvin was given two crucial tasks: first, to draft regulations for Geneva's church; second, to draft a secular constitution for the republic." By 1546, "Calvin was in a very secure position" in Geneva,[13] as a very influential figure on religious, social, and consequently political issues.

Calvin's ecclesiology enhanced both civil and religious spheres. The ways in which he structured the church with a pastor, teachers, elders and deacons, and the way he established the *ordinances* of the church clearly

---

1533; *Petit traicté de la saincte cène*, and *La Forme des priers et chants ecclésistiques*, 1542.

11. Some of the examples are Calvin, "Tract of the Relics," 287–341; Calvin, "Warning Against Judiciary Astrology and Other Prevalent Curiosities," 157–89.

12. Calvin as quoted in Bower, ed., *Companion to the Book of Common Worship*, 8.

13. Naphy, "Calvin's Geneva," 29.

reveal a political perspective on the ways people should behave in town. They include

> the sacraments, baptism and the Lord's Supper, and on marriage, Christian burial, the visitation of the sick, visiting prisoners, catechizing children, and a detailed specification of how the consistory of elders and ministers were to be chosen and exercise their task of "oversight of the life of everyone."[14]

For this reason, Calvin insisted that the church had to have the right to excommunicate, a right that the city council resolved to install.

As Haight affirms, "the role of discipline, that is, 'a comprehensive censorship of morals' which in his letter to Sadoleto Calvin judged to be one of the pillars of the church, finds expression in the several institutions and stipulations designed to promote and ensure it."[15] Calvin was not easy on those who violated the moral code that was supervised by the church so as to maintain not only the order and purity of the city but also the doctrine and the sacraments.

The excommunication issue came to a head in the case of Philibert Berthelier, who was excommunicated by the church, but appealed the decision to the council which ruled in his favor. On the next communion Sunday, Calvin reaffirmed the non-competency of the council in excommunication and warned any who were excommunicated not to present themselves."[16] What followed was a battle between the church and the city council over church power. The case was finally settled in favor of the church, as the council acknowledged the church's competence and relative autonomy. At that point Calvin's influence over the city was finally sealed.

Calvin also had to confront the refugee issue. In 1551, Geneva was invaded by more than 5,000 refugees, who constituted half of its population. These refugees had economic means and increased the cost of living in the city. "In response," says Naphy,

> xenophobia and confessional solidarity grew as one . . . the arrival of noble refugees with their prejudices and societal expectations exacerbated the situation. Geneva's merchant society resented the pretensions of refugee nobles. All these issues paled into insignificance before the greater questions: how many

14. Haight, "Calvin's Ecclesiology," in *Christian Community in History*, 2:98.

15. Ibid., 2:99.

16. Parker, *John Calvin*, 124, quoted in Haight, "Calvin's Ecclesiology," in *Christian Community in History*, 2:100.

refugees would stay and how was the city to limit their impact on Geneva's factional politics?[17]

The problem of having outsiders within the city was reflected not only in the economics of the city but also in a whole range of theological perspectives and liturgical practices which put the existing religious structure in danger. Calvin, a refugee himself,[18] came down on the side of the refugees and made a case for those who had died fighting for the city.[19] Most of these refugees were French people, some of whom eventually took political positions in Geneva's leadership and helped Calvin to win over some of the Genevan partisans.

Three people posed difficult theological problems for Calvin: Bolsec, Servetus and Castellio. Bolsec challenged Calvin's harsh doctrine of predestination which was not well received by some of the city authorities and ministers. Calvin won that battle and Bolsec was expelled from the city. Michael Servetus had an even more tragic end.[20] Servetus was against the doctrine of the Trinity and for that heresy was sentenced to death by the Roman Catholic church in Vienne. Castellio published "Whether Heretics Should Be Persecuted," a year after Servetus death. He was fostering an idea of tolerance but also questioned Calvin's understandings "about predestination, the trinity and Christ's descent into hell." Calvin saw Castellio's theological positions as "a deadly threat to faith in Christ."[21] He was then forbidden to speak.[22] Calvin, through controversies of different kinds with a range of opponents, established his position as theological spokesperson for a certain position within the Reformed movement (internationally), and this in a sense enhanced his position in the city of Geneva.

Calvin also had written against the Libertines and the Anabaptists. Against the Anabaptists, he wrote a treatise entitled *Brief Instruction for Arming All the Good Faithful Against the Errors on the Common Sect of*

17. Naphy, "Calvin's Geneva," 32.

18. Calvin only received his citizenship form the Council of Geneva in 1559, five years before he died.

19. Calvin had been a pastor of a church of French refugees in Strasbourg showing his pastoral care with outsiders. After his death, Calvin left some of his estate to the Bourse for Refugees.

20. It is interesting to see that the case of Servetus is rarely mentioned by reformed theologians.

21. Ibid., 18.

22. Ibid., 17; emphasis added.

the Anabaptist. His intention was to eradicate these errors by arming the faithful with the true gospel of Christ. As for the libertines, Calvin wrote *Against the Libertines* and saw them as "radicals [who] developed a hermeneutic that separated the 'letter' from the 'spirit,' and they likely propagated a pantheistic and speculative spiritualism."[23]

It was not without reason that the eucharist was also a place to symbolize the conundrum of the life of the city. There was power at stake and the eucharistic table was a privileged place that gave standing to political groups that took positions in favor of or against the city's larger project. This power was vested in the Consistory—and the Company of Pastors was an influential body in relation to this—and Calvin was an influential presence in both.[24] It was not Calvin who was fencing the table but the point here is the connection between the political, the social, and the theological/liturgical.

As Roger Haight reminds us, "Calvin lists what might be called the three pillars of the church: 'doctrine, discipline and the sacraments' and to these a fourth is added: ceremonies, by which to exercise the people in 'offices of piety.' These themes are subsumed into Calvin's systematic ecclesiology in the *Institutes* of 1559."[25]

> Some traditional Protestant congregations and some Pentecostal churches had decided that, in the following year, their missionary goal was to get rid of 50 terreiros, a liturgical space of a religion called Candomblé, with roots coming from Africa. These Christians believed that this religion was from the Devil and wanted to make those who practiced Candomblé disappear in a large metropolitan city. Every Friday night they would gather at church to pray and ask God to destroy the work of Satan in the city. After prayer, some of them would go to the door of the terreiros and throw stones at their roof in the name of Jesus trying to annoy and disrupt their worship services. After many years of intense evangelization, the Christians succeeded in many ways, since many terreiros had been discontinued due to the conversion of Candomblé leaders to Pentecostal churches. One woman, however, went the opposite way, and was converted from a Pentecostal church to Candomblé. She became

23. Gamble, "Calvin's Controversies," 190.

24. Calvin's "table is fenced, for one does not communicate without discernment" (Burki, "Reformed Tradition in Continental Europe: Switzerland, France and Germany," 443).

25. Haight, "Calvin's Ecclesiology," in *Christian Community in History*, 2:97.

> *a leader in one of these terreiros but she was scared. Nothing would*
> *deter these Christians from their mission. She would call the police but*
> *some of them were from some of these Christian churches and wouldn't*
> *do anything. She couldn't even talk to those Christians because every*
> *time she said something, they would start to cast her demons out and*
> *wouldn't listen to her. They couldn't dialogue. A religious war was burst-*
> *ing with rage underneath a society that thought they lived in so-called*
> *religious cordiality. However, a dispute over power was going on and the*
> *most violent group was "winning."*

As we can see, Calvin's power over the city of Geneva was broad and intense. The examples described above show the intricate links between Calvin's theology, liturgical understandings, ecclesiological structure, and his social, moral, economic, and political influence on the city of Geneva. Calvin's ecclesiology mixed civil and ecclesiastical affairs in ways that were very troublesome to those who wanted to see Calvin's influence only in spiritual terms. All of these cases of discipline and of relations between the church and political authorities were deeply related to the eucharistic table. Banishment from the eucharistic table was a sign of being on the outside of the small and large community (church and the city), that one was either missing something, dealing with sin, struggling with faith, or lacking the understanding of the true faith and consequently not able to acquire a proper place within the societal structure and the spiritual realm of God. As Ganoczy says, ". . . Calvin never tired of demanding a specifi-cally ecclesiastical moral discipline—especially of excommunication, i.e., exclusion of specific sinners of the Genevan community from the Lord's Supper."[26]

As mentioned before, Calvin's theological assessments had double perspectives. Calvin's *political ecclesiology* was central to the assessment of the sacraments and the relation between his ecclesiology and the politi-cal affairs demonstrate this complication. For him, church and state were two distinct institutions, each with its own autonomy, call, vocation, and spheres of actions. Both agencies shared a working relationship which was always ambiguous and tense, competing over the ownership of the issues at hand.

Calvin's writings and acts in Geneva show this ambiguous and yet clear relationship between the church and the state. His influence in

26. Ganoczy, "Calvin's Life," 18.

Geneva was definitely important. However, the way Calvin exercised power depended on his rhetorical gifts (he needed to persuade people) and not on some sort of episcopal dignity. His influence was seen in various ways. As Taylor suggests, Calvin helped theologically to support the economic decision of approving profit and interest, or in other words, approving of a *little usury* to the city council in order to expand business in the city.[27] This move, again, not done by Calvin alone but also influenced by other reformers (and perhaps from the Company of Pastors), ended up influencing the economic configuration of the world, and was later developed by Adam Smith. Even Smith's use of the image of the *invisible hand* to describe structural movements within the economic world was taken from Calvin who used it to describe God's providence. Thus, the difficult movement of approximation and differentiation between church and state, social and political themes were always complicated, and in need of constant negotiation.

Implicated in this constant wrestling and unending negotiations was the powerful symbol of the eucharist. As a theological symbol, it held in itself all of Calvin's dearest doctrinal emphases in the trinitarian Christian faith, namely, sovereignty, providence, incarnation, redemption, grace, faith, stewardship, and sanctification. Moreover, the eucharistic table served to identify the fences within the religious and civil battles, and consequently the issue of hospitality that interests us here. The ways that the church conveyed God's presence within the body of Christ were the ways that the entire world should receive God's grace and will. As Elwood says regarding the importance of the eucharistic symbol in Calvin's thought to delineate the social world:

> [B]ecause the eucharist served to symbolize power considered in a general sense, and not sacred potency alone, the effect of the Calvinist reorientation was not restricted to the realm of the theological definition. It influenced the way ordinary men and women conceived of political power, interpreted their social world, and established the relation between the sacred and society.[28]

Picking up the theological results regarding eucharist and its consequent incarnation perspectives, let us now analyze the political consequences of the political paradigm Calvin proposed in his eucharistic theology. First, if the eucharistic table was an important structure of social

27. M. C. Taylor, *After God*, 103.
28. Elwood, *Body Broken*, 4.

and political power within medieval times, one has to tackle the doctrine of transubstantiation to understand how that power was evoked and employed.

When Calvin proposes his own theological signification on the sacrament of the eucharist, he provokes drastic changes of power.[29] Calvin's defense of God's sovereignty and radical freedom emancipates God's restraints from the church and the sacraments and dislocates power. Calvin was not simply rejecting transubstantiation but rather, calling for a local bodily presence of God and his theology was developed out of a complex elaboration between the distinction of sign and thing. Against a tendency to reduce God's transcendent power to presence immanent within the bread, or to collapsing of the sign (Christ) into the thing (bread), Calvin managed to keep both God's presence in the eucharistic elements in a tensioned relationship. As Elwood points out:

> As Calvin's theory denied to physical signs any power independent of the agency of the Holy Spirit, the eucharistic elements were in effect degraded from their position as media for the appearance of divine power—bearers of God's body—and reduced to the status of mere instruments of the Spirit without any subsistent virtue.[30]

This change of signification shifted the *locus* of God's power from the sacrament of the altar, i.e., from the church, to a more transcendent inner power, the Spirit, who was now in charge of turning the elements into a sacrament and *pronouncing* the presence of God within the heart of the believer. With this theological re-signification and linguistic move, Calvin created an alternative economy of power. In Calvin, God's power in the eucharist signified by the Holy Spirit creates a distinction of the normative connection between the bread and body of Christ, sign and thing, while this connection is never lost. Calvin's theology emphasized a transcendent God, and that emphasis prevented any absolute claim by human institutions. Since God is and has absolute power and there is no figure, institution, event or sign that can clearly claim with certainty God's power, it is God as Spirit who ultimately decides. The irony of this theological move is that when God becomes totally transcendent, incapable of being conceptualized, God disappears.[31] Calvin's God was a transcendent one who

29. For this part I rely on Elwood, *Body Broken*, 56–76.

30. Ibid., 74.

31. "God can disappear in two ways: on the one hand, God can become so transcendent that He is functionally irrelevant, and on the other, the divine can become so

was to be attained by reason/knowledge rather than material elements. However, while Calvin's theology suppressed the corporeal, the magical, and the superstitious, it cannot be said that it lost its incarnational weight. Nonetheless this is how many have received Calvin. This transcendentalist emphasis over his incarnational one ended up having a serious influence on the liturgical practices of the church in our time. This reception has been so influential that Elwood says that "To an extent, then, the world inhabited by readers receptive of Calvin's view was becoming 'rationalized' or 'disenchanted,' to use Max Weber's terminology, as the symbols of immanental potency were displaced."[32]

However, Calvin's God does not simply disappear. Elwood is quick to say that even though Calvin's God was wholly transcendent, God "is nonetheless intimately involved in the temporal causal nexus."[33] God's incarnation is not only possible but necessary, accomplished once and for all in Jesus Christ. The sacraments not only hold the possibility of God's revelation through the Spirit but it gives the confidence that we are united with Christ in the sacrament. Calvin's sacramental theology, amplifies the acts of God in the world.

I conclude with Elwood's description of a paradigm shift on the structure of power in Calvin's thought. Using an analogy of the sacramental elements, Elwood offers a connection between the power of God and the power of governments and kings in Calvin's thought that was formed on the basis of the Eucharistic paradigm:

> Rather than being regarded as either sacred or secular, political and social orders, by analogy with the sacramental elements, were likely seen by the attentive reader of Calvin's writings as God's instruments, possessing no inherent or abiding virtue and exercising power only as a result of the active determination of God. This shift in paradigms, it should be stressed, was no subtle change in emphasis. To the extent that the paradigm of instrumentality stressed a distinction between the physical medium and the power deployed through it, it facilitated a critical approach to representations of power. Just as the physical media of the eucharist were subject to critical scrutiny, regarded in the Calvinist scheme as merely "earthly and corruptible elements," so too were those temporal instrumentalities laying claim to authority over the body politic, especially when a particular

immanent that God and the world are one" (M. C. Taylor, *After God*, 106).

32. Elwood, *Body Broken*, 75.

33. Ibid., 75.

exercise of power appeared to conflict with any given theological norm.[34]

The incarnation of Christ is now under intense and critical scrutiny. No temporal instrument of God's power can absolutely convey God's power. This power is open to be claimed and to be criticized at the same time. Where does the true power of God appear in this world? How is Christ to be incarnated in our world? Who can control the Spirit of God?

At a meeting with some members of the Presbytery's Task Force, a group of pastors and elders who were to work together with me and oversee, guide and offer companionship to our work in Fall River, I described my work and made observations about what I was seeing and learning. Our church was made up mostly of non-documented immigrants and I was helping them to find their lives around the city in many ways, which for some included breaking the law. After some discussion, an elder vehemently forbade me to break the laws of this country to help illegal immigrants. I told them that I could not be a pastor if I could not try to help them. Another pastor asked me if I could prevent myself from doing unlawful things. I kept quiet. Finally, another member of the group said: "Okay, do what you need to do, but do not tell us." I only asked them to help me in case I was caught. There was a general sense in that meeting that I was doing something wrong, but at the same time they knew this community was a group of people who didn't know anything about me besides my reports. I got home on that Thursday afternoon feeling at the same time encouraged and completely alone in this work. Of course the North American church could not comply with my unlawful actions. So, they stayed closed to me as they placed themselves away from me. My questions going home were: where do I belong? What community am I a part of? Who is my family? Where are the concrete signs and symbols that I can hold to tell myself to which community I belong? My schizophrenic feelings were just one of an array of symptoms of the dizziness that comes to those who work in and around borders. I was caught up between the rules of the Presbyterian Church (U.S.A.) and the laws of this country and the borders of illegality in my community. My split identity was brutally marked by my "Portuglish," neither properly Portuguese nor English. Moreover, I had to translate the Portuguese speaking community to the Task Force and the Task Force to the community.

34. Ibid., 74.

But the community didn't know about what had happened. Not only that, but the fact that I had proper documents to live in this country established an uncrossed separation between myself and my community, something that I could never figure out. On Friday, I decided to celebrate the eucharist in a different way. We had a liturgical team in the church and we decided to talk about family. We placed three large tables connected at the main corridor of the nave of the church and prepared it with fruit, water, honey, bread, crackers, different spreads, wine, and juice. On the table there were colorful flowers and many pictures taken throughout the four-year history of the community. There were pictures of former and present members of the church, from families visiting from Brazil, pictures of the white Anglo members of the Presbytery who either had visited us or had invited us to visit them. The pictures captured different moments in the life of the church. They were there to create a sense of family in constant transition. When people arrived at the church, they were surprised by the huge table that extended all the way from the main door to the front of the church. When the time for the sacrament of the eucharist came, I invited everybody to the table. When the community was gathered around the table, I asked them to look at the pictures and asked, "What does this table mean to you? Look at the pictures and the people around you, and think about what this community means to you. While you look at these pictures serve somebody who is around the table." After a period of conversation I asked them about what this church and this table meant to them. A variety of responses were forthcoming: people celebrated the fact that they had a community to worship and to live with; that the church was their family; that North Americans were also their family, even if they could not talk to them; that they hoped to get a Green Card and feel accepted in the country, that they felt oppressed by their superiors at their jobs, that they missed their home and families in Brazil; and that they did not know what family they belonged to anymore. In the midst of it all, eating and drinking, the words of the institution[35] were said and I affirmed that that table was the sacrament with other things on the table. People felt both connected and disconnected with this foreign way to celebrate the sacrament and with themselves. No single word regarding preconditions for participating in the sacrament was mentioned and nobody said anything. Guests and members, children and adults, baptized and

---

35. Within Presbyterian churches, the "Words of Institution" are so entrenched in the rite of the eucharist that they are often used as an instrument to authenticate the sacrament.

> un-baptized, all ate and served each other and talked about God, life
> and community through those pictures. A certain joy and estrangement
> about an uncertain belonging to the Presbyterian Church (U.S.A.) was
> also hovering around the table, due to the fact that they were not a legal
> part of this country. However, there were some assurances about being
> part of that church[36] and a feeling of being lost between many borders,
> of being unable to name what a family could be. Around that table we
> were caught by the unpredictable: we were neither at home, nor not at
> home. It was a ghostly, uncanny feeling.

Within the eucharistic table, God is free and moves freely. The Spirit
moves where the Spirit wants and God is not limited to the elements of
the table but works through them. Thus, the presence of God cannot be
captured by any human element since the presence of God always escapes
theological encapsulation. In a sense, God's presence is always elsewhere.

Elwood refers to a dialectic present in Calvin as freedom and communication which is the relation between the movement of the Spirit and
the ordination of God.[37] For Calvin, God's will is clearly an ordained
will—ordained in certain ways, even limited, in some ways, by God's free
willing and acting to redeem in actual, particular ways.

By defining the presence of God in the eucharist, Calvin was also
defining what was unfaithful, superstitious, and magical. He was at the
same time establishing his own structure of knowledge and, consequently,
the laws of God's ordination and manifestation. The result was that, from a
Scholastic view of God's absolute power, the sovereignty of God was also at
risk in Calvin's eucharistic table. Since Calvin, among his theological and
liturgical heirs, the freedom and communication/ordination/fencing of
God's movement around the table has shifted in many ways, through various theological receptions, differentiating forms of sacramental practices,
world views, and political movements.

To participate in the sacrament, to recite the *Sursum Corda*, to pray
the prayer of epiclesis, to eat the bread and drink the wine, to encounter
Jesus and be fed spiritually, is a constant way of shifting fences around
the table through the scrutiny of bodies of power, both theologically and

36. This sort of assurance came from the fact that they all had a direct phone
number to call, which was the pastor's cell phone, if they were caught up in any situation that they did not know how to handle themselves. Also, the church had two
lawyers on a stand-by basis in case of any emergency.

37. Elwood, *Body Broken*, 73.

political, individually and socially. The walls/borders of the Eucharist were marked by strong regulations of theological and political powers which also controlled acceptance, access and the limits of hospitality. However, the borders of the eucharist cannot claim in a way that establishes certainty either God's absolute presence within these fences or God's demand for impermeable fences. Thus, the eucharistic table claims both that God's presence is beyond any limit imposed on the table and at the same time that the table should be fenced. Any sacramental theology of the table should criticize a demand for absolute power that wants to define the guest list welcoming those invited to God's own table. In the end, God's table is always God's table, a space that is ours neither to define nor to leave unattended/empty of guests.

Taking on God's freedom in Calvin's thought, and not so much God's communication, we can say that God moves freely and unconstrainedly around the table. Moreover, since God's incarnation is not collapsed into the eucharistic elements anymore and, ideally, cannot be held by human constraints, the eucharist implies a theological principle where the incarnation of Christ in our world is irreducible to any material manifestation opening itself up to endless possibilities of cultural manifestations. Yet, in and through each of these endless manifestations of Christ, the table is a place where we wrestle with our theological, social, and political limits.

Taking our cue from Calvin's emphasis on God's freedom and bracketing for a moment his understanding of God's communication, we can say that God moves freely and unconstrainedly around the table. Moreover, since God's incarnation is no longer, after God's embodiment in Jesus, an appearance in flesh or matter and is not collapsed into the eucharistic elements—since God's presence, ideally, cannot be held by human constraints/instrumentalities—the Eucharist (then) underlines a key theological principle: the incarnation of Christ in our world is irreducible to any material manifestation and thus opens itself up to endless possibilities of expression and experience in multiple cultural manifestations/spaces. It is after God's endless possibilities of expression in Christ that God's communication comes to us, helping us stretch our boundaries and organize ourselves better. It is after our eating and communing together that we can figure out how God might have communicated with us and helps us structure ourselves for the next time we meet. Attentive to the free way that the Spirit moves in and thorough us we can hear God's communication to us.

Yet, in and through each of these endless appearances of Christ, the table is a place where we constantly wrestle with our theological, social, and political limits.

Theological Dimensions

Calvin belonged to the second generation of reformers. Martin Luther, Guillaume Farel, John Oecolampadius, Ulrich Zwingli, and many others had already written and disagreed about the eucharist. Reacting against the Roman church, they formulated their own understandings of the eucharist and found in different cities support from popular and/or political authorities who wanted to break ties with the Roman church. Calvin's sacramental theology is in many ways an answer to the many mistakes that he believed were associated with the eucharist coming especially from the Roman quarters but also from the Anabaptists and Libertines. However, it was also an answer to current theological debates among the reformers. In order to appreciate Calvin's sacramental theology we have to summarize how the Roman Church, Luther, and Zwingli understood the eucharist.

The Fourth Lateran Council established some of the concepts that the reformers were to attack later. The church wanted to administer the life of the Christian community from religious laws and hold control over other spiritual experiences that were happening outside of the church's official liturgical offices.[38] The very beginning of its decree sets forth the Councils view of the Eucharist:

> There is indeed one universal church of the faithful, outside of which nobody at all is saved, in which Jesus Christ is both priest and sacrifice. His body and blood are truly contained in the sacrament of the altar under the forms of bread and wine, the bread and the wine having been changed in substance, by God's power, into his body and blood, so that in order to achieve this mystery of unity we receive from God what he received from us. Nobody can effect this sacrament except a priest who has been properly ordained according to the church's keys, which Jesus Christ himself gave to the apostles and their successors.[39]

This doctrinal emphasis on the real presence gave more power to the clergy; meant less lay participation in the liturgy; required explanations by allegories (illustrations and paintings on the walls, liturgical objects, the

38. Tanner, ed., *Decrees of the Ecumenical Councils*, 227.
39. Ibid., 230.

altar as a place where Christ is sacrificed, the bread being held up by the priest, etc.); and viewed the sacrament as a magical mystery. The Fourth Lateran Council issued theological statements based on philosophical frameworks of the age in order to teach about transubstantiation. In addition, with the Fourth Lateran Council a whole set of liturgical changes regarding church architecture and new liturgical elements were set in course over time to honor the host. For example, gold and silver chalices and patens, monstrances and altar cloths. The festivities around Corpus Christi absorbed all of these changes.

The reformers considered the theological *deviations* in this decree to be the doctrine of transubstantiation, the Mass as a sacrifice, and the central role of the priest representing God on earth. The "changed in substance" vocabulary used by the Fourth Lateran Council to define the Eucharist was very problematic to the reformers. The doctrine of the transubstantiation later developed by the Council of Trent, affirms that the words of institution during the Mass change the bread, the host, and the wine, into the body and blood of Christ. The substance of the bread and the wine yields to the substance of Christ while the appearance of the bread stays the same. In linguistic terms, the bread, i.e., the thing, and the body of Christ, i.e., the sign of the thing were the same at the same time. Thomas Aquinas' use of Aristotle's categories of accident and substance became the philosophical and theological framework for defining transubstantiation. Thus, the presence of Christ is vivid, real, material, and corporeal (even if invisible).

The Mass, the celebration of the Eucharist, was also understood by Catholics to be the reenactment of the crucifixion of Christ. Thus, every time the Mass was said, Christ's sacrifice was offered to people. Due to that, the eucharist was called the "sacrament of the altar," where the passion and sacrifice of Christ was to be enacted through the transubstantiation of the bread and the wine into the body and blood of Christ.[40] Protestants, on the contrary, affirmed that the eucharist was not a propitiatory sacrifice but an act of thanksgiving only. The reformed also took issue with the Council's emphasis upon the sole authority of the priest over the administration of the "sacrament of the altar," and the consequent lack of laypeople's participation in the liturgy, as well as the Council's requirement that people should receive the sacrament of the eucharist at least once a year for the

---

40. For the Catholic Church, the altar became also a place where not only the death of Christ was presented but also the death of Christian martyrs.

sake of their personal salvation. The numbers of people partaking of the Eucharist in the Mass declined[41]

It was not until the Council of Trent (1545–1563) that the Catholic church responded officially to the Reformation attacks. The beginning of the Council's decree makes clear the theological affirmations about the doctrine of transubstantiation and consequently, the sacrificial aspect of the Mass. The Council of Trent affirms:

> In the first place, the holy council teaches and openly and without qualification professes that, after the consecration of the bread and the wine, our Lord Jesus Christ, true God and true man, is truly, really and substantially contained in the propitious sacrament of the holy eucharist under the appearance of these things which are perceptible to the senses . . . The body is present under the form of bread and the blood under the form of wine, by virtue of the words . . . And so this holy council now declares it once again—that, by the consecration of the bread and wine, there takes place the change of the whole substance of the bread into the substance of the body of Christ our Lord, and of the whole substance of the wine into the substance of his blood.[42]

While Trent strongly affirmed the doctrine of the transubstantiation in the eucharist, the reformers were divided in their understandings of the real presence of God in the sacrament. Luther's main theological act regarding the eucharist was to turn the outward ritualization of the sacrament into an inward search. Before Luther, the faithful gained assurance of salvation through participation in the sacrament at church at least once a year. Salvation was thus located in the church, on the altar, outside of the believer's body and mind, and in the faithful participation in it. Luther maintained an objective concentration, encouraging the Christian not to look to him/herself for what he/she possesses, but outward, to Christ. And this is reflected in his concentration, in his understanding of the eucharist, on an outward, objective, bodily presence of Christ. However, to turn to

41. Wandel says that "the ever close identification of the priests with the Eucharist seems to have had as one of its consequences the decline in lay participation in the Mass. Over those five centuries, the laity had been relegated to an increasingly passive role: to listen to an increasingly unintelligible text, to witness a miracle in which they did not participate, to be denied the wine, the blood of Christ, and to be given the bread on their tongues, so that they might not carry it away" (Wandel, *The Eucharist in the Reformation*, 33).

42. Tanner, ed., *Decrees of the Ecumenical Councils*, 694, 695.

Christ is, in many ways, to look inwards to oneself to find Christ. With this move, Luther helped turn the assurance of salvation into an individual, inward assurance; the believer's faith was now directed towards God inside of one's heart and subjectivity, not outside in the eucharistic Host. This change was huge and became one important trademark of the reformation movement.

This turn to subjectivity also reflects the way Calvin and other reformers understood the eucharist. God does not appear externally, in the elevation of the Host, but is experienced in what is essentially an inner event; Christ was to be united with the believer in his/her heart. For the reformers, the consecrated elements lose their intrinsic power of salvation and the priest loses his function as a mediator between the people and God. Even though the covenant community, i.e., the church, is essential to the development of the faith and life of the Christian, and the Eucharist is a powerful communal experience to be enacted as the church of Christ, salvation itself is not to be understood as mediated institutionally but rather, as an individual event.[43] What happens is that while Eucharistic practices in the late sixteenth century still have lots of institutional power being exercised, what comes after, with Calvin followers, is that the church starts to lose its power as the physical intermediary power between people and God, as God's holder of salvation on earth. Nonetheless, according to Mark C. Taylor, in the sixteenth century truth becomes a subjective matter, open to be negotiated between individual believers and God:

> Luther affirmed the priesthood of all believers. Since Spirit moves where it will, God can speak through anybody. This pivotal doctrine leads to what can be best described as the deregulation and decentralization first of religious and eventually political authority.[44]

These changes are important to Luther's notion of eucharist. Since his theology privileged an inner relation with God, the church as an institution could not be assigned unquestioned power anymore. The church could not hold power over Christ's presence or be regarded as offering a

43. M. C. Taylor, *After God*, 89

44. Ibid., 95. Elwood criticizes Taylor's oversimplification of Luther in many accounts, especially his take on Luther's subjectivity. Among other things he tells me he mentions the following: "The Reformation tendency to emphasize interiority (and this is present in Catholic figures as well as Protestants) could be used to undercut the absolute authority of the ecclesiastical institution, and (I would say over the long term) it had that effect for most Protestant churches" (email to author, July 2010).

sacrifice to God in every Mass. Moreover, the Mass loses its reliance on the role of the priest who, like Christ, was representing God as a channel of God's grace to the people present at the Mass. Contrary to that, the reformers proposed the universal priesthood of believers. In Calvin this meant that all the believers were equal before God. The church was to have governing offices to undertake specific vocations within the body of Christ—pastors, teachers, elders, and deacons, but none of these offices was to be higher in importance before God. Pastors, among other things, were supposed to minister to the people, functionally speak with the authority of God if they followed the Word of the Scripture and celebrate Eucharist. In this church of equality, with a functional differentiation, the laity were expected to render obedience to church leaders, even if the people should also obey the pastor.

She left her two boys with her mother at home in order to find a job in United States. Helped by a friend, she got a job and started to work in a factory. She shares an apartment with six other women from other parts of South and Central America. On the weekends, she works for a middle class family as a nanny and domestica. On Sunday morning she goes with the family to a Presbyterian church. After a while, she is able to send money to her mother and children. After six months she still does not speak English. One day her boss calls her into his office. She is shy and keeps quiet. The boss starts to say that she is not working well, that he knows that she does not have papers and that he will have to call the immigration authority on her. She can understand immigration and gets panicked. He locks the door and tells her that she can choose whether he calls immigration or not. She can't sleep that night and the next day she tells her friends that she is not going to work. Her friends convince her to go since jobs were getting tougher and tougher to find. She gets up and goes to work. The same thing happens the next day. She tells her friend and her friend invites her to go to a Pentecostal church. She does not understand what is going on there but feels her heart heavy and somber. She misses her boys. She meets a Mexican guy who works in the onion fields and they plan to see each other the next day at the church. They connect immediately. The next day they meet and she tells him what is happening with her at the factory. He tells her that he will try to get her a job in the onion fields. She waits the next day anxiously. She goes to the church but he does not show up. She hears that he was caught up by the immigration authorities. She sinks and thinks of going back home.

> *During the message, she cries so deeply that the leaders think she is pos-*
> *sessed with a bad spirit. She accepts Jesus as her personal savior and*
> *lord. Next day she goes to the factory. She hits her boss and runs away.*
> *She stays home until Friday. Saturday she goes to see the family. She is*
> *confused and exhausted. Sunday she goes to church. There is Eucharist.*
> *From the back of the church she watches everybody participate. She is*
> *taking care of the kids. Nobody speaks Portuguese. People barely talk to*
> *her after the service. She is always with the kids. At most she receives*
> *"Hola," "Mucho gusto," as if she spoke Spanish. Sunday night she goes*
> *back to her apartment. Her friends make her coffee. She does not know*
> *what to do. She misses her kids.*

For Calvin and many protestant reformers, God's presence, sacra-mentally experienced, was not a product of human effort or ritual action. God was in charge of the sacrament through the Holy Spirit and could appear without depending on proper human gestures, words, or physical conditions of the elements.

In place of the teaching of transubstantiation, Luther affirmed Christ's real, substantial presence along with the substance of the bread and the wine. The presence of Christ's body did not change the substance of the elements. For him, God was still materially present in the eucharist but not *in place of* the bread and the wine. The body of Christ was present "in, next to, or by the bread,"[45] not as a replacement for the substance of the bread.[46] Luther defended the presence of Christ in the eucharist as a necessary moment for forgiveness and also a moment to receive God's grace.

Luther debated many times against Zwingli about the eucharist. With Luther, Zwingli denied the Mass as a sacrifice but unlike Luther, he affirmed that the eucharist was only a sign of remembrance. Zwingli could not see the presence of Christ in any way in the Eucharist. Christ's body had ascended to heaven and could not "come back" to the earth every time the Eucharist was celebrated. He also could not agree with Luther's idea of

45. Luther, "Ain kurtzer einfeltiger bericht," quoted in Wandel, *Eucharist in the Reformation*, 89.

46. It is important to clarify Luther's so-called doctrine of "consubstantiation," El-wood says: "This view is sometimes referred to as consubstantiation, since the reality of Christ is thought to be present 'with' the essential reality of the elements." The point is that Luther insisted on nothing called consubstantiation, and certainly no "doctrine" or philosophical/metaphysical explanation of the presence of Christ. From an email.

Christ's ubiquity which he felt turned Christ's body into an abnormal body with many parts spread everywhere. Moreover, Zwingli was dismayed by the very possibility of tasting or even biting Christ's own body. However, Zwingli did not deny Christ's presence in the eucharist since it was a necessary way of identifying Jesus' incarnation. But he was clear to assert that the Eucharist was only a sign of Christ's presence, a pure spiritual presence completely detached from the elements.

Calvin's theology found a middle way between Luther and Zwingli. Calvin's eucharistic theology is more dualistic than Luther but his theology of symbol was deeper than Zwingli. He wanted to find a balance between these two positions. He denied both Roman transubstantiation and Lutheran consubstantiation. On the other hand, he could not agree with Zwingli's overemphasis on a merely symbolic aspect of the eucharist. For him, the elements did not hold any physical, immediate, or concrete meaning related to the body of Christ. Once ascended into heaven, the body of Christ does not return to the earth physically. Calvin deplored Luther's theological idea of the ubiquity for the same reasons Zwingli did.[47] What the sacrament did, however, was to affirm Jesus' real presence spiritually. In other words, the presence of Jesus was not in the elements, but in the experience of union with Christ, created by God through the work of the Holy Spirit. Moreover, through the sacrament the Holy Spirit was at work, using the elements, word, gesture, and the faith of believers to effect an intimate encounter with the reality of Christ.

Calvin's understanding of the eucharist distinguishes spirit and matter. To identify one with the other, i.e., the bread with Christ, would be to lose the main aspect of his theological construction which was based on *re-presentation*.[48] His sacramental theology entailed a *re-presentation* of God by means of grace, Scripture, preaching, and the sacraments, but they were always dependent on the work of the Holy Spirit. Without the Spirit there was no sacrament. Calvin's representational theology, especially related to Christ and the doctrine of incarnation, was a theological move done in connection to and in dependence on his emphasis on God's sovereignty and God's providence. If the body of Christ is truly (bodily) present in the Host and scattered all around, God becomes too attached and even dependent on the physical strictures of the elements. The result is that God loses sovereignty, since God's transcendence is collapsed into these

47. Calvin, *Institutes of the Christian Religion*, 4.17.30.

48. For a deeper analysis of Calvin's theology of signification, see Elwood, *Body Broken*, 56–76.

substances and God becomes not only dependent on them but disappears in them. In other words, once transubstantiated, God's transcendence is lost to finite modes of existence. God loses sovereignty and becomes contingent and equivalent to a piece of bread. Moreover, a God who depends on the human enactment of a sacramental rite cannot provide or sustain order for his people. What Calvin sees in transubstantiation is the collapse of the sign into the thing, God into the bread. The theological results go even further: Christ's glory and divinity is reduced to a local presence. The Host is not only the ultimate contradiction of God's sovereignty but also an idolatrous movement away from Christ's glory, one that detaches what belongs to Christ and superstitiously identifies His Glory with material things.

Calvin's use of the sacrament as a *medium* of grace preserves both the glory of God which is and must remain untouched, and, at the same time, habilitates and enhances the human heart to be transformed by an encounter with Christ who cannot be seen by the material elements of the Eucharist but can be known only by the eyes of faith. For the believers, the Holy Spirit conveys the true substance of Christ. As Elwood says, "[w]hile Calvin affirms the representational character of the sacrament, he insists on 'true' representation, to the extent of claiming that the substance of Christ's body is conveyed to the believing communicants."[49]

The spiritual and theological transformation does not rely on the elements solely, but on the heart of the believer. Therefore, the sacrament is more than "merely" symbolic because it entails an involvement between the believer and the Holy Spirit. The believer, through the inner work of the Spirit, is taken into heaven to encounter Jesus seated at the right hand of God. As part of this inward/spiritual/faithful exercise, the community affirms the *Sursum Corda* (Lift up your hearts/We lift them up to the Lord) and believes that by the Holy Spirit they encounter Jesus, their spiritual food.[50] Elwood explains that Calvin's use of the word *substance* is "an attempt to express the *efficacy* of the signification operative in the eucharist: the sacrament really conveys the whole Christ and all Christ's benefits to faithful communicants, and in the Supper Christians become one with him."[51]

The spiritual/material communication, or the eucharistic efficacy, relies on the Holy Spirit who uses the means of the sacrament of the

49. Elwood, *Body Broken*, 67.
50. Calvin, "Short Treatise on the Holy Supper," quoted in ibid.
51. Elwood, *Body Broken*, 68; emphasis added.

eucharist. This power makes this ritual not a purely human action but rather, *a sacrament*, i.e., an instrument that channels God's grace. The efficacy of the sacrament happens every time one participates in the Eucharist when the Holy Spirit unites the believer with Christ and the body of Christ. In order to be taken by the Holy Spirit to be united with Christ, one has to receive the gift of faith, given by God. This in turn provides a proper understanding of God and participation in the sacraments.

The relation between the sacraments and the participant happens through faith and faith is given and nourished by the Holy Spirit. Faith is what makes knowledge of God *firm*. However, one is never sure of one's faith and must find ways to reinforce it constantly, which, by logical conclusion, also makes uncertain the proper knowledge of God. As Calvin says, "there is no faith save that which leans unshakingly, firmly, and undividedly, on the mercy of God . . . a perfection of faith which none of the sons of men ever attained, none ever shall attain, in this life."[52] Both God's knowledge and faith are a process effected by the Holy Spirit—a process in which the Eucharist plays an instrumental role. This is why Calvin insisted on the importance of frequent attendance at worship and sought to have Eucharist celebrated at least once a week.

The intelligibility of the world of Christ, and of the sacraments comes from a proper understanding of the Scriptures, which comes from the efficacious work of the Holy Spirit. Christ, the Word of God, is the center of the sacraments. The Word of God is received by means of preaching and sacraments. The preaching of the Scriptures is the preparation for the sacraments and the ritual actions of the sacraments are the completion of preaching. Scripture, Word, and the Lord's Supper belong together, words and ritual actions channeling God's grace through the Spirit. The correlation and inter-dependency of pulpit and eucharistic table for Calvin is fundamental.[53]

The presence of Christ among us is only possible through God's *accommodation* in the Scripture and in the sacraments, mediums of God's self revelation. The scripture read and preached is God's way of getting into the heart of the believer. Within the ritual process of the eucharist the believer is drawn by the Holy Spirit to encounter Jesus and challenged to love his/her neighbors. As for the materiality of the ritual, the preacher and the preaching, the bread and the wine are not themselves God's presence.

52. Calvin, *Institutes of the Christian Religion*, 4.14.7.

53. See Hageman, *Pulpit and Table*.

However, they convey God's presence; they signal God's presence; they manifest God's presence.

Talking, writing and teaching were Calvin's ways of doing his ministry. Calvin could hardly do anything without words. In Geneva he preached three times every Sunday and taught the Scriptures every single day of the week. The singing that he added to the liturgy was the singing of the words of the Psalms. As Martha L. Moore-Keish has pointed out that

> Words are a crucial element in the eucharistic ritual. Perhaps he [Calvin] overemphasized words as a reaction to the Mass, but he was supremely concerned that people understand what they are doing. The ritual is not effective if they cannot hear the words or understand the language in which they are spoken . . . Moreover, not only the words of the worship leader, but also the words of the community are crucial elements in sacramental practice. Calvin insisted that an "outward confession" of faith should be part of the Lord's Supper. He interpreted Jesus words "Do this in remembrance of me" to mean that we should "with a single voice . . . confess openly before men that for us the whole assurance of life and salvation rests upon the Lord's death that we may glorify him by our confession . . ."[54]

This seeing/faith/knowledge/action around the eucharistic table is centered in Christ *the* Word of God and depends on the speaking of proper words around the Word. Words, which form a grammar, which form words and worlds, are the ways to bring clarity to the mind of the believer, to produce proper knowledge, to create intelligibility regarding the sacraments, to require an answer from the heart of the believers, to "beget faith." As Calvin stated, "the Word must explain the sign . . . the sacrament requires preaching to beget faith . . . let us understand that these words are living preaching which edifies its hearers, penetrates into their very minds, impresses itself upon their hearts and settles here, and reveals its effectiveness in the fulfillment of what it promises."[55]

Calvin used the *Institutes* to teach. Catechesis was one of the means of grace, so much so that eucharistic ritual was both a way of teaching and converting people. As one repeated the actions of the Eucharist, one was to improve the knowledge of God and receive God's grace for salvation.

---

54. Moore-Keish, *Do This in Remembrance of Me*. She quotes Calvin's *Institutes*, trans. Battles, 4.17.37. Moore-Keish advocates a broader and deeper perspective on ritual action in Calvin's thought against the usual concentration of interpretation on doctrine.

55. Calvin, *Institutes of the Christian Religion*, trans. Battles, 4.17.29.

This continuous process of *learning* the faith was also linked with Calvin's understanding of ecclesiology. Even though the experience of faith was irrevocably personal and individual, it was not unrelated to the communal aspect of faith since this experience was lived among the faithful believers. The spirituality fostered by this experience of faith in God was to be developed and lived within the church, among one another. Thus, the learning and the living of this inner experience was ecclesial. Education is a trademark in Reformed faith and was fundamental to Calvin who also instituted a school of theology for pastors in Geneva. His radical emphasis on the teaching/learning process of faith is linked with the idea of being nurtured, nourished, and fed by God, and it can be best captured by two images he uses of the church: mother and school.

> Calvin was fond of another saying of Cyprian: that one could not have God for a father who did not have the church as a mother. The image of the church in whose womb the faithful are conceived, born and nurtured was an ancient and powerful one. To this traditional image Calvin added a second when he called the church mother and school. The notion that the church was a school underscored for Calvin the centrality of the teaching mission of the church and the theological responsibility of the whole people of God, lay as well as clergy.[56]

The church as womb and a mother for God's people was a clear image of his understanding of God's providence, and the mission of the church as a school was to help the believer to strengthen his/her faith. A womb, a mother, and a school would warrant the continuous education for the believer and a continuous obedience to the church. This relation would ground a proper understanding of God, would spark (beget) faith, and open up possibilities for the believer to encounter Christ and receive God's promises. It would also guarantee that the sacraments were not rituals *ex opere operato* (efficacious by virtue of the rites themselves) but were rather the *work* of faith through grace effected by the Spirit. It is now easier, I hope, to understand how Calvin defined sacraments. A sacrament, he said,

> it is an external sign . . . a testimony of the divine favor toward us, confirmed by an external sign, with a corresponding attestation of our faith towards Him. You may take your choice of these definitions, which in meaning differ not from that of Augustine, which defines a sacrament to be a visible sign of a sacred thing, or "a visible form of an invisible grace."[57]

56. Steinmetz, "Theology of John Calvin," 123.

57. Calvin, *Institutes of the Christian Religion*, 4.14.1.

The sacraments are instruments of God's grace. They were to show materially what could only be experienced spiritually. God's invisible grace was given not through the materiality of the sacrament but by the spiritual connection enabled by the Holy Spirit to the faithful believer who could then encounter Christ. Therefore, the sacraments served to help believers to use the grammar of faith, to clear the reasoning of people's belief, to help the participants to grow in their understanding, and feel more comfortable in their knowledge. Calvin defines sacrament in the catechism he wrote for the church in Geneva as "an outward attestation of the grace of God which represents to us by a visible sign spiritual things in order to imprint promises of God more firmly in our hearts and make us *more certain of them.*"[58]

This certainty that we need in regard to the sacrament was very important for Calvin. Faith and reason are always an uncertain and shifting ground needing constant supervision, relocation and correction. Human cognition was affected by sin, always going astray from God. "The audacity of the human reason"[59] was a mind that was not under God's corrective grace. Thus, salvation from God also involved a correction of our own ways of thinking and relating to God. The sacrament of the eucharist should be free of theological errors. The pedagogical aspect of the worship service reflected in the minister's preparation of the believer before participation in the sacrament was a way to avoid magical or naïve beliefs about God, like the doctrine of transubstantiation that led many people into "many superstitious observances." Human cognition can be deeply affected by mistaken comprehensions around the table and be led astray. No wonder social and theological discipline was a constant and fundamental theme in Calvin's ministry.

Calvin had two main guidelines for his liturgical work: biblical warrant and faithfulness to the ancient church. One passage illustrates the recurrent use of these guidelines throughout the *Institutes*, "That such was the practice of the Apostolic Church, we are informed by Luke in the Acts, when he says, that 'they continued steadfastly in the apostle's doctrine and fellowship, and in the breaking of bread, and in prayers (Acts 2:42)."[60] Scripture and eucharist had to go hand in hand since in the Roman church, the "the ministers of Satan, whose usual practice is to hold the Scriptures in derision"[61] dissociated the sacrament from the Scriptures.

58. Calvin, *Catéchisme*, quoted in Elwood, *Body Broken*, 62; emphasis added.

59. Calvin, *Institutes of the Christian Religion*, 4.17.47.

60. Ibid., 4.17.44.

61. Ibid., 4.17.48.

The sacrament of the eucharist was an institution initiated by Jesus and practiced by his disciples. Every time the eucharist is celebrated, it has to be related to the reading and the preaching of the Scripture. In that way, Calvin could prove the legitimacy of his own work by its close relation to the gospel and its fidelity to the ancient church which celebrated the eucharist on a weekly basis. More than that, he could also avoid the plentiful liturgical deviations of the Roman Church and have the ancient church as his witness.[62]

For all these reasons Calvin wanted the eucharist to be celebrated every week. It was a central part of the order of his Sunday worship service. However, he was not able to convince the Geneva Magistrates or the city council to have it weekly. He called the Geneva custom "defective."[63] His objection to the Roman practice requiring reception of the eucharist no more frequently than yearly was stronger: it was, he said, an "invention of the devil."[64] He admonished his readers that they should be fed frequently with the sacrament, summarizing in the following way the reasons for frequent participation:

> What we have hitherto said of the sacrament, abundantly shows
> that it was not instituted to be received once a year and that

62. Thompson, *Liturgies of the Western Church*, 190.

63. Ibid., 190.

64. Calvin, *Institutes of the Christian Religion*, 4.17.46.

perfunctorily (as is now commonly the custom); but all Christians might have it in frequent use, and frequently call to mind the sufferings of Christ, thereby sustaining and confirming their faith; stirring themselves up to sing the praises of God, and proclaim his goodness; cherishing and testifying towards each other that mutual charity, the bond of which they see in the unity of the body of Christ. As often as we communicate in the symbol of our Savior's body, as if a pledge were given and received, we mutually bind ourselves to all the offices of love, that none of us may do anything to offend his brother, or omit anything by which he can assist him when necessity and opportunity occurs.[65]

It is clear that for Calvin participation in the eucharist was a source of both spiritual nourishment and fraternal love. The believer is supposed to be constantly reminded of Christ and thus confirm and persevere in his faith. Singing, proclaiming and testifying was the enactment of words and the ritual actions around the table as the believer sees the table and the elements, drinks the wine and eats the bread. In this action, one is always proclaiming God's glory. Through participation in the eucharist, one enters into the economy of a pledge, "giving and receiving," which grounds the ethical consideration for the other as one is considered by God. This economy of reciprocity marks Calvin's ecclesiology.

With his sacramental theology, Calvin stimulated a new way of relating eucharist to common life and to power.[66] The reformers created for the people/laity possibilities for new dimensions of participation. People were to become involved in a more active participation around the table with songs, prayers, eating, and drinking.[67] This can be seen in Calvin's design of the eucharistic rite.

The ritual structure of Eucharist approved by Calvin was established as follows:

> "All this Mass of ceremonies being abandoned, the sacrament might be celebrated in the most becoming manner, if it were dispensed to the Church very frequently, at least once a week.

65. Ibid., 4.17.44.

66. We will see that aspect more detailed in the political dimensions of his eucharistic theology.

67. "Both Martin Luther and John Calvin called for changes in communion practices that renewed the congregation's role and participation. At the center of these changes was an understanding of the role of the assembly in the practices of praying and coming to the table" (Galbreath, *Leading from the Table*, 11).

The commencement should be with public prayer; next, a sermon should be delivered: then the minister, having placed bread and wine on the table, should read the institution of the Supper.

He should next explain the promises which are therein given; and, at the same time, keep back from communion all those who are debarred by the prohibition of the Lord.

He should afterwards pray that the Lord, with the kindness with which he has bestowed this sacred food upon us, would also form and instruct us to receive it with faith and gratitude; and, as we are of ourselves unworthy of the feast by his mercy.

Here, either a psalm should be sung, or something read, while the faithful, in order, communicate at the sacred feast, the minister breaking the bread, and giving it to the people. The Supper being ended, an exhortation should be given to sincere faith, and confession of faith, to charity, and lives becoming Christians.

Lastly, thanks should be offered, and praises of God should be sung. This being done, the Church should be dismissed in peace."[68]

Calvin kept the ritual to a bare minimum of actions to avoid idolatry and any distraction from Christ. The ritual and theological borrowings for this ceremony entailed the meaning of a communal meal.[69] The eucharistic service was intended to be a communal and corporative activity and not celebrated individually or in honor of specific persons as in the Roman church.

Both elements of bread and wine were fundamental at the table. They were food for the body, but they essentially represented food for the soul. Around the table, the body of Christ was to be given, faith invigorated and expanded, and the soul nourished and replenished. Moreover, mirroring the Last Supper lived by Jesus with the disciples, the Christian community was to eat together and remember Christ's deeds for the community and for the world. Calvin's theological distinctions, influenced by Augustine and the church fathers, distinguished the material and the spiritual elements of the eucharist. The body was fed by the bread and the wine but it was the spiritual food that was the main element of the eucharist.

68. Calvin, *Institutes of the Christian Religion*, 4.17.43. (formatting altered to reflect my own classification).

69. "His first move, logically, establishes the imaginative framework of understanding: the fundamental metaphor for the Eucharist is a meal" (Haight, "Calvin's Ecclesiology," in *Christian Community in History*, 2:117).

As bread nourishes, sustains, and protects our bodily life, so the body of Christ is the only food: *invigorate and keep alive* the soul. When we behold wine set forth as a symbol of blood, we must think that such use as wine serves to the body, the same is spiritually bestowed by the blood of Christ, and the use is to foster, *refresh, strengthen, and exhilarate.*[70]

The bread and the wine were the liturgical marks of the spiritual nourishment present in the meal. They were not to be confounded with the presence of Christ and the movements around them should be small but precise since they were there to point to the spiritual fulfillment in Christ. It is good to remember that Calvin was reacting against the Roman Church and the way that he and many reformers acted in regard to the materiality or physicality of the rites was to pare down the liturgical order and reduce the ritual ceremonials to a bare minimum of actions by the assembly. As a movement of reaction to what was considered the main deviation from the true Christian faith, everything that represented the Roman Church, especially its rituals and symbols, should be avoided, denied or dismissed.

Images and paintings were used by the Roman church to educate the people, especially because of rampant illiteracy. Their use was in accordance with the custom developed by the early church as a means of teaching and remembering Christ's life. This educational aspect of the liturgical rite was not part of Calvin's catechesis since he denied any use of images by the early Christian churches during the first five centuries. In the church, images should be peremptorily avoided since images could easily distract people's attention from Christ. However, Calvin was not completely closed to the use of images (outside of the church) but they had to be used carefully, ". . . because sculpture and painting are gifts of God, I seek a pure and legitimate use of each, lest those things which the Lord has conferred upon us for his glory and our good be not only polluted by perverse misuse but also turned to our destruction . . ."[71]

Calvin's erasing of liturgical symbols from the church was a theological mixture of avoidance of idolatry, focus on the Scriptural knowledge of God, and care for the people participating in the service. In this sense, the *seeing* of faith which was related to the construction of knowledge should be linked with the "gripping and sharp" eyes of adoration and not the eyes of the sensual body.

70. Calvin, *Institutes of the Christian Religion*, 4.17.3; emphasis added.

71. Calvin, *Institutes of the Christian Religion*, trans. Battles, 1.11.12.

Calvin related art to the sacraments by saying that instead of using paintings in the worship services it is better to stay with the images of water, bread, and wine already provided by the Word of God in the sacraments. He preferred "[t]hose living and symbolic ones which the Lord has consecrated by his Word. I mean baptism and Lord's Supper, together with other rites by which our eyes must be too intensely gripped and too sharply affected to seek other images forged by human ingenuity."[72] Since Calvin's theology was representational, there was nothing that could fully present God to us, and he was always suspicious of most of the artistic material aspects and ritual movements of the faith that could engage in idolatry, replacing God with gods of our creation/imagination. Fearing the superstition and magical gestures which Calvin thought were present in the Roman Church, he avoided any possible misuse of the ritual realm by structuring it minimally because that is what is required "biblically."

The result was a dramatic simplification of the Christian rites. In the Roman church, the shape of the church building, the placement of the liturgical elements, the altar as a place of sacrifice, the sculptures and paintings describing the life of Jesus, and the various elements/objects of the eucharistic rite were not only decorations of the Christian faith but rather composed the core of the Christian faith. More than representing faith they were the presence of Christ, not as a sacrament but as icons. That is why Roman Catholics make the sign of the cross in front of an image or touch the feet of the sculpture of Christ.

The change of the visual aspect and ritual action within Calvin's liturgy was enormous. Instead of the colorful vestments of the liturgical seasons, and "crosses stitched on albs, crucifixes and altars," priests were to wear sober black robes in naked churches that had only the pulpit, the font, and a bare table. Instead of the "choir and the antiphon, the verbal multiplicity of an episcopal Mass, and the aural complexity" of the liturgy, it was now to be simple, without ritual complications and marked by words, and few gestures, and songs. No more "procession, blessing, elevation, genuflection—all the priestly performance."[73] Instead, the ministers were to make few movements and allow the people to participate. As for eucharist, since the body of Christ was not materially present in the Host, there was no need for golden and silver patens or chalices or embroidered altar cloths. Simple chalices and patens were used instead.

---

72. Ibid., 1.11.12.

73. Wandel, *Eucharist in the Reformation*, 92.

These changes were powerful and entailed a whole way of relating to God and to power in general. *Sola scriptura* was the liturgical principle, simplicity became central to ritual, and people's participation in the Eucharist was a mark of sharing and commonality. In some ways, the ordinary life of people was mirrored in this space since most people led simple lives with simple things at home.

As for the place of the human body, Calvin was also very suspicious about that. His thinking on the body is marked by his account of human fallenness. The body was a prison of the soul, a powerful device prone to mistake that could betray the main purpose of the worship service, the adoration of God. Calvin does not deny the human senses but again, cannot trust them fully since bodily senses are always on the verge of corrupting the proper understanding of God. As stated before, his mistrust of the body was related to the fact that the body could distract human attention from God and falsify God's knowledge. The body properly placed in the actions of the worship, not tempted by exterior elements, could fix its eyes on God. The audible and the edible would only enhance the concentration of our eyes in God. Then, the singing of the Psalms and the drinking and the eating would heighten the senses instead of leading them astray. For instance, Calvin said that songs should "incite us to pray to and to praise God, to meditate on his works, that we may love, fear, honor, and glorify God."[74] When focused on God, and God alone, pleasure was a possibility, not so much for the body but for the soul, once related to the participation of Eucharist and to the honoring of God.

One can say that the general doctrinal and liturgical emphasis of Calvin's theology was based on the whole principle of order, exhaustively repeated in the *Institutes*. Order, proper decorum, reverence, and purity were key elements that must surround the sacraments. The worship service has to be done in order, according to a proper structure. Any deviation would entail distraction, dangerous misguidance of knowledge, corruption of our minds, and unlawfulness.

I have been emphasizing the need of a proper knowledge in Calvin's thought so far. However, and paradoxically, the dualistic thought of Calvin also encompasses the impossibility of knowledge. God's sovereignty lay beyond any human grasp. There can never be a proper knowledge capable of understanding God, no clear vision that could entail a proper seeing, no proper action that would leave us with the totality of God's self-revelation.

74. Calvin, *Institutes of the Christian Religion*, quoted in Haight, "Calvin's Ecclesiology," in *Christian Community in History*, 2:115.

Even when corrected by God, our understanding will be slippery, our eyes will still be myopic, our actions will fall behind, and we will not be able to attend to the fullness of God's mystery in the sacrament.

There is a relation between bodily experience and the experience of understanding, or lack thereof. Calvin said that the mind cannot grasp God's presence in the Eucharist, with the result that one has to *experience* it instead of understand it. That bodily knowledge entails what E. A. Dowey calls an "existential apprehension."[75] Even with the event of God's accommodation, we can never comprehend God's insurmountable sovereignty and glory which creates a gap between us and God. This gap between human reason and God's sovereignty impels Calvin to turn to matters of the heart, spiritual adoration, and contemplation, activities which in themselves are devoid of proper reasoning and final understanding. This approach brings Calvin close to the mystical tradition of Christianity. Here's a passage from the *Institutes* that reflects a more mystical Calvin:

> [W]e are called to a knowledge of God: not that knowledge which, content with empty speculation, merely flits into the brain but that which will be sound and fruitful if we duly perceive it, and if it takes root in the *heart*. For the Lord manifests himself by his powers, the force of which we must feel within ourselves and the benefits of which we enjoy. We must therefore be much more profoundly affected by this knowledge than if we were to imagine a God of whom no perception came through to us. Consequently, we know the most perfect way of seeking God, and the most suitable order, is not for us to attempt with bold curiosity to penetrate to the investigation of his essence, which we ought more to *adore* than meticulously to search out, but for us to *contemplate* him and his works whereby he renders himself near and familiar to us, and in some manner communicates himself to us.[76]

There is a point at which knowledge fails: speculation, rational arguments, and reasoning cannot grasp God's fullness. At this point, one is left alone with one's feeling and the experience of contemplating an inexpressible God to whom one owes adoration. Away from the real strictures of logical reason, perception becomes a tool to adore God. If one *duly*

---

75. Dowey Jr., *Knowledge of God in Calvin's Theology*, quoted in Wheeler, "Use of Visual Art in Reformed Places of Worship," 352.

76. Calvin, *Institutes of the Christian Religion*, trans. Battles, quoted in Wheeler, "Use of Visual Art in Reformed Places of Worship," 61–62; emphasis added.

perceives it, in another sense of knowledge, one attains to the matters of the heart in which one meets this awesome God.

As mentioned before, when Calvin comments on how the presence of Christ happens in the eucharist he says: "Now, if anyone should ask me how this takes place, I shall not be ashamed to confess that it is a secret too lofty for either my mind to comprehend or my words to declare. And, to speak more plainly, I rather *experience* than understand."[77] This passage shows that the eucharist was not only a cognitive experience, but also an experience of the body. Therefore, it is not correct to say that Calvin thought that the body could add nothing to worship. I want to suggest that Calvin anticipated that human movement would add too much meaning to the eucharist and would draw too much attention to the elements. This caution over the impact of materiality led him to resist the implications of his *mystical thought* and to deny a more open manifestation of the body. Moreover, as he was surrounded by a splendid variety of eucharistic practices and incarnational devotions around the table, Calvin knew too well that actions could create unruly words and worlds, a knowledge that encouraged his efforts to domesticate the body in favor of higher concerns for the soul and the mind.

Surely the use of space, material elements and performative actions are entangled in the theological, ecclesiological, and liturgical gesturing of Calvin's sacramental thought. All of these elements work in their own way to expand the doctrine of the incarnation. The theological challenge of Eucharist is deeply related to the ways the community of the believers understand and *practice* the incarnation of Christ and how it is handled theologically, liturgically, materially, and consequently politically today. As Wandel affirms,

> The Eucharist confronts the mystery of the Incarnation more explicitly and more variously than any other sacrament. The sixteenth century debates on the Eucharist agonized not only over what "body" was present in the moment of communion. They also confront directly: How did the Incarnation confound the temporality, the boundedness, and the natural propensity to decay of the material world?[78]

Moreover, a central aspect in the eucharistic framework proposed by Calvin is that he leaves open the possibilities for the doctrine of incarnation without much theological constraints. Killian McDonnell's interpretation

77. Calvin, *Institutes of the Christian Religion*, 4.17.32.; emphasis added.
78. Wandel, *Eucharist in the Reformation*, 10.

of Calvin suggests this, negatively, in his critique of Calvin's resistance to uniting Christ to the elements in material way, a resistance that challenges the incarnation as a theological reality. The connection of Christ to physical reality remains spiritual, vaguely concrete, or incarnated. On the other hand, Moore-Keish says that "Calvin's emphasis on the 'spiritual real presence' of Christ tries to avoid confusion of Christ's body with the material elements of bread and wine, but it is not therefore less 'real.'"[79]

This movement within the eucharist is crucial for the doctrine of incarnation. Even though there is a connection between Christ and the elements, this relation seems to rest entirely on an act of faith. However, the understanding of the Eucharist in Calvin must also take into account his notion of God's accommodation. God accommodates Godself to the sinful human condition, to human finitude, and limitations. In Calvin, God's accommodation is, in many ways, an embodied accommodation. So God comes to us, and communicates with us, in "familiar" ways. Thus if God does accommodate Godself to our bodies, a Calvinist theology of embodiment should not only concentrate on human sinfulness and fallenness but also on the fact that our bodies can be a privileged locus of God's revelation.

In that way, if our Eucharistic theologies could consider the body as fundamental to God's manifestation in the Eucharist, the act of faith of taking the elements and meeting Christ would not need to be only a participation of the mind and heart over in an *ex opere operato* kind of ritual. Rather, the Supper might become a manifestation of our bodies, with all their embodied limitations, ready and eager to receive God around the table. The result is that, if we can consider that God's accommodation can render bodies capable of receiving and sharing in God's grace, we might more easily trust the people's active and imaginative Eucharistic participation. We might be able to leave behind feelings of suspicion and insecurity that lead us to prepare rituals in which believers must be wholly passive, participating only by walking, mute, to the table, putting forth only hands or tongues to receive the pastor's gift.

As we will see later, the presence of the assembly is fundamental to any celebration of the Eucharist and the members of the assembly should also be able to move their bodies beyond the minimal movement allowed in most worship services. Instead of being aural receptacles in a lecture hall, people should engage their bodies, interpreting their ritual, their Bible, and their faith with and through their bodies. For their bodies also,

79. Moore-Keish, *Do This in Remembrance of Me*, 32.

not only their minds or hearts, are part of the presence of God. If God's grace can be accommodated in sinful bodies, these bodies can be more than the elements, and become a place, a channel, a dispenser, a sharer, a holder of God's grace to God, to each other, and to the world. By trusting our bodies we together undo the negativity of the body imaged as only limited, shamed by sin, and incapable of holding God's mercy, miracles, and glory. The sharing of our faith must be done also through our bodies and to celebrate the Eucharist is to share God's love in and through our bodies, a full force liturgical-theological embodiment of our faith.

Thus, unending possibilities of the ritualization of the Eucharist can be called into our worshiping communities without fear! But if we are concerned with our limitations and our sinful nature, we must remind ourselves that in Calvin's understanding of God's radical sovereignty, God can reveal God's self in or in spite of those who are an embarrassment to the gospel or those who deal with the sacrament preposterously, either with their minds or bodies.

> Hence Paul, addressing believers, includes communion with Christ, in the sacraments . . . But when he speaks of a preposterous use of the sacraments, he attributes nothing more to them than to frigid, empty figures; thereby intimating, that however the ungodly and hypocrites may, by their perverseness, either suppress, or obscure, or impede the effect of divine grace in the sacraments, that does not prevent them, where and whenever God is so pleased, from giving a true evidence of communion with Christ, or prevent them from exhibiting, and the Spirit of God from performing, the very thing which they promise. We conclude, therefore, that the sacraments are truly termed evidences of divine grace, and as it were, seals of goodwill which he entertains towards us.[80]

What we see here is that the sovereignty of God exhibits the Spirit of God performing "where and whenever God is so pleased," even against those who try to impede, suppress or obscure divine grace. Thus, the mystery that the eucharist holds in many possibilities of ritual embodiment can be God's ultimate freedom to be and manifest Godself anywhere God wills. Stretching Calvin's understanding of God's freedom, God's irreducible freedom can turn sacramental even what was denied, dismissed, negated or never considered before. In a sense, the embodying aspect of

---

80. Calvin, *Institutes of the Christian Religion*, 4.14.8.

the Eucharist can never be reduced to any particular incarnational act or thought, be it theological or liturgical.

This wide open movement of God's sacramental embodiment in the world is an open space whose incarnational actions, writings, and movements give themselves up to the community of believers, or in Charles Sanders Peirce's term, "community of inquiry," to meet Christ at the sacramental table of the eucharist. What are God's incarnational movements around the table? Who is going to pledge what and how? The economics of God's incarnation is framing the table and the Holy Spirit is hovering over the table calling us to meet Christ. Who is to say "this is my body" at the table? How do the body movements of the people present interpret the event named by the words "this is my body"? And around what kind of hospitality are these words uttered?

In spite of God's *dangerous freedom* and this irreducible reminder, what Calvin does in his Institutes is to frame "this is my body." He says where and how the Spirit moves and that has to do also with access to the table. Calvin could not allow anybody participating in the rite without high concern for the sacrament, deep self-examination, a certain understanding of the sacrament, a desire to believe, and, all in all, the keeping of order and decency. Well aware of the fallen human condition, biblically shown in Adam's sin and clearly demonstrated by the social upheavals of his time, Calvin tried to safeguard the table with high fences. He knew he had the office to protect the table from disrespect and dishonor. Referring to Augustine and Chrysostom's epistle to the Ephesians, he said: "But since, as we have said, the people were sometimes remiss, holy men urged them with severe rebukes that they might not seem to connive as their sluggishness."[81]

The criteria to gain access to the table were both objective and subjective. Sincerity of faith was an inward experience and holiness of life was to be overseen by the church consistory. It had to fit the norms proposed by the church, theological doctrines, and right moral behavior. In the Middle Ages, the Eucharist was a gate to God's power. For Calvin, the Eucharist served as a kind of symbolic embodiment of the church, and that is the main reason why issues of access become so important for Calvin and some of his contemporaries and successors. So there are, indeed, issues of fencing.[82] Not everybody could hold this power and those allowed within

81. Calvin, *Institutes of the Christian Religion*, 4.17.45.

82. Elwood helps clarify a less well-explored point here: "There are also issues on the other side, namely, Calvin's opposition to those whose practiced ecclesiology

the gates could never be "unbelievers or scandalous sinners, both of whom would shortly reduce this 'communion' to a sham."[83] The table was a sacrament and demanded purity. Profanation was always a deep concern. Moreover, the table had its extensions not only to those who professed the Christian faith but it served to create the social and political identity of the city. In Calvin's second stay in Geneva, the church expanded its control over the city and the borders of the church slowly helped shape the civil laws of the city.

Again, cognition and understanding played a key part in the access to/fitness for the table. The worship service to God was also an educational moment when people were reminded of the dangers and promises of such participation. When it came to leadership at the table, women did not fit. Strangers, coarse and ignorant, were to be educated before their participation in the church's sacraments. This care with the table was also related to the belief that people would incur dangers to themselves. However the main point was to protect the church against squanderers, libertines, and sinners. Within the liturgy, the part of recommendation before participation was utterly necessary. Christian Grosse describes the liturgical acts around Supper in Geneva. After the sermon, the minister in Geneva had to read I Corinthians 11 and then fence the table with the following admonition:

> I excommunicate all idolaters, blasphemers, those who hold God in contempt, heretics, and all people who have made sects apart, rending the unity of the Church, all perjurers, all those who are rebels against father and against mother, and against their superiors, lewd, thieves, plunderers, avaricious, drunks, gourmands, and all those who lead scandalous and dissolute lives.[84]

Summarizing this part, the eucharistic table was a densely charged place during Calvin's time. It involved much more than theological doctrines or proper beliefs. What was at stake was the very notion of power and who was to hold it. Calvin's dualistic thought, theological anthropology,

---

called for higher and more carefully policed fences. Calvinist practices of discipline are well-known, and because of this it is easy to overstate the experience of fencing—as though there were strenuous efforts to determine suitability for admission to the table in sixteenth century Geneva." From an email.

83. Ibid., 187.

84. Grosse, *Les Rituels de la cène*, quoted in Wandel, *The Eucharist in the Reformation*, 169.

and doctrine of the Holy Spirit led him to develop a powerful theo-political sacramental eucharist. In the eucharist, God's transcendence could not be constrained by human predicament or earthly element. That made him loosen the connection between God and any human event, figure, or institution, even the institution of the eucharist. On the other hand, the eucharist was a sacrament and the elements should somehow convey God's presence.

However, at table, the Eucharist was surrounded by God's communication, fences that entailed a process, by faith through grace, within the life of a Christian believer to regain God's image. "The goal of Christian life, for Calvin, is the restoration of the image of God which sin has distorted and defaced."[85] Regular participation in the eucharist would induce discernment and activate a proper knowledge/action of God's will, effectively deploying God's self-revelation and life among community of neighbors.

This process proceeded from words and eventuated in deeds. One begins the worship service with welcoming words and adoration of God and then sends the congregation forth with the commitment to act in the world with God's love. Calvin writes, teaches, and preaches, preparing the believer to believe properly. But later, when he is working in Geneva for the second time, he is worried about the deeds of the believers and the church in relation to the local political power. The Eucharist becomes not only a place for words, but a place for gestures, liturgical, social, political deeds. Mark C. Taylor goes as far as to say that "[i]n terms of the word/deed polarity, the former Calvin gives priority to word over deed and the latter privileges deed over word."[86] The radical and revolutionary ways that Calvin understood the sacrament of the Eucharist helped foment a huge transformation of great political and social significance. He helped compose a "radical reformation"[87] that deeply affected not only Geneva and the entire Europe of the sixteenth century but continues to live everywhere around the world.

3. Eucharist and Hospitality in the Presbyterian Church (U.S.A.)

The Presbyterian Church (U.S.A.) is the largest church in United States in the Reformed tradition. It is my intention to analyze the ways in which this

85. Haas, "Calvin Ethics," 95.
86. M. C. Taylor, *After God*, 99.
87. Elwood, *Body Broken*, 172.

historical Protestant church understands the sacrament of the eucharist and hospitality in relation to Calvin's thought by examining its *Directory for Worship, Book of Common Worship* which is part of its Constitution; and a recent document entitled *Invitation to Christ* (September 12, 2006).[88]

The *Directory for Worship* contains an expanded vision of what the liturgy of the church is supposed to look like. At the very beginning it affirms: "[t]his Directory for Worship reflects the conviction that the life of the Church is one, and that its *worship, witness,* and *service* are inseparable."[89] In this affirmation there is a strong definition of the correlation between theology, ecclesiology, liturgy, and ethics. Faithful to Calvin's anthropological theology, the church believes that human beings do not initiate their movement towards God; worship is always a response to God's grace, to God's "self-revelation, redemption, and forgiveness."[90] Believing with Calvin that the Holy Spirit is God's moving within us, the Directory says that "[t]he Holy Spirit calls, gathers, orders, and empowers the new community of the covenant."[91] "Freedom and communication," the dual theological reasoning of Calvin on the Holy Spirit is present here too. The free movement of the Holy Spirit is made immanent by proper channels of grace, "Through Scripture, proclamation, and Sacraments, God in Christ is present by the Holy Spirit acting to transform, empower, and sustain human lives."[92] However, this immanent movement cannot be completely circumscribed by any of these human channels. It is the impermanent action of the Spirit through these elements that manifests God's presence. This concession to immanence is heavily outweighed by the transcendence of God. Nothing can constrain the free movement of God in the world and no human vessel can hold God's absolutely transcendent power. Thus, the way one offers an account of God's communicative presence is always improper, impermanent, fractured, lacking, a rendering as if in hope that God is really here and we are working from God's manifestation to us. Therefore, when people respond to God's grace, and communicate

---

88. The theological, liturgical, and ecclesiological grounds of the Presbyterian Church (U.S.A.) can be found in the two-part constitution of the church, namely, *Book of Confessions*, and *Book of Order*. These two books along with reports and documents issued annually by the General Assembly, the highest office of the national church, forms the evolving rationale of the church's identity, theology, and mission.

89. Preface to *Directory for Worship*, in *Book of Order*, a.

90. *Directory for Worship*, in *Book of Order*, W–1.0000, c.

91. Ibid., W–1.1005, a.

92. Ibid., W–1.1004.

> to each other their experiences of God, they must use symbolic means, for God transcends creation and cannot be reduced to anything within it. No merely human symbols can be adequate to comprehend the fullness of God, and none is *identical* to the reality of God. Yet, symbols human beings use can be *adequate* for understanding, sharing and responding to God's gracious activity in the world since God has chosen to accommodate to humanity in self-revelation.[93]

This theological understanding reflects Calvin's pneumatology of carefully handling God's incarnation without turning or letting anything become identical to God. Even the presence of Christ "is present by the inward witness of the Holy Spirit."[94] God is thus ultimately irreducible to the human experience. Nonetheless, God accommodates God's self to humans through the work of the Spirit in a lesser way in creation, but mostly in Scripture, preaching and the sacraments. It is the Holy Spirit who, through these channels of grace, makes Christ's presence "real" both inwards to the heart of the individual believer and more publicly in the shared worship of the community.

Since God is present "through Scripture, proclamation and sacraments,"[95] there is always an expectation built into participation in the Lord's Day, a hope that Christ will come to the gathered community at the worship service and that an encounter with God will happen. It is the presence of God "*through* the Scripture, the proclamation and the sacraments" that offers grounds for such bold expectation and anticipation. As the Directory affirms, "[t]he Reformed tradition has emphasized the importance of the Lord's Day as the time for hearing the Word and celebrating the sacraments in the expectation of encountering the risen Lord, and for responding in prayers and service."[96]

The worship service is caught between the promise of Christ's presence and the freedom of the Holy Spirit who, if one takes God's sovereignty to its limits, is free not to show up. However, it seems that there are some "other" ways besides Scripture, preaching, and the sacraments to assure God's presence within the worship service. In the Reformed tradition, the presence of God is always under the scrutiny of proper language, proper enactments, proper symbols, proper understanding, and proper *order*.

93. Ibid., W–1.2002; emphasis added.

94. Ibid., W–2.2001.

95. Ibid., W–1.1004.

96. Ibid., W–1.3000.

The Directory is fond of *order*, as the title of the constitution shows. It reaffirms this priority throughout the text with expressions like: "appropriate language" that "creates ardor and order;" "each place was ordered to invite and express God's presence;" "proper administration of the sacraments;" "in worship, the church is to remember both its liberty in Christ and the biblical command to do all things in an orderly way." Each presbytery has the responsibility to check whether the "standards of governing" the worship services are being done accordingly.

This preoccupation with order is not different from any other historical Protestant church. Perhaps because of a very cerebral faith tradition received over time, the Presbyterian Church cares for rationality and order. Perhaps, and in spite of the regulations provided by the *Book of Common Worship*, this pressing for order also comes from the fact that local congregations are not required to follow a fixed order of worship or are bound to a specific liturgical format as, for example, are the Episcopalians. The *Directory* is clear to say that "[t]he church is free to be innovative in seeking appropriate language for worship. While respecting time-honored forms and set orders, the church may reshape them to respond freely to the leading of God's Spirit in every age."[97] This freedom might be a shocking possibility for some Presbyterians today for whom order is what makes a worship service proper. As the Directory says: "[w]hile Christian worship need not follow prescribed forms, careless or disorderly worship is both an offense to God and a stumbling block to the people."[98]

This freedom for Christian worship can be very disorienting since it demands a search for cohesion or unity within local communities. A principle for this cohesion is found in the Word of God: "In Christian worship the people of God (1) hear the Word proclaimed, (2) receive the Word enacted in Sacrament, (3) discover the Word in the world, and (4) are sent to follow the Word into the world."[99] The *Book of Common Worship* defines the *ordo* of "The Service for the Lord's Day" in four parts: Gathering, the Word, the Eucharist, Sending.[100]

In order to link this *ordo* of worship to the early Christian church and find a common ground for the celebration of the eucharist, the Directory relies on New Testament scholarship. Scripture suggests that the Last Supper was an historical event celebrated by Jesus with his disciples,

97. Ibid., W–1.2005.

98. Ibid., W–1.4000.

99. Ibid., W–1.1004.

100. *Book of Common Worship*, 33, 46–47.

specifying the exclusive use of water, bread, and wine by Jesus and stating that the early church was faithful to this singular tradition. At one point, the *Directory* says that "[t]he early church, following Jesus, took three primary material elements of life—water, bread, and wine—to become basic elements of life to God as Jesus has offered his life." Then it expands this by saying:

> During his earthly ministry, Jesus shared meals with his followers as a sign of community and acceptance and as an occasion for his own ministry. He celebrated Israel's feasts of covenant commemoration. In his last meal before his death, Jesus took and shared with his disciples the bread and the wine . . . He commended breaking bread and sharing a cup to remember and proclaim his death.[101]

The Companion to the Book of Order explains that the first Christians had full meals, but in the second century those meals were outlawed by the Roman Empire. The church then gathered around the Word and Sacrament (bread and wine) which is the source of the fourfold ordo present in the *Book of Common Worship*.[102]

This understanding of the eucharistic meal as the sharing of bread and *wine* alone, i.e., outside of the larger structure of the social institution of the Greco-Roman meals, turns it into a sign of small proportions, narrowing and diminishing possible meaning of the sacrament. As we saw in chapter 2, the early church meals entailed a larger, broader, and fuller communion among the participants and within the society at large, thus expanding the possibilities of the sign of the sacrament.

When the Christian churches shrink the eucharistic meal to a morsel of bread and a sip of wine, the church turns what was supposed to be an experience of plenty into a feast of scarcity, and it loses many connections with the outside such as the world's hunger, and runs the risk of turning a table that was created for others into a celebration of an inner club. If the church is to follow a radical ministry of hospitality mentioned in the *Companion to the Book of Common Worship*, its gestures and movements should reflect openness and food for all. "In the words of St. Benedict, 'Let all guests be received as Christ.' Our meeting with Christ at the Table must be an exercise of 'hosting people unable to host us in return' (see Luke 14:12–14) and, therefore, seeing the face of Christ."[103] If we were to see the

---

101. *Directory for Worship*, in *Book of Order*, W–1.3033. and W–2.4001.

102. Bower, ed., *Companion to the Book of Common Worship*, 15–16.

103. Ibid., 45.

face of Christ in every guest, we would never deny food to anybody who approached the table. Moreover, we would take the food to the streets to feed the hungry. Unfortunately, the companion reduces its description of a radical "ministry of hospitality" into tips for ushers to help people to get a place in the parking lot or find a seat in the church.

If the Presbyterian Church (U.S.A.) claims its origins in the early Christian church and follows the freedom of worship found there, the celebration of the Eucharist can be made to *fit* this radical "ministry of hospitality." It would welcome the many Christs disguised as neighbors/ strangers by being open to a broad use of movements and gestures. Instead of repeating the same sequence of contained gestures around the sacrament as the *only* way to have Christ present in the eucharist, it would manifest its prophetic capacity to denounce injustice, "heal the nations," and expand its connections and commitments with the communities completely ignored or forgotten because of the world's political and economic borders.

With Calvin, the Presbyterian Church also sees the eucharist through the metaphoric lens of a meal, a place of nourishment. But if this meal is to be eaten at the margins of the world with poor people and the excluded, our borders within and around the table (God's presence, a sense of community, the gesturing around the table, and the living out of our theological beliefs), should be re-examined. Within this space of communion with the forgotten other, ethical commitments are constantly being developed, fostered, shaken, challenged, and replaced if necessary. This communal meal not only defines us our place in our community and in the world but also reveals the displacement of many others within our communities and around the world. At the same time it shows our hospitality and the ways in which the church deals with the spiritual and the material hunger around the world.

The question of an open table for all was addressed in a recent document entitled "Invitation to Christ" in which the members of the Sacraments Study Group of the Presbyterian Church (U.S.A.) offered a new and expanded interpretation of the sacraments to the whole church. This document does not hold the same weight as the "Directory of Worship" but it is an approved study document of the church that develops an understanding of the sacraments and encourages congregations to renew their sacramental life. Moreover, it relates the sacraments to various aspects of the life of the church and culture, offering new challenges and dealing with the demands of our time.

"Invitation to Christ" responds to challenges from presbyteries that were asking the General Assembly to reconsider the "current language of invitation to the Lord's Table." These presbyteries were asking the church to change the language of invitation in the "Directory of Worship" that makes baptism a requirement for access in the eucharistic table. Questions regarding the participation of children were also raised. The petitioners wanted the invitation issued to "all persons of faith" instead of "all the baptized." The document interprets the phrase, open table, "to mean open to all who want to respond to Christ, whether or not they are baptized,"[104] and thus frames the notion of hospitality.

While theologically supportive of the Eucharist as an open table, the study fails to clearly affirm that. Perhaps, the writers of the document knew they were dealing with a divided church and didn't want to stretch this divide. Nevertheless, the document missed a great opportunity to expand the borders of hospitality through the Eucharistic table. The document concludes first with a note about the need to enhance "sensibility to the variety of circumstances from which people come to the church and its worship in Word and Sacrament," and, finally, invites believers to pay closer attention to baptism.

It is important to say that even though the document leans toward an open table, it fences the table with the necessity of baptism perhaps because of the many theological understandings of the Eucharist within the church. In regards to baptism, the study is mostly powerful when it invites the churches to expand their use of water as the vehicle and symbol to renew the vows and commitments of baptism. This invitation is bold enough to encourage the use of large amounts of water even to the point of "getting wet," which for Presbyterians is a daring and even shocking invitation. The incarnation of Christ symbolized with great amounts of water in and around the baptismal font achieves a certain dramatic effect.

The study is ritually driven i.e., the group emphasizes the ritual practices as ways of fostering theological understandings. While the study offers innovative practical-theological reforms related to baptism, its treatment of the Eucharist is more cautious. There are no challenges, no other possible practices or words and movements around the table, and no urging to place more bread or wine at the table, let alone additional kinds of food.

In regard to the historical relation between the sacrament as presented in the New Testament and the sacrament performed today, the

104. Sacrament Study Group, *Invitation to Christ*, 18.

document still relies on the centrality of the narratives of the Synoptic Gospels without analytical or redactional perspective on these texts. It treats them as if they are all undifferentiated, thus keeping the Last Supper of Jesus with the disciples to be the central and historical referent of the sacrament. However, the study makes a powerful shift away from the *Directory of Worship* as it emphasizes the context of varied meals in early communities. The most fascinating part is the theological reflection on the meaning of the sacrament growing out of various practices within the early church, with blurred perspectives and uncertain definitions regarding the sacramentality of the meals. It says: "The narratives of the early church in Acts suggest that they shared different kinds of meals and that there were initially fluid boundaries between what we would differentiate as sacramental and non-sacramental meals."[105] However, without mentioning how the process of "basic patterns for baptism and the Lord's Supper develop in the early church, once these practices are placed in the context of a *distinctive Christian narrative*," it concludes that in the case of ". . . the Lord's Supper, a shared meal becomes connected to this same central gospel narrative."[106]

What stands out from this interpretation is that the current practice of eating a bite of bread and drinking a sip of wine is closely related to this *distinctive Christian narrative*. Thus, when the sacraments are put in an historical perspective, the liturgical order gains what has been repeated over the history of liturgical studies, that is, that within this *distinctive Christian narrative* there is a clear link between the liturgical *ordo* practiced today and a consistent *pattern* repeated by the early Christian church since its first meal practices. The study affirms: "From the beginning of the church we see that there was an order, a pattern, to the way the Word, baptism and the Lord's Supper were celebrated."[107]

The document takes a step forward, when it describes the flexibility of a liturgical meal experienced through various practices supported by a plurality of theologies. However, it ends up repeating the standard interpretation of the sacrament as based on the *natural* configuration of the liturgical pattern of celebration with the elements of the bread and wine. This ends up restricting the gestures around the bread and the wine. The sources of New Testament research used focus only on the patterned ritual

105. Ibid., 18.
106. Ibid., 18; emphasis mine.
107. Ibid., 24.

use of "word, preaching, baptism and eucharist,"[108] thus, limiting any reading of the eucharist to the same elements. The document does distinguish between *who is served* at the table and *who is invited* to the table, but does not elaborate on that. Unfortunately, the document does not help us think about the significance of this difference.

In the document, the table is open but there are some fences around it. One must respond to Christ in order to participate. Without the desire to respond to Christ one cannot sit at the table. Perhaps one can sit a few times around the table without baptism. However, what would be the point of giving access to the table to those who do not want to confess Christ? A more theological question thus comes to fore: is it possible to have an open table even for those who do not want to be united with Christ but want to share the solidarity of the gathered community? Does this openness turn Christ's costly grace into cheap grace? How does one deal with Bonhoeffer's *costly grace*[109] of Christ at a table when fellowship seems to be more important for the participant than the contents of faith expressed in baptism?

Thus, reflecting the "two sides" of Calvin, the Presbyterian Church (U.S.A.) does acknowledge the free movement of the Spirit within the norms of the eucharist's established ritual. However, it never really pushes forth or even trusts enough this freedom. Instead, the church prefers to emphasize the structures of the known *order* of the worship through the strictures of gestures and words around the eucharistic table.

> *In the Christ is Life Presbyterian Church (U.S.A.) in Fall River, MA, there were two men in their fifties who wanted to participate in the eucharist. It was common practice in the church for the eucharistic table to always be open to anybody without any questions asked. The invitation to the Table was different every Sunday. One of them was the following: "This is God's table. There is food for you here. If you want to participate you have only to decide whether your neighbor is important to you. You*

108. Ibid.

109. "Cheap grace is the preaching of forgiveness without requiring repentance, baptism without church discipline. Communion without confession . . . Cheap grace is grace without discipleship, grace without the cross, grace without Jesus Christ, living and incarnate . . . costly grace is the treasure hidden in the field; for the sake of it a man will gladly go and sell all that he has . . . Costly grace is the gospel which must be sought again and again, the gift which must be asked for . . . it is costly because it costs a man his life and it is grace because it gives a man the only true life" (Bonhoeffer, *Cost of Discipleship*, 44–55).

> *are responsible for everyone who is here and we are connected to every-*
> *body around the world. So come! As you eat food prepared by people of*
> *this congregation, pay attention to your neighbors, to the church who*
> *is hosting us and to the continuous flux of immigrants across the world*
> *crossing the borders at this very moment." Joe and Paul felt that they*
> *were able to participate in the table. They both loved the congregation*
> *and were very active participants of all the programs of the church. But*
> *baptism is a pre-requisite for reception at the table. When baptism class*
> *started, they both joined but soon decided not to continue. Both of them*
> *could not believe a thing about the Christian faith but loved the fellow-*
> *ship. Each one came to ask me if they could continue participating in*
> *the eucharistic table. The session got together and decided to let them*
> *participate without a hint of belief in their hearts. (Perhaps that decision*
> *can be related to the suggestion of the document about considering the*
> *various circumstances before making any decision.)*

EXPANDING LITURGICAL PRACTICES AND HOSPITALITY IN AND AROUND THE REFORMED TABLE

The Presbyterian Church (U.S.A.) has a powerful eschatological perspective on the meal. Every meal points to a future of joy and justice represented in a final meal with Jesus.

> In this meal the church celebrates the joyful feast of the people of God, and anticipates the great banquet and marriage supper of the Lamb. Brought by the Holy Spirit into Christ's presence, the church eagerly expects and prays for the day when Christ shall come in glory and God be all in all. Nourished by this hope, the Church rises from the Table and is sent by the power of the Holy Spirit to participate in God's mission to the world, to proclaim the gospel, to exercise compassion, to work for justice and peace until Christ's kingdom shall come at last.[110]

This passage marks a difference between Calvin's table and the table of the Presbyterian Church (U.S.A.). Calvin's eucharistic table, like the Presbyterian Church's view of the table, was a place to encounter Christ. However, due to the historical situation of Calvin's time, it was also the very place to wrestle with the most striking issues of his time. It was in and around the eucharistic table that power was heavily disputed and reconfigured and

110. *Book of Order,* W–2.4007.

where contact with God also involved social, political and economic decisions. The theological, liturgical, and ecclesiastical fences Calvin created were also symbolic constraints on political and theological views which along with bold affirmations of the presence of God, established the place of the church in society.

In the Presbyterian view of the table, the Eucharist is seen primarily as spiritual nourishment. When the community is spiritually fed, the "church rises from the Table and is sent . . . to the world . . . to work for justice." This ritual movement entails a distinct ethical perspective that separates the church sacraments from society. The ritual encourages the Christian believer to live in the presence of God in the church and a life of testimony to this presence outside the church. This split places the political outside of religious space. That becomes apparent when people receive the benediction and are sent out into the world to exercise compassion and so on. This sending forth to the world is connected with the welcoming of the believers into the house of the Lord, a place of refuge, of personal and spiritual retreat, where one moves away from the world into the safety of God's place, where God is present. In a sense, life and its complications are to be left at the door while the soul is reinvigorated, very different from the radical and revolutionary marks once seen in the Eucharistic table in Calvin's time and thinking, not to say the early Christian churches.

Even though the eucharist table reminds the believer of the ethical aspect of faith to be lived out in the world—and this includes the work of consolation, reconciliation, and justice—pressing issues of injustice and death are not brought to the table. These discussions or movements might help people rethink and even alter the ways power is exercised in society. The eucharist is often a silent, somber ritual where nothing is said or done besides the proper words of the minister and the eating of bread and sip of wine. The world might be present but it is present in a silent mode.

What it is often absent at and around the table is what the table indeed represents, what is going on around the world. The ordo shows the split between what the word proclaims and the lived liturgical Eucharistic practices. The table announces life but prevents people from participating; it proclaims God's unconditional love but retains its sacramental actions only for believers; it speaks of compassion but cannot demonstrate compassion with the neighbor who has a different theological, liturgical, religious perspective; it boldly proclaims Jesus as the bread of God to the world but offers a meager tiny piece of bread; it raises the cup and says this is the cup of salvation but it does not follow it with acts of mercy; it proclaims comfort but does not extend the comfort of the table to those who cannot believe; it offers a warm welcoming to all the baptized but does not extend this welcoming to those who are baptized but are illegal immigrants; it announces healing to the nations but closes its borders; it declares the need for solidarity but keeps away those who belong to different social class, language, or skin color. With this schizophrenic tension, the ethical is always postponed to the public space, safeguarding the private religious space for those who belong to the community. Even the offer to belong to the community entails the erasure or the adaptation of one's specificities, singularities, and attributes into those acceptable to the community in order to *fit*.

The understanding of liturgy exclusively as worship of God, a self-reflexive act, aiming only at God[111] runs the risk of becoming a ritual more preoccupied with keeping a certain correct ordo and praising gestures to an disincarnated God in heaven than with pressing ethical problems of our world. When the worship service becomes a reflection in and of itself, it mirrors itself and reproduces patterns of cultural consumerism while it undoes the very purpose of the proposed ordo, becoming more concerned with itself than the people who are part of the worship service. To gather together in praise and thanksgiving to God without acts of love and mercy and hospitality offered to neighbors renders the euchartistic service a performance of self and communal alienation. Worship services must be embedded in a world where cruelty, injustice, conflicts, and social exploitation are newspaper headlines every day. As Lukas Vischer says so poignantly:

> Again and again worship is being celebrated as a self-contained event. Again and again worship becomes a refuge from the

111. This view is exemplified in the following statement from the *Companion to the Book of Common Worship*, 6: "From a certain point of view, worship is use-less. It may be, of course, that people found worship to be useful. It may have been useful in reducing stress; in developing closer ties to family members, friends, and even strangers: in introducing us to a deeper appreciation for the Scripture and to the doctrines of the church; in making contacts that proved to be fruitful personally and professionally. However useful worship may have proved to be, the church does not gather to worship as a strategy to achieve some useful end. Worship is first and foremost, a people's meeting with the God who has taken the initiative to gather that people. It is a gathering intended for no other purpose than to offer our praise, our thanksgiving, and our lament, while trusting the Spirit to bring us into the presence of the risen Christ. It is not adult education. It is not socializing. It is not therapy. It is not networking. It is not a rally to support programs or causes. For all practical purposes, it is and ought to be use-less."

> world and its challenges. Often, the community succumbs to the temptation to leave the world to itself. But the truth stands: God so loved the world—this world—that he gave for it his only begotten Son. The credibility of worship depends on the willingness of the community to share in God's movement of love for the world. Worship will always have an impact; it can either lift up God's love for the world or it can, on the contrary, hide that love behind spiritual walls.[112]

Vischer is right when he says that worship will cause an impact anyways, either by moving the world towards justice and thus, towards the open table of God, or towards injustice and away from the table of God. Instead of only announcing the eschatological gathering in God's table, instead of sending people forth to the world to do the work of justice, instead of only patterning itself spiritually in "Christ's bread and wine," the eucharistic table should bring to the core of the church's liturgical practices, ways of addressing the uneasiness and the brokenness of the world in a more fully embodied way. Issuing a tantalizing note against the rampant exclusion of poor people around the world, the table of Christ should have its mission of compassion and justice within and around the table of Christ. If that mission is to be lived on liturgical grounds, the Eucharist should issue an open invitation/admission and radical hospitality to all. Moreover, eucharist should not only issue an open invitation but also provide real food to those who come to the church from of any circumstance of life. Instead of this split between God's table in the sanctuary for members/citizens and a soup kitchen in the basement for poor people/strangers, the church should have the soup kitchen *as* God's table.

Turning the eucharistic table from a little piece of bread and a sip of wine to a whole meal could entail an enlarged communion, one that could *mark* and perhaps tear down the economic borders of exclusion and offer hospitality to those who are in flux, those who cannot believe, those who have no idea what this ritual means, those who cannot understand, and those who are excluded.

Moreover, this change would also entail the change and expansion of liturgical practices beyond the gestures that, in Presbyterian Church (U.S.A.) understandings, assures the presence of Christ. Consider these affirmations: "[i]n the name of Christ, by the power of the Holy Spirit, the Christian community worships and serves God (1) in shared experiences of life, (2) in personal discipleship, (3) in mutual ministry, and (4) in

---

112. Vischer, "Worship as Christian Witness to Society," 415.

common ministry in the world,"[113] and "[t]he church is nonetheless, free to be innovative in seeking appropriate language for worship," and "working in and through . . . material things," and "[t]o the extent that forms, actions, languages, or settings of worship exclude the expression of diverse cultures represented in the church or deny emerging needs and identities of believers, that worship is not faithful to the life, death, and resurrection of Jesus Christ."[114]

These are bold affirmations that could enhance a much larger process of renovation within the church according to occasions, situations, challenges and dilemmas lived by local congregations in its relation to the world. They provide a whole set of new actions that could help the participants at the table to position themselves theologically, politically and liturgically around those current events. They would thus gain an expanded vocabulary of gestures, body movements, artistic expressions, and personal contributions.

For example, if desolated places such as Darfur, Syria, or Palestine are not only prayed about during the service but become an issue at the table, then one could imagine the following taking place. Let us imagine Darfur. The table is filled with pictures from Darfur, food is scarce and not enough for everyone, movements are slow, and the participants at the table might sense the incarnation of God differently. If sounds of wind and sand and whipping are heard, stories/testimonies of people from there are voiced along with the cries of people from the Old and New Testament, and people walking aimlessly with veils over their heads around the church, these attempts might help believers to gain a glimpse of the experiences of the people without much hope in Darfur. Then the death of Christ is announced in the midst of this dreadful scenario. People are then asked to provide accounts of resurrection for such a situation. People sing, the table is poor, and people are sent forth into the same world. Perhaps, and only perhaps, these movements might intensify the ways that the eucharistic table, and the people around the table, not only internalize a small portion of the lives of those who are dying in Darfur, but also become concerned about power relations in society. By connecting Eucharist with this tragedy, in this way, the "ministry of hospitality" and the conditions for the access of the table might change abruptly.

Many questions come out of this liturgical practice. First, there is no relation between host and guest. The hosts are walking aimlessly without

113. *Book of Order*, W–1.1005, b.
114. Ibid., W.1.2006.a

guests to entertain. Perhaps the guests are missing for some reason. Perhaps they are at pains with their suffering and trying to imagine in their bodies what it would be like to live in that situation. Moreover, there is not enough food at this table for everybody and that says something of God and of this community. It contradicts the gospel, the hope of the sacrament, and interrupts the joy of the community.

However, in this eucharistic meal, the sacramentality of the event will depend on the actions of the Holy Spirit through our actions, our bodies in movement and our actions will be seen as a response to God in relation to the situation of Darfur. The gospel of Christ is still there, incarnated, with faces and historical contingencies. However, the sacrament comes without the promises that accompany it. Is a sacrament where God perhaps is not there, still a sacrament? Nonetheless, the demand for the Christian faith and discipleship are there. The love of God cries out loud, and the walking of a *covenant people*, a theological theme so dear to the Presbyterian Church, will be challenged and hopefully strengthened. The sovereignty of God will, of course, have to be understood differently. God will only be able to change things as we are able to change things. By way of lack of power, God shows strength by empowering us to do justice.

Since "Invitation to Christ" says that the use of water and practices with water and around the font are possible ways to enhance one's faith, then to expand gestures, language and movements with, in and around the eucharistic table might also empower people in their lives. It will also involve a much needed welcoming of a greater variety of hosts and guests around the table. By fostering other movements, words, gestures, and ways of eating together, different practices of hospitality will appear, and, perhaps, the table will not be fenced against those who don't believe in Jesus. Therefore, performing our liturgies will not be only a spiritual statement but also an ethical one. It will not claim political power for the table but rather challenge any source of the power in and around table.

The result could be the expansion of the notion of sacramentality to include more realities as places of God's incarnation. Calvin's sacramentality which entails an always fleeting presence of God within the gestures surrounding the sacrament, might offer glimpses of radical hospitality within the Reformed tradition. Christ's hospitable incarnation in our world through the eucharistic table can *dis-order* the laws of hospitality presently written in the theological, liturgical, and ecclesiological beliefs of the Presbyterian Church (U.S.A.).

Pneumatic Liturgical Border(less) and the Reformed (Un)Framing of the Spirit

"The wind blows where it chooses, and you hear the sound of it, but do not know where it comes from or where it goes."[115] How do we control the wind? If the Spirit is like the wind, what do we do with the free motion of the Spirit? How can we affirm it is here or there? How can we organize God's communication to us? How can we be sure it is here where the words of institution are said properly by an authorized leader, and around a proper table, where nobody eats anything? How can we be sure it is not where homeless people eat at the soup kitchen without words of institution and with no leader leading the meal?

In spite of all of our theological and liturgical bordering of these events, the Spirit is ultimately free to move where it wants. Surely no reformed theologian/liturgist would be against the fact that the Spirit moves where it wills. The drawing of the Spirit is like an open gate, and the communication of God about the Eucharist is a constant re-drawing on the Spirit by communities made of the people of God, moving in and out of our traditions, re-creating and expanding the circles of traditions. To talk about the moves of the Spirit is to be in a dangerous field where, ultimately, everything can easily become improper. To talk about the Holy Spirit is to guess, through the complicated maps of the Bible, tradition, and our experiences, not necessarily in this order, where God might be moving. To find God's communication to us is like walking in a foreign land with temporary maps that we cannot read correctly or with which we have much assurance or certainty. The fear of getting lost rushes people to create fixed maps (Book of Order, Directory for Worship, Book of Common Worship and the Book of Confessions) to give a sense of seeing and knowing God's whereabouts and consequently our own. We must consider these maps carefully as we go along, we must love them and we must rewrite them as well.

Our theological and liturgical task is a very difficult endeavor. How do we talk about the Spirit if, in sovereignty and freedom, God might be here and there, or neither here nor there, or perhaps there and not here? The Spirit of God comes and goes without necessarily announcing its arrival or its departure. What if God does not show up even if we do our order of worship according to the "best practices" and our best tradition? We

---

115. John 3:8 (New Revised Standard Version). I am not considering any exegetical analysis of the biblical texts used here.

take God's presence for granted, perhaps because reformed people have a deep trust in God's grace. However, and if that is the case, the practices we create around the table do not need to be always the same. If we are to meet Christ in each other around the table, we must consider carefully our Eucharistic practices as temporary maps to our existence in this earth. The eucharist should never detach us from the world and we should never turn the sacrament into a mirror of ourselves to serve primarily our own beliefs. Our maps are collective, the food is for all and this feast should help us mirror here the new earth and new heavens where we are going to live together.

Our theological and liturgical work can indeed enhance or restrict the possibility of the movement of the Spirit, or even stand between the Spirit and its freedom. If our task is to unveil the works of the Spirit, how do we do that without at the same time veiling the Spirit? As hard as it might be, it can be a joyful event, even if we cannot see properly the ways that the Spirit manifests itself among us. Thus, we will ask ourselves: what are the proper practices, beliefs, venues, theological conduits, liturgical orders, or experiential paths in which the Spirit can help us meet Christ? How shall we proceed?

All we do are acts of faith! It is indeed our acts of faith, once they are moved by the power of the Holy Spirit, that have the power to turn our guesses into assurances, our hopes into definitions, our inventiveness into theological affirmations, our love into reality, our illusional maps into temporary territories. If we are to live by *faith alone*, a trademark of the Reformed faith, we are to have this faith as if we are wandering around the earth clinging onto God through our fragile theological-liturgical acts.

In our worship services, it is neither the leader, nor the church space, neither the table, nor the elements, neither a proper ritual nor lack thereof that are able to manifest God's presence. For some time, Reformed people relied on the fact that the repetition of the words of institution would assure God's presence. However, the Eucharist both in Calvin and for Reformed people has to do with the presence of the assembly. It was the assembly that warranted the presence of God.[116] Thus, our assurance rests more on the fact that when two or three are gathered, God is there, than in the repetition of the words of institution. If that can become the moving roots and ground of our Eucharistic celebration, then all the ungraspable movements of the Spirit will be a work of discernment of the community

---

116. "For where two or three are gathered in my name, I am there among them." Matthew 18:20.

of interpreters trying to figure out together God's communication to us through actions, prayers, singing, eating, and reading, proclaiming the word of God, offering hospitality, and living together.

In this process, we will always lack proper interpretation. Instead of being a frustration, there will always be a graceful excitement in not being able to see/interpret/figure it out properly, which is a constant call for ourselves to depend entirely on the mysterious work of the Spirit. There is grace in keeping the word of God suspended, open, refusing certainties that close ourselves to others and tend to diminish the powerful unlimitations and expansive possibilities of God's hospitality offered to us. In this process, by the grace of God, we do find certainties by the presence of each other; we do encounter promises of presence, of God coming to meet us, of God having been there even without our knowing it.

The imperfection of our faith will keep a division within us, moving between the impossibility to properly grasp God's word and the joy of being enveloped by the promise of the gospel. This division is attested by Calvin:

> . . . the godly heart feels in itself a *division* because it is *partly* imbued with sweetness from its recognition of the divine goodness, *partly* grieves its bitterness from an awareness of its calamity; *partly* rests upon the promise of the gospel, *partly* trembles at the evidence of its own inquiry; *partly* rejoices at the expectation of life, *partly* shudders at death. This *variation* arises from imperfection of faith, since in the course of the present life it never goes so well with us that we are wholly cured of the disease of unbelief and entirely filled and possessed by faith.[117]

Our liturgical movements are also to take into account these variations, being partly connected, partly assured, partly confident, and partly at loss. Our eyes can only see things partially, without measuring anything accordingly, much less the unveiling of the Holy Spirit, which leaves every Eucharistic sacrament incomplete, unending, unfinished.

However, when we get together we expand it through the movements of the Spirit in our practices and we complete it partially. By being together we gain the possibility to give measures to our meeting with Christ, and assert proportions, locations, senses of our borders, ways to believe, to engage, and experience God. In our worship services, we live with the risk of trusting more in ourselves than in the sovereignty of Christ. We move like a pendulum between restricting the free movements of the Spirit,

---

117. Calvin, *Institutes of the Christian Religion*, 3.2.18.

narrowing its flow, circumscribing its territory, and naming the powerful movements and miracles and wonders of God in the world. Through the grace of God, we have hope and faith that this immeasurable love will always come to us without ever knowing exactly how, where, or when God is visiting us. But we keep coming together and celebrating the very presence of Jesus Christ. This double movement is what keeps us coming and continuously excited to celebrate the eucharistic sacrament.[118]

> People knew that they had to be more political in order to fight for their legalization. They were attuned to everything that had to do with immigrants and immigration in the United States. One day I went to the mayor of the city and asked him to attend the celebration of the Brazilian Independence Day that our community was organizing. He not only agreed but invited us to raise the flag at the door of the city hall. The community was thrilled. On that Saturday morning we had a huge crowd. We sang hymns, read the Bible, and sang both the Brazilian and the United States national anthems. I spoke briefly about the Brazilian history of independence and the mayor said he was happy to see this immigrant community, which he did not know was illegal, making progress in the city. We ended with "Our Lord's" prayer. After the service everyone took pictures with the mayor and we went to the church to eat together. We were having a big lunch party for anyone who wanted to taste the Brazilian cuisine. We had lots of guests and the celebration was filled with joy. A sense of not having to hide from the major authority figure of the city and a feeling that our community was welcomed brought happiness to our table that day. In a way, a sense that the borders of this country were widened that morning as the symbolic gesture of the mayor made everybody felt welcome for awhile. Nonetheless, the meal that celebrated that feeling was never mentioned as a sacrament. God was there but not fully, as when God is in the "real" sacrament. At most, what we had there was a sacramental meal, but not even that was spoken. In any case, a sacrament, a sacramental act, or "just" a meal, that afternoon was a moment when this community felt, for a very short while, that they were welcomed in this country.

118. Nonetheless, the condition of our unveiling of the Spirit will always bring forth, as the condition of this action, this seeing, this un/veiling of the work/presence/apparition of the Spirit. Thus, with fear and trembling we guess the Spirit's unveiling by murmuring what cannot be properly heard. Not to see properly is not to hear properly as well. As Cixous puts it: "The joy of the unbridled eye: you can hear better like this. To hear you have to see clearly" (Cixous and Derrida, Veils, 12).

CALVIN'S EUCHARIST, BORDERS, AND HOSPITALITY

In this chapter we saw the Calvin that was hospitable to the refugees and worried about the excluded in his society. However, we also saw the other Calvin in the case of Servetus, when he not only fenced the eucharistic table and the doors of the city to exclude Servetus but, most importantly, denied his right to live. We too, out of our faithfulness to construct our own borders to protect the Christian faith and the eucharistic table, run the risk of protecting a particular systems of belief, a safe space, and a common worldview at the cost of someone else's life. Thus, the main question posed by Calvin's fences in regards to the death of Servetus can be: "what are the consequences of the borders we build around the eucharistic table?" This question should haunt us day and night in every worship service we create and/or participate.

Also, concerning these two Calvins, in one we see a very rigid doctrinal emphasis on proper understandings and practices of the sacrament of the eucharist for those who wanted to participate, as if we know exactly what we must do. The admonitions prior to the taking of the bread and the wine were rigorous and clearly showed the borders around the Lord's Supper. The other Calvin has a pneumatology that avoids idolatry and there is nothing that is completely apprehended, nailed down, named, fenced, called, or fully understood. In a sense, no one can say that God is, or is not, ever fully there. As for the sacraments, the elements might point to God's presence but they are not God's presence. The eucharistic elements might take us to Christ but they do not hold Christ. We could say the same in regards to the use of the words of institution in the Reformed worship services today. The wonder of Calvin's sacramental theology was to say that what makes God present in the sacrament is the Holy Spirit and the gathering of the assembly. It is the Spirit of God who does the work of passing through the people of God, of showing up, of doing the work of hospitality in God's house, of making Christ present in the hearts and bodies of the participants.

Thus, we make ourselves available to the Holy Spirit, starting from the free movement of the Spirit in our midst using the things we have received from those who came before us. Since the presence of God is a work of the Spirit, and neither rites nor anyone can actually make the Spirit do this or that, we are at the mercy of the givenness of the Spirit. This givenness of the Spirit in the sacrament can take us to different places or point Christ to us in unexpected situations, people, and borders. Like the Quakers, we listen to the Spirit first and then we say what the Spirit might have said to us. Everybody is welcomed to the house and everybody can speak.

In this process, while theological borders, ecclesiological fences and liturgical boundaries cannot assure the presence of God, we cannot live without borders. Borders are necessary and can even enhance our lives and our faith. Take the lives and experiences of African-American people and we will see how much fences were/are God's protection to their lives. As the spiritual says:

> Sometimes the way get so rough y'all
> And the nights are so long
> In my hour of weakness, that old enemy tries to steal my soul
> But when he comes like a flood to surround me
> My God will step in and a standard he'll raise
> Oh Lord be a fence all around me everyday
> Ohhh Jesus
> Jesus be a fence (Jesus be a fence)
> Be a fence right now (Jesus be a fence)[119]

We are caught up in this liturgical space where unmovable borders can be idolatry and lack of borders can be irresponsibility and death. In other words, if we don't listen to the Spirit we can harm ourselves either by building or destroying fences. We must then proceed very carefully, drawing from the wisdom of the past and the experiences of the present, uttering, wailing, moving, crying, singing, laughing, walking, sweating, and begging for God's presence. Since we cannot know for sure, we expand the spaces around eucharistic tables for others, constantly negotiating our borders and re-orienting ourselves and the sacraments towards God, each other, and the world. Then, by worshiping God *with* the stranger, *with* those who are the least of these, we can call upon the Spirit in hope and faith that, in this process, God will come and tell us what to do, and change our sacramental tables, our liturgies, our lives, and the life of the world. Now and forever!

119. "Jesus Be a Fence Around Me." I want to thank Professor Wil Gafney for mentioning this spiritual once on Facebook.

4

Feminist Liturgies, Borders, and Hospitality

The eucharists will be both festive and mournful, so connected are
they with what has been done and left undone in this world. It requires
breaking down barriers and crossing the boundaries of gender, class,
race, age, physical abilities. Reconstructed celebrations will not only
recall what has been missing in traditional retellings of the covenant
story but also correct what has been oppressive.[1]

—Janet Walton

This is her home, this thin edge of barbwire.

—Gloria Anzaldua

FEMINIST LITURGIES HAVE GREATLY expanded the notion of liturgy, sacrament and liturgical theology. They have challenged the field by rereading
and offering corrections to white patriarchal male views not only of wom-
en but also of tradition, God and life. Feminist liturgies have identified the
oppressive nature of implicit normative forms of ritual practices as foreign
to their bodies, stories and experiences. The hierarchical, patriarchal and
exclusive structures of Christian liturgies have often denied them voice,

1. Walton, "Eucharist," 92–93.

space, thought, and work, while trying to control their imagination. Feminist liturgical theologians are clearly aware of the ethical imperative of the liturgy and have challenged many boundaries of liturgical and sacramental practices and understandings. What I want to show in this chapter is how feminist practices have negotiated some of these boundaries and, by doing that, expanded notions of hospitality.

In order to do that, I first look at how liturgical patterns of normativity have established the law of belief, practice and consequently of life, patterns to which feminist liturgies have responded in their work. After that, I introduce some principles that guide feminist liturgies in order to have a better understanding of their liturgical work. Then, I develop three main aspects from their work, namely, sacred bodies, juxtapositions and "eucharists," and after each topic I establish connections with borders and hospitality. I finish by proposing broader negotiations at our unfolding eucharistic tables by challenging feminist liturgies to help us make our liturgical communities become *trans-national communities* as we redraw the lines of our worshiping practices by engaging with international groups and issues of women.

Lex Orandi, Credendi, Vivendi

As mentioned in the previous chapter, the historical reading of early Christian liturgical practices in the Western world has generally focused on a sole and integrated pattern of worship practiced and transmitted since the fourth century. This reading of the tradition has provided criteria to fence and validate *authentic* expressions of liturgical practices around the table at the same time that it has dismissed or avoided other actions that do not fit these norms. Moreover, this reading of a normative liturgical pattern also formed a theological and philosophical categorization that not only fenced but constituted liturgical practices and eucharistic understandings around metaphysical grounds.[2]

From a pluralistic beginning marked by many theologies and a variety of liturgical practices, the early church saw a change in its practices when it was co-opted by Constantine. From that time on, rituals were developed and enhanced, but at the same time began to be turned into normative public worship, limiting their plurality as a way of giving coherence and

---

2. Garrigan does a superb job in surveying and analyzing the metaphysical underpinnings within the field of sacramental theology and liturgical studies. See Garrigan, *Beyond Ritual.*

social consistency to the new situation. As Teresa Berger affirms, "With the so-called Constantinian revolution, the Church emerged publicly and its liturgy became a *cultus publicus*. Elaborate rituals flourished, and liturgical celebrations more and more became the ritual focus of surrounding society."[3]

The form of the *cultus publicus* slowly became a pattern that became accepted as a foundational structure, from which the church developed both its continuing identity and power. In the fifth century, Prosper of Aquitaine elaborated the maxim *lex orandi, lex credendi*,[4] which emphasizes the primacy of worshiping practices as enacting and confirming necessary beliefs. Liturgical scholar Aidan Kavanagh describes his own understanding of this sacramental principle:

> (I am a) creature of a deeply sacramental tradition of orthodoxy, which means first "right worship" and only secondarily doctrinal accuracy. This is very radical. It implies that worship conceived broadly is what gives rise to the theological reflection, rather than the other way around. In Prosper of Aquitaine's phrasing, it is the law of worship which founds or establishes the law of belief—rather as a foundation establishes a house or as the virtue of justice founds the law. The axiom in all three cases is irreversible: it is not law which makes justice possible, not the house which establishes the foundation, not beliefs which enable worship.[5]

Important here also, is the fact that liturgical practices acquire the status of law (lex), which regulates itself through the regulation of beliefs and liturgical practices. This regulation turns the *lex orandi* into an affirmation of a right worship.

Moreover, the right worship entails a right belief, or, in other terms, *ortho-praxis* becomes *ortho-doxa*. Therefore, the doxa in the Christian worship follows the right order of the normative praxis, holding up proper ways of speaking, moving, gesturing and believing in God. The law of right worship (ortho-praxis, right practices) collapses belief into a theological proper (ortho-doxa), and sets the ground for the development of the taxonomy of the right Christian discourse.

---

3. Berger, *Woman's Ways of Worship*, 13.

4. *Legem credendi lex statuat supplicandi* ("the rule of supplicating [in the church assembly] establishes the rule of believing"). See Lathrop, *Holy Things*, 9.

5. Kavanagh, *On Liturgical Theology*, 4–5.

In the sixteenth century, there was a profound theological/liturgical shift of ground. The *lex orandi* was replaced by *lex credendi* with the church officials (reformers and Catholics) naming a correct theology that was "now determining rather than interpreting liturgical text and form."[6] *Ortho-doxa* became "correct doctrine to be maintained by centralized ecclesiastical authority having exclusive power to enforce an absolute standard in liturgical texts by law."[7] Liturgy became correct doctrine by means of the theological law. The law of belief becomes primary theology, making the law of prayer dependent or secondary to the beliefs/dogma elaborated by theology. In Kavanagh's words:

> . . . liturgy no longer serves as the constitutive foundation for secondary theology, but is reduced to a doxological *envoi* which concludes the secondary enterprise and is wholly controlled by it. *Lex supplicandi legem statuat credendi* is effectively reversed, with the law of belief founding and constituting the law of worship. [8]

In the last twenty years, liturgical theologians have attempted to continue this debate, wrestling with alternate views, trying to re-enact the *lex orandi*, the law of liturgy, as primary theology.[9] The discussion entails a shift of focus from the primary of worship (*lex orandi*), or belief, *lex credendi* (lex credendi), to law (lex) and *ortho*, right laws. To attend either to *ortho-praxis* or to *ortho-doxa*, one accepts the discourse of those who establish and hold the *lex*, the *ortho*, i.e., the power of control of right Christian practices and beliefs. To confess the right beliefs is to sign up for the right practices and to do the right practices is to confess the right beliefs. One does not go without the other. Moreover, they circumscribe the *vivendi*, i.e., the ways life is lived and understood.

Feminist liturgies came to the debate by showing that the marks of the *lex* of the *doxa* and the *credendi* established borders of exclusion, leaving their *vivendi*, their lives, on the outside. The women's *vivendi*, the history of women in Christian liturgy is not only about the absence of women at the table as ordained leaders but also, and primarily about the *impropriety* of women within the compounds of the *lex*. Their work has been challenging the *ortho-doxa* of the *credendi* and *vivendi*, and reclaiming the unified

---

6. Ibid., 81.

7. Ibid.

8. Ibid., 80–83.

9. See Wainwright, *Doxology*; Kavanagh, *On Liturgical Theology*; Irwin, *Liturgical Theology*; Lathrop, *Holy Things*, Garrigan, *Beyond Ritual*; and many others.

dignity of their lives, bodies, and stories, widening the tradition with their own ways of worshiping. By doing that, they have shown how tainted official liturgy was by patriarchy, heterosexuality and racism. With their own ways of thinking and *liturgizing*, they helped us see the constraints embedded in the prejudices of the patterns of the traditional liturgy and how these patterns leave outside of the borders what the *lex* says is not acceptable or authentic. I will mention five aspects from feminist liturgies that can help us see how they explore, expand, break and negotiate the borders of the *lex orandi, lex credendi* and *lex vivendi.*

"Widening the Circle of Traditions"[10]— Principles of Feminist Liturgies

Marjorie Procter-Smith, who is a powerful voice amidst women doing liturgical theology, starts by *naming* and *re-claiming*[11] the places where women have historically been dismissed in most parts of the Christian

---

10. Walton, *Feminist Liturgy*, 81.

11. These words have been historically important to the women's movement. It consisted in making real what has been silenced for too long, giving materiality to what has always been unattended in women's experiences. Moreover, the re-claiming was the process of taking back what had been theirs all along but was denied: a place within the worship service, value, dignity, and even humanness.

tradition. In a process of re-valuing women, she claims that women's ways of doing liturgy prioritize

> shared leadership and responsibility . . . diversity . . . women's bonds . . . women's bodies and bodily processes as loci of divine revelation . . . interconnection and non-hierarchical . . . intentional experimentation . . . critical to traditional loci of authority . . . an ethical act . . . designed as particular and specific to a community, a gathering . . . a moral vision of the world . . . and an experience of empowerment of all oppressed.[12]

In marking the borders of the liturgical tradition, women name the issues and concerns that were left out and those that have exploited women for too long within the Christian tradition. Exploding the axis of proper liturgies enacted by centered and focused orders, Procter-Smith lays down the guiding principles that feminist liturgies should pursue. Her intention is to find a place, a liturgical place, in which women's experiences can be shared, memory and imagination freed, and movements open to perform what could show the truth of their lives, instead of following a preset rule that failed to give adequate consideration to women's lives as important to be mentioned or *liturgized*. In their worshiping practices, they saw liturgy as an emancipatory space of action for women to consider liturgically their social power and limitations, their interpersonal issues, their suffering, their gifts, and their exploitation within society and the liturgical traditions of the church.

> On the one hand, women need to be free to gather together as women-church to lament our losses, celebrate our joys, remember our history, tell our stories, and claim our power as women. The experience of solidarity that comes from participation in groups of women for discussion, study, or strategy finds its liturgical expression in the worship of women-church. On the other hand, women also need to be free to claim the church as our church, to place our griefs and joys, our stories and memories, at the center of the liturgical gathering of the whole church.[13]

This double-edge project intends to empower women by creating a space in which they can talk about their faith, connecting the variables and contingencies of their lives. Women expect to relate these celebrations to the church at large. They do not see themselves as heretics or what they offer as based on personal idiosyncrasies, but rather they are

12. Procter-Smith, *In Her Own Rite*, ii–viii.
13. Ibid., 156.

re-discovering what was always already there, what they were or could be, bringing these new discoveries to engage into an expanded reading of the Christian liturgical sources and tradition.

Within the same approach to the feminist liturgical movement, Mary Collins identifies five principles that challenge the patriarchal order and guide the "feminist consciousness and feminist liturgy:"[14]

> First, feminist liturgies ritualize relationships that emancipate and empower women. Second, feminist liturgy is the production of the community of worshipers, not of special experts or authorities. Third, feminist liturgies critique patriarchal liturgies. Fourth, feminist liturgies have begun to develop a distinctive repertoire of ritual symbols and strategies. Fifth, feminist liturgies produce liturgical events, not liturgical texts.[15]

The historical project of the feminist movement in various forms and places has impacted Christian churches and made entire denominations change their laws regarding the place of women in worship, ecclesial, and power structures including the ordination of women to the ministry of "word and the sacrament." This process of change has been quite dramatic because the patriarchal patterns were so entrenched. In Collins's words, feminist liturgies had to find a source of life that "could not be found in any existing liturgical order."[16] They had to imagine a world that did not exist. Imagination is a central element in the liturgical process. They rely on activities that are "typically exploratory, local and occasional,"[17] or as Susan Ross puts it, "event based, multiple and particular."[18]

At the outset of her book *Feminist Liturgies*, Walton describes these new liturgical experiences and in so doing also reveals what she feels is lacking in "normative" liturgical rites:

> (this work) represents my longing for liturgies that are more expressive of what we know about God and ourselves, a knowledge that changes and grows, for liturgies that are more connected to the choices we make daily, where risk-taking as a mandate of liturgical action, for liturgies that extend what is holy to what is not yet imagined.[19]

14. Collins, "Principles of Feminist Liturgy," 9–24.

15. Ibid., 11.

16. Ibid., 24.

17. Ibid., 22.

18. Ross, *Extravagant Affections*, 27.

19. Walton, *Feminist Liturgy*, 9.

The "not yet imagined" stimulated the imaginations of women who had to invent themselves in order to become real not only for God, but for themselves and for the liturgical tradition. Following Marjorie Procter-Smith, Walton works on a topic that has been very important to the feminist movement, namely truth telling.[20] She voiced the concerns of the women who were left out of the dialogue and practice of the ordo, of the liturgical structures that not only denied the existence of women, but also avoided what really mattered to them.

For many years, just before the Mass, a group of elderly women gathered together in the pews to chat for few minutes before the priest began the liturgy. During these few minutes, they shared with each other about their days, their lives at home, their sons and granddaughters, their pains and their new discoveries. The priest would then start the Mass on time and when it was finished they went home promising each other to meet again the next morning. Not even once, in 30 years of celebrations of the Mass, has a single priest ever asked these faithful women about their conversations, much less about their lives. Worse, the priest never knew that the Mass could be a place to talk about their needs, their pains, their hopes, their fears. Some boundaries could never be thought to exist, even though they have been there for so many years.

Walton describes two main qualities within feminist liturgies as honoring and correcting. "Honoring God, ourselves, one another and other-kind, involved naming what was inaccurate, distinguishing what was true, believing what we learned, and resisting naysayers. The next phase required correction, (which includes) self-image, God's image and stories."[21] Within these two principles there is a clear movement, based on an ethical claim that searches for social justice for women.

Breaking the patterns of disinterest, uselessness and self-referentiated borders of the traditional liturgy, this movement marks the walls of liturgical thinking and practices with intentions, proposals and reforms by honoring what has never been understood as valid, correcting what

20. "Liturgies typically described as 'feminist' began to emerge in the late 1960s when women and some men realized that what they were experiencing in the liturgies of churches and synagogues was not only not 'enough,' but in fact, was not 'true.' Moreover, based on the ways women establish their relationships, she affirms that feminist liturgies 'promote truth-telling'" (ibid., 12).

21. Ibid., 39–45.

has pushed people away from the patterns of worship and naming what is present and what is absent within these enclosed walls of Christian celebrations. With their hard work and powerful voices, they mark the official liturgy with human contingency.

Feminist liturgical work challenges these liturgical borders that have imprisoned women and many others on the outside of the liturgical patterns of authenticity and what tradition declares is acceptable. Against an unfair liturgical order, with a bundle of words and movements that often did not touch on the most pressing issues of women's experiences, Walton says that "[t]raditional liturgical patterns have been shaped by patriarchal values, where males, particularly privileged white males, are accorded power and authority while everyone else, including all females, are without status or identity."[22] By "extending what is holy to what is not yet imagined," feminist liturgies take the realm of the sacred from the hands of male gatekeepers and connect it to the experiences of women too. By shifting the power of the sacred, inventing other ways of interpreting and performing liturgies and reclaiming their space, feminist liturgies are able to expand the borders of the proper, of the acceptable and the authentic, offering hospitality to people and things that have often been ignored within traditional liturgical orders.

A TURN TO PRAXIS[23]—CONTEXT AND STORYTELLING

Feminist liturgies are hard to understand if one does not participate in them. What might sound strange and make most men dismiss these liturgical practices comes from the newness of their work with different sets of resources and actions. The logical "male" aspect of the formal Christian liturgy cannot be found there. The structure is not hierarchical, the ground is moveable, the movements not necessarily expected, the texts used not limited to the index approved by the tradition. Due to that, every ritual has a life of its own, depending on the context and the story to be celebrated. The ritual is not pre-fabricated but organically created from the experiences lived by the group of women gathered. Diann L. Neu, an experienced leader of WATER: "Women's Alliance for Theology, Ethics

---

22. Ibid., 39.

23. These are Garrigan's words to define the turn from a linguistic approach to liturgies to a more practical method one of accurate documentation. See her chapter 1, "Crisis of Institutions," in *Beyond Ritual*, 38.

and Ritual," proposes a process for creating liturgies designed to mark rites of passage in the lives of women.

> Think of a particular liturgy that your community needs; Focus the theme; Discover a symbol that will visibly carry the message of the liturgy; Identify readings, prayers, and blessings that make your message concrete; Select music that conveys your message; Choose an environment that enhances the theme of the celebration; Share the leadership for various parts of the service with several people; Include body expression; Involve children in the celebration.[24]

These guidelines show the need for a variety of resources and practices that for some will lose the authenticity of the "common" and expected Christian rituals. However, these feminist liturgies will not rely on fixed forms of rituals that will impose form, text and movements to the liturgical gathering but rather, will start organically, based on the story to be shared and the context from whence this story comes.

An emphasis on the practical aspects of the liturgy has brought different lenses and perspectives to the liturgical field. The living/lived experience is what creates the narratives of the event and the context where this liturgy is to be shared will prepare the ground for the texts that are going to be used. Garrigan calls this a turn to praxis. She explains:

> By coming to understand through the various liturgical movements and reforms of the twentieth century that sacraments must be studied as lived events, systematic and liturgical approaches have both posited as the object of analysis not text but context, the "juxtapositions," the narratives of the experience.[25]

This turn to praxis comes from the fact that women's experiences were consistently not considered in the liturgical documents or practices of the Christian church. What feminist liturgies do is to bring people's lives to the crux of the liturgical gathering. As Megan McKenna says: "People are not just the first priority in liturgy and sacraments and rites: they are in a real sense the *only* priority."[26] Moreover, by focusing on the lives of women, feminist liturgies bring their experiences to the core of the liturgical space, honor them, make them sacred, and use them as text and context of liturgical practices. The result is that the liturgical space

---

24. Neu, *Women's Rites*, 44–46.

25. Garrigan, *Beyond Ritual*, 38.

26. McKenna, *Rites of Justice*, xi.

becomes a populated space where God is not spoken about or controlled univocally by one person, but rather, debated, shared and lived by the gathered community.

Storytelling then becomes a necessary tool in feminist liturgies. From the monolithic discourse of the Christian message imposed from a top-down system to the lives of people, the liturgies of the gathered women open up spaces for everyone to tell their stories. In these liturgies, each is exposed to the other and everyone has the potential to be transformed. Also, by lending one's ear to another, the one who tells the story gains a human face in the process of becoming a person who unfolds the pains, the joys, and the mysteries of one's life in many directions. Then, one gets support and challenge from the community to keep going with her life. What feminist liturgies do is to perform their autobiographies the same way that women writers do in more formal texts. What Estelle C. Jelinek says about theories of autobiographies and women can be related to women's liturgies and "liturgical theories:"

> Any theory of autobiography that excludes experimentation—shapes that suit individual personalities—and relies on absolute definitions and forms, dooms the genre to extinction. Fortunately, autobiographers write on, undaunted and unaware of theoreticians . . . Many of these women are creative writers—poets, novelists, and playwrights—long silent in autobiography, who are now "telling their story" in the same aesthetic mode as their other writings.[27]

Thus, instead of relying solely on the meta-narrative of the Christian discourse, or on liturgical studies that do not include women's perspectives, feminist liturgies understand that individual stories can in fact widen the Christian tradition, and effect in great ways, the way people live and understand life. These liturgies are a continuous process of layering perspectives, of correcting and converting their vision, their attention and resources, and of placing these perspectives in relation to other situations, other experiences, other challenges. This process is also the way that feminist liturgies elaborate their knowledge of God, from the context and stories of the participants in relation to the tradition received. The knowledge of God keeps changing, as one gets to know the experiences of other's lives in relation to God. Moreover, certain knowledge of God can only be known through the concrete bodies and lives of those who are *liturgizing* together. Feminist liturgies are open to *liturgize* the multiplicity

---

27. Jelinek, *Tradition of Women's Autobiography*, 189.

of ways that life happens in the lives of women and the ways that God is manifested in these diverse situations.

Thus, the contextual narratives of experience bring a vast array of meanings and possibilities that expand greatly the scope of liturgical studies and practices. They break down the universalizing and a-historical Christian discourse that does not see the local constructions of meaning in people's lives as important, or necessary. Moreover, these possibilities entail an empowering of the worshipers, bringing them new tools to create and re-create their own lives, their understandings and relations to God and at the same time create resistance against oppression.

Feminist liturgies by breaking down the monolithic constructions of Christian discourse and liturgical forms in these ways end up hosting a vast array of guests and opening possibilities where God can be manifest. Each woman's life becomes a source for liturgical practices. Even though the scope of the understood context does always include the larger social-economic-political perspectives, feminists do get to the center of the exclusionary structure of church and society by claiming an undeniable place of importance and honor for the lives of women. In order to make each story count, they have to open wide the doors of acceptance, so that every one, no matter what story they bring, is welcome in the liturgical spaces where God is encountered in the life of the community. Moreover, each story is engaged by the group that is exposed then to different situations that can transform understandings of the world, of the other, and of oneself. Due to the variety of contexts, stories, and praxis, these liturgical performances carry a potential challenge to formed theological understandings by opening up other possibilities to think and practice hospitality within the liturgical space.

Thus, feminist liturgies not only fracture some borders but also tear down some other fences that exclude women's lives from the table of God. Prevented from being fully welcomed in the "official" Christian liturgies, women create a space where they constantly welcome each other as they open themselves up to others who want to participate.

SACRED BODIES

Truth, in feminist liturgies, comes also through the concrete experiences of women's bodies. The spiritual discourse of the Christian message was developed, among other things, over and against the concrete specificities of women's bodies. Women were always associated with their bodies, while men were associated with the spiritual and higher aspects of faith. To quote Susan Ross,

> In the history of religion and culture, women traditionally have been associated with the body. The biological processes of menstruation, pregnancy, and lactation have served to define women as "more bodily" than men. When interpreted as lower than the soul, the body is seen as particularly prone to sin.[28]

This process can be seen historically in the way that Christianity has *desecrated* women's bodies by adding contrary signs, i.e., as a locus of the devil's possessions, as instruments of the devil's actions, as a dangerous, sensual weapon against the faith of any true (male) believer. Thus, women's bodies were considered inferior to men's bodies and a stumbling block to God's purity, lacking proper reasoning, and intrinsically incapable of doing anything noble, holy, or of higher value.

Thus, the recovery of the importance and meaning of the body to the development of faith is central to feminist liturgies. "Feminist theologies have emphasized that human experience and knowledge are rooted in the body. They have stressed embodied thinking."[29] Since women's bodies were not only dismissed but often abused, violated, raped or killed, women's liturgical practices honor women's bodies as ways of resisting oppression, of adding significance and value to their lives, of capturing the truth of their lives, and re-membering what matters to one's faith. It is in and through the body that the life of faith happens and is articulated.

Around the table, women's bodies and experiences not only add perspectives to the eucharistic sacrament but most importantly, they change the very understandings of the sacraments and their theological suppositions. By entering through the limited spots of the male liturgical structures, women's presence, thinking, and work have challenged many norms around the table. Commenting on Latina liberation theologians, Susan Ross says that "when women's experiences are incorporated consciously into worship, they do not simply add on to it but also transform it."[30]

Within virtually every woman's body there is an experience of pain, of exclusion, of avoidance, of mistreatment, of abuse which must be considered through shared liturgical practices of communion, support, strength and wholeness. Thus, feminist liturgies deal with emotions and affections

28. Ross, "Body," 32.

29. Ibid., 32.

30. Ross, *Extravagant Affections*, 177.

that have for too long been silenced. The power that these practices carry *touches* deep moments and memories in women's lives, providing them with a larger community of solidarity to cope with the past as well as strengthen them to fight for the present and future. They end up offering a more intense relational perspective of what it means to be human and so shed new light on understandings of God. From feminists, woman-ists, and Latinas we learn that through the body, everything is connected: people, earth, cosmos, and God.

The eucharistic table has been a central liturgical place which wom-en's bodies have not been allowed to approach. Their tainted bodies did not, could not hold the holy sacrament of the altar/table. Moreover, they were placed as recipients of the sacraments or, at most, as caregivers of the sacrament, preparing the elements or bringing than to the table, but not participating as celebrants. With the work of many feminist liturgists and liturgical theologians, women's bodies became a central challenge to the historical denial of hospitality practiced by Christian liturgies. They show how the bodies of women are taken only as "Fragments of Real Presence,"[31] and not as wholly, full bodies expressing the real presence of God.

In this way, women's ways of worshiping have expanded the borders of understandings and practices regarding definitions of what liturgy might be: spaces are changed, new intentions are stimulated, alternative texts are chosen, specific prayers are crafted, songs close to heart are sung, guests are welcome—all of which offer a vast array of interpretative connections where God can be found in multiple ways. In other words, the welcoming of bodies into liturgical practices has enabled women to consider, analyze, and open space for a whole range of both human possibilities and divine interactions never considered in the formal orders of official liturgies.

One morning, almost thirty immigrants, adults and children, more women than men, crossed the border of Mexico and were left by the coyotes at the door of a Reformed church on the other side of the fron-tera/border. They go inside the church and sit in the pews waiting. The assistant pastor sees them coming and thinks that it is a robbery. He immediately decides to call the police but when he sees children he stops and calls the senior pastor who tells him to watch over them and make sure they don't touch anything. The assistant pastor hangs up the phone and tries to speak with them. The women carry their kids on their arms

31. See Berger, *Fragments of Real Presence*.

and one of them burst into tears. Everybody starts to talk and the assistant pastor is completely lost. The senior pastor arrives. People start to
arrive. Nobody knows what to do. The immigrants are scared to death
and the congregants pass around them without saying anything. The
immigrants stay at the back of the church as the members go to the front.
They try to connect but only one church member says that he speaks
a little Spanish and cannot understand the words that the immigrants
speak. The immigrants try to speak English but they cannot. The service
is about to start and there are lots of strange people standing and sitting at the back of the church. The session decides to send them to the
basement while a social service organization is called to come and pick
them up. The crying of the woman does not stop and at this point it
is really annoying. By now the service is really late. The van from the
social service agency arrives and picks them up. Members go back to
their usual pews. The pastor finally sits in his front chair and the organ
starts with the prelude. The liturgist says: "Welcome to the house of God
where everybody is welcome." And the church replies reading the bulletin
"Thanks be to God who has shown his love to us."

JUXTAPOSITIONS: SPACE, THINGS, SYMBOLS, AND MOVEMENTS

With this turn to practices, feminist liturgies have employed an ample
range of symbols, literature, experiences and juxtapositions, mostly to the
dismay of "classical liturgical authorities."[32] They have created a vast array
of liturgical possibilities where, in the words of Walton, the holy was linked
to "what is not yet imagined." Feminist liturgical juxtapositions did not
only subscribe to the proper juxtapositions of liturgical accepted orders,
but also, turned and twisted God's possibilities as well as our constructions of God's possibilities which were re-oriented through a kaleidoscope
of many colors, patterns, textures, scenes, languages, movements, senses
and vibrancies. The whole sense of juxtaposition here is not positioning
known elements of known Eucharistic elements but rather, juxtaposing
apparently foreign elements of women's lives into the traditional elements
of the liturgy. The process of *juxtapositioning* strange things, symbols,
movements and even strange spaces into the Eucharistic prayer is the
powerful movement that creates different theological thinking and practices not only into the *lex orandi* and *lex credendi*, but also into the *lex
vivendi* and *lex agendi (laws of life and agency/ethics).*

32. Collins, "Principles of Feminist Liturgy," 12.

The most powerful result that this unfolding variety of juxtapositions brings is the challenge to the rational, linear process in which liturgical rites have been bound. With unexpected correlations, or even *dis-relations*, feminist liturgies stir up the deep-rooted rationality that has marked the onto-theo-logical project that keeps God as the "unmovable mover."[33] Even though these juxtapositions by themselves cannot undo the metaphysics of God present in the liturgical studies, it can crack the self-enclosed liturgical system and show other interpretative understandings of God that were never allowed. Through a dazzling movement of push and pull practices, they turn God into a polidoxy of events, a dizzying polysemic scattering of possibilities of meanings and practices, not only defying some unshaken definitions of God but, also, exposing and educating the worshiper into a cultivation of emotions and affections that are present in the official liturgies mostly through prohibitions, denial and guilt.

This process of cultivation of the multiple liturgical practices, which has historically not been allowed in official liturgical spaces, entailed women's use of their imagination and the invention of themselves within the liturgical space. This process realizes that the liturgical space is a foreign space for women. The architecture of the church is hierarchical: the sacred space is male-oriented, the liturgical objects, or things, are chosen and handled by men; and movements are always constrained according to the gesturing of certain male (often white) behavior required by the liturgical rite. Thus, women's stories are surrounded by that which is not their own, and asked to ascribe to forms and contents that in some ways are foreign to their living. As a result, women started to look for their resources somewhere else, namely where their lives grew ordinarily and organically. They started to look where their hearts and minds and bodies were attached, celebrating within a space that they could claim as sacred, with things that were closely linked to their stories and could point to something related to their lives, using an unfixed set of gestures that would make sense to their bodies and hearts.

Since feminist liturgies are "ordinary, organic and for everyone,"[34] they are open to negotiations regarding arrangements of space, use of objects, choice of music, preference of gestures and range of symbols and movements. Here is a small description of what feminist liturgies offer, or of what "doing liturgy differently" means.

33. Aristotle, in Edel, *Aristotle and his Philosophy*, 129.
34. Walton, *Feminist Liturgy*, 12.

As in our homes, in our feminist liturgies we want our space
to be evocative, honest, connected to our everyday lives, all its
heartaches, terrors, and accomplishments; as well as what we
yearn to know and be. In planning our liturgies, we intentionally gather whatever we need to meet this goal, whether it be
pictures, objects, or traditional liturgical symbols such as water,
candles, oil, or food. Some things are used once, others reappear
regularly . . . Horizontal gestures prevail in feminist liturgies;
they suggest equality and interdependence . . . We pray with our
eyes open and without bowing our heads . . . Feminist liturgies
intend to provide occasions to practice gestures of resistance
and expressions of shared power . . . we search for music that
has been forgotten, composers or performers made invisible
throughout history because of their marginalization . . . Though
we may be self-conscious and awkward, we dance, we move
together, we touch each other in actions of solidarity, play and
blessing . . . Symbols, texts and sounds are drawn from various traditions . . . we intentionally do this work in light of our
relationship with God. [35]

This whole spectrum of physical and material possibilities makes
feminist liturgies not only a world to be imagined but also an instrument
to discover how our lives are structured in layers of historical oppression,
social injustice, racism and violence. Both things and themes that are so
important to people's lives are to be considered. In the feminist worship
services that both Walton and Neu write about, one can see that these
feminist groups address a variety of issues: advent, madness, healing from
childhood sexual abuse, memorial, mastectomy, Sophia, honoring wom-
en's blood mysteries, reproductive choices, mourning loved ones.[36] In this
endeavor, they are trying "to discover how to use symbols, texts and forms
that express . . . relationships with God, one another and our created world
more accurately and more authentically. The quest is a matter of justice."[37]

Women's liturgical spaces have always been a challenge to the liturgical structure: its ambiguity, outside source of symbols, movements and
language, moveable places of worship, often (un)recognizable ways of developing spiritualities, naming of desires and bodily experiences, contingent thematic structures, marked material references, open-ended use of
juxtapositions, along with challenges to the male control of the liturgical

35. Ibid., 36–38, and Neu, *Women's Rites*, 48–49.

36. Walton, *Feminist Liturgy*, 48–80.

37. Ibid., 12.

order and consequent narrowing of the liturgical tradition, serve as a harsh critique of the liturgical tradition and its borders of control. Moreover, it is an embarrassment to those who avoided or ignored the place of women in their liturgical studies, as well as a challenge to an open, fairer and just celebration of the rites of the Christian tradition.

Women's ample use of objects, space and movement challenges the many borders of what has been considered proper or authentic in Christian worship and the proper juxtapositions of the liturgical orders. The self-referentiated liturgical axis that has kept the normativity of the official ways of worshiping is then bent out of shape. The borders within which to gain access to God are amplified and expanded through women's liturgical practices. From their hands, everything can become a liturgical element or a sacramental action.

> . . . "women's experiences" as a source for feminist theological reflection on the sacraments constitutes a multiple, diverse, and continually changing source. Unlike traditional sacramental theology there is no clearly defined set of texts or practices that constitute a given for liturgical or sacramental reflections by and for women.[38]

The instability and interchangeability of their practices, aligned with the power of imagination, provide powerful tools to promote the widening of the borders of hospitality. The juxtaposition is not a lack of respect with the known orders of tradition. Instead it is an expansion of its possibilities. In this sense, one can understand what Walton says when she defines feminist liturgies as "widening the field of tradition," i.e., adding to the tradition a vast array of liturgical possibilities, bringing other theological and liturgical perspectives on God and women, thinking "what is not yet imagined," and so expanding borders of hospitality.

EUCHARISTS

The most fascinating and constructive definition of Eucharist that I have encountered in feminist liturgical and sacramental studies of the Eucharist has been written by Janet Walton in the *Dictionary of Feminist Theologies*. She starts by presenting the scope of the ritual saying: "Eucharist describes a ritual meal that embodies memory, imagination, power, encounter,

38. Ross, *Extravagant Affections*, 27.

freedom, relationship, presence, blessing."[39] Due to her liturgical experiences with other women, she embodies and thinks of eucharist not as a spiritual a-historical exercise but rather as an exercise in incarnation, a ritual that "embodies," that lives, moves, and alters the body through a vast range of human predicaments. The relational aspect of the Eucharist is tantamount to the construction and passing on of justice that must happen within eucharistic practices. Throughout the article, she stretches the definitions of what a reconstructed Eucharist could be and breaks with the idea of "the" sacrament by writing the word eucharist in the plural, eucharists, a plurality that has to do not so much with enacted times of the ritual, but rather with the plurality of its practices, i.e., the real sacrament in the plural. In order to reconstruct eucharist into eucharists, she gives powerful open-ended guidelines:

> Such a reconstruction implies a reorganization of power and a sharing of authority. It requires breaking down barriers and crossing the boundaries of gender, class, race, age, physical abilities. Reconstructed celebrations will not only recall what has been missing in traditional retellings of the covenant story but also correct what has been oppressive. These eucharists will be both festive and mournful, so connected are they with what has been done and left undone in this world.[40]

The sacrament finds here possibility for expansion. There is no negotiation of the sacramental, but the very notion of the sacrament changes through the notion of a plurality of Eucharists. The possibility of the sacrament in its plural perspectives is almost impossible, since it demands a painful and difficult work in which people lose their power, their space, and their most cherished assurances, for the sake of the other, for the sake of the sacrament, and for the sake of God. In this unending process, the work of the Spirit goes beyond the confinements of boundaries. To give thanks in a world such as ours is a challenge in and of itself. However, these Eucharistic practices, difficult as they may be, if illuminated by the Spirit, can surround us with trust, help us redefine the story of the covenant between God and people, and boost our bodies into heartfelt thanks. As she affirms: "[t]o give thanks, eucharistia, is an expression of confidence in the persistent stirring of the Spirit . . ."[41]

39. Walton, "Eucharist," 92.

40. Ibid., 92–93.

41. Ibid., 93.

The reorganization of power implies the displacement of meaning, and the reconstructions of the eucharists entail a dialectical use of Derrida's "Law of hospitality" and the "laws of hospitality." The breaking down of barriers is not the absence of barriers since feminist liturgies are very aware of (necessary) borders. However, "the breaking down of barriers" aligned with "the *crossing* of boundaries" is a clear movement towards a radical inclusion in the Eucharist, a very disturbing and almost unbearable step,[42] since the crossing of "gender, class, race, age, physical abilities," implies a space heightened with various kinds of differences. To proceed with this step is to engage in a dangerous work of moving boundaries, which seems, at first, to be an impossible task. However, Walton's "Law of Hospitality" is marked by the ethical conditionals of the "laws of hospitality," namely justice, and embodied relational power. The negotiation of power and the work of hospitality are to be found in the junctures of the reconstructions of these eucharists, a work that never ends; we must keep recalling what was left out and forgotten, as we keep correcting what has been oppressive.

Women know quite well how it is to live in and around borders of exclusion. They have worked against unjust boundaries and fostered the creation of fairer ones. No wonder Walton's language is marked with words like borders, boundaries, crossing, etc. With the possibilities of creating eucharists, feminist liturgies have widened the borders of hospitality and given us tools to expand the place around the eucharistic table and redefine the sacrament.

NEGOTIATIONS, UNFOLDING EUCHARISTS, AND TRANS-NATIONAL COMMUNITIES

It has been already mentioned that the expansion of the notion of hospitality entails negotiations, negotiations of many kinds, be they within the framework of social democracy where issues are debated and voted in a democratic way, such as Gandhian and Martin Luther King Jr. pacifism, or pacifist liturgical social movements such Quakers, or even within the more revolutionary frameworks of The Landless Movement in Brazil,[43] or

42. As mentioned in the introduction, Derrida says: "The crossing of borders always announces itself according to the movement of a certain step [*pas*]—and of the step that crosses a line." See footnote 25 above.

43. To see the connection between grassroots movements for justice and liturgy in Brazil, see Adam, *Liturgia com os Pés*.

the Sanctuary Movement in Unites States[44] and the use of worship spaces to protect immigrants, or the work of early feminist liturgies.

Hospitality is not a given and when it is offered, it is surrounded by high fences. The transnationality of our world, globalization, impoverishment and human migration have made countries around the world pass tighter and tougher laws regarding immigration and citizenship. As feminist Trinh T. Minh-ha said: "The globe is evoked in terms of both a closely knit village, and a new, dishomogenous metropolis. Yes, the talk on the world political page is all about closing down, curtailing movements, reinforcing borders, building new fences."[45] This building of new fences has to do with the social classes struggle, the enrichment of few and the impoverishment of many. The Occupy Wall Street movement has shown the battle between the 99% of the population over against the 1% who holds the wealth of the United States. A place "under the sun" has increasingly become more difficult to find and a place at the eucharistic table in the United States mirrors all these world/national events. Since feminist liturgies place the ethical dimension at the top of their practical and theoretical thinking, they can help us to establish a prophetic voice of discontent, a way to fight against injustice and provide a variety of negotiations at the table and approximate incompatible worlds through hospitable bonds.

> *A member of the church learns she has cancer, but no health insurance. Her treatment is expensive. The church decides to take away the money form their endowment and offer a good treatment to the member. Some people are against it but they all decide to do that. They believe they are each other's keepers and they have a commitment to care for each other. While the person goes through treatment, they start to invite more people who have cancer to their worship services to give their testimonies of struggle, losing and winning their battles. People with the HIV virus also come to tell their stories. During their testimonies, they share the Eucharist. The bread is for the sustenance of those who were strangers and now are their families. The blood is for the healing of them all, those in good health and those who are sick. Their lives are entangled in and around the Eucharistic table and there, they promise to live together in life and in death.*

44. Among others sources, see Coutin, *Culture of Protest.*
45. Trinh, *Elsewhere, Within Here,* 1.

Eucharist and Globalization

The Eucharistic table has its location in various parts of the world. It functions like a rhizomic fold[46] that refolds and unfolds itself with a plethora of meanings and possibilities of life that are horizontality spread on the surface of the ground instead of vertically grounded on a certain depth that holds deeper truths. The folding and unfolding of the Eucharist embraces the "'inconstant feeling' (half hope, half fear, becoming shadow; the peacefulness of sleep, and the anxiety of transformation) that arises when the sun capsizes."[47] The folding of the eucharist captures the fabric of our lives, the borders of our communities that spread out the edges of our tables and touch invisible communities. The fringes of the Eucharist scream to the center its delusions, its utter fears of abandonment and detachment, the brutality of violence against women, the trafficking of women's bodies, the tiredness of an unending fight.

The eucharistic table should help us see ourselves and our beliefs not as limitations to the correlations with the world but rather, a rhizomic flux, a work of fluidity, polidoxy, liminality, in which the table moves and is moved, changed, and occupied by others. A privileged place for the disfranchised to find tools to fight. In this process, we must be, in Homi Bhabha's words, "'a community of negotiation,' since there is no such thing as a community or body of the people, whose inherent, radical historicity emits the right signs."[48]

The crossing of boundaries should be the crossing of spaces unknown to us, the grasping of the fact that we are all inter-related and inter-connected, not necessarily by a universally fixed meaning but by a sense of being the people of God living in the same world. Within this world we must negotiate borders, expand them to protect the poor or even take them by storm as to destroy the capitalist walls of disconnection and the *muros de odio (walls of hatred)*, always bearing in mind that, for poor people, to negotiate is always difficult, since they do not have power. This

46. "Above the soul sings of the glory of God inasmuch as it follows its own folds, but without succeeding in entirely developing them, since 'this communication stretches out indefinitely.' A labyrinth is said , etymologically, to be multiple because it contains many folds. The multiple is not only what has many parts but also what is folded in many ways . . . If we go back to the model of the Baroque fabric, it could be stated that knowledge is known only where it is folded. Ideas are so folded in the soul that we can't always unfold or develop them, just as things themselves are inextricably wrapped up in nature. Malebranche's error is to have believed that in God we see completed unfolded Ideas. But even for God's notions have folds that adorn infinite understanding" (Deleuze, *Fold*, 3, 49).

47. Trinh, *Elsewhere, Within Here*, 75.

48. Bhabha, *Location of Culture*, 27.

brings us to the need for acts of revolution, for movements that go beyond the limits of our accepted rationality and venture into new possible worlds that God has in store for us. The subversive memory of Jesus Christ reenacted at the Eucharist is an eternal spring of revolutionary movements.

When women are at the table they transform the sacrament. As Susan Ross suggests, their movements affect the theological and liturgical nerve of the Eucharist and press changes to the existing configurations of practices and understandings of the sacrament. Unless the boundaries of the sacrament are pressed and we check the universal language, movement and ordo of its structures, the laws of conditional hospitality will continue to make the priest/pastor pass by the elderly group of women at the church every morning; non-documented immigrants will continue to be hunted by military border patrol; the homeless will continue to sleep at the doorsteps of Fifth Avenue Presbyterian Church; and Carmelo, mentioned in the introduction, will never get a visa to come to the US to help feed his family.

Feminist liturgies challenge to help us unfold the corners of the eucharistic table by including other parts of the world. Since their spaces are open to everyone and especially to excluded women around the world, they can help us make bridges between other groups of women who are isolated by economic, social, and religious borders. For example, there are one million women treated as sexual slaves around the world today according to the International Labor Organization.[49] How can feminist practices help us think about ways to worship/practice that might extend the corners of the eucharistic table to these women in solidarity, freedom and justice? What liturgies, what spaces, what movements, what languages, what sounds and songs, what commitments must be made at and around the sacrament of the altar/table to honor God and these women?

Gayatry Spivak Chakravorty, postcolonial thinker and professor at Columbia University, presents four groups of "women in the transnational world" that need to be considered:

> 1) homeworking: the women (who) stay at home, often impervious to organizational attempts through internalized gendering as a survival technique; 2) population control, (which) is the name of the policy that is regularly tied to so-called aid packages, by transnational agencies, upon the poorest women . . . the policy is no less than genocide and war on women . . .

---

49. Pablo Uchoa, "Exploração sexual escraviza 1 milhão de mulheres," *Folha de S. Paulo*, March 26, 2007: http://www1.folha.uol.com.br/folha/bbc/ult272u61697.shtml.

because it identifies women with their reproductive apparatus and grants them no other subjectship; 3) groups that cannot become diasporic: larger groups within this space of difference subsist in transnationality without escaping diaspora; (as part of these non-diasporic groups are the) 4) indigenous women outside of the Americas: (which in the words of Gramsci) "are ranked among the subaltern," are an important part of the 'transnational world.[50]

The situation of these women begs us to sit at the table and think/practice about encounters and politics that might undo this oppression. How can the eucharistic table reach out and be transformed by them? Again, what words, gestures, movements of un-folding would challenge us to think/eat with them at table? How can we offer (and receive) hospitality in this unwelcoming world? If we think about the relationship between the Syrophoenician women and Jesus, as Hal Taussig has shown, we can also think about the negotiations of the social spaces in which these women live and struggle today.[51] Can we find a place at the table for them with us? Michael Nausner suggests a "discipleship of Christ that negotiates (at) the boundaries and follows the traces of divergent tracks across the common land. Through this practice a new conception of belonging to the (home) land can emerge, and multiple boundaries may reveal themselves as places of encounter and solidarity instead of division and exclusion."[52]

Even though there is no such a thing as a boundary of encounter without exclusion, we might gain some insight if we think about eucharist and hospitality as an ever unfolding place with multiple boundaries where we negotiate under, around, and even on the table these encounters and exclusions, always looking for the poor, the most vulnerable, the disempowered and the disfranchised of the earth. In this way, the unending feminist reconstructions of the eucharists with its ethical juxtapositions will help us in the formation of hospitable and plural communities of people. Using the words of Trinh T. Min-ha, we can define just for now, the work of the eucharists:

Slowly repeats, slowly modifies itself, slowly disintegrates, and then, slowly begins anew. Multiplication of periods and pauses. Words decomposed, repeated, sometimes misspelled, sometimes mispronounced, isolated and incomplete. If failure there

50. Spivak, "Diasporas Old and New," 88–89.
51. See H. Taussig, *In the Beginning Was the Meal.*
52. Nausner, "Homeland as Borderland," 132.

is, then it is a failure à la Beckett (fail again, fail better)—a failure that retains its agency in a supposedly non-failing, successful society.[53]

53. Trinh, *Elsewhere, Within Here*, 119.

5

Latin American Hospitality
and Sacraments

The world is gone, I must carry you.

—PAUL CELAN[1]

IN NOVEMBER 2006, WHEN twenty-two presidents got together in Latin America for the "16th Ibero-American Summit," Kofi Annan, then the general secretary of United Nations, said: "in this region (Latin America), inequality and poverty are permanent challenges. The region has the highest level of inequality in the world in regards to the distribution of its wealth and 220 million people live in poverty."[2] Since its colonization and subsequent decolonization, the processes leading to an unfair distribution of land and wealth, have made Latin America one of the most degrading places as regards differences between poor and rich people, in which to live. Out of this disastrous situation, Latin American theologians created their own way of talking about God, with their own specificities and challenges to the universal and normative ways of doing theology.

Liberation theologians started to do theology from below, from a harsh social reality where millions of people were living in abject poverty. What motivated Liberation Theology then was a powerful movement called Base Ecclesial Communities (BECs) comprised of poor people who,

1. Quoted in Derrida, *Sovereignties in Question*, 161.

2. Annan, "Desigualdade na América Latina é a maior do mundo," *Folha de S. Paulo*, Nov. 4, 2006: http://www1.folha.uol.com.br/folha/mundo/ult94u101501.shtml.

in many ways, reinvented the church. This movement developed its own specificities of being the church and its *alterity*[3] created problems with the normative way of being church. However, mostly welcomed by local priests, theologians and some bishops, the BECs grew immensely and fueled the movement of liberation theology. It became a powerful movement spread throughout Latin America.

This chapter seeks to offer an overview of liberation theology and BECs and analyze ways in which hospitality, Eucharist practices and borders function both in this new theology/ecclesiology and within social reality. In order to do that, I will start by analyzing how the notion of alterity has always been avoided in liturgical studies and practices and how poor people have always been left out of the eucharistic table; then, I give a brief and general introduction to some characteristics that mark liberation theology; I proceed to explain some of the new ways the BECs developed the idea of a new church and how its alterity annoyed the official church until it was accommodated by the mainstream church; lastly, I will explore Brazilian hospitality and note how poor communities create hospitality in relation to sacrament and eucharist.

1. Liturgy and Alterity

One main question runs throughout this dissertation: Who has not been invited to the eucharistic table and is thus left out from our liturgical practices? From this question we might wonder about the idea of alterity. Who is the other who is not here at the table? What has this liturgical code forgotten, denied, repressed, and negated? And, how should liturgy deal with alterity, that which has to do with *difference*, that which alters its order, confuses its scripts, as something akin to an intrusion, a foreign matter, a deviant behavior, an iconoclast move, an improper performance? In other words, how should liturgy host a possible parasite, that which undoes the condition of its possibility, that pierces and scatters the very element of its structure? Or, more succinctly, is it possible for liturgy to express that which it denies?

To answer this question, it is necessary to recognize that the logic of the modern liturgical codes, based on a structured kind of rationality, delineates the liturgical space and practices into hierarchical dichotomies:

---

3. "Alterity: otherness; specifically: the quality or state of being radically alien to the conscious self or a particular cultural orientation" (*Merriam-Webster's Collegiate Dictionary*, 11th ed. [CD-ROM], s.v. "alterity").

good and bad, altar/table and pews, ordained and unordained, safe and dangerous, us and them, black and white, clean and dirty, true (proper) and false (improper), men and women, and etc. These binary structures have set aside and denied that which they cannot understand, whose presence cannot be identified or accepted, since it disrupts and disfigures the figural status of the liturgical rationality. Yet, the very identity of the Christian liturgical code can really only be defined by its own alterity, that which is different from and unknown to it. In the last chapter, we saw how the alterity of women defined the values of the liturgical code. Here we use the alterity of Latin America within the normative discourse to further define it.

Liturgical colonization imposed the white male missionary (both Roman Catholic and Protestant), a certain civilization placed at the center of the altar (Roman Catholic) and table/pulpit (Protestant), and a code concerning what was proper for Christian worship which had consequences not only for worship but also for life in general. Now, with the arrival of hundreds of people from these colonized countries (myself included) there is an annoying disturbance that challenges the ways that local churches deal with their own liturgical structures. Many mainline protestant churches in United States have dealt with new immigrant communities by helping pastors and missionaries to start ethnic churches and worship God in "their own way." One cannot deny the wonderful hospitality that these churches have offered to unknown immigrants who found a religious community which helped them develop their lives in a much fuller way. However, what often happens is that Anglo and immigrant churches rarely get together. Anglo churches do invite immigrant churches to sing their local songs, which are often said to be very alive and powerful, but immigrant pastors are not invited to preside at table or share power in higher levels. When an immigrant community invites an Anglo church, their pastor often preaches and plays a much more prominent role in the worship. Moreover, it is common to see two ethnic churches worshiping in the same space, but it is rare to see the two sessions working together. It seems that a very safe distance between these two communities is carefully kept. One does not bother the other. Another colonizing process continues to be at work. The colonizers spreads and forces their familiar rationality upon the colonized so as to move the *other* into sameness, turning the *other* into the colonizer's self-realization and making the unknown knowable, safe, and easy to deal with or even to control.

This liturgical code/ordo is what makes Barbara Brown Taylor, a prominent Anglican thinker and preacher, feel *at home* in the worshipful service in a "small, tin-roofed (Anglican) church in Western Kenya."

> I did not understand a word of the service, but I understood perfectly what we were doing that morning. I had learned it halfway around the world in another language, including the part that begins: "We believe in one God . . ." Essentially mysterious but entirely accessible, the sacraments are pure genius for teaching us what we need to know about our relationship with God.[4]

This *pure genius* of the sacraments teaches and establishes the limits of the familiar, the figurable, the representable, the controllable, and the attainable. This *genius* turns the other and its unfamiliar, threatening assets into a mirror, turning the unfamiliar, what does not resemble *us*, into familiar, recognizable terms, elements, postures, rationality, behavior, practices, gestures, and so on. This strange familiarity came to Barbara Brown Taylor with the fact that the *liturgical code* was pulsing at that small church the same way it pulses in her own denomination in the United States, giving frame, meaning, rhythm, authenticity and thus security to that moment. The *otherness* of the Kenyans was shadowed by the light shone through the structures of the inherent liturgical and theological logic that made Taylor say *I understood perfectly*, and felt it *entirely accessible*. In the proper

4. B. B. Taylor, *Preaching Life*, 66; emphasis added.

performance of the sacraments, she *knew* everything she needed to know about her relationship with God. So much so that the people of Kenya, the *other*, became a joyous surplus, since they were not actually needed once the liturgical frame and theological words were already given. This surplus could come then as a native dance or an offering by Kenyans in colored clothes that shy away from the idea that it was *all* about a colonized universal logic that framed, structured and imposed the whole reasoning of religion over *the other*. Moreover, in her experience, *the other* was turned into her sameness so that she did not have to deal with any foreign element of a strange faith.

This overarching control of modern and colonial rationality permits anybody from Europe to the United States, Latin America to Asia, Azores Islands to Papua New Guinea, to reasonably sense some kind of familiarity within the logic of Christian liturgical representations. Outside these *meaningful ways*, there are only shadows, the shadows of the *other*, the shadows of the unpresentable, the absence of a proper knowledge.

When poor people celebrate in Latin America, they do not always rely completely on the meaningful ways that the church has always taught. They create ways out of their own ways, their cultural traditions, knowledge, as well as five hundred years of colonization and syncretism between Christianity, African religions, and Indigenous wisdom and practices. As "a forceful adaptation to a necessity unknown to us,"[5] they celebrate other ways of being church. They are bearers of their own noises, the absurdities that they live and how these absurdities make us deaf and blind. They blur things without knowing *systematically* why they are doing it. They undo some dichotomies by adding what is not supposed to be added, annoying that which is settled, loosening up the structures of truth, and making uncomfortable that which seems to be safe. Moreover, they are on the go to create borders to help them map the *unmappable*. Their lives are always at stake and only their faith promises them that their lives will be better tomorrow. And once their faith encounters the gospel of liberation, it gains the capacity to fight for their future in ways that no political party or state can do.

Poor people are the social negative in Latin America, the defacement of every country. They are the excess of a society that despises them and has no respect whatsoever for their lives. Worse, they are treated like dogs and are often held responsible for urban violence. God does not seem to live among them, and their social situation feels like the death of God.

5. Breton, *Mad Love*, 28.

They have become the *social secret* of society, that is, the *truth* of a society that nobody can know. This social secret, Michael Taussig affirms, "is the most important social knowledge, *knowing what not to know.*"[6]

For too long, the church, its theology and liturgical actions, along with the larger society, have treated the poor and the destitute as the *social secret* of society, as that which keeps the inequality of the system functioning and privileging only a few people. At the end of the nineteen sixties, liberation theology discovered the social secret and by telling us all that secret—which was in front of us but we could not see it—it shook the structures of the "well-being, well-meaning, and well-doing" of both the church and the society. What liberation theology has done, is to invite us to linger a little longer within the unmapped territory of poor people, the negative aspect of society. In this lost territory, where *the labor of the negative* happens, liturgical performances become similar to what Taussig calls writing:

> So our writing, becomes an exercise in life itself, at one with life and within life as lived in social affairs, not transcendent or even a means to such, but contiguous with action and reaction in the great chain of storytelling telling the one always before the last. Yet, how can you be contiguous with the not merely empty, but negative, space?[7]

The only difference is that the liberation theology writings placed God in relation to this *negative space.* Or better said, it discovered the ways in which poor people would relate God to their destitute lives. The presence of God in Latin America has always been there for poor people. There is no doubt that God permeates their reality. When Leonardo Boff writes that the sacrament can be placed in a symbol of the quotidian like a family's mug or his father's cigarette butt, he is telling us what poor people see, God is everywhere, holding these ordinary objects with a bonded human depth, amplifying an encounter between him, his family and his father. Boff, whose father died of coronary thrombosis,[8] lives with this sacramental object, which reminds him of joy, of hope, of what was so dear to him—his family and his father—and what was an intrinsic part of his life. The social negative, that which was repressed, becomes bearable, or even a blessing, with the presence of God. It is the consideration of forgotten

---

6. M. Taussig, *Defacement, Public Secrecy and the Labor of the Negative,* 2.

7. Ibid., 7.

8. Boff, *Sacraments of Life, Life of the Sacrament,* 15-19

aspects of the life of poor people in relation to God that creates other ways of thinking about church, liturgy and theology.

> *She was carrying her baby on her arms. It looked like a five-year-old boy. She was alone and did not have anybody. She would sit on the main street of her neighborhood. With one hand she held her child and with the other hand she would alternate between hiding her weeping face and stretching it out to beg for help. On that day, there was a presidential rally around that area and this candidate, who would later become the president of the country, was campaigning. She did not know who he was. She saw many people walking alongside of this man whom she could barely see. All of sudden, she gathered all her strength and moved in the direction of the big crowd. Forcing her way in, without knowing how to get to this man she didn't know, she finally approached him. Squeezed by so many, she touched him and he felt her touch and looked at her. She said something that he could barely hear, "'Moço,' my son died of malnutrition yesterday and I don't have money or a place to bury him. Would you please help? The president-to-be stopped smiling and looked at that woman with a scared face. When he was going to say something to her, his security agents took him away and he never saw that woman again.*

Most often, the borders within the liturgical practices of poor people in Latin America move around shadowed spaces outside traditional liturgies. These shadowed spaces, however, are places where the poor shed light of their own creation, by structuring ways to resist, to survive and to change exactly that which seems to be bigger than they are. The liturgies of poor people mix gestures and thoughts (sexualized incarnation), personal interrelations and faith (church/community), remembrance and politics (eucharistic anamnesis), presence and absence (sacraments), reality, struggles and resistance (political faith), and help us re-visit the possibilities of God who is incarnate in a common meal together, in the fight for a health care unit, for national changes, or even in a cigarette butt.

Liberation Theology—New Ways of Doing Theology

In comparison to European and North American theologies, the main shift proposed in Latin American theology was to place poor people and their concrete situation at the center of every theological project. One had to start from below, from reality, and not from God's revelation in the Bible. Imported theologies based on a-historical situations in which God was imagined without taking the political, economic, and social situation of believers into account would not be accepted anymore. Poor people became the hermeneutical axis, the epistemic ground, and the social and theological criterion to access both human reality and God. Trying to move the periphery to the center, this theology strived to be faithful to those who were excluded from society. Liberation theology wanted to make up for what had been left out of the main theological discourses up to that point in Latin American history. *Listening to poor people* was their way of shifting the center of theological production from theological cabinets to the street, from conversations between well-trained theologians to poor people on the street, from theoretical to practical ways of doing theology. Enrique Dussel explained it thus: "There is a privileged subject who produces the theological discourse, and almost always, the theological discourse is marginal, implicit, spontaneous, resistant and it is the popular theology."[9]

In order to do liberation theology, one has to understand the situation of where poor people are located, on the margins of the economic and social system, and make sense of the reasons why they are there. Thus, liberation theologians had to make theology take a *second step*, a *second action* that would depend on a first act, namely an analysis of concrete material reality. It was this analysis of reality that would give poor people tools to understand their situation and to discover what their faith in God meant in their situation. Fed by Marxist categories and Socialist movements around the world, liberation theology adopted a Marxist reading of reality with strong emphasis on the notions of ideology, material reality, the power of the proletariat, and *class struggles* as integral to Latin America societies.

Believing that poor people had become the new subject of their own history and of God's liberation project, liberation theologians made material life the source of theological thinking, rather than speculative, a-historical spirituality, philosophy or theological tradition. In that sense, the church was not supposed to tell poor people what God wanted, but rather to encourage poor people to discover what God was telling them through their own lives and praxis as they read the Bible in community. Ortho-*doxy* was replaced by ortho-*praxis* in all the Basic Ecclesial Communities.

9. Dussel, "Hipóteses para uma história da teologia na America Latina," 188.

The mediation of the social sciences rather than the theological canons of the church was a major source of this change. However, as Clodovis Boff affirms in his seminal book that explains the difficult relation between praxis and theory:

> In fact, the ultimate originality of Liberation Theology relies not in its method, i.e., in the use of social sciences, including Marxism. The roots of this method are in what bestow itself a "spirit," a "new way" of using the method. And this spirit is the root of the spiritual experience of the poor.[10]

Poor people, the *new subject* in liberation theology, the agents of its own destinies, were not only to become conscious of their situation of oppression and injustice but also to fight against it through a politically engaged faith. The educational method of Paulo Freire[11] was key in the pedagogical work of catechists within basic communities. He prescribed the following process to access reality: *to see, to judge, to act.* That sequence of first looking at reality and its mechanism of oppression, then making necessary decisions about what to accept and what to fight against, and finally the mobilization to change the situation was the process of what in Latin America was known popularly as *conscientization.* Through *conscientization,* liberation theologians insisted that poor people could transform their own historical situation. Religion would be understood not as an ideological tool to hide injustice and oppression but as an instrument to detect the powers that organize as well as oppress society, so as to dismantle them.

The figure of the theologian was also transformed. Instead of sitting in ivory tower offices, theologians were required to live among poor people and understand their reality. The term used to describe this new theologian was taken from Antonio Gramsci's *organic intellectual.* Gustavo Gutierrez describes the theologian as an organic intellectual:

> Theologians will be personally and vitally engaged in historical realities with specific times and places. They will be engaged where nations, social classes, and peoples struggle to free themselves from domination and oppression by other nations, classes, and peoples. In the last analysis, the true interpretation of the meaning revealed by theology is achieved only in historical praxis.[12]

10. Boff, *Theologia e Prática*, iii.
11. Freire, *Pedagogy of the Oppressed.*
12. Gutiérrez, *Theology of Liberation*, 10.

This theology has created new hopes and new dreams of transformation. It has helped to create what is now one of the most influential political parties in Brazil, called PT, or "people's party," that much later elected Lula as president of Brazil in 2002 and reelected him in 2006. However, in time, liberation theology encountered problems within its own intellectual structure, while at the same time being bombarded by those powers structures that once held control over poor people. The Roman Catholic Curia was not happy with the directions of the movement, especially its ecclesiology, and started to implode the movement by moving archbishops associated with Liberation Theology from influential positions within the church throughout Latin America.

Moreover, the political and economic situation in Latin America seemed to be too harsh to be transformed and the utopian thoughts that fed the grassroots movements (mainly Basic Ecclesial Communities) lost its power. The promise of *liberation* could not contain the frustrations over lack of historical changes of the poor. Meanwhile, Pentecostal movements sprouted up promising healing and miracles, easing somewhat the most immediate anxieties of poor people regarding the disorders of daily life: illness, unemployment, difficult relationships, and lack of money.

With the end of the Sandinista government in Nicaragua, and the implosion of the Berlin wall in 1989, the end of socialism in Eastern Europe, liberation theology has lost its external references as a powerful theology capable of changing social reality. The fact that liberation theology did not expand or rework the sources of social tolls, or reinvent its theological tools to interpret reality, ended up ignoring other needs and activities of human life (e.g., sexual life of the poor, social disruptions, drugs, fantasies, consumerism, violence) as well as women's struggles, African Brazilian historical exploitation, indigenous rights, domestic violence, racism, battered children.

Questions have been raised about the death of liberation theology in Latin America. For a while, I also believed that it had died. But not anymore. I do believe that it has a core structure that can help new ways of thinking and practicing theology, liturgy and church. There are many theologians working from within its perspectives who are correcting its mistakes[13] and amplifying its possibilities while reclaiming its option for poor people as a radical commitment for theological as well as, liturgical

---

13. There has been a great production of theological material in Latin America that is not available in English. In English, Althaus-Reid, ed., *Liberation Theology and Sexuality*; Althaus-Reid, *Indecent Theology*.

work. In September 2006, Gustavo Gutierrez gave a talk at the II Congress of the Social Doctrine of the Church in Latin America at which he reaffirmed his life as based on the option for poor people. After his talk, he addressed this question:

> A friend of mine went out to fish. Later in the day, when he was carrying back the fishes he felt a bite in his back and then said: "There are dead bodies that still bite." Is it the same with Liberation Theology? Gutierrez listened to the question with humor and said: I don't worry whether Liberation Theology will die or not, that does not trouble me. What is immortal is God's option for the poor. This truth never dies. Moreover, I am more interested in the liberation of people than in Liberation Theology; and added, but if Liberation is dead, nobody invited me to their funeral.[14]

BASE ECCLESIAL COMMUNITIES— NEW WAYS OF BEING CHURCH

The Base Ecclesial Communities (BECs) are a movement within the Roman Catholic Church in Latin America. The origin of those in Brazil is very difficult to determine. Most of the literature, written by priests, traces their beginnings to 1956 with Dom Agnelo Rossi in Barra do Pirai in Rio de Janeiro.[15] They argue that lay people didn't begin these communities, spontaneously but rather it began with Dom Rossi, who wanted to evangelize regions of Brazil that had no priests to serve them and so used lay catechists to reach them. At the outset of his book on BECs, Frei Guimarães makes this note:

> the Brazilian BECs are not contesting groups that are born at the margins of the church. On the contrary, people responsible for the pastoral animation of the dioceses, members of the hierarchy and pastoral plans are at the origin of the birth and

14. Roberto (Gogó) Malvezzi, "Gustavo Gutiérrez: 'esqueceram de me convidar para seu funeral,'" *Adital*, 22 September 2006: http://www.adital.org.br/site/noticia.asp?lang=PT&cod=24550.

15. Boff, *Ecclesiogenesis*, 3; and Guimarães, *Communidades de Base no Brasil*, 18. Interesting enough, the second part of the title of Guimarães book says that the BECs are "A New Way of *Being In Church*," differently from Boff and others who would say something like "different ways of *being church*." Emphasis mine.

development of these groups. They are not at the margins of the official life of the church.[16]

It is understandable that the "explicators" of the movement want to associate it with the church, by describing them as an intrinsic part of the church (as legitimate ecclesiology), and not as a movement of excluded people trying to create an autonomous sect. The theologians thus gave to the movement a ground within a solid institution that had many priests and bishops fighting for them. The first generation of priests and bishops were influential men within the church power structure who were deeply committed to poor people and used the church's resources to help people organize themselves and fight against injustice.[17] However, the process of institutionalization made the BECs lose their flexibility. Some of them depended on the supervising of leaders (priests, bishops): all were subject to constant theologizing, (i.e., formatting of their practices and the constant explanation of what it is to be church); and the constant "inter-ecclesial encounters" with the presence of priests and bishops giving lectures to the delegates and animators of the communities structuring the movement under the radar of the hierarchy of the church.

However, according to other people, especially lay people who were in the BECs or still are in the movement, the movement was started spontaneously by lay people and was later embraced by progressives in the church. Due to the unchanged alterity within the parts of the movement, which did not abide by the laws of the church, some BECs were excluded from the larger movement. Marcella Althaus-Reid affirms that

> during the past decade, many BECs have been dissolved by the decision of Roman Catholic dioceses in Latin America. This has happened because BECs have never been inscribed into canonical law: They were spontaneous, non-hierarchical movements of the church, outside the legal arrangements of ecclesial institutions.[18]

---

16. Guimarães, *Communidades de Base no Brasil*, 12.

17. In Brazil, there were several priests and bishops that fought for poor people. Without them, the history of Brazil would not have been the same. We can name just but a few: Don Paulo Evaristo Arns and Don Luciano Mendes in Sao Paulo, Don Pedro Casaldáliga in São Feliz do Araguaia, Don Frei Xavier Plassat in Pará, Don Ivo Lorscheiter in Ceara, Don Helder Camera in Olinda and Recife, Frei Tito, and many others.

18. Althaus-Reid, *Indecent Theology*, 131.

She also reminds us of the neglected aspect that the BECs were created mostly frequently by women, who were never mentioned in the historical accounts of the movement.[19]

The question of the origin of BECs stresses different perspectives on ecclesiology and the work of the Spirit. To be fair to the movement, one has to consider the following: even if the movement was not an initiative of the church, and it seems that it was not, but rather initiated by lay people who organized themselves due to the lack of priests in their regions, the movement spread and gained strength only when the church embraced the movement as its own, especially with the support given by radical and libertarian bishops and priests who were committed to poor people. In any case, this ecclesiological "turn" was due to the theologizing of the movement by many theologians and especially by Leonardo Boff. In fact, the vast accounts of the BECs are marked by strenuous and fascinating theological and ecclesiastical moves that were trying to turn these communities into a "real" church.[20] As one goes through the literature, it is clear to see an apologetics that attempts to adjust the movement [by connecting the ways people were gathering together and celebrating the gospel,] to the normativity of the juridical theological structure of ecclesia as seen in the official church. I will rely mainly Leonardo Boff's texts of "militant ecclesiology" to explain the ways that the BECs moved so many grounds in society and within the Roman Catholic Church.

SOCIAL CLASS STRUGGLES

The BECs were a powerful locus that liberation theology used to base its challenge to the unequal structures of both church and society. The economic system that shaped society and the hierarchical structure of the church were called into question by the ways that BECs were being church, doing theology and markedly exposing the inequalities perpetuated in

---

19. Ibid., 33–35. Even the celebration of Eucharist by the coordinator of BECs was done sometimes by women but only men were mentioned as the "coordinators" and "celebrants" of the Eucharist.

20. Boff, *Ecclesiogenesis*; *O Caminhar da Terra Com Os Oprimidos. Do Vale de Lágrimas Rumo à Terra Prometida*; Conferência Nacional dos Bispos do Brasil, *Comunidades Eclesiais de Base no Brasil, Experiências e Perspectivas*; Betto, *BECs*; Nóbrega, *BECs e Educação Popular*; Guimarães; Jiménez, *La Iglesia Popular en America Latina*; Torres and Eagleson, eds., *Challenge of Basic Christian Communities*; Bebblethwaite, *Base Communities*; Azevedo, *Basic Eclesial Communities in Brazil*; Hewitt, *Base Christian Communities and Social Change in Brazil*.

society. Boff uses a Marxist analysis of *class struggles* to point out that the church has been part of this social injustice as it took the side of the minority hegemonic class. Society is structured by its modes of production. In the western world,[21] this mode of production is based on an unequal distribution of material resources which ends up placing the national wealth in the hands of those people who manage the modes of production and control those who have no access to these resources and end up becoming the low paid workers. Moreover, these modes of production are *dissymmetrical*, which in Boff's definition, is a capitalist way of organizing society

> that is characterized by the private appropriation of the means of production by a select and permanent minority, by the unequal distribution of the work force (there are those who do not exercise any productive function) and by the unequal distribution of the final products among the population. This dissymmetrical mode of production originates a society of classes, with power dissymmetrically distributed, with relations of domination between classes with divergent interests . . . A class is continuously in a process of construction (or deconstruction) according to its position in the social division of labor . . . As the modes of production is asymmetric, the dynamic of classes is also asymmetric, that is, conflictive and unequal with unequal forces contending (independent of will and as a dynamic inherent to an objective position that each actor occupies in the structure of classes.[22]

From this reading of reality, nobody is absent from participating, in one way or another, in the economic social system; classes, institutions and communities are social agents that either perpetuate or fight against that dissymmetrical and oppressive system. Boff's battle against the church comes from the fact that the church itself, as any other social agent, is also intrinsically related to this system and is ultimately responsible for it:

> The church does not operate in an empty field but in a society historically situated. It means that the church, *nolens volens*, is limited and oriented by the social context, with a population and limited resources structured in a determined form. The

---

21. At that point in time, globalization was not as it is today with international markets sustaining the global flux of money and defining the neo-liberal structure of the economy throughout the world.

22. Boff, *Igreja, Charisma e Poder, Ensaios de Ecclesiologia Militante*, 189–90.

religious-ecclesiastical field is a portion of the social field; the
latter influences the former dialectically and not mechanically.[23]

That situation makes the faithful internalize this larger system of oppression and it becomes the unquestioned law of society. That structure is repeated in the church where the "faithful ones occupy objectively distinct social places according to the situation of their class. This situation makes them perceive reality as corresponding to its social condition, and make them interpret and live the evangelical message according to its class function . . ."[24]

Liberation theology sees the rise of the BECs as the poor people's united response to these structures and forces of power. The church has the power to change sides and resist this hegemonic system by trying to break its unchallenged unequal structure of production. Jesus of Nazareth is the historical figure who feeds the community, helps them organize themselves and become active and resistant subjects within history, fighting the oppression that serves the rich and excludes poor people. Thus, the BECs call for a double transformation: one within the church, helping the church to break down its own power structures of religious domination, and the other within society, helping poor people become conscious of their power and reject their status as a subaltern silenced class. Instead, poor people should have a voice of protest and resistance. In both cases, the despised and forgotten class of the oppressed now takes their lives into their own hands. As Boff defines this double transformation in the BECs: ". . . it has to do with a true ecclesiogenesis (genesis of a new church, but not different from that of the Apostles and Tradition) that realizes itself at the base level of the church and society, that is, in the subaltern classes, religiously and socially powerless."[25] With the BECs, the church has now the chance to shift allegiances to be on the side of poor people and against the hegemonic powers that exploit and keep them in their oppression. In that sense, the BECs are seeds of a new church, a new future and a new society.[26] The BECs carry the dream of a just society, are fed, and mirror the early church in their following of Jesus.

23. Ibid., 188.

24. Ibid., 189.

25. Ibid., 196.

26. See Betto, *BECs, Rumo À Nova Sociedade.*

CHARISMA AND POLITICS

Boff argues in his book, *Church, Charisma and Power: Liberation Theology and the Institutional Church*, (in Portuguese the subtitle is "Essays on a Militant Ecclesiology,") that at the core, of the definition of a church is not the canonical definitions but rather in the vitality of its *Charisma*. The church is born out of the encounter with Jesus Christ through the work of the Holy Spirit and from the Spirit receives its life and progress. Thus, every ecclesiology must depend exclusively on the free work of the Spirit. In order to be in faithful continuity with the early church, the church today depends on the guidance of the Spirit; it finds its strength in its gatherings as it shares its life in light of the gospel of Jesus. Thus, the church is not a static entity framed by heavy institutional contours, but rather it is, under the Spirit, a movement, an event, a happening, always being transformed, always re-inventing itself. "In this primitive way," says Boff,

> the church is more a happening (event) that might happen under a mango tree, in the house of a coordinator or even within the edifice of a church than an institution with all its goods, services, laws, doctrines and mysteries, with historical continuity.[27]

The church must be an *event* because it is based on the sustenance of the Spirit who endows the church with a plurality of charismas and gifts (I Cor 12:5). A charism is God's loving offering to people giving the community the capacity to live together; making sure that their needs are met by the plurality of gifts given to each individual in the community; and sustaining its life in God and with one another. A charism can be measured by the ways that God's gift given the individual is lived in the service of the community. No charism or gift is self-centered, nor is it used for the sake of one individual; it only exists if the charism offers itself to the service of others. As Boff defines it, "charisma is a manifestation of the presence of the Spirit in the members of the community; assuring that everything they are and do must be done and ordained to the benefit of others."[28]

With these charismas the members of the church are called to serve and depend on one other. The church does not need hierarchical power structures. Charismas do not eliminate leadership but place everybody in perspective, at the same level in light of the universal priesthood of the church. Boff reminds us that "the charismas are not held to any institutionalization of the sacramental order. When Paul talks about the charismas,

27. Boff, *Igreja, Charisma e Poder, Ensaios de Ecclesiologia Militante,* 252.
28. Ibid., 257.

he does not mention those related to the Order."[29] The abundance and simultaneity of the gifts within the community limit the church's ability to assign more power than to another, as if one charisma would exercise more power over the others. This simultaneity is sustained by the Spirit and not by any system that a church might create. What structures the community then is not any official structure of power with its departmentalization of gifts and honors and merits but rather, the horizontal experience of the charisma within the Christian community as they are received from God by the Spirit.

That idea of charisma that Boff takes from Paul can be related to the larger rubrics of utopia held and expressed in the early Christian meals or banquets. The charisma lived and experienced within the community serves to feed the larger charisma of radical "isonomia" within society, or in today's Marxist terms, the classless society. It also places strong limits on the power that any group or individual should exercise. The abundance of the charisma shared in the simultaneity of the lives within the community is what prevents the charisma from becoming a totalizing power organized and determined in hierarchical structures of unquestioned dominance. In addition it helps the Christian believer fight for a reality that holds itself up to the utopian claim of a society without classes, at the same time realizing that society's literal deliverance will never be realized. As Boff declares:

> Thus in a certain sense, it is unrealistic to struggle for a "classless society"—a society that would be simply and totally a community of brothers and sisters, without any conflict at all. Realistically, one can only struggle for a type of sociability in which love will be less difficult, and where power and participation will have better distribution. Community must be understood as a spirit to be created, as an inspiration to bend one's constant efforts to overcome barriers between persons and to generate a relationship of solidarity and reciprocity.[30]

In other terms, the Christian community holds the trust that the *charis* of God might happen more justly now, within the living communities with better distribution of wealth and opportunities. However, the Christian community also holds an eschatological hope that expects that its fullness will come only one day when the realm of God is gathered. Meanwhile,

29. Ibid.
30. Boff, *Ecclesiogenesis*, 5.

this eschatological utopia is fed by the political struggle that anticipates its final glory.

> *She was afraid she was lesbian. She realized that after a long struggle against these evil desires. She couldn't believe that she could be attracted to other women. She dated some men and with one or two she had even made plans to get married and have kids. She was raised in a very traditional protestant family and learned all the good things the Bible said about God's love for God's children and God's hate for those who persisted in their sinful ways. When she finally realized that she was gay and decided to live with another woman, her mother accused her of being possessed by Satan and told her she would despise her if she didn't change her ways. Her aunt wrote her a lovely e-mail saying how much she loved her but unless she changed, she could not love her anymore because she had to love in the way that God loves people. She decided to live separately from the woman she loved. They kept seeing each other without everybody knowing it. She still does that, but she is struggling against these desires as much as possible. And more than anything else, she is afraid of being possessed by Satan.*

Again, it is the givenness of the Spirit within the community at the service of others that prevents any charisma from belonging to an individual, or political, economic, social system under the rubrics of charis. The charismas present in the communities are important factors that help destroy any empire, be it religious, economic or political. This relation between the Greek term *charis* and Paul's *charisma* are correlated in the perspective of the realm of God. This is the same relation between the dissymmetrical and the symmetrical means of production seen in Boff's interpretation of Marx:

> The religious-ecclesiastical field holds in itself an inevitable contradiction: on the one hand it realizes itself historically within the dissymmetrical means of symbolic production, holding, on the other hand the basic ideal entails a symmetrical means of production, participatory and fraternal. Because the church lives this contradiction, it is always possible to see the irruption of the prophet and the libertarian spirit that turn the church to walk in the direction of those who search for fairer relations in

history and organize themselves in the marks of a revolutionary practice.[31]

The revolutionary practice of the church is not borrowed from social systems but rather, it is an intrinsic part of the Christian project and faith. Thus, the politics of faith is already embedded in the charisma, in the communal life of the Christian believer. At first, this faith is less a partisan faith than a faith lived in the *polis*, in the daily life and struggle of the city, the country and the world. It is not prevented from taking the form of a political party and/or a political system but it does not start there. The Christian faith, born in God, based on the life, death and resurrection of Jesus, and offered by the Holy Spirit, realizes itself in and through the simultaneity of the charismas within the community, where it ordains and gives meaning not only to the system of faith but also to human existence, to the political practices and the structures of the world. At this juncture, it is important to remember that "Everything is political but politics is not all."[32] The component of faith is an important partner to politics. Without faith, politics lacks an important component, and without politics, faith lacks its ground to establish social justice. Thus, the Marxist saying, "Religion is the opium of the people," has no resonance. Religion is what feeds consciousness and social transformation.

RELATIONALITY, NOT HIERARCHY

The church of Jesus Christ has lost its contact with poor people. It has surrounded itself with levels of power that have reflected its own self-sufficiency and avoided the (alterity of the) poor. Against that structure, Boff tries to give a historical, theological and ecclesiological account to the ecclesiastical structure present in the BECs. He is struggling against the sectarian way that the church understands the notion of the ecclesia and tries to relate the movement of the BECs with the most genuine evangelical understandings of what the church should be, both universally and in the context of Latin America. He critiques the church by condemning its hierarchy, which prevents people not only from actively participating in it, but also from connecting with one another and creating other kinds of relationships. The church, for him, is an organism that has perpetuated injustice:

31. Boff, *Igreja, Charisma e Poder, Ensaios de Ecclesiologia Militante,* 192.
32. Boff, *O Caminhar da Terra Com Os Oprimidos,* 106.

Through the latter centuries, the church has acquired an organizational form with a heavily hierarchical framework and a
juridical understanding of relationships among Christians, thus
producing mechanical, reified inequalities and inequities.[33]

The BECs are to change that system and challenge the hierarchy of
the church. Here is a scheme that Boff provides that shows the differences
of structures between the hierarchical system of the official church and the
structure proposed by the BECs:[34]

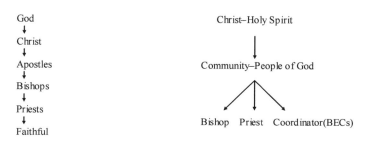

The BECs break down the hierarchical structure of the church by
giving people the chance to participate actively in every instance of the
church, defining goals and directions for the struggles that each local
community has to concentrate upon. It also opens up a vast array of relationships within a horizontal church structure where power is understood
as relational and horizontal. The new way of being church involves the
decision of the people within each community to define their own future
without having to follow pastoral guidance from the larger church. Boff
locates the BECs, this new relational way of being church, with the early
church that is born out of a relationship between Jesus and his disciples.
In both churches, primitive and BECs, the Spirit was the initiator and the
sustainer, and relationships were kept without super power structures of
division. Thus, the BECs should be a continuous counterpoint to the institutionalized church, a community to be considered as ecclesia but still
living as a community, open to change, not relying on the institution but
on its own evolving relational mutations.

33. Boff, *Ecclesiogenesis*, 1.
34. Boff, *Igreja, Charisma e Poder, Ensaios de Ecclesiologia Militante,* 222.

Boff says that Vatican II defined the church "in terms of diocesan reality, with bishop and Eucharist."[35] In the process of turning the community into ecclesia, Boff characterizes the BECs as a movement of baptized people who are living the gospel of Christ under the precepts of the New Testament. Boff mentions CELAM and Medellin in 1968 to show that in the official document of the conference, the presence of the bishop. or even the presence of the eucharist, were not seen as necessary elements to turn the community into a church. However, since the movement was increasingly taken over and placed under the control of the bishops, as the Fifth Inter-Ecclesial Encounter of BECs already shows clearly,[36] it ends up meeting the institutional demands of the official church for a diocesan control under the authority of the bishops. Notwithstanding, the celebration of the eucharist by the coordinator was a huge problem for the church.

EUCHARIST AND LITURGICAL PRACTICES

Once or twice a week, the BECs gather together around the community to share the gospel and talk about life. There are usually fifteen to twenty families. When they are together, they read the Bible, make their own comments, and decide what to do. As mentioned before, each community uses Paulo Freire's pedagogical tools "to see, to judge, to act," to which they added "celebrate." The liturgical component is central to the practices of the community and they do it in various ways. They use different local materials and symbols, they sing their own songs, they move around any space that they decide is liturgical, and the whole community participates. Previously, they had gotten together only once or twice in a year when the priest was present to perform baptisms, weddings, and celebrate the eucharist with them. Now that they gather together every week, they face the problem of how to celebrate the eucharist, if the eucharist can only be performed by a priest? To solve this problem and legitimate their own celebration of the eucharist, Boff tries to elevate the role of the coordinator of the community as high as he can in order to make the church allow the coordinator to celebrate the eucharist.

Through a long biblical, theological, and historical process, Boff shows that the coordinator should be allowed to celebrate the Eucharist

35. Ibid., 11.

36. At this encounter, a large number of Bishops are present and some lead the encounter and participate in the liturgies of the event. See Betto, *BECs, Rumo À Nova Sociedade.*

on special community occasions, acting as an "extraordinary minister."[37] His reasoning is based on the fact that everybody in the community is baptized, gathered according to "right doctrine," functioning as a priestly community where Christ is present.[38] However, since the "Mass is a rigorously defined reality, theologically, liturgically, and canonically,"[39] he cannot affirm that this gathering is a Mass but should be called "the celebration of the Lord's Supper, however, as it would have a ritual organized by the community itself, in which would clearly appear the memorial character of meal, sacrifice, and eucharistic presence of Christ . . . the precept would be fulfilled: 'Do this in remembrance of me.'"[40]

Then Boff describes a "celebration of the Lord's Supper" and shows how congregants worship together. For the celebration, they do not use bread and wine but a "cake of sweet cassava and tea or other refreshing drink."[41] The words of institution from the Bible are recited by the coordinator and the elements distributed. Songs, readings, and sharings of the gospel stories are also performed. Throughout the description, one does not find once the word Eucharist. There is a careful attempt to avoid the correlation between the Lord's Supper with the Eucharist. The elements of the Lord's Supper are not the same as the Eucharist as not to confuse the sharing of cake and tea with the bread and wine of the transubstantiation.

The celebration ends up *feeling like* a sacrament, *appearing like* a eucharist, but is not performed as the eucharistic sacrament, as the *sacramentum* of the church. What Boff says of the sacraments being "sacrament-sign and sacrament-instrument of liberation,"[42] happens only in and through the official performance of the Mass by an official priest. Beyond the Mass, everything is reduced to sacramentals, which strengthen the people in the necessary stubbornness of faith to keep fighting the good fight but it does not, and cannot, carry the same weight of the sacrament. The sacrament of the Eucharist is not challenged by the BECs or if it is, it is not reported anywhere. The distinction between Eucharist and any meal celebrated by the people is still maintained. The notion of the sacrament is never challenged. The eucharist is a sacred liturgical action, connected to a place (the altar of the church) and performed by a priest. Beyond that,

37. Boff, *Ecclesiogenesis*, 72.
38. Ibid.
39. Ibid., 73.
40. Ibid.
41. Ibid., 74.
42. Boff, *Igreja, Charisma e Poder, Ensaios de Ecclesiologia Militante*, 187.

everything can look like a sacrament, function as sacrament, but not be a sacrament.

It is very unfortunate that the construction of Boff's argument throughout his book "Ecclesiogenesis" leads not to the authentication of the sacrament of the eucharist performed by poor people within the BECs but instead, to the re-affirmation of the uniqueness of sacrament performed at the altar by the official church by abashing the sacrament of the eucharist among the poor. The disconcerting treatment of the eucharist among the poor by Boff only affirms poor people's inability, impropriety, and incapacity to lead the sacrament.

His critique of the authoritative hierarchy crumbles with his inadvertent adjustments of the sacrament. It is the poor who have to adjust, and change the elements of the Eucharist so that they will not run the risk of perhaps committing a sin against God. There can be no bread but cake which alludes to a local element but without the propriety of the eucharistic bread. The same thing happens with the tea. It points to, and alludes to the rite of the eucharistic sacrament, but they cannot do more than that. His reluctance to allow poor people to lead the Eucharist sounds like the same boundaries that the church has historically held against women, whose impropriety would certainly be both a danger to the people around the table and an insult to God.

Moreover, Boff even changes the name of the rite. It must be called "Lord's Supper" which is a clear indication that the ritual performed by poor people cannot be "Eucharist," but only a lower form of manifestation of the sacrament. In a word, it is a liturgical meal without being a sacrament. The irony in Boff's efforts are that he leaves poor people with the crumbs of the real table, showing them that they must be happy and empowered with that.

The alterity that the poor represent in the universal liturgy of the church in Latin America is maintained in a worse scenario since it is done in the name of the poor. Why do poor people need a substitute sacrament which will be inexorably lower, unreal and inauthentic? Poor people can *inflict* the table with damaging theological, ecclesiastical, and sacramental consequences. Thus, it has to be taken away, away from the vicinities of the altar and placed far away from it, where poor people live, which is in itself an un-sacramental place. Moreover, the watering down of the Lord's Supper by poor people in Boff's argument shows that the contingencies of people's lives cannot be related to the monolithic divine aura of the sacrament or the official liturgy. In the same way that women's liturgies could not challenge the practices of the sacrament of eucharist, so the contingencies of people's stories cannot break the borders of the sacrament which is eternal, self-referential, and worthwhile only in itself.

I am in no way inferring that Boff is consciously going against poor people. Boff was and is one of the most important and powerful theologians who has given his life to the cause of poor people, and helped expand the whole movement of liberation theology to claim the centrality of the poor in the life of the church. However, specifically in this book, Boff falls short and cannot go all the way and break with the notion of the sacrament or affirm that what poor people celebrate can be a sacrament. Besides Boff, only Juan Luis Segundo has paid attention to the sacraments.

HOSPITALITY, SACRAMENT, CRUMBS, KNEES, AND CHURCH IN BRAZIL TODAY

In this part, I will demonstrate some aspects of the Brazilian hospitality and show how it has a deep impact on the ways that poor people live and celebrate the eucharist today, challenging the borders of inclusion/exclusion. I will also show how poor people still eat the crumbs that fall from the table of the Eucharist and use their bodies to turn the eucharistic tables upside down in Latin America as they depend on each other to survive.

4.1. Brazilian Hospitality

The Brazilian body and soul is plural. Natives, Europeans and Africans compose what we have become(ing). The mixture of these ethnic groups along with some other waves of immigrants that came literally from everywhere, have made Brazil a plurality of cultures that form the various Brazils we have today. We are made of many and these many have created what the Brazilians are, even though we do not know exactly who we are or what identity we have. Nonetheless, we know, for sure, or at least we have a strong guess, that we know something about ourselves. Among these things, joy and hospitality are certainly everywhere within the many *tupiniquim*[43] culture.

---

43. The word *tupiniquim* comes from the tribe Tupi and today it is used to refer to things typically Brazilian.

> *La Migra comes to a factory where many immigrants work. For some reason they know it in advance and they run to the church in town that has declared their worship space a sanctuary. The pastor opens the door for all of them and then closes the door. The immigration officers come by but the pastor says they cannot come inside for it is a sanctuary. Pastors around town get together for an urgent meeting and they hire lawyers who fight for immigrants. The press comes to see what is happening and the churches stand behind these immigrants. They say these immigrants are working for a very small wage to help our economies and they demand that the immigration authorities treat them with dignity. Meanwhile, inside the church members, pastors and the immigrants do a vigil and pray for each other. They celebrate Eucharist every day until the case is solved.*

Brazilian hospitality was always a mark of indigenous tribes that formed Brazil. The hospitality I am referring to can be seen in the description of Jean de Léry, a Calvinist "anthropologist" who came to Brazil in 1556 with another thirteen missionaries, sent by John Calvin, to form what was to be "the first Protestant mission to the New World."[44] In his fascinating description of his time in Brazil, he felt in love with the "noble savage" which later he would miss when he saw the nobility of his French fellows "roasting and eating other Frenchmen's hearts" during the "siege and famine of Sancerre."[45]

It is worth quoting a long passage where Léry describes the ritual of hospitality give to him by the Tupinambas:

> Let me now set forth the ceremonies that the Tupinamba observe when they receive friends who go to visit them. In the first place, as soon as the visitor has arrived in the house of the *moussacat* whom he has chosen for his host (the moussacat being the head of a household, who offers food to people passing through the village, and whom one must visit first in each village before going anywhere else if one is not to offend him), he is seated on a cotton bed suspended in the air, and remains there for a short while without saying a word. Then the women come and surround the bed, crouching with their buttocks against the ground and with both hands over their eyes; in this manner, weeping their welcome to the visitor, they will say a thousand

44. Whatley, "Introduction," xvi.
45. Ibid., xvii.

things in his praise. For example: "You have gone to so much trouble to come to see us; you are good; you are valiant." And if it is a Frenchman, or some other stranger from over here, they will add: "You have brought us so many fine things that we do not have in this country." Spouting big tears, they will string out this kind of applause and flattery. If the newly arrived guest who is seated in the bed wants in turn to please them, he must assume the appropriate expression, and if he doesn't quite get to the point of tears (I have seen some of our nation, who, upon bearing the bleating of these women next to them, were such babies as to be reduced to tears themselves), at least when he answers them he must heave a few sighs and pretend to weep. This first salutation having been graciously performed by the American women, the moussacat, busy making an arrow or some other object (as you see in the illustration), will meanwhile have spent a quarter of an hour or so pretending not to see you—a blandishment quite contrary to our embraces, hugs, kisses, and handclaps upon the arrival of our friends. Then, approaching you, he will first use this style of speaking: "Ere-joubé" that is, "Have you come?" and then "How are you? What would you like" and so forth; to which you must respond according to the forms of conversation in their language which you will see hereafter. Then he will ask you if you want to eat; if you reply "Yes," he will immediately have prepared and brought to you, in the fine earthen vessels, the flour that they eat instead of bread, as well as meat, poultry, fish, and other food; but since they have no tables, benches, or stools, the service will be right on the ground in front of your feet. As for drink, if you want a *caouin*, he will give you some if he has any. After the women have wept beside the visitor, they will bring him fruit or some other small gift from their region, to obtain him combs, mirrors, or the little glass beads that they put around their arms. If moreover, you want to sleep in that village, the old man will not only stretch out for you a fine white bed, but also, even though it does not get cold in their country, he will place around the bed, against the night's humidity, four or five small fires, which will often be relit in the course of the night, along with some little screens that they call *tatapecoua*, made like the masks that the ladies over here hold in front of them when they are next to the fire, to keep from spoiling their faces.[46]

---

46. Léry, *History of a Voyage to the Land of Brazil*, 165–66.

This radical hospitality is offered not without borders but with an almost unbearable joy and welcome, a hospitality that is hard for the guest to take, relate to, and to respond. In regard to the welcoming in this hospitality, the borders are gone and guests are exposed to the hosts in a way that the guest is completely disarmed of any fear or power to react negatively. An unprecedented welcome that is felt as an excess, an over-abundant givenness that carries such fullness that it is difficult to receive. No previous knowledge and yet the words of surprise and gratitude: "Have you come? How are you? What would you like?" Words of a gracious welcome and then tears from the Tupinambas women. Radical hospitality with tears and praise, the guest is honored by wonderful words of bravery and a friendship that never existed before but seems to have always been there. After tears and praise the abundance of food on the ground and a warm place to sleep.

However, without knowing it, the Tupinambas were hosting parasites, welcoming Europeans who later, would destroy their history and kill their people. These radically hospitable "noble savages" were also cannibals. Léry describes with great detail how the Tupinambas would slaughter their enemies, eat their bodies and keep their skulls.[47] It was among the cannibals Tupinambas and other noble savages that Protestant and Roman Catholic savages fought for the first time in the New World over the meaning of the Eucharist, reflecting the high tensions present in European debates.

The hospitality present in the welcoming ceremony of the Tupinambas, with growing mixtures of Europeans and Africans, created a trace of the Brazilian culture that Sérgio Buarque de Holanda, one of the most famous Brazilians "explicators," called in 1935, the "cordial man." The cordial man was an expression that Holanda used to explain the ways of being of the Brazilian people, a mark that was present in the Brazilian soul:

> Somebody already told in a happy expression that the Brazilian contribution to civilization will be the cordiality—we will give to the world the "cordial man" [sic]. The kindness to treat the other, the hospitality, the generosity, all of them virtues that foreigners proudly confess when they visit us, represents a definite trace of the Brazilian character."[48]

47. Ibid., 122–33.
48. Holanda, *Raízes do Brasil*, 106.

While along with such generosity and hospitality, there were other characteristics "cordial man" exhibited that are not as virtuous as one might think. The cordial man acts for his own purposes, negotiating public matters under the table by making politics a private, "familiar" affair for personal interests. Moreover, the Brazilian character is also marked by the difficulty of joining rigid rituals, the difficulty of becoming institutionalized, rigid schedules, last minute tasks, and etc. Tridentine Catholicism offered a religious faith that emphasized the cordial virtues and freedom within the religious space that the Catholic Church offered to move within and outside of the Catholic faith. Protestants never flourished in Brazil (Holanda said they were too "austere")[49] until the event of the neo-pentecostals who, leaving behind the heavy moral codes of the first wave of pentecostals, accommodated their somewhat morally loose gospel to the central aspect of efficacy, not seen or experienced in the Catholic Mass.

The consequence is that Brazilian hospitality has to do with a certain flexibility in everything, such as a flexible schedule, an availability to adjustments, no time constraints, a space for a surprise visit, an embodied notion of life, and an openness to experience. As Holanda puts it:

> The Brazilian is free and abandons herself to entire repertoires
> of ideas, gestures and formats that he encounters on the way,
> assimilating all of them frequently without much difficulty.[50]

This abandonment generates an openness to find ways around things. To live life is to find ways of approaching it differently, as one needs, as social life permits. Moreover, this Brazilian openness to other things entails openness to the other as well. Every guest is invited to eat together with the family he/she is visiting, if the guest arrives around meal time. Or, if the guest arrives at any other time, the host will prepare coffee immediately. I learned from my mother that Brazilian hospitality is to receive everybody who is visiting with food and drink, an eucharistic hospitality without theological names or ecclesiastical categorization.

4.2. EUCHARIST/SACRAMENT IN POOR PEOPLE'S COMMUNITIES

Poor people do not see eucharist as something to discuss, to change, or to work for or against. In fact, the Eucharist becomes an issue when it comes

49. Ibid., 112.
50. Ibid.

with the discussions of other problems, as cause and result of other things, such as exclusion, abandonment, and being left out. The eucharist has to do not with its elements or movements or gestures but with inclusion/exclusion. In a succinct and yet, powerful email, Nancy Cardoso Pereira, a Methodist pastor and theologian who has been working with poor people for a long time, told me recently:

> As far as I know people who are there fighting don't talk about the eucharist per se . . . we talk about the sacraments in the midst of other things! The sacraments of those who do not have access to the upper side of the table . . . we get together under the table . . . and with the crumbs, the holy and miraculous leftovers we do theology like the way people live: with crumbs! With our soul on things, the picnic that re-creates the mystery: nobody will go hungry!! Under the table, the crumbs touched by the ritual of life turns into something else and becomes the total inversion of the religious forms of oppression . . . the table turned with its legs up (tables and ourselves) we sing Elsa Tamez song: ". . . may women not forget to bring the salt and men bring the leaven. We hope many people will come: blind, deaf, crippled, jailed people, poor people. Ready. Let's follow Jesus's recipe. Let us all prepare the dough with our hands and we will see how the people grow. Because today we celebrate the encounter with Jesus . . ."[51]

In this context, the eucharist is a symbol, a symbol of social and theological exclusion. It is represented by a table and a table not to be around but under. The Eucharistic table exposes the gifts of life to which poor people do not have access. Jesus is offered under the table. It offers a religious moment that vanishes when misery is in and out of one's home or quasi-home. The most significant religious movement happens when things in life gain correlation, connection, attachment. They receive the religious weight that structures life a bit and become a sacrament without necessarily being named or called a sacrament. The organic theologian who is in charge of theologizing over this community, doing his/her due theological work, always as a *second step*, as a subsequent movement to what poor people do and think, might call these moments of connection, a sacrament. Within the life of the poor, however, the first step, the living of life, *is* the second, the third, and the fourth steps. There is no severance between God and life, faith and life, they are pulled together as one, pretty much collapsed into one another. Thus, theology is already there

---

51. Nancy Cardoso Pereira, from an email received on March 18, 2007.

without being named, and sometimes even denying any possibility of being named. Life happens with or without theology.

And that is because poor people do things with "their soul on things." Poor people are always struggling to live their lives in fullness. The presence of God as *sacramentum* happens when life encounters this human dimension (un)folded in things or events, and life gets densely populated with stronger ties of conviction and the horizon is stretched beyond the limits of their lives. A sacrament can also be seen or experienced when "the soul is on things," when some things create other connections. For instance, it happens when Boff talks about his father's cigarette butt. Flavio Silveira and Manuel Filho describe the anthropology of Boff's cigarette butt where one finds the "soul on things:"

> That object apparently deprived of material value takes on a pro-
> found human dimension before the tragedy of the event (Boff's
> father's death). In this moment, a kind of metonymic repercus-
> sion seems to appear, since the part (the object) that was trans-
> formed in the whole (family, city, Brazil), unchained a series of
> feelings on the subject (Boff) in exile (he was in Germany when
> it happened). It is in this sense that we can talk about a memory
> that impregnates and restitutes "the soul on things" . . . [52]

Little things are all that they have and these things carry a weight that is saturated in their relations with other little things. Are they saturated with God? Yes, without having to be theological, canonized, approved by any church. Things are not only things but they are touched by a human dimension that folds and unfolds God without the necessity to name this (un)folding process, God. Nevertheless, God is always named. God is always already there but perhaps disguised, under other names, watching over everything. God's unnoticed presence does mean neither absence nor lack of care. Life goes on like that, with God being there without being named there. This does not mean that God is in everything. God surrounds things but cannot be identified as a rock, a river, and so on. When things in life lose their grip, when someone is violently killed, when there are fights with the police, when a disaster happens, the *Ave Maria* and the *Pai Nosso* will always be said. Not much because of a theologi-cal injunction or deference, but out of "human need." With the "soul on things," a new dress, a cup of coffee, can so expand life and its connec-tions as to become God's redemption. These moments when the "soul is on things," when abject poverty, unspeakable needs, utter longings and

---

52. Silveira and Filho, *Por Uma Antropologia do Objeto Documental*, 43.

overwhelming lacks are enmeshed and intertwined with the joys of life, and an unexpected moment spurs and breaks open into a thread of bonds, tied in with larger aspects of life, laden with memories and hopes that the sacrament happens. The sacrament happens when salvation and redemption occur in the quotidian of life with others in community. It is in this daily life in community that we can see the occurring of a quotidian sacrament, a "quotidian salvation."

> Salvation seems to be a movement toward redemption in the midst of the trials of existence, one moment of peace and tenderness in the midst of daily violence, beautiful music that calms our spirit, a novel that keeps us company, a glass of beer or a cup of coffee shared with another . . . salvation is a get-together, an event, a sentiment, a kiss, a piece of bread, a happy old woman.[53]

The experience of salvation in these terms is the experience of repeated events of *mini-salvation*, which are, in the midst of death, daily sacraments, daily encounters with God, daily resurrections. This *dailiness* of life where God's mini-salvation occurs does not preclude the larger social perspective of life but it does help us turn our focus to the lives of poor women to see what belongs and pertains to their daily lives. Therefore, for Gebara, God's salvation can only and overtly be called mini-salvation. There is no space for a metaphysical idea of salvation if salvation cannot be considered an event in the daily life of a poor woman, happening on the streets, in the backyards of one's house, at the school, or in the small rooms of shanty town. Following Gebara's steps, we could also say that what they see as redemptive are also sacraments or even mini-sacraments happening in life here and there.

> *Mary was a mother of two kids, one 13 and the other 8 years old. She had lived alone with them since the day she decided to send away her husband who had beaten her up so many times. Now she had to handle her life with her two boys. She was unemployed for a while and was trying to work in small jobs here and there. She lived in a shantytown, far away from the small church where she was a member. The new pastor had started his ministry in this far away congregation about two months earlier. One morning, after Sunday school, the pastor approached her and said: "Mary, I want to visit you and your boys this afternoon, can I go around 4 pm?" "Certainly, pastor, it will be an honor" she said. When*

---

53. Gebara, *Out of Depths*, 124–25.

the pastor was eating at another family's house, another woman came to visit him and said "pastor, you cannot visit Mary today." Why, he replied. "Mary is unemployed and has no money. She cannot buy anything to offer to you to eat and she will not go through this shame. She will tell you when she is able to receive you." Mary was so ashamed that she never came to church during the following months. The pastor felt so guilty. After six months she came to the Sunday school and joyfully said: "Pastor, can you visit me today?" And the pastor, finally relieved, said, "Yes, I can." He was guided by two other women from the church. After a long walk in dirty streets, they arrived at her door. The two boys were clean and had just finished their shower. She was so happy. "Come in pastor, this is your house, I am so happy I can have you here, sorry I could not receive you before," she said pointing to this tiny one bedroom with no restroom. On the small table there was coffee, sweet bread, corn cake, cheese, ham, and a liter of Coke. "They told me you like Coca-Cola, don't you, pastor?" It took her six months to buy these things. And during these six months she could not go to church. The pastor held his tears throughout the visit. He could barely talk but forced himself to show how grateful he was. At the end, he prayed without knowing what words to use. Her life was so difficult. In the evening service, he couldn't preach.

Eating the Crumbs Under The Table

In 1972, Leonardo Boff addressed the notion of the *symbolic and the diabolic/demonic*.[54] Boff's main argument is that reality in its largest perspective, i.e., human beings, nature, the world, the cosmos, the universe, and God can be understood through the two categories of *sym-bolic* and the *dia-bolic* or demonic. Taken from Greek etymology, the *sym-bolic* is that which is thrown together, that unites, organizes, balances, and structures reality. Various elements thrown together create the idea of a re-union, of a re-grouping, of order, forming structures of meaning, value, and location. The *dia-bolic*, from which the demonic derives, suggests that which is thrown away without cohesion, without connection. It is the principle of disarray, disorder, of what is scattered, loosen, dismantled, disorganized. The *dia-bolic* is that which disunites, disestablishes, and keeps things

54. Boff develops this metaphor first in his dissertation in Germany. Recently, he revisits this metaphor in more accessible ways in Boff, *Águia e a Galinha*.

apart, creating a sense of purposelessness, chaos, lack of meaning, place and time.

The sacrament of eating together, eucharist, is *sym-bolos*, that which unites, connects, provides correlates, and weaves the threads of life in community. The *sym-bolic* aspect of the common meal is what sustains people's lives. However, once this thread of commonality is shred, the *dia-bolos* happen, when life in community loses its amalgam; when life happens without "the soul on things" as it is taken apart, life itself is turned into an even thinner line, now suspended over the precipice of helplessness.

In order to hold the symbolic threads of life together against the constant disruption of the diabolic, the poor try to interrelate everything in life. Marga J. Stroher writes an intriguing study of John 6:1–15, where she affirms that breakfasts, picnics, eucharist, and ecology cannot have distinction. Ecologies of tenderness and sharing are to be shared in the lives of people without separation:

> There cannot be any distinction between sacred and profane meals, between picnic and eucharist. An ecological reading of the text does not allow distinctions between the fragments of the bread in the altar and on the breakfast table. To eat in each meal is to live by the sustenance of the body. To reaffirm the connection between sustenance and spiritual life, between bread and faith and the bread of the table is an ethical and religious responsibility for the bread in all tables and for the awareness of the ecosystem as home and sacred space, as planetary community, like the body in communion.[55]

There is no distinction between sacred and non-sacred meals. However, to affirm that there is no distinction does not mean that everything is either sacred or secular. It is for both to live together without tension.[56] God's illumination is the tangible *trace* of the sacrament under the table, where the crumbs expose the profane exclusion that poor people live religiously and socially. The crumbs also show that the poor live under the shadows of the big tables where abundance and opulence overflows. Nonetheless, the crumbs, the leftovers of other tables, illuminate life in community, since the crumbs are shared with everybody. And this is the

55. Stroher, *É Preciso que Haja Pão!*, 120.

56. This correlation is something akin to what Walter Benjamin's calls *Profane Illuminations*. M. Taussig asks "What exactly is illuminated?" and answers, "In Benjamin's coining of the phrase, the illumination in a 'profane illumination' bears the emphatic trace of a religious illumination it has surpassed" (class lecture, "Interpretation of Culture," Fall 2004). See also M. Taussig, *Walter Benjamin's Grave*.

clearest sign of a radical hospitality, where no one goes hungry. The food is not distributed only among those who are part of the community, the sacrament is offered to all, even if the community does not know the one who is arriving in order to partake the crumbs. They show what Clarice Lispector once said: "bread is love among strangers."[57]

However, the social displacement of being under the table all the time, eating crumbs when there is plenty of food on the table for everyone attests to the social and religious *diabolic* aspect, a radical disconnection that turns the official celebration of eucharist into an empty and even demonic action. This is what Gustavo Gutierrez unmistakably affirms:

> Without a real commitment against exploitation and alienation and for a society of solidarity and justice, the Eucharistic celebration is an empty action, lacking any genuine endorsement by those who participate in it. This is something that many Latin American Christians are feeling more and more deeply, and they are thus more demanding both of themselves and of the whole church.[58]

If the eucharistic action around the table is empty, the eating of the crumbs under the table is not. The sacrament is precisely there, under the table. Crumbs and leftovers are the vanishing theological material for us to theologize, and liturgize, and invent a new ecclesiology. They are indeed the borderless borders of any Eucharistic meal. Thus, as scavengers, both symbolically and literally, how should we liturgists and theologians talk and act about the crumbs? How should we create liturgies, do theology and talk about the incarnation of Jesus under the table with poor people? The Syrophoenician woman did change her place in her negotiation with Jesus. She embarrassed Jesus who had to change his ideas.

How then can poor people in Brazil negotiate their places under the table? We learned to be under the table as our proper place. No movements to go away from there, no stretching or bending of our knees as ways of resisting the expected movements within the liturgical order. At first, the Eucharistic table was an offering of God to us, to help us go through life and fill it with meaning, and joy, and trust. The Christian message of love within the table came to our hearts through the bending of our knees. Once our knees were bent appropriately, we were evangelized, converted. And we believed in this love. Kneeling to God, what better expression of

57. Lispector, "Repartição dos Pães": http://www.releituras.com/clispector_paes.asp.

58. Gutiérrez, *Theology of Liberation*, 150.

surrender? The table was given to us with care and proper ceremony. But then, when we tried to stand up, and sit around the table, and eat with our own hands, we were told that we could not do that. Over time, we forgot that we had knees to move, and that there was a place around the table. We were left believing that the crumbs were enough. Cardoso continues to relate liturgy and the domestication of our knees when she affirms that "kneeling at the ringing of the bell at the Angelus is to accept the Church as owner of time and the sacred history as the fountain of order.[59]

In the official liturgy, our liturgical gestures are done with a purpose, a sense, a history, or an intention. The religious structures of power take over our hearts, minds, and bodies and place us under the table, suppressing and controlling our bodies according to the rules.

> The bodies learned to obey first the weight of violence and of the punishment that were accompanied by the catecheses and the homily. Nobody was invited to be convinced. The knees were co-opted to bend and then belief was invented.[60]

We learned to repeat what we received without any change in regard to those ways tradition was displacing our lives away from a better life, always keeping us away from the access to the social, and economic and religious table.

> Seated: legs crossed. The repeated aspects of learning by generations of women: the gap within the legs avoided. The gap between the legs and its cartography . . . All the effort placed on the knees with the learning of yes! And the no! The knees as collective knowledge, deposited in the joint and its capacity to bend. To transit between allowed positions and through the vortices of abused movements, absorbing what centuries of culture and biology had developed for the female knees: obedience, seclusion, grace.[61]

To undo this abusive control over the cartography of our knees and legs is to undo the metaphysics of patriarchy, heterosexuality, racism, and centuries of learning the "proper" under the table. Who controls our knees? It is crucial for us to rediscover the table as a place to move about and around. What has the church done to our knees? Our knees could not jump up and down, could not be shown, could not misbehave. Knees

---

59. Pereira, "Des-Evangelização dos Joelhos," 164.

60. Ibid., 165.

61. Ibid., 166.

became the location in our bodies where we were put to shame. To bend our knees is a sign of giving up, of surrender. With our knees bent we cannot go anywhere, cannot escape, cannot run, cannot affront, cannot move under the table. The bending of our knees is the controlling of our movements and finally, the usurping of our own lives, in the name of the proper, for the sake of sameness and safety for the other.

The only way to reclaim a place at the table is to turn the tables *and* our legs up, iconoclastically up, providing food/hospitality for all. Cardoso powerfully affirms it in this way:

> No distinction between the crumbs of the bread on the breakfast table and the eucharistic altar . . . people do live like that! They take the leftovers, respect them, reinvent them in other foods! And this is how the miracle happens always and again! Nobody will go hungry (and from now on let it be declared that this is the beginning and the end, the middle and the always forever more of the eucharist!).[62]

To turn the table up is necessary to move our knees. At every table, coffee table, dinner table, friends table, picnic table, eucharistic table, in all of these meals we move our knees to undo the domestication and colonization that taught us to move according to a set of sym-bolic movements prescribed by a given behavior which was named as given by God. When we move our knees, we discover that what we thought was *symbolic* gestures under the table, was actually a *dia-bolic* system of severance, disconnecting understandings of poor people's obedience to God from their bodies, their sexualities, their stories, their dignity and their capacity to resist.

The church is reinventing itself, in the forgotten places where there are no organic theologians to call them church. This church is a project, living and slipping under the norms and marks of ecclesiological authentication that might be a true church of Christ. The "new" base communities may never be ecclesial in the official sense, but they might be ecclesia on their own way. They are small communities of fisherman, in shantytowns,

---

62. Pereira, email to author, March 18, 2007. It is worth mentioning that Pereira is talking about eucharist over against a country that has disastrous inequalities. Just to offer some numbers: Brazilian agriculture is one of the most developed in the world and has climate conditions to plant almost any kind of food. However, ten percent of its population suffers from malnutrition and from this eighteen million people, five million are children and elderly people. Brazil wastes more than US six million dollars of food every year which could feed thirty million people or eight million families throughout the year.

in the camps of the landless movement living under plastic tents, and on the streets. In all these communities, anyone can come and be received well. Perhaps not with weeping, but certainly with joy, a plate with food (even if Eucharistic leftovers), and a conversation about life.[63]

Within these communities they only have each other to hold and help. And God! The world is always escaping them, as if they had no right to have it, no strength to fight for it, and no humanity to deserve it. And yet, they live because they know they have the right to inherit the earth, even if it was stolen from them: they fight because they have no other choice, and they hope because their humanity overflows. It is as if they say to each other every morning, right after the *Hail Maria* and the *Lord's Prayer*: "The world is gone, I must carry you."

---

63. In Portuguese we say "dois dedinho de prosa."

6

Christians and Yorubá People Eating Together

Eucharist and Food Offerings

We only live by doing. Without doing, we are just existing.

—PADRE VIEIRA

I am only interested in what is not mine.

—OSWALD DE ANDRADE

Religions and religious differences are an active and inseparable element of the cultural and political dynamics that are transforming the meaning of social and political connections in our time, when expressed from below, as emancipatory.

—JOANILDO BURITY

I would say that there can't be dialogue between Christians and Muslims if there isn't a common practice. Any other dialogue outside of a common practice is just discussion. Byzantine nonsense.

—FREI BETTO

Eucharist and Globalization

THIS CHAPTER PRESENTS THE possibility of a broader form of Eucharistic hospitality which builds on early church practices and is consonant with the ongoing work of our spiritual/faithful *reformata semper reformanda* "reformed and always reforming." By exploring a possible relation between two religions in Brazil, Christianity (the Reformed branch) and Candomblé (an African-Brazilian religion), I am trying to expand the inter-religious, racial and global vocabulary, practices and notions of Eucharistic hospitable prayers. The issues at stake in Brazil's reality and the format of praxis proposed here can perhaps illustrate the growing need for churches everywhere to engage with strangers through new forms of theological dialogue and liturgical practices that can in some ways provide dialogue, justice, peace, and hospitality. Moreover, our globalized world continues to spread many forms of religions everywhere and Christians need to learn how to relate, dialogue, and live together with different forms of people's beliefs, practices and worldviews.

Candomblé is such a religion that is apt to live in a globalized world with a strong and malleable capacity to adapt and adjust to new places and situations. Candomblé's gods travel with their people and welcome local gods where Candomblé people are received. Traveling from Africa, Candomblé changed and took on a new configuration in Brazil. Rachel E. Harding defines Candomblé this way:

> Candomblé is a rich and complex portico of ritual actions, cosmology, and meaning with deep and obvious roots in several religious traditions of West and West Central Africa—especially Yorubá, Aja-Fon, and Bantu. It is a (re)creation of these traditions, and others, from within the matrix of slavery, colonialism, and mercantilism which characterized Brazil and other new societies of the western hemisphere from the sixteenth through the nineteenth centuries.[1]

I am choosing Candomblé for what I am calling an inter-religious dialogical-praxis for three reasons: (1) Candomblé is not the type of religion, like Hinduism or Islam, which other scholars normally pick for considering inter-religious dialogue or praxis and thus may offer new insights into the inter-religious work we need to do; (2) it is a religion, somewhat like Christianity, in which food and eating together play a central role in worship and thus provides an excellent inter-faith case study for reflecting upon boundaries in Eucharistic practice; (3) Candomblé has been a religion of which Christians have long been highly suspicious and

1. Harding, *Refuge In Thunder*, xiii.

have attacked throughout Brazil's history. It has become a radical other, especially for Protestant Christians, and my own faith has been deeply defined by the negation and condemnation of Candomblé people and their religious activities. Let me explain:

Candomblé is not found in the textbooks on the so-called world religions. It has no founder, no sacred texts, no normative traditions like Hinduism, Buddhism, or Islam to which most Christians interested in inter-religious dialogue normally turn. Like Christianity and the aforementioned world religions, it is also a religion firstly grounded in oral history and practices formed in local communities that reads the universe from their own social structure. However, Candomblé did not take the next step of forming sacred texts. Instead, it continued its movement and continuous formation through the passing of its own secret (awó) by oral history to those who belong to the group. As for its various traditions, they are not defined primarily by dogmas, religious, or theological ideas but rather by their practices defined by social groups (tribes in Africa) that move, transform and give structure to their world. That is why it only makes sense for us, Christians, to establish a dialogical-practical relation with Candomblé people. In addition, Candomblé happens to be a religion, somewhat like Christianity, in which food and eating together play a central role in worship and thus provides an excellent inter-faith case study for reflecting upon boundaries in Eucharistic practice.

In Brazilian history, both Roman and Protestant Christianity fought fiercely against African religions. In general, Christians considered them to be lesser forms of civilization and their believers less human, engaged in superstitious and magical religious practices that belong to the Devil. Thus, Candomblé and other African religions are seen as a threat to the Christian culture and well-being of the "free" religious life of Brazil. Moreover, since most of the members of these religions were black, one cannot disassociate this low view of African religiosities from a heavily marked system of racism underlying Christian views, concepts, and perceptions.

The widespread fear, anger, and suspicion of African religions in Brazilian culture have made African religions a mission field for Christians to conquer. Lately, this fear, anger, and suspicion have even taken more violent forms. To cite just one example, Yalorixá Dulce left the *Assembly of God* to become a mother-of-saint (a spiritual leader, a kind of pastor) in Candomblé. She told me that Christians came to her house, where her *terreiro* (worship space) is located, sang Christians songs loudly and even

threw stones to interrupt and destroy the Candomblé worship celebration.[2] This attack, I might add, was not out of step with Brazil's history of
racism and Christian theological reasoning.

Finally, Candomblé has become a radical religious other hovering
around the Christian faith in Brazil. Once Prof. John Makransky asked the
following question to a group of scholars who were doing inter-religious
dialogue: "What is your (personal) fundamental motivation for doing
this work and how does that influence your theology? Is it related to your
predilections or is it something else deeper in you?"[3] My faith can only
be understood when I look back and see that most of what I affirmed
was grounded in a negation and denial of other people and other beliefs,
including African religions. At school, church, and on the streets of São
Paulo, I learned that Candomblé was a religion dominated by demons and
controlled by the Devil. I could not cross the front door of a *terreiro*, a
Candomblé worship place lest I be taken captive by those demons. Very
early in life I became a fervent evangelist and my mission was to convert
these *demonized* people who were made captives by the Devil and were
going to hell.

It was much later that I started to learn that Candomblé people were
not people of the Devil but my brothers and sisters. The movement away
from fear and into a space of trust and admiration was neither quick nor
easy. I had to meet them, I had to visit their own worship spaces, I had
to invest myself, I had to see their rituals, I had to eat their food, I had to
invite them to be part of my own life. Thus, engaging new forms of relation
here, I want to find and foster a somewhat safe space where Christians can
connect with Candomblé people and through practical movements, create
a process of restitution for Candomblé people and a space of shared joy,
care, respect, and hospitality.

This chapter holds the belief that by searching for sacramental possibilities through interreligious dialogue/praxis and by exploring the
relationship between Christianity and Candomblé, we can find a space
for dialogue, reconciliation, connection, dismantling of racism, healing
peace, and hospitality. Thus, my initial questions are: given the Brazilian
history of slavery and racism, can we provide a space of reconciliation
and hospitality through common rituals of eating, praying and dancing?

2. Some Christian friends tell me that several churches have as their mission
goal to close down a number of *terreiros* every year.

3. This question was asked in a plenary of the "Cohort II of the Luce Seminar
on Theologies of Religious Pluralism and Comparative Theology," developed by the
American Academy of Religion, Chicago, May 2011.

Can we offer sacred food to each other and can we eat together? Can the Eucharistic table carry food offered to *Orixás* (gods of the Candomblé)? Can the Orixás allow Christians to eat their food? How can we do such things while respecting our own limits and expanding our possibilities?

One might ask why we must bring the history of colonization and slavery to the Eucharistic table. As we have also seen, the Eucharistic table establishes not only theological, liturgical and ecclesiastical boundaries but also social/economic/political borders that delimit the ways in which a community defines itself, engages issues of power, and determines the norms and standards of its own identity and worth. In one word, the Eucharistic table offers a certain understanding of humanness. By tapping into the ways in which Christianity in Brazil dealt with black people and their religion, the question of what it means to be human is open again. We, who are at the table, are also responsible not only for ourselves but also for those who are not there and for what is going on in our society.

SLAVERY AND CANDOMBLÉ IN BRAZIL

The history of Brazil is the history of Indians, Europeans, Africans, and their religions. It is around these encounters that Brazilian cultures and identities were formed. The African people have been fundamental to this cultural, religious, and identity polydoxy. Africans enriched Brazil's ways of thinking, literature, music, food, religions, and ways of relating. Nonetheless, Brazil's history is deeply tainted by almost 400 years of slavery perpetrated by Portugal. The Portuguese, unhappy with the work of the native people, imported African people from their colonies in Africa. In 1590, there were as many as thirty-six thousand slaves in Brazil; by 1817, there were 1.9 million, and by 1850 there were 3.5 million slaves. "In total," says Luiz Felipe de Alencastro, a Brazilian historian,

> more than 4 million Africans were deported to Brazil between 1550 and 1850, making Brazil the American country that received the largest amount of slaves arriving in the New World. If compared to United States in the same period mentioned above, Brazil received 43% of Africans, while the United States, from 1650 to 1808 received five and a half percent of Africans brought to the Americas.[4]

4. de Alencastro, "As Populações Africanas no Brasil": http://www.casadasafricas. org.br/wp/wp-content/uploads/2011/08/As-Populacoes-Africanas-no-Brasil.pdf, 2.

In 1888 Brazil became the last major country in the world to enact a law ending slavery. However, slavery continued in many different
ways, deeply affecting the people and religions of African descent. The
impact of 400 years of slavery is still very much alive in Brazil today, but
is made nicer by the Brazilian cultural apparatus. Brazil's racism is not
an "in your face" movement with public signposts saying "blacks are not
welcome here"; it is subtle and "nice," making people think that they live
"in harmony" while it keeps black people at the bottom of society. This so
called "cordial racism" shows the ideological myth of racial democracy
in Brazil. Its niceness is so pervasive that it makes fighting against it way
more difficult.[5]

This does not mean that there was no African resistance to it. One of
the most significant was *Quilombo dos Palmares*[6] in the seventeenth century. Slaves fled from their owners and created these free cities in remote
areas and were joined by the disfranchised. More than twenty thousand
former slaves and other socially rejected people, including Europeans and
indigenous people, lived in freedom in their own sovereign place.

Brazil is slowly starting to delve more deeply into these differences
and into the acculturation of Afro-descent peoples. As Africans arrived
in Brazil, they brought their religions with them. However, slaves were
forbidden to practice their religion and were forced to learn the Christian
faith. Especially during the nineteenth century, the Portuguese made clear
attempts to destroy the religious practices of Africans and *Criolos* (blacks
born in Brazil). Candomblé beliefs and practices were considered to be a
sign of an uncivilized culture, featuring magic and premodern elements
of religion that were not part of the modern civilized European Christian

5. "Cordial man" is an expression created by historian Sérgio Buarque de Holanda
to describe the ways Brazilians live. See Buarque Holanda, *Raízes do Brasil*. However, "cordial racism" was an expression created later to capture the kind of racism
in Brazil that is constantly denied. Marcelo Coelho says: "Perhaps, one of the horrors
of the 'cordial racism' is that prejudice expresses itself when somebody says 'I don't
have prejudice.' To say that 'there is no racism is true to a certain extent (there are no
benches on public square dividing whites and blacks as it was in the United States)
but this is misleading in a deeper analysis" (Coelho, "Estranhamento conduz 'racismo
cordial,'" *Folha de S. Paulo*, 28 de Junho de 1995: http://www.cefetsp.br/edu/eso/com-
portamento/racismocordial.html).

6. *Quilombos*. These places still feed the memory of black people in Brazil in their
struggles today. As new *Quilombos* continue to exist, African religions are still powerful strongholds of resistance, empowerment and transformation even though mostly
forgotten by the government. For more information about Quilombo dos Palmares,
see Carneiro, *O Quilombo dos Palmares*; Gomes, *Palmares*.

project for Brazil. Forceful attacks on Yorubá and other African religions continued in different forms until the end of the twentieth century.

Nonetheless, Candomblé and its people were able to survive in spite of continuous persecution by the Brazilian government and systematic repression by the police force until 1975 when a federal law was finally issued to protect *terreiros de candomblés* (worship places) from invasion, abuse, and destruction. From that time until now, it has been a continuous struggle for the Candomblé people, called "people of the saint," to survive and live freely in this nice and cordial racist South American country called Brazil.

CANDOMBLÉ[7]

Candomblé is grounded in the mystery of *Awô*, the *secret* that is transmitted orally to new generations of believers over time. Candomblé is passed on by the initiated as they live its religious precepts together. It has a non-structured orality at its core and only recently have efforts to write about African religions been made. In Candomblé, the tradition is sung and danced. The synthesis of the whole process, says Alessandra Osuna, would be

> the search for an energetic equilibrium between the inhabitants of the material world and the energy of those beings who inhabit the *orum*, a space dimension that could be called heaven, the interior of the earth or a place beyond anything that is known, according to different understandings of tribes, peoples and traditions. Each human being has an Orixá who protects him/her and that person will only know if s/he gets in touch with the Orixá through a ritual. By fulfilling the obligations ascribed by the Orixá, the person receives a reserve of energy and will gain more equilibrium."[8]

The same way that we cannot talk about Christianity but Christianities, we also need to talk about Candomblés, in the plural. Candomblé varies according to its various traditions: congo, jejê, nagô, queto, ijexá, angola. Roger Bastide says that, "It is possible to distinguish each of these

7. I ask for Agô (permission) to the Orixás, to the Candomblés of Brazil and people of saint to delve into a little their beliefs and practices.

8. Osuna, Osuna, Alessandra. "Significado do Candomble," Oxum a Deusa da Fertilidade, April 3, 2008: http://ebomealessandraosun.blogspot.com/2008/04/significado-do-candomble.html.

'nations' from the way each nation plays the drums (with sticks or hands), their music, the idiom spoken, songs, liturgical vests, names of divinities and for certain aspects of the ritual."[9] Moreover, "'each house of Candomblé is a sentence' that is, each house of worship finds notions of right or wrong, its theologies and religious understandings of their histories and antecessors."[10]

Gisele Omindarewá Cossard, a very well respected Yalorixás, engages three essential African traditions in the Yorubá line: "the Yorubá aspect of the houses of Ketu tradition, the Fon aspect in the houses of Jejê tradition and the Bantu aspect of the houses of tradition Congo/Angola . . . The world of Candomblé is multifaceted."[11] However, the differences in the African traditions do not mean that the Africans are polytheists. Olorum, Olodumarê, Zaniapombo, are names for the same God creator of all. According to Vilson Junior, "Candomblé is grounded on three pillars: 1) Secret-Religion or orality; 2) Respect-hierarchy; 3) Precept-liturgy."[12]

Pierre Verger, a French scholar who went to Brazil to study Candomblé and became a father-of-saint, a Babalorixá, defines Candomblé this way:

> Candomblé is for me very interesting because it is a religion of the exaltation to the personality of people. Where one can be what one is and not what society makes you be. For people who have things to express through the unconscious, trance is a possibility for the unconscious to show itself.[13]

Candomblé carries a powerful view of the world, known and unknown, including myths of creation and offering ways that people can realize the potentiality and the fullness of their lives. Candomblé is a way of balancing the energy of the individual, the community and the world. The movement between the visible and the invisible worlds, the connections with gods and entities (thus with oneself, communities, past, present,

---

9. Bastide, *O Candomblé da Bahia*, 29. This book is a great resource for understanding the structure, meaning and movement of the ritual services of the Candomblé in general, but most properly of the services done in Bahia.

10. Oliveira, ed., *Diálogos Fraternos Contra a Intolerância Religiosa*, 14.

11. Cossard, *Awó, O Mistério dos Orixás*, 12 (my work will rely heavily on this work).

12. de Souza Jr., "A Relação da Comida no Candomblé: 25 Anos de Logun Edé. Part II," interview by the students of gastronomy of the Faculdade FTE/RUY, Barbosa, Salvador, BA, June 2010: http://www.youtube.com/watch?v=VuGlStsTVBc&NR=1.

13. Verger, cited in Motta, *Estratégias e culturas da comunicação*, 240.

and future), the ways one can find healing and protection, the ways one is charged to live a just life are all part of the private sessions/rituals and public festivities. Everything happens ritually and the connections and responses to the Orixás conveyed through the rituals. The composition and demands of this very difficult and committed religion are fascinating ways to understand humanity in all its complexities.

Let us consider some of the main known elements in Candomblé:

Hierarchy and Structure

The respect of hierarchy is based on the religious structure that has Olodumarê as the main God creator, Orumilá who holds all the wisdom, and the Orixás, voduns, and inquices who live in between the natural and the supernatural world. Within the social organization of Candomblé, there is a strong hierarchical structure where the Babalaôs and Yalawôs are the main leaders of the Candomblés, something like pastors/priests in Christian Churches, and the *iawôs*, the initiated people, and then those who participate in one way or another way but are not necessarily members. The hierarchy is grounded in the line of ancestors of the African people and is the result of the ways in which the ethnic, sociocultural system with kings and queens of different nations on the one hand, and the religious system with Iorubás and Nagôs on the other, were established in Africa. Kings and Queens were responsible for the well being of peoples and communities and controlled the powers of nature. They were treated like gods. When they died, their reign was spiritualized and they became part of the history, memory, and strength of a community who made them sacred. They then became their guides and Orixás.

Worship

Candomblé is worship; it is service. Only those who are initiated know the secret and continue to grow into the knowledge of this secret. Candomblé is a religion that connects the material and immaterial world, giving space for the unconscious to reveal itself as part of the totality of the sacred. A religion that balances out the energies of these worlds and struggles with the imbalance of our attitudes and the balance of the world provided by Olodumarê, the main God creator, also called Orumilá. Candomblé is a service to the Orixás, gods that come from all forces of nature: earth, fire, water, and air. Babalorixá Aragão describes Candomblé as a monastery where people are in the world and the function of Candomblé and its priest/ess (Yalorixás /Babalorixá) is to take care of the initiated and the entities. Service is an exchange in Candomblé. The omniscient, omnipresent, omnipotent God (Olorum) does not need worship. The Orixás need worship! Most of the festivities are centered around singing, dancing, and eating.

Worship Spaces: Terreiros

Candomblé is an extension of the house, of the family. That is why the terreiros are always at the back or around of the house of the Yalorixás / Babalorixá. Terreiros/worship places are often located at the house of the mother- or father-of-saint. The terreiro has to be close to trees and gardens and plants since Candomblé is fundamentally related to nature where its sources come from. At each terreiro, often one main Orixá is the head of the worship place but all of the Orixás are welcomed and worshiped. It is their choice to appear or not. During festivities and specific works, the terreiros are the place where people stay, sleep, dance, eat, and live. The terreiro are the sacred places where "Orixás, voduns and inquices dance; the font where the iawôs (initiated) bathe, the sacred trees where Iroco and Tempo live; the little houses for Exú and eguns."[14] Grounded in African societies, Candomblé has complex social, cultural, and religious structures and its practices and beliefs are multiple, varying according to each terreiro. Terreiros became spaces for resistance and wrestling with old and new worldviews. At these spaces, thin and thick movements of memory, resistance, engagement and solidarity were at work against oppression and death. As Harding puts it, these spaces refer "to socio-political, cultural, psychic, and ritual-religious locations within Afro-Brazilian experience . . . locations contain the implication of both boundary and movement."[15] These religious spaces kept by the African people were places that would contrast and offer alternatives to the streets (where poor, "worthless," abandoned people lived), and the *senzalas* (plantation slave quarters), destitute of dignity, value or pride, social locations imposed by a racist and slavocratic society. Terreiros, also called axé, the vital energy, were locations that helped Africans and African Brazilians to re-position themselves in relation to the new world of slavery, destruction, and death. Harding establishes the relation of Candomblé to the African and African descent people.

14. Carneiro, *O Quilombo dos Palmares,* 20–21.
15. Harding, *Refuge In Thunder,* xvi.

for these people and their descendants, Candomblé was an important means for the engagement of trauma. It represented an integrative process—pulling together and (re)organizing that which had been rendered asunder: family, identity and psyche . . . Candomblé provided a means of re-membering and re-creating an identity of value and connectedness—to Spirit, to a pre-slavery past, to ancestors, to community. It also provided, cultivating African material and cultural elements in its rituals, an alternate meaning of Africanness, an alternate identity of blackness. And where the myriad of ignominies of life in Brazil created crises in psychic integrity, Candomblé offered transformative music and dance, community, and magico-pharmacopoeic healing. In the mutual embrace of humanity and spirit in Candomblé emerged intimations of wholeness—representations of the reciprocity of devotion and responsibility, the sharing of burdens and joys.[16]

Candomblé's terreiros were *places* where people participated fully, and this way of participating gave them a certain assurance of identity and self-worth, conditions to resist, restoring their strength and living their lives under the crushing power of slavery.

Priest/ess

Babalorixá, or Father-of-saint, is connected to *Knowledge*, while the Mother-of-saint, Yalorixás, is connected to *Wisdom*. Long before, Babalorixás and Yalorixás were called servants. They are the ones who took care of the Orixás. The priest/ess (Babalorixás and Yalorixás) organize the worship event and make sure everything is done appropriately. They are the ones who hold the secrets of the religion and to whom the initiated owe respect and obedience. Also, they are the ones who receive and give the messages to the Orixás (entities/gods) and they decide what the worship acts, offerings, and work are to be made for the enjoyment of the Orixás and for the safety, blessing, and protection of the initiated. Rituals are corporeal and the priest/ess' (Babalorixá's/Yalorixás') speaking generates energy.

Orixás

Orixás are bodiless, energetic forces that feel and think and experience things like us humans. The African understanding of the world divides neither the sacred and secular nor the human and godly behaviors of the

16. Ibid.

Orixás. Orixás manifest themselves to human beings by possessing their bodies during worship at terreiros. A person chosen by the Orixá is an *elegum*, who has the privilege to be mounted by the Orixá. Anyone can ask and know and engage their Orixás without having to do the ritual of initiation. However, if a person is chosen by the Orixás, s/he will be asked to do the Orí, the making of the head, which is the ritual of initiation. Those who invoke the Orixás have to offer greetings, do liturgies, perform gestures and movements, sing, dance, and drum, cook, dress up with their proper colors, and follow the demands ordained by the Orixás. They have to offer food desired and spread it around the city but mostly within forests, as ways of fulfilling the Orixás desires. In everything, the believer has to obey the Orixá who in turn will offer miracles, healing, and a balanced life to the person. Orixás cannot be irritated. If they demand a work and it is not done, the believer will suffer the consequences.

Feasts, Sacrifice, Food, and Offering

Festivities in Candomblé are powerful events with many people participating. However, as Roger Bastide said, "the public festivity constitutes only a small portion of the life of the Candomblé. The private rituals are more important than the public ceremonial. African religions will color and control every part of the life of its members, and (by ways of living its religion) the black person feels more African and ends up belonging to a different mental world . . ."[17]

Kitchens are fundamental parts of the worship inside of the terreiros. As Edson Carneiro puts it:

> The kitchen ritual, filled with clay pans and stones, with its novices and iabassês (kitchen chefs) is a fundamental point of any terreiro of any Candomblé nation . . . where the cook prepares the obligations, the food offerings and the drinks to the black gods. Everything is spotless. These kitchens used to be different from people's daily kitchen but now they look alike. But then and now, these kitchens hold secrets only those inside know. The way of preparation and to serve must follow some precepts.[18]

Kitchens have all of the proper tools and ingredients for the cooking and preparation of the food. There is a high office, so to speak, in the work of the kitchen and a person, called Iabassê or Adagam, designated by the

17. Bastide, *O Candomblé da Bahia*, 27.
18. Carneiro, *O Quilombo dos Palmares*, 20–21.

Orixá of the house, prepares the special food. Babalorixá Luis de Logun Edé says that, "Nobody is asked if one is formally educated or not. The gift is perceived by the Babalorixá/Yalorixás and chosen by the Orixá to occupy the office. Often the person is born with this gift. Then she/he is trained so she learns how to do the many offerings for each Orixá."[19]

After it is prepared by people specially trained for it, the food/offering is a) offered at specific sites in a procession to the sound of songs; b) then brought to the forests or nature where the Orixá live; c) offered during the festivity of the whole terreiro, and eaten by the participants. Moreover, the offering of food to the Orixás is usually done in the evening since Orixás do not eat when the sun is up. Often Candomblé feasts end very late and with food. Gisele Cossard describes the end of a ceremony:

> It is usually too late for people to go back home . . . some of the yawôs (the initiated ones) go help serve the meal that is offered to the people present. This food is a generous offering of the terreiro to the whole community who came to the feast. However, according to the ancient people of the Candomblé, there is another meaning for this offering: the Orixás like plenty and they desire that all present leave with their belly full.[20]

However, there is way more to the meaning of food to the African religions. In fact, it was the women of the Candomblé who preserved and made known the African religions by ways of their ability with the preparation of the food and the making of their art crafts: necklaces, wristbands, sewing, embedded cloth work, etc.[21] Rituals in Candomblé involve

19. Babalorixá Luis de Logun Edé, "A Relação da Comida no Candomblé: 25 Anos de Logun Edé," interview by the students of gastronomy of the Faculdade FTE/RUY, Barbosa, Salvador, BA, June 2010: http://www.youtube.com/watch?v=8IxS7vQUQNg.

20. Cossard, *Awó, O Mistério dos Orixás*, 123.

21. Farelli describes the essentials in the Candomblés terreiros founded in Bahia: "Black princesses with ivory smiles conducted their god to the dirty streets of the cities and the moonlight of the countryside. And for their divine lords they prepared the best spicy food, cooked with wood in within their mysteries. Were it not for them, queens and African priestess, brought as slaves from Benin and Angola, how would their gods come live in Brazil? . . . Foods for the saints are traditional, necessary, and they make the beauty of the religious festivities . . . Around the terreiros people live in order to adore their gods and ancestors and to them they prepare drinks and food that constitute one of the links between aiê (earth) and orum (heaven) through the axé (the magical force). All of the African-Brazilian supernatural world likes food. They must be fed. Blood, dendê (palm oil), and ataré are part of the menu. If you haven't eaten the delicious food and the nectar drinks you should experience. If you follow the precepts, the food will be done so well that all of the gods will come from Africa and Haiti. Let us

offerings of mineral, vegetable, and animal kingdoms, healing, dancing, and percussion. The sacrifice of animals is a very important part of the religion. Only those who are part of the terreiro/axé can see it. Mostly, the fear is that non-believers will see it as uncivilized or barbaric. Each animal relates to a different Orixá. In each festivity, if the terreiro has the means, one two-legged animal should be sacrificed for Exú and a four-legged animal to the appointed Orixá of the house. The sex of the animal has to follow the sex of the Orixá. The Oxogum is the one who makes the sacrifice. Then the sacrificed animal goes to the person in charge of the kitchen who prepares the food and makes it ready to be offered. After the food is offered to the Orixá in a separate room by the Babalorixá/Yalorixás, the food will be consumed by the faithful and also given to guests. [22] Every food offered to the Orixá has the power to change people's lives. Everyone can receive a blessing from the food. The food not eaten is kept for three days and after that thrown away. It was the African kitchen preserved in the African rituals that ended up going to the table of every person.

Vilson Caetano de Souza Junior says that "during the festivity, food is shared among people and means commensality. People share, live and memorize it. Food is memory and provokes emotions. Food in Candomblé has to do with the rescue of the memory of the people. The food during the service is to energize the Orixá, people, and the place." [23]

The Babalorixá Luis de Logun Edé says that, "Orixás eat the food that humans eat." However every offering has its own wisdom and ways of being prepared that include: enchanted words (fó), prayers (àdúrà), evocations (oriki) e songs (orin) connected to sacred stories (itan), essential elements that are vital to the transmission of the axé. Life, power, and creativity are what we use to do good."[24]

The structure of the food ritual is described by Bastide as follows: "In the morning, the sacrifice is done; the culinary preparation and the offering to the divinities happen in the afternoon; the public ceremony properly done is done when sun goes down and enters deep into the

---

salute our Orixá, the owner of our ori (head) and live without the notion of sin, which brought so many bad things to the African who didn't know what sin was. Axé to my ancestors white, black and indigenous, for it is time for the delicious food form Bahia" (Farelli, *Comida de Santo*, 12).

22. Bastide, *O Candomblé da Bahia*, 31. This is a practice in most terreiros/axé but some babalOrixás like Luis de Logun Edé do not like to offer food

23. de Souza Jr., "Relação da Comida no Candomblé."

24. Babalorixá Luis de Logun Edé, "Relação da Comida no Candomblé."

evening."[25] The eating together is a fundamental part of the festivity. Below Roger Bastide describes an experience of eating together at the end of the ceremonies. He says

> . . . and before we all break up, a fellowship meal will allow the gathering of deities, members of the fraternity and the specta-tors who still remain in the worship room. The daughters of saint bring in dishes from the color of their Orixás, a little food, some of which had been placed in peji: white for Oxalá, blue for Yemanja, violet for Nanã . . . They sit around a towel placed on the same ground on which they deposited the sacred food. Each person takes a bit of the food from their god's plate, with both hands cupped, then the person scoops the food in his/her hand and raises it to their mouth. After that, it is offered a bit of each dish to the sons of other Orixás in order to cement the solidarity of the group through the sharing of the food. The leftovers are placed on banana leaves, are offered to the spectators who are standing near the daughters of saint who are seated—the vari-ous food offerings from the multiple Orixás fraternally mixed in a kind of fraternal mixed vegetable tray; it is mandatory to eat with your hand. One should not confuse this repast, which is a communion, with the collation sometimes served to impor-tant guests between a calling dance and the dance to the gods. This is something very different, a kind of triple solidarity to happen before returning to the mundane world: first, between the divine and human, then the fellowship among the members who belong to different deities, and sometimes even rivals; and finally among the fellowship of the uninitiated so that a little bit of Africa that was lost can be found again and penetrate into their lives. The group of the faithful goes beyond the fellowship of the sons and daughters of the saint. Entering a Candomblé is done gradually and there are many degrees of inclusion . . .[26]

The food/offering is an essential part of the life of the religion and the community, a way of re-enacting a relation with nature, commensality, memory, resistance, offering, joy, and celebration between the deities, in-ner and outer community. Once we have gained a brief knowledge of Can-domblé, how do we frame this dialogical-praxis? What is at stake here?

25. Bastide, *O Candomblé da Bahia*, 34.
26. Ibid., 40

INTER-RELIGIOUS DIALOGICAL PRAXIS

In Latin America there has been a great movement of theologians working on "Intercontinental Plural Liberation Theologies."[27] These theologians are aware of the need to expand the dialogue and create opportunities for theological conversation and sharing life together. As a result, they are trying to expand the discourse of liberation theology into the field of religious pluralism and engage indigenous and Afro-descent religions, spiritualities, and worldviews. This new way of engaging theology has been called "a new and positive look," "pluralism as principle," "new compassion," and "macro-ecumenism, a new word to replicate a new reality and a new consciousness."[28] This liberative inter-religious dialogue is challenging us to engage ecology issues affecting the life and beliefs of the poor and to include women.[29] At the core of this Christian work, says Teixeira, "there is a convocation to hospitality, to courtesy and acceptance to alterity."[30] As we all engage into this project, Marcelo Barros calls our attention to an important aspect of its methodology.

> Why, all of sudden, theologians and anthropologists start to see positively what was called syncretism, that historically, authorities and intellectuals always saw as negative? The only explanation we have is that such an opening happens when we are able to look at this question not with confessional eyes or from the perspective of the institution, but rather, with an eye of love towards the people, worrying about their life and liberation."[31]

This call is very important since intellectual thinking without emotions and feelings and the body being involved, as obvious as it might be, cannot entail a full inter-religious dialogue. Love is a fundamental presupposition for Christians and worrying about people's life conditions and possibilities

27. Vigil et al., eds., *Teologia Pluralista Libertadora Intercontinental*.

28. Teixeira, "A Teologia do Pluralismo Religioso na América Latina," in Vigil et al., eds., *Teologia Pluralista Libertadora Intercontinental*, 31.

29. Gebara calls this study to include women since the "principle that structures it cannot be only male. Its expression has to be multiple, plural, infinite." Quoted in Teixeira, "A Teologia do Pluralismo Religioso na América Latina," in Vigil et al., eds., *Teologia Pluralista Libertadora Intercontinental*, 34.

30. Teixeira, "A Teologia do Pluralismo Religioso na América Latina," in Vigil et al., eds., *Teologia Pluralista Libertadora Intercontinental*, 39.

31. Barros, "Multipla Pertença, o Pluralismo Religioso," in *Teologia Pluralista Libertadora Intercontinental*, in Vigil et al., eds., *Teologia Pluralista Libertadora Intercontinental*, 54.

of liberation is more important than any methodological tool we choose to work with.

This present project hopes to contribute to this field by expanding what liberation theologians have been thinking about inter-religious dialogue in Latin America by bringing into the heart of this dialogue the need of radical hospitality described in previous chapters. In so doing, the relation between Christians and Candomblé people becomes grounded in practical ways to welcome each other. Starting from the gospel's love commandment as requiring radical hospitality to one another, this way of understanding inter-religious relationships hopes to move beyond detached dialogues to provide down-to-earth tools that can possibly, give practical shapes and forms to the notions of multiplicity, plurality, and infinite love as envisioned by Gebara, Barros and many other inter-religious thinkers.

Theologies of religious pluralism and comparative theologies are based on reflection and practice. From a Latin American perspective, we must return to Antonio Gramsci's notion of the "organic intellectual."[32] Liberation theologians in Latin America have viewed the notion of the "organic intellectual" as a facilitator, one who gathers information hidden by ideologies, connecting it with the formal knowledge that can serve as critical tools, and engaging the pulsing reality and wisdom of the poor in order to create a different praxis that will transform the social situation and bring about liberation.[33]

The organic theologian assumes the need to change Brazil's social threads, especially those of Christian hatred that endanger the living and the religious reliefs of Yorubá people. Thus, starting from our "religious-interreligious" perspective, we must assume that the organic theologian must take a step ahead and enter other's religious communities in order help facilitate the dialogue and the sharing of life together. In addition to

32. "Every social group, coming into existence on the original terrain of an essential function in the world of economic production, creates organically, together with itself, one or more strata of intellectuals which give it homogeneity and an awareness of its own function not only in the economic but also in the social and political fields" (Gramsci, *Selections from the Prison Notebooks*, 5).

33. Priests, pastors, and professors, such as Carlos Mesters, Ivone Gebara, Leonardo Boff, Milton Schwantes, Richard Shall, Nancy Cardoso Pereira, Pedro Casaldáliga, Dom Helder Camara, Don Paulo Evaristo Arns, just to name a few, have deeply engaged the life of the poor and, with them, organized local and national movements of liberation in Brazil (Pastoral of the Land Commission, Landless Movement, Romaria da Terra, workers rights, violence against women, etc.), as well as created discourses that were marked both by the intellectual academy and the concerns and needs and wisdom of the poor.

the organic theologian, the *organic liturgical-theologian* in particular must take steps as she/he is the one who considers rituals and performances, gestures, body postures, prayers, voice, hearing, vision, touch, taste, dancing, and songs as key "texts" for inter-religious dialogue.

Since Yorubá religions do not have a sacred text but are grounded in non-structured orality, the *organic liturgical theologian* must learn how to best engage this dialogue through religious and non-religious practices. Thus, ritual theories, liturgical reasoning, performance studies, everyday life theories, affect theories, constructive inter-religious theologies, and so on can and must engage dance, songs, bodily movements in order to help frame this inter-religious dialogue. In Christianity, the law of prayer/ *lex orandi* is what helps the law of belief/theology—*lex credendi*. In this dialogue, the law of dancing, drumming, dancing, and eating in the Axé, along with the law of prayer and singing and eating in the Christian services are the *lex agendi*, that is, the laws of respectful ethical living. As a result, a *lex vivendi* is constantly re-formed, a life where spaces of generosity, commitment, love, and care are fully lived.

It is the doing of religion that is at stake here. As J. Edgar Bruns puts it theologically, "God is the doing of something."[34] How can we understand each other from our religious practices, or, our very doing of God? What *methodology*, what journey, path, or road, is the organic liturgical theologian to take here?[35]

Gebara suggests what the articulating point might be: "the recognition of the pluralistic founding principles of our existence and life itself, invite us not only to understand ourselves, again, as human beings, but also, to create politics of dialogue that will help us get once again, to that which we call common good."[36] Moreover, according to Diego Irarrázaval, this process includes the ability to be open to and to appreciate the symbols of salvation that are present in other's religious search. From a Christian point of view, this process involves a recognition of the sacramentality of somebody else's religion and how the sense of the sacred is fluid and permeable in our living together.

---

34. Bruns, cited by Betcher, "Take My Yoga upon You," 72.

35. Vigil renews Latin American liberation theology's methodology based on Paulo Freire's work: to see, to judge, and to act and frames it around theologies of religious pluralism as "a new way of living religion, a new practice" (Vigil, *Teologia do Pluralismo Religioso*, 15).

36. Gebara, "Pluralismo Religioso, Uma Perspectiva Feminista" in *Teologia Latino–Americana Pluralista da Libertação*, 297.

Sacramentality (according to the Catholic perspective) runs through the veins of the Latin American population. However, it does not limit itself to this or that church. So much of Latin American ritualism shows the importance of symbols that configures the spirituality and praxis of the daily life of people. God is loved in the everyday life and concrete realities that always carry symbolic value.[37]

Ararrázaval sees the notion of *symbiosis* as a perspective to approach the systems of symbols of Black people, which engage "different elements that conjugated, make space for a bigger life."[38] It is through a symbiotic process of dealing with opposing forces without dichotomy or contradictions that Africans and their beliefs and practices have engaged the new land, Brazil. Christians could learn from this symbiotic movement.[39] We don't start with orthodoxy but with orthopraxis. Everyday life is the criterion of religious truth, and in that regard every religion might carry the possibility of holding a *sacrament*, that which is vital, important and necessary for the living of one's life. Thus, while Candomblé has its own set of beliefs and sacraments, it does not need to undo some other faith structure, or sacrament, in order to relate or engage in dialogue; it respects and engages somebody else's sacrament for everything belongs to everybody.

Irarrázaval ends his work by offering four main points of dialogue in the Christian-African religions:[40] 1) to celebrate and to think, meaning that the celebratory way of the African religions are ways of thinking, of constructing their lives, and recreating the world; 2) to identify ourselves and our continent as African-American, calling ourselves Africans so as to

37. Irarrázaval, "Salvação Indígena e Afro-Americana," 69.

38. Ibid.

39. This notion can be also correlated to the notion of *inclusivism*. While Christian inclusivism sees value in other religions, it appropriates things to itself but retains only what it recognizes, turning what it appropriates into its own system, holding within itself notions of salvation, truth, and revelation that are valid only within the Christian system. What it does not authenticate it demonizes/destroys and dismisses. What Aragão advocates in Candomblé as inclusivism is very different and pertains to symbiosis. Candomblé embraces other beliefs and practices and make it part of its own system without devaluing it into or making it turn into its own categories as a way to destroy other's alterity and relevance in its own way. Instead, this symbiotic process engages different realities to live together to fight a stronger adversary that might want to destroy the larger system. This way of relating to other religions allows Yoruba believers to live religious-interreligiously since any religion can be of help for the struggles of daily life.

40. Irarrázaval, "Salvação Indígena e Afro-Americana," 69.

help us embrace the life, history and the religious elements of the African religion as common to us all; 3) to celebrate the mystery of the African way, which is the celebration of the sacred in our bodies, and to realize that the body is a privileged foci for the revelation of the sacred; and 4) wrestle with syncretism and belonging. While Irarrázaval does not explicate what belonging means, he quotes Maria Cristina Ventura to say that Afro religiosity has the power to recreate their worlds from the available religions that they have at hand. Thus, a disposition to this form of syncretism, of recreating our worlds from each other religious wisdom and tools, is a way of relating with the African religions in Latin America.

One point not mentioned by Irarrázaval but fundamental in this process is the connection with the earth. Ecology is a central aspect of this dialogue since the African religious practices are markedly steeped in elements of the earth. Every Orixá has a connection to some aspect of the mineral, vegetal, and animal world and every terreiro is always around earth, trees, and plants. Without the eco-system, Africans would not be able to live their religions. (Neither would Christians for that matter.) For a pluralistic theology of liberation to happen in Latin America between Christians and Yorubá religions, the commitment to peace and justice must accompany the commitment to the defense of the environment. "This is the ground from which we try to build a true communion between different religious communities with their own doctrinal, ethnic, linguistic and ideological elements."[41]

She was a Methodist pastor, a faithful one to her church. However, for some reasons unknown to her, her heart was very much attuned to the drumbeats of the terreiros. So much so that she decided to study Quilombo Zeferina and the presence of powerful women in that community. A great solid academic work. However, this work got her body closer to her heart and she started to participate in the Candomblé festivities. So much so that she was called to do the initiation process. She then said no because she was faithful to her Methodist tradition. Then one morning, while she was preaching about the Holy Spirit, she was taken by her Orixá and started to move the way she did at the terreiro one night. The people of her congregation thought it was very strange but she said it was the Holy Spirit and while people had their concerns, they believed God had manifested Godself in her. She was fine to move

41. Barros, "Multipla Pertença, o Pluralismo Religioso," 66.

in between these two religions but on that day she said: "I can't do that."
I must honor my Orixá and must leave the church. I will always love the
church and Jesus Christ but my work is at the terreiro now.

CHRISTIANITY-CANDOMBLÉ: MOVEMENTS AND CHALLENGES

The opening to an other in Christianity is neither a new thing nor a choice. Rather, it is a demand built into the core of the gospels and grounded in love. As Sharon V. Betcher, using Jean-Luc Nancy, says- Christianity has an "obligation" to use "the great open."[42] As part of this obligation to the "great open," which is an unknown, unforeseen space, Christians must always learn again the ability to offer a radical hospitality, and eating together with strangers and expanding the table of Jesus Christ must be a common practice. Again, this "great open" does not mean doing away with Christian beliefs, for the Eucharist must always carry the powerful message of the revolutionary memory/*anamnesis* of Jesus Christ given, broken, and shed for all, food for the world. For Candomblé people in Brazil, these theological claims are not foreign. However, if these claims are made by Christians who respect and care for Candomblé people instead of Christians who want to destroy their religion, that change would create an open space of respect for each religion to make their claims without avoiding what they believe. On the other hand, Christians could learn the claims Candomblé people make and honor their faith. At these crossroads, Christians will have the opportunity to live the gospel as a culture of hospitality, embrace and healing. How we deal with each other's theological claims will be decided along the way. The only demand is that we must be near each other, preferentially at the Eucharist/food offering table(s). What than, should we consider for a possible dialogical praxis?

Holy Spirit

Every beginning depends upon the Spirit, both for Candomblé and for Protestants. For Christian Reformed people, we cannot start anything if not first deeply moved by the Holy Spirit. Our acts of praise and work to God are always a response to God's love, generosity, and demand. For Candomblé, the Orixás and entities move the energies and make us respond to their calls and demands.

42. Ibid., 67.

For Reformed people, the emphasis on the Eucharist is not the table or the elements but rather the Christian assembly called by the Holy Spirit. At the table there is common food/common good and under the power of the Holy Spirit, we gather as strangers and become a family. At the table, we engage God's sources of power and healing that invite mutual conversation and transformation. Reformed people are able to say boldly that "Through 'eating Christ' in the meal, this community is strengthened and preserved in its task to be the body of Christ in and for the world. With these meanings foregrounded, the meal becomes a central symbol for this new community."[43]

A radical trust in the work of the Holy Spirit is issued so that the table of Jesus Christ becomes open, breaking down walls of self-enclosed religious membership and sameness. The presence of the Spirit at the table calls us to live radically in an egalitarian manner, sharing food, wisdom, resources, love, and care for the world. The table of Jesus Christ, empowered by the presence of the Holy Spirit, offers forgiveness, healing, and reconciliation, even if continuously interrupted by fear, hatred, anxiety, injustice, death, and the perils and conflicts of the world.

Since God is the one who manifests Godself where God wants, and makes a covenant with whomever God wants, we are the ones, inspired by the Holy Spirit, to create channels for God's grace to be experienced in ways that we may not yet have been able to experience. Here we are trying to find ways in which the covenant of God can be expanded and offer hospitality to people of other faiths. We are the ones who become channels of God's incarnation.

Around the table, Christians have their Bibles, their food, their songs, and their prayers praying "Come Spirit Come." However, in this dangerous prayer, the coming of the Spirit can become the coming of a stranger, a guest, one whom we were not expecting or even desiring. Once we pray "Come Spirit Come," the move of the Spirit cannot be controlled any longer. Perhaps, after our prayer we might have to welcome Candomblé people dressed in their white dresses, dancing and singing, asking for the Orixás to come and move energies through the primal energy Axé.[44] Once the Holy Spirit takes over, we must follow. At the table, we share

43. Presbyterian Church (USA).

44. "Axé is the primal force, life principle, sacred force of the Orixás . . . is power, is charisma, it is the root that comes from the ancestors; we can gain and lose Axé, Axé is a gift from the gods . . . it is above all, the very house of the Candomblé, the temple, the roça (place where you plant for your family) the whole tradition" (Prandi, *Os Candomblés de São Paulo*, 103–4).

food and struggle together to find balance in the life of individuals, of our communities, and of the world.

The Holy Spirit and the Axé are the moving forces that establish, shift, and balance the world and all of our respective universes. The Holy Spirit and Axé can transform whatever it wants and are the very source of life. Christians and Yorubá people are totally dependent on their movement and they are the sources we tap into so that we can engage each other around the table and become able to expand our religious horizons.

The engagement with Axé and Holy Spirit can become a vital theological response to the globalized world we live in. The increasing sense of dislocation marked by the growing flow of people around the globe, the hybridity of immigration, the accumulation of capital in the hands of less than 500 people around the world, the trafficking of people, the brutality against women, the shifting markets of labor, and the growing new diverse local neighborhoods are just some of the signs that demand our theologies and communities to deal with the constant flow of identities and "mobile personalities."[45] The force, potency and agency of the Holy Spirit/Axé can help us engage challenges and dismantle deadly world realities.

The Holy Spirit/Axé can also help us find plural identities not in the de-ritualizing of our religion's rituals but rather, in the renewing processes of the ritualization (the expansion of our rituals) of our beliefs as we encounter others along the way. In a lecture given at Union Theological Seminary after the beginning of the Iraq war, Professor Janet R. Walton asked us: "Would your service be the same if a person from Iraq enters our churches?" For some people, this question must be answered immediately with a "No," since what we do is who we are and we cannot change who we are. Nonetheless, if we could entertain the possibility of a "Yes," we would need to change our worship. We can become better with the presence of an other who talks about his/her own experiences and we can start attending to the words and gestures we use in our communities. If a person from Iraq is with us, we can learn about ourselves and wrestle with ways to live out our faith in more expansive, powerful, and welcoming ways. This attention to someone else does not mean to silence ourselves or to shy away from who we are or what we believe, but rather the presence of another can be an opportunity to expand who we are. The Scottish Council of Churches said: "We become human through our relationships—with ourselves, others, creation, and God. Reformed spirituality is first and foremost about being grounded in what holds us in common with one

---

45. Betcher, "Take My Yoga upon You," 58.

another and grounded in what it means to be human." While concerned with Christian unity, this message can be of help us to broaden our own liturgies and theologies as well as help us embrace those who differ from us in large or small ways.

The Spirit of God shows itself through movements of unfolding, openness and alterity, movements marked by dis-placements of generosities. The Spirit of God must be seen in my responsibility to myself, but always in relation to some-body else, even if this some-body-else throws me at an abyss of inescapable inner and outer workings and challenges. The presence of *some-body-else* at the table of Jesus Christ connects me to unexpected obligations towards this other and that person's people, a people that I might not have paid attention to until that moment. Thus, the movement of the Spirit in us can be a call to us to pay attention to some-body-else.

From this place of unexpected openness given by the Spirit, Christians can find a common ground to welcome Candomblé people. There are common elements for a theology of the Spirit in Christianity and Candomblé. Some of them are: 1) the Holy Spirit/Axé have a deep connection with the body and without our bodies there is no community. In both religions the Spirit/Orixás can possess bodies; 2) The Holy Spirit and the Axé/Orixás help us not only deal with our daily life, our struggles, our wounds, but also give us strength, wisdom, and vision to go through life; 3) The Holy Spirit/Axé always make us engage with a guest or visitor; 4) The Holy Spirit/Axé are deeply connected with creation; 5) It is the Holy Spirit/Axé who create and sustain the gathered communities; and 6) The manifestation of the presence of the Holy Spirit/Axé is both worship and work.

In Candomblé, the relation between the Spirit and human bodies is seen in the possessions that occur during the public and private festivities, when the Orixás choose some of the initiated people in order to "ride" on their bodies as if the Orixás were *mounting on horses.* Believers become horses of the entities. In Christian communities, prayer for the Holy Spirit to come and take our bodies, and control our minds, mouth, and gestures are common. The surrendering to the Holy Spirit is something that Christians search for while worshiping God. In Pentecostal churches, bodies are literally taken and they shake, dance, move, and are at the mercy of the leading of the Holy Spirit. The possession of bodies seen in both Pentecostal Christian and Yorubá gatherings have almost the same body postures, gesturing, and general movements.

Candomblé and Christian believers pray for the Holy Spirit and entities for guidance and wisdom in their daily lives. They bless the Spirit, they walk in their daily life in ways pleasing to the Holy Spirit/Entities. Both religions have a deep commitment to the transformation of society through their beliefs and practices. For both religions, God is always doing something through us. Or, using J. Edgar Bruns words, "God is the doing of something"[46] in our religions.

It is in, under, through, and around the Spirit/entities in our diverse bodies and rituals that we can re-create our daily and common life within and among ourselves. In both religions, God/Orixás are doing something in and through us and we are also doing something in and through our liturgies/worship recreating the world, recreating life. As Maraschin says, "It is in the body that we are spirit especially when our bodies are ready to recreate life. Let us, then, make of our bodies our main instrument of worship."[47] Open to the unknown movements of the Spirit and the Axé, we move along together.

Being at the Table

The gathering of Candomblé and Christian people around the Eucharistic table can issue a powerful call to that part of Brazilian culture which hates and fears Candomblé, which continues to demonize them as a "Godly" way to destroy them. Gathering together and sharing each other's food is a way of offering a version of the Christian gospel that is committed to keeping each other alive, in love and care, with the right to live and share faith fully. This is a gospel that continues to require us to love, day and night, God and our neighbors, no matter what faith these neighbors profess and live.

Each community will be open to the Spirit and to the calls both going around the table and inside their minds and hearts. Baptism will always be a call to the Candomblé people to engage more fully in the Christian faith. And the Orixás will also invite Christians to "make their head," which is the initiation ritual to become a Candomblé believer. These calls should never be understood as threats but as loving offerings of our best to our friends, as circular movements of the Spirit/Orixás to each other to expand our hearts and minds. And each one of us will decide what to do. Then, the words of institution or Christian prayers and songs will be carefully and

---

46. Cited by Betcher, "Take My Yoga upon You," 72.
47. Maraschin, "Transient Body."

powerfully said/sung as will as the sacred words and songs of Candomblé spoken by the Babalorixás and Yalorixás.

For the Candomblé people, the ability to make their own theological claims freely at such a central Christian event can represent a Christian request for forgiveness, a historical restitution of the Candomblé's own worthiness, as well as the undoing of the historical stereotype of Candomblé people as the Devil's presence in Brazil. For Christians, the Devil has no place at the table of God, and it is always undone there by claims of truth, life, justice, and hope. By being at Jesus' table offering gifts to the Orixás, Candomblé people and Candomblé theological beliefs gain a new and privileged place, both religiously and culturally, expelling a complex misunderstanding and demonization of their faith within the Christian circles and the larger culture, because at the Jesus' table, they are deeply honored by those who worship the God of Christianity.

Eucharist and Food Offerings

Part of this mutual knowledge has to do with our respective understandings of food and of how we should engage each other through our sacred food. Most religious discourses around food have to do with the delimitations of others and ourselves. Food establishes the distinctiveness of our faith and creates boundaries that can present mixture and impurity or, in other words, to impede some relationships from occurring. Notions of foreignness and otherness are very explicit in the inner definitions of sacred food and we must pay attention to it.[48] In 1 Corinthians 8:1–13, the Apostle Paul discussed eating food sacrificed to idols. He argued that the freedom we receive from God does not prevent us from eating that kind of food. As we grow into knowledge of God's freedom, we slowly lose our fear to face the difficulties involved in accepting food that is marked as beyond our customs or religious regulations. Thus, we must be careful with those in both Christian and other communities, who cannot understand this freedom and prefer the freedom of sticking to their norms. Each community should discuss these regulations and delve into the reasons of their own and other's belief system's regarding food and identity. As Paul said, "food will not bring us close to God,"[49] but certainly, it can bring us closer to each other. God's call to us comes before our gathering, laying down the very ground for our gathering and demanding that we figure out how

48. For a fascinating work on this topic, see Freidenreich, *Foreigners and Their Food*.

49. 1 Cor 8:8.

this love should be lived, through practice. Once we have welcomed each other to our common tables/ground, we can start to lose the fear that the other re-presents to us.

As the apostle Peter received God's command to eat everything he saw, we are also commanded to be open to attend to our neighbor's food through and beyond our regulations: "The voice said to Peter again, a second time, 'What God has made clean, you must not call profane.'"[50] If Paul tells us to be open, Peter's dreams show God demanding him to eat. How can we move around Paul to Peter as we ponder about the precious food of Candomblé? An honest conversation between these two communities will help us dispel the notion that Candomblé people eat food prepared for the Devil. To be religious-interreligious is not only to deal with intellectual religious differences but also to eat one another's food. The aphorism "we are what we eat" is especially true with regards to religion and to being religious-interreligious life. Moreover, we *become* what we eat and it is precisely because of that possibility of *becoming* that people of saint and Christians need to eat together: to establish connections of love and care, to dispel hatred, to recreate Brazil into a more welcoming religiously diverse country. At the end, as Paul again said, "love builds up."[51]

Eating together has to do with creating love, building community, sharing memories, and acceptance of the other as God's gift to me. As we gather together we start to see the theological as well as the social, political, and cultural possibilities that this gathering, this eating together, can create among our people. I believe that a whole new chapter in Brazil's history would be inaugurated. Forgiveness and reconciliation would be worked out not by state authority as in South Africa, but by two religious groups showing themselves to each other, finding ways of mutual reconciliation, asking for ongoing forgiveness, engaging our cordial racism, and learning to honor each other's faith.

Since the central questions of this book asks how the borders of the eucharist might be negotiated so that other people who are not used to being part of it can participate, we believe that occasions of generosity are possible for these different peoples of faith. When we start the conversation, Babalorixá Aragão tells me that we need to return to the original Eucharist which was a meal, a whole meal. As a former Roman Catholic seminarian he knows well what he is talking about. Christian meals at the beginning were not about the blood and flesh of Christ but about memory.

50. Acts 10:15.
51. 1 Cor 8:1.

He says: "God makes Godself food, food for the community. It is not the mythic element that counts at the beginning of the meal, but the way that Christ chooses to be remembered. From all of the possible ways that the disciples can use to remember Jesus, they choose the sharing of the bread. The most divine part of Jesus, the most powerful moment that Jesus manifested as a Messiah, as a divine being was his sharing and his sharing of a meal. Later on, it was around a meal that they remembered Jesus stories. The most original Christianity, the most charismatic, the most Pentecostal is exactly it: the sharing of bread and life."

In Candomblé however, there is not the same type of remembrance that Christians have of Jesus Christ, since the entity is there, present at the service. For Candomblé, the presence of the entities does not point back to a primal event, as Christians do with the Last Supper in the Upper Room. However, the possibility of the presence of the entities and the presence of Christ in a worship service where there is sharing of food is a common theological aspect for both religions.

The blood and sacrifice in Candomblé, the slaughter of the animals has to do with the scapegoat, can be compared to the Jewish Day of Atonement, when a goat was offered to cover people's sins. In Candomblé, the animal is offered for the sake of the community and in this process, the animal has to want to offer itself to the community. If the animal doesn't eat the leaves it is given, it is not ready to offer itself and the celebration can only happen when the animal offers itself to bless the community. This ritual is important because it keeps the energy flowing and moving, and it continues the encircling of the relations humans and animals and entities have. Animals are messengers to the entities and they serve as connections.

Babalorixá Aragão reminds me that Africans do not have problems with blood. It is not dirty or impure as some of us believe. Everything is sacred in the African worldview. Blood is food and a precious food, the best offering we have. When the animal dies, he transfers the energy of the blood to the stones and reinforces the connection between the entities. Blood is a channel for deep communion, energy that gives life to the relation between animal-entities-community. In this process, the interconnectedness of life is assumed, the inter-related participation deeply connected with honor and respect. Each sacrifice is done with care, devotion, libations, ritual objects properly consecrated, and follows a ritual order.

Each entity has some kind of food prohibition. There are two types of food: dry (grains) and wet (blood) food. Food offerings are offered to the Orixás and are eaten by the initiated. The food that is offered and is not eaten is given to nature: to the river, sea, or earth, where the entities live, encircling the movement of life. We can offer our simple food and the Orixá will receive it. The places prepared for Orixás at terreiros called *assentamentos* and these places have a heightened sense of the sacred. We could say that these *assentamentos* do not symbolize the Orixás but instead, they *are* the Orixás. In the same way, the bread and blood in the Eucharist for Catholics do not symbolize the Eucharist but *are* the Eucharist. The Christian God is present in the bread and the wine, and in the Candomblé, the stone, the house, the place prepared for the Orixás are *assentamento*, are the Orixás. For instance, the bowl and the food that are offered to the Orixá are not containers of the Orixá but are the Orixás themselves.

Expanding Each Other's Faith, Practices and Theologies through Commensality

Food and drink are precious liturgical-theological elements in the life of these two communities. Both celebrate God's creation and providence. The entire cosmogony of Candomblé is grounded on the meaning and importance of earth. God and Orixás are deeply related to the earth and herbs, plants, food, drink, etc, all things from the earth, do the connections between this and the outer world. Moreover, the elements that mark the liturgical objects and worship in Candomblé all come from nature. Both rituals need food and they have deep connections with creation, ecology and can only be sustainable if understood as part of a larger eco-system where life is lived at the table and on the floor, in gatherings, and in rivers and forests, in the air, and in every part of God's creation. Together, we can fight for our common good, the ecosystems and the biodiversity which is a powerful way of working for peace.

The sacredness of these worshiping events is a common mark in both religions. Through this food, God is manifested through Jesus/Holy Spirit, and Olodumarê through the many Orixás and other entities. The doing of the sacrament of Eucharist is a way of worshiping God by obeying God's command to do this in memory of Jesus Christ. As for Candomblé, food offerings are carrying out promises and works of praise to please the Orixás so they will continue to bless the lives of the community.

It is interesting to see how women are at the center of the preparation of these sacred foods. The worship can happen only if the food is properly prepared. I remember my mother preparing herself in order to prepare the food for the Eucharistic table. Jan Rudolph, s student of mine at Louisville Seminary, once mentioned in class how her African-American grand-mother used to literally iron all of the breads the day before Communion Sunday. In Bahia, I participated in a ceremony to the Orixá *Ogum* and the women carefully prepared the food many days before. Good and well prepared food and drink are keys to making the festivities efficacious.

Both the Eucharist and the Candomblé worship are rites of passage and political acts. Historically, while in Brazil we can say that the Eucha-rist, since it was attached to the powers that be, it was more attuned to a rite of imperial reinforcement, in Candomblé, the food offerings were liturgical acts of resistance and resilience. In any circumstance, both ritu-als enact ongoing passages in the life of the individual, larger community, and the country.

Christian Eucharist is grounded in the ecclesial understanding of a cloud of witness that surrounds this community of faith. The presence of the ancestors can also be related to the presence of Christ in history. As for Candomblé, the belief in the ancestry offers the assurance that this community of believers is continuously empowered by the presence of the ancestors who have prepared the way for them. Both religions can share these commonalities of their cloud of witness and ancestry.

Eucharist is celebrated around the table and food offerings are done around a table or on the floor. For Christians from Reformed traditions, the table reminds them of the place that Jesus had the last supper with his disciples. For Candomblé people food on the ground emphasizes the deep relation of the food with the earth, and to those places of nature that are related to each Orixá. The sharing of each one's food around the table and on the floor can be a powerful way to engage each other rituals and experience the differences and commonalities between their rituals.

At the common table/floor Christians will have their sacred book, the Bible, and the Yorubá people will have their oral culture. Each group can share their stories of faith and transformation in different ways.

Candomblé has way more theological connections with the Eucharist where the Eucharist is understood as a sacrifice, as in the Roman Catholic Church. The shedding of blood and the expiatory event of Jesus can be related to the animals sacrificed in Candomblé. If the Christian sacrifice brings forgiveness, the Candomblé sacrifice brings protection. Some Protestant understandings of Jesus' death as a ransom can also relate to the animal slaughter and food offerings that honor/pay/negotiate with the Orixás.

Perhaps, Candomblé people can teach Christians how to engage more deeply with the cooking and the relation between food, preparation, and the sources of its food. Candomblé people can also help Christians to have a sense of commensality around sacred foods. The food offerings are always plentiful in worship services and are offered not only to the Orixás but also to the community. For Reformed people, the Eucharist is not often thought of as an open table with enough real food for all. Instead, it is a reminder of a full meal, a memory of a feast and not necessarily a joyful celebration. People don't actually eat the food from the Eucharistic table but join in sharing a meager piece of bread and a tiny sip of wine/grape juice. Perhaps Candomblé people could learn with Reformed people about the Protestant principle that confronts power, hierarchical unbalanced religious structures, and works for social change.

At the end of our conversation I blatantly asked Babalorixá Aragão if it is possible to place food for the Orixá at the Eucharistic table/altar. And he answered with a loud, "Yes!" and continued: "We gather the food of our extended family and everything belongs to God. Or better said, is not everything God?" Aragão's answer affirms the conditions of the possibilities for this dialogue, connections and relationships.

Learning with Christian Ancestors—Holy Kiss as a Liturgical Practice to Be Engaged in Inter-Religious Praxis

In this rehearsal for a possible future for our societies and religions, I call upon the early Christians and their liturgical gesture of holy kissing to help us engage in this relationship-dialogical praxis. Kissing is a common practice in many religions and I am not claiming that Christians invented the holy kiss. Instead, the idea here is to learn about the liturgical kissing from the early Christian practices and how it can enhance our own religious communal living. The holy kiss from the early Christian churches is one that combined the liturgical gesture of getting close to each other, the sharing of the breath/presence of the Spirit, and the eating together and the negotiation of social structures. The holy kiss was a practice that wove together several layers of life. Paul and Peter will write to different communities to kiss with a holy kiss and a kiss of love. (Romans 16:16 and 1 Peter 5:14).

Early Christian scholar Michael Penn says that in this gesturing, "Family, spirit, reconciliation—seemingly abstract concepts—the kiss transformed these into embodied actions." For the Greco-Roman world, any gesture in public space was an "exercise of power . . . the exchange of the ritual kiss (should be viewed) as praxis—the combination of interpretation and action . . . the kiss was not just an object of discussion, but also a physical action."[52] This liturgical embodied gesture can help us go from the secure mode of inter-religious dialogue to the more scary space of praxis.

More than that, the ritual kiss became a way of life, a connection between faith and familial kinship, a social bond. For a brief moment, the ritual of kissing each other would break the class boundaries and social status, the insurmountable divisions that were existent in that society. Michael Penn writes about the ritual of kiss as social bound and community building that has similarities with our inter-religious dialogical praxis. While he is writing about the Christian communities, one can say that the blurring of boundaries during that time can be correlated with the blurring of social and religious boundaries of our time. He says:

> First, the familial connotations of the Greco-Roman kiss help portray the Christian community as family. Second, its connections with spiritual exchange emphasizes community member's pneumatological bond to each other. Third, especially as the kiss moved from a seal of prayer to part of the Eucharist service, Christian leaders attempted to decrease internal tensions by

52. Penn, *Kissing Christians*, 15, 35, 50.

fashioning the kiss into a reconciliation ritual. Finally, the kiss as a physical action uniting two individuals was correlated with the creation of a unified body.[53]

Expanding on these reasons, we could say that liturgical kiss can enable us to expand the idea of family beyond the boundaries of Christian beliefs. As Philip Penn notes, "the parameters of kissing could be expanded regularly to include nonfamily members, or those whom one kissed during Christian rituals could be redefined as family."[54]

Second, since the kiss emphasizes the connectivity through the breath, the belief that one would share one's very soul to another through the kissing, we can also say that the pneumatological presence of the Holy Spirit/Axé can be our common sharing, the offering of our best gifts. In this offering to each other what we have as the most precious, we can engage our bonds of affection and belonging to each other through the exchange of our kisses. To kiss is to draw one's heart into somebody else's, it is to receive his/her breath, his/her very life into my body. To kiss somebody is to establish a bond of peace and I cannot withdraw my body and myself from this person anymore. I am bonded to this person now. That is why a kiss might be a scary gesture, especially when we are trying not to interfere in each other's lives and being civilized and respectful in this a individualistic culture. The "spirit" of our culture is a spirit that does not want to share, to exchange, to live together. The promise and hope of the exchange of the Spirit is what these religions can offer to the Brazilian culture and to the world. The holy kiss is a collective practice that goes against the tide, one that perhaps can challenge this narcissistic culture that pushes people into withdrawing from one another.

Third, the holy kiss as a bond, a gesture of deep commitment, of forgiveness, a familiar gesture of affection, an affirmation of belonging, an act of love, social and communal love. That is why it was done first during the Eucharist. Penn reminds us "the ritual kiss can unite the participant's souls and cause individuals to forgive any wrongs."[55] There is a powerful event happening when we kiss each other. John Chrysostom wrote: "The kiss is given so that it may be the fuel of love, so that we may kindle the disposition, so that we may love each other as brothers [love] brothers, as children [love] parents, as parents [love] children. But also far greater,

53. Ibid., 8.
54. Ibid., 36.
55. Ibid., 42.

because those are by nature, these by grace. Thus our souls are bound to each other."[56]

Finally, The holy kiss is a liturgical gesture that connects individual bodies to a larger body, the social body that we might call the body of God. Michael Penn says that, "several early Christian writers connected the kiss, spiritual exchange and group cohesion."[57] When I kiss somebody, I give this person a part of myself that only this person will know. Moreover, I offer to this person my social group; I open the entrance door for the other to be part of my family and life. Thus, through the participation of several groups of affection and social connections, we become responsible for each other. When we do it in an inter-religious dynamic, the radical other changes its status: from a threat, the Candomblé people become a blessing to me, a help for my Christian living in society, an assurance of larger double belonging, an expansion of my soul, a respectful touch in my body, a gift to my faith, and vice versa.

REFORMED/CANDOMBLÉ PEOPLE EATING TOGETHER— A PRACTICAL ITINERARY

If Christianity works around the spiritualization of the body through acts of sanctity such as Eucharist, penitence, fasting, privation, etc; Afro-religions work around the embodiment of the spirit through the coming of the entities that possess the bodies and dance, eat, celebrate, talk, laugh, etc. These different forms of movement around the sacred are both a challenge and a blessing and must be considered as we plan this dialogical-praxis.

Both religions have embraced foreign elements into their structures of faith and practices, adapting themselves to their surroundings through different processes. Neither Christianity nor Candomblé is a pure, autonomous, culture free, and homogeneous religion. Moreover, it was the presence of each other that ended up defining their ways of being in Brazil. After living together for almost five hundred years, offering an open table to share the Eucharistic food with Candomblé brothers and sisters and having Christians eat at a Candomblé festivity should not be a strange move or an act of infidelity from both parts but instead, a mutual offering of a blessing and a gift.

---

56. Chrysostom, *In epistulam II ad Corinthios* 30.2, cited in Penn, *Kissing Christians*, 34.

57. Penn, *Kissing Christians*, 39.

This movement of mutually pursuing each other must be carefully crafted and created according to the conditions of possibilities that this impossible gathering might be. The itinerary has to be done by the two communities once they have established a bond of trust and accepted that this dialogue/engagement entails a great amount of vulnerability. Christians should be reminded by what Paul Knitter said: "to be loyal to Christ, one must be vulnerable to others."[58]

As we ponder about possibilities of dialogue and life together, we must consider strategies that come up from practice through and across the folding of differences. Starting points, movements of the sacred, and end results are completely different. What can we learn from each other? Around the relation spirit/body body/spirit, we can expand the possibilities and understandings, practices and of faith.

In order for this dialogue to happen, a lot of misunderstanding will happen. Our theological work is to help each other undo, as much as we can, these misunderstandings, knowing however, that the incommensurability of each religion will always remind us of this impossible dialogue.

From the Reformed tradition's perspectives, this impossible dialogue must carry that aspect of the *Protestant principle* which is to call into question any and every aspect of the Christian faith so it does not run the risk of becoming an idolatrous worshiping community and continue the perpetual movement "to be" reformed: *ecclesia reformata semper reformanda.*

Her daughter became very ill. She asked the pastor and her beloved Presbyterian church to pray for her daughter. Everybody did but her daughter continued to be seriously ill. She went to the doctors and after many opinions nobody knew what to do with her daughter. Out of utter despair she brought Diane to a Candomblé terreiro and to a mother-of-saint. Her heart was beating so hard in her chest she had trouble breathing. At the terreiro, the mother-of-saint asked her to do a couple things and she did. In one week her daughter was healed. After she received the blessing, she started to feel guilt. All of her life she had been taught that Candomblé was being a place for the Devil. She began to wonder whether it was the Devil himself who healed her and now she belongs to the Devil. She got so scared that she went to her Presbyterian pastor and told him in a confessional mode how she had sinned and now needed to be converted and ask God's forgiveness, even if the price to be paid would

---

58. Knitter, *Introducing Theologies of Religions,* 209.

> be her daughter's getting deadly ill again. *The pastor had learned about the sovereignty of God and God's providence in Calvin and said to her: "Sister, God's love and care go beyond the boundaries of church limits or religious walls. God can act wherever God wants, the Spirit of God is free to do what pleases God. God's Spirit also breaks rules and does what we don't want or allow God to do. Perhaps in this case we must trust that the sovereignty and love and provision for you and Diane is such that God decided to heal Diane in a very different way. We believe that God loves Diane, right? So even if we don't understand, we will thank God for God's love and for our brothers and sisters from Candomblé who were a true blessing to you and Diane. Would you pray with me? Let us fill our hearts with gratitude and lift up our hearts to God. And after the prayer she rejoiced leaving the church in tears holding her baby healed and beloved by God who moves and acts in very wonderful ways.*

This itinerary imagines God coming after, as after us helping us to get together, but coming after as showing up later, after we have gone through the hardships of a possible dialogue and engagement. Concrete steps might attend to the following: first, we visit each other's sacred spaces to see each other in our own worship services. Then, we gather to eat a common non-religious meal together and bring about questions on our practices thus initiating the conversation. For this gathering we start by greeting each other and kissing each other's cheeks. Then, when we eat together. Before we eat, the Yorubá people explain why and how they do what they do, especially their food offerings. Then Christians explain why they do what they do and explain the Eucharist. Both show each other what is at stake in their celebrations and the living of their faith. Then we decide what we can or cannot do/eat together for now and try to formulate possibilities within these fundamentally different rituals. Then we go back again to each other's worship services and try to participate as we are allowed. Songs, prayers and passing of the loving kiss of peace are shared. Then we eat again and we bring the elements of our celebrations to show people how we do it. Then we allow those who want to take a step further to participate at each other's tables. We start with the hospitality of the Eucharistic table, writing a Eucharistic prayer that welcomes our brothers and sisters from Candomblé and evoke Axé and the powerful history of Candomblé in Brazil to make who we are. As we continue, the next time at a Eucharistic table, Candomblé people are invited to talk and bring foods offered to the Orixás. Every time we celebrate the Eucharist we eat a whole meal at the table.

Within this process asking questions is fundamental: Besides the questions about practices we, as Christians, must engage questions regarding our own involvement and mutual knowledge: 1) If we are to eat together how should we do it? 2) If I participate in the Yorubá meal, what and how will this participation change in my own view and practice of the Christian Eucharist? 3) What might the Yorubá meal change in my own understanding of community, resistance, memory, ancestry, commensality, thanksgiving, possession of the Spirit? 4) Can we share prayers and songs together? 5) What is community for me as a Christian after that experience? 6) What is the memory process here and how does it affect my own understanding of memory here? 7) As a Christian, if I participate in the Yorubá meal, what does this participation change in the Christian Eucharist? 8) What does the Yorubá meal/food offering change in my own understanding of memory, of resistance, of community? 9) What is the sharing of the meal invested with? 10) What are the theological aspects of it? Learning form religious others engages our total being. Emotions, feelings, body, mind, and spirit are all intertwined in this process. How can we be informed and re-formed in this bodily engagement?

In this process, we might educate each other by teaching each other about the history of our faith and practices. Both communities could search the history of Christianity/African Religions in Brazil, face the "cordial racism" in the Brazilian culture, and find places where connections between Christianity and Candomblé were not only about destruction but also about help, protection, and mutual care. In other words, look for ways in which reality supplanted what the official rhetoric proposed and how Africans, Europeans, and indigenous people constructed small harmonies and communal experiences. *Zumbi dos Palmares* can be a beginning. What were the accommodations made between Christianity and Candomblé? Find where the connections, symmetries, commonalities and sound parallels were and are. As a theological process, a more socially and historically oriented research could be done to foment a solid theological ground.

We are feeding each other here not only because we are morally obligated to do so. We are gathering together and feeding each other because we must create not only a possible new world but a necessary one, one that will expand our possibilities and make our lives and our country bigger and better for us and for the future generations. We are feeding each other because we must heal the wounds of our common history, and turn to each other in respect and honor. We are learning and practicing and gathering because it is God's demand that we love and care for each other. We are eating together around our tables/floors because we are offering a radical hospitality to each other and this hospitality can only come if we are bounded by the Spirit.

CONCLUSION

It is impossible to offer a lucid and honest introduction to Candomblé in these pages. However, the idea here is for us to have a glimpse of this religion so we can honor the people of the Candomblé and start to think why such inter-religious dialogical praxis is not only possible but truly necessary.

Symbiosis and phagocytosis can be key theological elements to be developed in this dialogue. Also the notion of ritualizing/*ritualization* as proposed by Catherine Bell and Ronald Grimmes and explained in the next chapter, is also an important element of this dialogue as we welcome each other into our rituals and invent other common rituals to enhance our dialogue and mutual care. We have also learned from ritual theorist Jonathan Z. Smith that rituals are also forms of engagement with that which we hope to see happening. When we create our rituals, we are struggling between the reality we live, the reality we strive for, and the reality we want to see happening. In this inter-religious dialogical liturgical praxis, we also struggle between a reality that puts these two religious groups at odds and a reality that sees them eating, drinking, praying, and dancing together.[59]

As we are able to explore some of the history of slavery and Yorubá religion and raise new challenges related to the so-called Brazilian religious diversity and its "cordial racism," also engage the hospitality of the Eucharistic table and the sharing of a holy kiss, we can find a common space to transform this history and break down historical alienation and religious hatred. The hope continues as we try to foster dialogue and rituals between Candomblé and Christianity as a way to stop violence, engage in deep appreciation of each other's religious choices and enable each other to be fully human in and through our deepest religious callings.

At the end, we must remember that our commitment is grounded in love. Marcelo Barros reminds us once again:

59. "Ritual is a means of performing the way things ought to be in conscious tension to the way things are" (Smith, *To Take Place,* 43).

Evidently, every spiritual path is an itinerary of love and cannot be explained intellectually. It is a mystagogy. It is a mystery that can only be explained through an intimate relation of life . . . We can be lovers that offer ourselves to serve. From what is divine, there is title of property. Access is free to all to search what makes our hearts alive. No mortal can tame the wild wind. Mystery is our peace and the religious paths, our parables of love.[60]

And as Ivone Gebara says,

the question of pluralism invites us, again, to the thinking, to the proximity to wisdom, to the friendship with the different, with those who are close by and afar as expressions of this amazing complexity of life. And that is the same for our theologies, because, at the end, its certainties have to do with the weak, uncertain, plural and always renewable trust in this love that sustains us: "Where there is love, God will be there . . . "[61]

So this love lived around food and communities. Christians and Candomblé people creating a space of care, love, and welcome that currently does not exist in society. A place where people are what they hope to be, where their identities are forged, developed, transformed. Like the early Christian churches or the Quilombo dos Palmares. A place to be not what society wants us to be necessarily but a place for free exploration of one's hopes, beliefs, and dreams. Spaces where respect and protection are intrinsic and where we reimagine our lives and our world. A space to dance samba and sing hymns and Yorubá songs. A rather impossible space for sure. However, we will never know if that is possible or not if we don't try, practically, moving towards one another.

60. Barros, "Multipla Pertença," 60.
61. Gebara, "Pluralismo Religioso," 298.

7

Performing Hospitable Eucharistic Borderless Borders

Living with the world at heart.

—MARTIN HEIDEGGER

To tolerate the existence of another, and allow the other to be different
is still very little. To offer toleration is only to concede, and this is not a
relationship of equality, but superiority of one over the other.
We should create relationships between people that excludes
any sense of tolerance and intolerance.

—JOSÉ SARAMAGO

And I shall clothe myself in your eternal will, and by this light
I shall come to know that you, eternal Trinity,
are table and food and waiter for us.

—CATHERINE OF SIENA

Let all guests who arrive be received as Christ . . .
let all kindness be shown them.

—RULE OF SAINT BENEDICT

It was Easter day. The church was getting filled at 6 o'clock and there was incense around this church of indigenous people from Guatemala. People were gathering at the sanctuary and making conversation as they prepared for the service. Children were already running around playing with each other. The band got to their space and talking started to wind down. A man came to the microphone and said: "Buenos dias hermanas y hermanos. (Good morning brothers and sisters) We are here today very early in the morning to remember the day when the women went to Jesus' tomb just to find out that the tomb was empty. Alleluia! We are here at this Easter Sunday to celebrate that the tomb is empty, that the women saw Jesus resurrected and that Jesus had won out over death forever. Praise be to God!" He prayed and invited people to sing. After a time of singing hymns and coritos, people sat down and the pastor started to preach from the pulpit: "Hermanos y hermanas, in the midst of the life that Jesus gave to us, we must remember our brothers and sisters who died trying to cross the desert looking for a better life for their families. We must remember those who are still on their way, and from whom we no longer hear we must remember those who cannot come back and those who have no means to try a new life. We must remember the families that stayed here and are fractured by the absence of a mother, a father, a son, or going through illness without means to be treated. As we remember Jesus Christ, the way he passed from life to death and back to life again, the Passover is very important for us too. Because like the Hebrews in Egypt, who were trying to find a promised land, we are too trying to pass over the desert both ways to keep our families fed and alive. Sometimes the crossing of the desert for us is like the cross of Jesus Christ, crossing from death to life, being crossed by so many border fences, injustices, and with a high price to pay. The sacrifice of Jesus becomes our sacrifice as we also try to search for more just ways to live. Ai hermanos y hermanas, we all belong to Jesus, who crossed so many borders and distances, hatreds and antagonisms, self-righteousness and arrogance. In Jesus, a migrant himself, we understand ourselves. It is through his cross and the cross-ing over so many borders that his life, death, and resurrection entails that we understand our attempts to cross whatever prevents us from having a dignified life. Let us not forget that Easter was only possible because of Good Friday! So, if you are crossing the desert alone or with your family in the future, among bandits and robbers, rapists and drug dealers, don't forget that we must keep the promise of Easter and the hope of a new life! Let us pray for all of those who are passing/crossing over places and doing it for the love of their families. Let us pray that God gives them and us, crosser people, a promised land as well, be it here, in our pilgrimage or anywhere else . . ." He paused, took a breath, and said "Let us pray . . . As the church started to pray, the space was filled with loud prayers and soon, overflowing tears. For about an hour, people prayed alone, then together, then alone again, standing, shouting, jumping up and down, crying quietly on bent knees, supplicating God's mercy and favor towards them and their families. We could hear several people asking for children without fathers and mothers, and for those who were deported and had nothing else to do in their homeland; for kids who learned about gangs in the U.S., were deported to their countries, and started gangs as a way of belonging somewhere; for women raped and abused by coyotes (people who lead migrants across the border) and border patrol police along the desert . . . We could hear about split families, torn down by the lack of jobs, threatened by people who lend them money to cross the desert but had to come back home without any success, couples estranged by such a long time without seeing each other . . . The prayers made the building become heavy and after a while it started to slow down. As prayers started to lose intensity, people sat down and remained seated in the pews. A deep silence took over the worship space and the whole congregation didn't say a word or make a move . . . After what seemed to be a very long time, the pastor came to the Eucharistic table and helped by two women, uncovered the bread and the wine for the Eucharist. The pastor said: "Hermanos y hermanas, hay aqui alguno que quiera dar un testimonio? (Brothers and sisters, is there anybody here who wants to give a testimony?) People were so tired that very surprisingly, silence was kept intact. From the table the pastor continued: "Don't give up! God has given us life! God has provided for the journey. Look and see, we have food for the journey! Especially at this Easter day, as we eat and drink this food, we MUST remember and never forget that life is bigger than death! No matter what you or your family are going through, or where you might be in your pilgrimage, there is promise of life for you to keep going. Today is the Easter of our Lord Jesus Christ and because of Jesus, it is our own Easter as well! Like the women who went to the tomb, we are called to go there and see that our Lord is risen! Let us keep going brothers and sisters. We cannot stop or we will die before our time like so many of our people! Here at this table are the signs and the promises of our new life, life always renewed to us. Like Jesus with his disciples and friends, it is the eating and drinking together that help us continue our journey. Here we stop and renew our strength, here we stop and find rest, here we stop and gain new perspectives, here we stop and are reminded that we are not alone, that God almighty is with us and that the church of Jesus Christ, God's family is with us, here in Guatemala, in El Salvador, in Honduras, in Mexico and in Estados Unidos. As we are about to eat this bread and drink this wine, remember the powerful life and death and resurrection of Jesus Christ. Jesus fought against the injustices of his time and was killed. Now, in Jesus' memory, get your portion of strength and renewal and transformation and go back to the road trusting that God in Jesus, through the work of the Holy Spirit will walk with you, will be part of your pilgrimage and will give you a new Jerusalem, a promised land here and also when you die. See, we can still be thankful for God's love in our lives can't we? Let us do this: as you take a piece of this bread, give it to somebody else and receive it from somebody else as a gesture of our life together, of our dependence on each other, as a reminder that we are not alone and that is here in our midst through each other. And raising the bread he said, "On the night when Jesus had his last supper with his friends . . ." People started to share bread and wine and somebody gave them the idea to take the bread and wine to families who were suffering because of immigration author-ity. Various groups were divided right in the midst of the Eucharistic ceremony and they left the church with bread and wine and Bibles and visited about ten families. The Eucharist continued in these ten homes and from there, to other homes, healing the city from the wounds of loss, death, sadness and many other illnesses . . .[1]

THROUGHOUT THIS BOOK, THERE has been an attempt to link the safe li-turgical borders of the sacrament of the Eucharist to a larger world where life is always at risk. The hope is to expand Eucharistic practices and conse-quently spread and open the frontiers of the church in the world. The praxis and the idea are to go beyond the self-enclosed relation exemplified by J. M. R. Tillard: "The eucharist is explained by the church and the church is explained by the eucharist."[2] The hope is that the eucharist should be more visibly marked by the troubling global migration, by situations and places of death, oppression, poverty and disasters around the world, so that, the church and the eucharist could explain and be explained by the *lex agendi*,

1. Another version of the story can be found in Carvalhaes and Galbreath, "Season of Easter."

2. Tillard, *Carne de la iglesia, carne de Cristo,* 39

by the daily life of people, and by the movements of Jesus Christ around us. In other words, it is not only the Church that can explain the Eucharist and its practices and theories and vice versa. The ways in which we live in the world also explain the Eucharist and the Church. An example: when the Roman Catholic Church moves the altar to the borders and celebrates the Eucharist right at the wall, and the altar is then suddenly broken by the walls separating people from each country, the location, the wall, the unjust immigration, and the erection of a symbol of hatred explains the Eucharist that in turn, by its practices, prayers, and songs tries to undo the wall's power of death.[3]

Thus, this book is an attempt to move the borders of the eucharistic tables of Reformed and other churches to the margins of society and other unexpected places. We need to name, to have present, to engage more consciously with the *materiality* of oppressed people and oppressive systems. As mentioned in the introduction, the questions that have guided me in this process were: how do we connect the somewhat ordered world of the eucharistic sacrament to a terribly disordered world? How can the borders of the eucharist be openly marked by the markers of the world?

3. See the movie *One Border, One Body*, directed by John Carlos Frey: http://oneborderonebody.nd.edu/. Also, see here the liturgical guidelines and questions that implicate the Eucharist with our witnessing of Jesus Christ in the world regarding the migration issue: http://www.jfimn.org/One%20Border%20One%20Body%20Discussion%20Guide.pdf.

In what ways are we working as a people of God, practicing our Christian faith, from a liturgical space that is *tainted* by the blood, hunger, violence and exclusion of the world? On the other hand, how can we celebrate the Eucharistic ritual so we can live and work with the poor? As we negotiate the borders around the table we honor God and open up spaces for the unwanted, the disfranchised, the immigrant, and create visions of justice and practices of solidarity.

The connection between worship and the world happens in the double movement of the altar/table[4] to the world and from the world to the table. Unless these worlds start to consciously see their intrinsic relationship, how they belong to each other, and keep interacting and changing each other, the inherent dualism of the Christian discourse will not be undone and our offerings of hospitality will be lacking. One possible understanding and practice of this connection between the altar/table and the world is provided in this book.

In chapter 1 I set the conceptual framework of the book around the main issue of borders. I started showing how globalization, especially international migration, is deeply connected with liturgical spaces and how this interconnectedness challenges Christian churches to rethink Eucharistic hospitality. Since the notion of borders is intrinsically related to the idea of hospitality, I developed this notion in the thought of Jacques Derrida, and then coin the concept of *borderless borders* which becomes the main thread of the argument/practice. *Borderless borders* performs a collective way of creating borders to *live with* as we continue to undo these same borders with the developments and discoveries of our liturgical practices, our living and thinking the gospel together, and experience the injustices and claims of the world to us. In this Sisyphean process, we expand the limits of our borders searching for a radical hospitality.

Since I focus this book on the sacrament of the Eucharist in the Reformed tradition, in the second chapter I examined the theological and liturgical foundations of this sacrament as understood and practiced in the Presbyterian Church (U.S.A.). In order to do that I retrace the ways in which John Calvin dealt with the sacrament during the time of the Reformation in sixteenth-century Geneva. What one can see from that analysis is that the Presbyterian Church (U.S.A.) grounds the interpretation of the sacrament more on one side of Calvin, namely, order and discipline, and forgets a little the other side of Calvin, which has to do with sovereignty

---

4. And here I depart, however only conceptually, from the Roman Catholic *altar* in order to work more closely with the *table* of the Reformed churches.

and freedom of the Spirit. This unbalanced approach makes the church interpret the eucharistic table as a self-enclosed ritual, forgetting the heavy political tones that both constrained and determined the very theological and liturgical borders of the Eucharist during Calvin's time. In Calvin, the world and its structures of power were at the table being negotiated, stretched and challenged. For the Presbyterian Church (U.S.A.), the eucharistic table becomes a self-referentiated, liturgical event, having to do with *God alone*. The world, however, with its contingencies and impropriety, is often set apart from the table and its official worship book. The result is that the sacrament ends up dividing faith between the ordered sacred space, its proper doctrines, self-contained liturgical practices, *and* the disordered world outside. There is much of God acting in these liturgies and very little of humans acting and when we do act, it is only to receive properly (liturgical practices) what the right doctrine has decided to give to us.[5]

Because the Presbyterian Church (U.S.A.), like Calvin, has used the New Testament as its chief warrant for celebrating the Eucharist by linking the sacrament to Jesus' Last Supper, what I try to do in chapter 3 is to examine this claim of historical continuity by looking at more recent New Testament scholarship on the relationship between early Christian churches and the Greco-Roman banquet. One of the things that this study reveals is that, besides the impossibility of proving the historicity of the Lord's Supper, there is such a diversity of meal practices within the early churches that the link between the sacrament of the Eucharist and the historical event of Jesus' Last Supper is at least open to serious questions. Moreover, it opens up a vast array of ritual practices that can help us engage the Eucharistic sacrament in its aim to offer hospitality. Due to that, the second and third chapters serve to establish the conditions of the possibilities for a critical engagement with the normativity of the Christian eucharistic sacrament in general.

Chapters 4 and 5 show how two marginalized groups have dealt with the standardized and normative structure of the sacrament of the Eucharist. Chapter 4 engages the feminist liturgical movement in U.S. and

---

5. Moore-Keish, quoted earlier on, has ventured into this dichotomy and offered wonderful work around this divide. She challenges reformed believers for a more engaging participation in the Eucharistic ritual believing that people's participation in this ritual can effect transformation in the world. She says: "[R]ituals are about doing in the sense of affecting the world as a whole: presenting models for a different world and even changing social structures. Rituals can transform" (*Do This in Remembrance of Me*, 90).

shows how they challenged the notion of the sacrament through their own thinking and practices. It also shows how their liturgical and theological alternatives expanded and enriched the ways one can think about and practice the sacrament, and consequently, redefine the borders of hospitality. Chapter 5 deals with the difficult relation between poor communities and the official liturgical and sacramental theology of the Roman Catholic Church in Latin America. Leonardo Boff engages the power structures of the church by trying to *elevate* poor people's liturgical practices to a sacramental status. Notwithstanding, his mediating role did not do the job because the church never recognized the liturgical practices of the poor as truly a sacrament. Engulfed by the normativity of the proper, the notion of a sacrament developed by poor people never found expanded expression in the church. By being allowed to celebrate their worship services as a *quasi-sacrament*, poor people were placed under the table of the authority of the church, where the sacrament proper was to be protected. However, away from the official table, poor people create another church and another table, without proper ecclesial borders, where bonds of inclusion/ hospitality, usually not present at the official table, are present and alive. They challenge many borders of exclusion around the world. Their sacramental crumbs were fully theirs, and fully a Sacrament.

Chapter 6 ventured into uncharted waters. By trying to engage Christianity and an Afro-Brazilian religion called Candomblé through an examination of ritual practices with food, this inter-religious dialogical-praxis investigated the possibility of talking, eating, and even perhaps worshiping together as a way of showing the marks of honor, appreciation, joy, and blessing that can strengthen local communities. This mutual sharing around the Eucharistic table and food offering provides a way of undoing racism, of creating a path to forgiveness, dialogue, and of sharing of acts of love and hospitality. All of these chapters showed how understandings/ practices of the sacrament can put borders around practices of hospitality. By challenging theological and liturgical thought and practices, one can see that these conceptual borders can be troubled, pushed away, expanded, replaced, and enriched as they negotiate God and life itself around the table. In other words, no border is definitive. Inspired by the thinkers and practices demonstrated so far, I will now show possible ways to negotiate borders and how Reformed and perhaps other churches need to be challenged in their theological and liturgical understandings and practices so as to expand their eucharistic tables/borders towards the margins, towards an-other, towards especially the poor. In order to do that, the discussion follows in this order:

First, I will point to the liturgical order that structures Reformed worship as the main obstacle that cements its liturgical borders and denies requests for negotiation. I will show how the Presbyterian Church (U.S.A.) warrants its eucharistic ordo and practices in the commission given by Jesus in the gospels at the Last Supper, and how this warrant is challenged biblically and theologically by some New Testament scholarship. Thus, without warrants of assurance that a Last Supper was experienced, we can hopefully move beyond the rigidity of the form of the eucharist as structured around the words of institution and we might be able to open the ritual up to other practical and no less powerful eucharistic possibilities.

Second, I will show how the borders of the eucharistic tables in United States are already *tainted* by showing how the presence of non-documented immigrants are a strong presence even in their absence of the liturgical actions of the eucharistic celebration. Moreover, since this country acts like an empire, the Eucharistic table celebrated in this country runs the risk of stretching its imperial borders in many ways to the world at large.

Third, deeply influenced by my Brazilian upbringing and feminist liturgies, I show how the liturgical experience must consider the body as a central element, as a way to attend to personal experiences and stories as a global event, as well as to try to understand both the locus of a local community and the social structure of the larger society.

Fourth, I propose that the ritual practices of the sacraments of the Eucharist should be framed around *ritualization* and *ritualizing*. As I explain these words and locate eucharistic sacraments as installations, border crossing, and rites of passage, I develop ways in which local communities can create different Eucharistic liturgical practices and develop different forms of hospitality.

Throughout this process, I am looking for ways to help us renegotiate our liturgical and eucharistic borders, share power and find ways to provide a space for the marginalized, in an attempt to get at borderless borders Eucharists.

As I said before, this chapter does not intend to propose all the answers but to show some ways that we can expand the borders of the sacraments of Eucharists and try to construct, endlessly, a borderless borders liturgical space.

FROM BIBLICAL WARRANT AND FIXED ORDO
TO MULTICENTRIC EUCHARISTS

Much traditional liturgical scholarship infers from the earliest patterns of eucharistic meals that there was mainly one predominant meal pattern mirrored in the historical account of the Last Supper of Jesus with his disciples. Based on biblical accounts and "codified forms"[6] in posterior data, traditional liturgical studies have patterned early Christian liturgies and later "standardized liturgies"[7] with specific words and gestures that have been generally followed by many Christian churches.

However, as recent New Testament scholarship shows, the early Christian meals were more varied, and more complicated than that. It also demonstrated that the event of the Last Supper can hardly be uncritically accepted as historical and that the words of institution most probably were never spoken by Christ. Thus, this scholarship *re-values* the tradition by offering another view of the "center" of the tradition, first, by moving the eucharistic meal from a one meal format to a plurality of meal practices, and second, by challenging the historical event of the Last Supper and Jesus' words of institution.

As we saw in the second chapter, Calvin promoted various changes to the Eucharist, re-orienting the sacrament theologically and ritually, socially and politically. He invited people to the eucharistic table, the center of power at that time. People could be active participants in the Eucharist and the emphasis in eucharistic rituals shifted away from the celebrant and the elements on the table. To Calvin, no material element, human or non-human, can contain, and for that matter, "manage" God's presence. As a result neither the celebrant nor the eucharistic elements could hold the power to carry God's presence. The sinful situation of the world and the human predicament prevent God's presence from manifesting fully and completely anywhere and in anyone.

With this theological move, Calvin reoriented the presence of God away from the human or material element to the Holy Spirit amidst the Christian assembly. The Holy Spirit is the mediator between God and God's people. However, the Holy Spirit is not the sole warrantor of the sacrament.[8] Since the sacraments must carry the certainty of God's pres-

---

6. Smith and Taussig, *Many Tables*, 37.

7. Ibid.

8. "(Calvin) was hesitant to regard the Spirit's power as a permanent endowment immanent within the church life, for that might seem either to compromise God's freedom or to divinize the church as though it were simply 'identified' with God's

ence, Calvin relied on the Biblical narrative to assure the believer of the presence of God at the sacrament. The words of institution provided this assurance.[9] However, this assurance could not be attested, even by the saying of these words, if not moved and provided by the presence of the Holy Spirit in and through the Christian assembly.

His country was entrenched in civil war. After the colonizers took all they could, they left the country with such an unbalanced division of power that only a few years later, the two major ethnic groups were fighting each other. The smaller ethnic group decided to kill the rival group in order to gain power. They started to do an ethnic cleansing by going to every village in the country and mercilessly killing their rivals. In one of these villages, there was a pastor of a Protestant church. He was at church on that morning when people started to scream on the streets. He knew they were coming to kill them all. He decided to run to his home but he was impeded by his parishioners who said that they had already invaded his house and that he was going to die if he left the church. The better thing to do was to stay and hide in some corner of the church. After a few hours of waiting for the massacre to end, he finally left the church and went to his home. There, he found his wife and all seven of his children, from ages two to fifteen, murdered. They were killed by guns and machetes. He fainted and couldn't move. Somebody came to him and said that the rivals were coming back and that he had to run. He ran to the next village and asked the mayor to help him find a place to stay, but this man was co-opted by the other group and tried to kill him. He had to escape and kept running for hours until he arrived at a friend's house. They were foreign missionaries and were "safe" from the massacre. The missionaries told him they couldn't keep him there because they could be killed too. They told him to run to the banana fields and stay there for as long as he could. They said they would make contact with him. After three months living in the banana fields he was found by these friends who had made contact with the World Council of Churches. The Council brought him to Geneva. He was first placed

own activity and power" (Mitchell, "Sacrament," in Bradshaw, ed., *New Westminster Dictionary of Liturgy and Worship*, 414).

9. For Paul Galbreath, Calvin uses the Words of Institution for two reasons: first as a biblical argument to reduce the sacraments from seven to two; second, as a rationale for the sacramental occasion and not as an instrument that will produce anything; from personal conversations.

> *among an ecumenical group that was living in Bossey for a semester.*
> *He arrived and we were in silence. The love of God, the peace of Christ,*
> *and one meal after another, together, created our bonds of affection.*
> *From there he had to rediscover what his life would become, somewhere,*
> *somehow and the church was his only and last refuge.*

As mentioned earlier, Calvin had two main guidelines for his eucharistic re-orientation: biblical warrant and faithfulness to the ancient church. Thus, the eucharist gets its authenticity as a sacrament from the "words of institution" allegedly spoken by Jesus and registered in the Gospels and in Paul's epistle to the Corinthians. Even though these words do not have the power to enact God's presence, or make God present, they serve as warrants to attest to the link between the sacrament and Christ. This connection ends up assuring that the believer is in fact celebrating the sacrament of the eucharist. As Paul Galbreath, a Reformed liturgical theologian, says, Calvin "had to keep the Words of Institution in order to proof-text the rite—even while he reoriented the entire ritual action."[10]

However, the church was not necessarily endowed with the presence of God, the saying of the words of the gospel was not the sole warrantor, and the gathering of believers didn't make it the sacrament. It was the meeting of these elements that propitiated the possibilities, not the assurance, of the presence of God in people's lives through participation in the sacrament. Nonetheless, one can say that first, the efficacy of the sacrament comes from the Holy Spirit, who is the only "authority" to carry and manifest God's own presence in the sacrament; second, the sacrament has to manifest its authenticity by showing its embedded connection with the gospel, which serves as the warrant that authenticates the rite through the repetition of the words of institution taken from the New Testament; and third, that the assembly of Christians gathers to receive the movement of the Holy Spirit.

Since the gathering of baptized believers is a given for the worship of God, Reformed churches in general seem to have turned to the words of institution as *the* assurance of God's presence in the Eucharist. As was shown in the first chapter, the Presbyterian Church (U.S.A.) "Directory for Worship" bases its Eucharistic warrant on the New Testament historicity of the Last Supper celebrated by Jesus with his disciples.[11] While it is a

10. I am grateful to Paul for helping me frame this whole part; from personal conversations.

11. "Directory for Worship," W-2.4000 and W.2-4002.

very open document in regards to a variety of practices, it requires that the words of institution, "1 Cor. 11:23–26 or Gospel parallels"[12] be said at some point in the eucharistic celebration. Besides that, it requires a prayer, that the bread and the "fruit of the vine" are on the table, that the Bible is read and preached prior to eating and drinking, and that there are restrictions in the invitation to the table. "The invitation to the Lord's Supper is extended to all who have been baptized."[13] Moreover, the celebration of the sacrament can only be done when authorized by a governing body.[14] The *Directory for Worship* also affirms that "[f]or reasons of order the Sacrament of The Lord's Supper should be administered by a minister of the Word and Sacrament or commissioned lay pastor when invited by the session and authorized by the Presbytery."[15] In this strict sense the church preserved the notion of a proper celebrant and a proper sacrament.

While the *Directory of Worship* has both a baptismal language to fence the Eucharist, and the words of institution to warrant the sacrament, the rubrics of the *Book of Common Worship* (BCW), never directly invoke the language of baptism and only one of the four invitations uses specific language, "Our Savior invites those who trust him to share the feast which he has prepared,"[16] while the other three invitations simply avoid it altogether. However, the use of the words of institution is a must, and has to be said at some point in the Eucharistic prayer.[17]

A recent official study document called "Invitation to Christ," takes a significant and considerable step forward when it affirms the multiplicity of the eucharistic meals by the early church, claiming the plurality of meals and relaxing the baptismal language that tightens the borders around the table. It says: "Regarding whether or not the unbaptized might commune at the Lord's Supper, the biblical texts do not give a specific command . . ."[18] On the other hand, while the document does not claim the need to use the

---

12. Ibid., W–3.3612

13. Ibid., W–2.4005, W–2.4008 and W–24011.

14. Ibid., W–2.4012.

15. Ibid., W–2.4012.

16. *Book of Common Worship*, 68.

17. "The minister, or the authorized person to preside, invites the people to the Lord's table using suitable words from Scripture. If the words of institution (1 Cor 11:23–26, or Gospel accounts: Matt 26:26–30; Mark 14:22–26; Luke 22:14–20) will not be spoken at the breaking of the bread or included in the great thanksgiving, they are said as part of the invitation" (ibid., 42).

18. Sacrament Study Group, "Invitation to Christ," 22.

words of institution, it still holds its foundational ground on the *distinctive Christian narrative* found in the gospel.[19]

June Christine Goudey, a reformed theologian, makes a poignant critique of the ways in which the Reformed tradition depends on the Words of Institution.

> These words of institution have been used as a "warrant"—an administrative guide—for why we do what we do in this sacrament; nevertheless, they are often seen to function as magical words, without which God's presence would be absent. Ironically, absence not presence is what too many services reveal. We are absent from our embodied souls, we are absent from our communal ties, and we are absent from our this-worldly ties to all of creation. Despite Calvin's significant nod to the Spirit's work in our midst, we seem to have taken Zwingli's memorial as a literal manifestation—the remembrance of a past event that has no power to change our lives here and now. This is sacramental travesty. To commune under the notion that God is absent more often than present denies the sacramental nature of our world.[20]

Goudey strikes a powerful chord in the ways that the Reformed tradition celebrates the Lord's Supper. The Reformed tradition relies on the repetition of proper words to have a sense and a feeling that the sacrament is warranted.

Roman Catholic theologian Robert Taft engages the pertinence and presence of the words of institution in the history of the Eucharist and says that the Institution Narrative is a later addition to early Christian Eucharistic prayers. He says:

> Furthermore, although theories on the origins and evolution of the pristine Anaphora remain in flux, one point of growing agreement among representative scholars, Catholic and non, is that the Institution Narrative is a later embolism—i.e., interpolation—into the earliest eucharistic prayers. For pace Renaudot's mistaken assertion, not only Addai and Man but several other early Eucharistic Prayers do, in fact, lack these words

---

19. Ibid. The document does not require the use of the words of institution in the celebration of the eucharist neither does it link the baptismal language to the entrance into the Eucharistic sacrament. However, it does work from the perspective that the words of institution are a given, since it is clearly stated in both the *Directory of Worship* and the *Book of Common Worship*. It is important to say however that the "words of institution" was not an issue set to be engaged by the group who wrote the document.

20. Ibid., 167.

... Furthermore, it seems probable that ca. 150, Justin Martyr's Eucharistic Prayer did not have them either. In addition, Cyrille Vogel lists six eucharistic prayers in the apocrypha without any trace of an Institution Narrative, and at least twenty-one later Syriac anaphoras either lack the Words of Institution completely (8 anaphoras) or partly (4), or give them in a form considered defective (9)—e.g., in indirect discourse.[21]

Also, the most recent New Testament scholarship explained in chapter 2 weakens the ground of authenticity of the eucharist through the use of the words of institution. Without this historical warrant to connect the "original" Lord's Supper to the sacrament of the Eucharist today, the theological reasoning that structures this choice has to be remade for the good of the Reformed tradition. It does not mean that the church loses the possibility of celebrating the Lord's Supper or loses the power to celebrate the sacrament, or that the church cannot use the words of institution. That is not the point. The quest here is for what authenticates the sacrament and the argument made here is that it is ultimately the presence of the Holy Spirit that authenticates Christ presence and not any proper uttered word or enacted gesture.

In this way, Smith and Taussig give us plenty of reasons to celebrate the eucharist in various ways, based on early church historical evidence. More than that, what gives strength to the celebration of the eucharist then, is the messy plurality encountered in the various Eucharistic practices of the early church.[22] As Smith and Taussig say, "[t]hat multiplicity reflects the fact that for these churches liturgy was not seen as a means to preserve a relic from the past but rather a dynamic way to address the church of the present."[23]

It is this "dynamic way to address the church of the present" that must be pursued by the Reformed Church. To lose the warrant of the words of institution does not imply not using them anymore but rather, first and foremost, to depend on the warrant of the Holy Spirit in the gathered assembly as the main criteria of sacramental authenticity in Reformed Eucharist. Thus this dependency could break open the church into new ways of serving Christ in the world and offer a vast array of possible encounters with Christ, even when gathering with people of other faiths.

21. Taft, "Mass without the Consecration?"

22. Smith and Taussig, *Many Tables*, 15.

23. Ibid., 15, 16.

Smith and Taussig also challenge churches today to look for differ-ent kinds of eucharistic meals that would foster an amplified experience of living in community. Church potlucks, a meal at somebody's home, a picnic gathering, a lunch after the wake of a friend or family member, tea and cookies among friends, coffee in the morning with the family or with a guest who has just arrived, or even a meal around pictures and feelings of strangeness, the church can celebrate many *eucharists* in its plural sense, and practice in a multi-centric perspective. Through the patterns of the banquets, which were always open to unexpected guests, and new under-standings of eucharists and sacraments, a borderless border hospitality becomes a possibility, since it redraws the lines of liturgical actions and provides the eucharistic tables with moveable borders.

Bread and wine can be and should be part of the Eucharist. However, the presence of bread and wine does not need to be there in order to make the eucharist a sacrament. The argument here is not against the presence of the bread and wine or to say anything goes, but rather, to see that what we call Eucharist, the elements we use, and the actions we portray, are open to the movement of the Holy Spirit around different communities. It is the Holy Spirit who is truly free to decide what *Eucharist* might mean. Logically, this freedom also entails the possibilities of the Spirit to warrant traditions to celebrate the sacrament in specific ways that are important for the community. But what we gain is the openness to other possibilities that the Holy Spirit might offer us. Thus, we don't need borders against my brothers and sisters, be they baptized or not, or from one or another denomination or religion, since what is at stake at the celebration of the Eucharist is our deep care for these sacred things as an assembled com-munity, under the movement of the Holy Spirit. The borders that we need are to protect those who are bruised, harmed by the system of exclusion; those who cannot afford a dignified life, the least of these. We need bor-ders to save the lives of those who are in danger. The Eucharist gains its specificities as the people of God do it in different contexts by listening to the movements of the Spirit.

What is at stake here is the engagement of traditions in order to fos-ter and expand it, and not the appeal to dismiss it. This discussion has resonance even in Roman Catholic quarters. When speaking of tradition Robert Taft says:

> There is no ideal form of the liturgy from the past that must be imitated. Liturgy has always changed. We don't study the past in order to imitate it. Tradition is not the past. Tradition is the

life of the church today in dynamic continuity with all that has come before. The past is dead, but tradition is alive, tradition is now.[24]

In keeping with the engagement and *aggiornamento* of tradition, we are trying to honor tradition and make it alive to our day. For this matter, the measures of the sacrament are grounded on *koinonia*, friendship, love, and hospitality and not on any material assurance, be it words of institution, gestures around the table, prayers, proper liturgies and so on, in order to make the Eucharist a true sacrament. A true sacrament is a table filled with people trying to make contact by connecting their lives and challenging each other with each other's stories of love and pain, experiences, needs, perspectives with the stories of Jesus, the visions of and from God, and the movements of the Spirit moving us towards the other and the world.

Perhaps, if we celebrate the eucharist once in a while without the biblical, historical warrant, it might shift our attention from "mere" words to a broader horizon where new situations are created and new solutions are offered. Perhaps, if we start talking about the ways that the food that is served on the table got there, we will make ourselves responsible for the people who prepared it. Thus, this other horizon provides connectedness to other people and things around us. Moreover, a broader notion of the sacrament would also expand conscious connections to other communities that are not part of the table, either by remembering them or by committing ourselves to invite other people to eat with us.

In this way, immigrants and other silenced communities will be remembered and invited to eat with us around a variety of food and multiplicity of gestures known by many communities. We would move around from one table to another not being afraid of stepping in each other's tools. We might even leave our liturgical spaces and knock on someone else's door, inviting them to eat with us and bring their food, stories, and experiences to the table. In addition, the food will remind us that it comes from nature and that we are responsible for the safety and preservation of the ecological system of our planet. Then, the real presence of Christ will neither be in the words of institution nor in Christ's presence in heaven, but rather in the presence of the Holy Spirit in, under, through, and around us, in the presence and absence of those who are there with us, in the care of each other and the ecological systems that sustains us. In one word, Christ

24. Taft, "Mass Instruction: Fr. Robert Taft on liturgical reform."

incarnate in the people, in the food, in the hands of those who planted and harvested it, in those who prepared it and those who are eating with us: Christ incarnate in my neighbors.

These ways of doing the Eucharist might bring a sense of relativism and the use of the Bible can be seen as superfluous. However, since this is always a story of thanksgiving, *anamnesis*, and Jesus Christ, nothing can be done without the Bible, its stories, and texts, and people. Using the words of Kevin J. Vanhoozer, even more than he might like, I'd say that the dramatic liturgical approach to the celebration of the Eucharist fits the "dramatic fittingness" of the Scriptures. The place and importance of the Scriptures are key to this project and its "dramatic fittingness will require different performances in different situations. This is a kind of relativism that *establishes* rather than undermines biblical authority."[25] Improvisation, invention, imagination, creation, and a sense of fidelity to the many Christian liturgies are all at stake in this movement.

The variety of eucharistic meals can also open endless possibilities for biblical words, as well as other liturgical movements according to the Reformed and other traditions. Everyone can participate and lead at the table, since no one holds an exclusive privilege of carrying God's presence, except and solely the Holy Spirit of God who is free to make any meal a "real" sacrament. This radical possibility of a guest leading the Christian meal is not a break from Christian traditions but rather, a faithful heir to some forms of liturgy lived by early Christian churches as evidenced in the second chapter of this book. In fact, it is the radicalization of the "Priesthood of all believers" already lived out in many Christian churches.

This variety also defines the spirituality of the liturgy-sacrament. Paying attention to Johann Baptist Metz, the liturgical theology at stake here deals with power, with a deep criticism to the Christian middle-class and its bourgeois style of life that takes prayer and collects money for the poor but never prays *with* the poor or shares their belongings with the poor. The spirituality of the sacrament taps into the dangerous memory of Jesus Christ and its revolutionary gospel and asks for our prayers and liturgies to be "political and influential."[26] Spiritualities incarnate in our bodies, ignited by actions, visions and prophetic dreams of justice. Spiritualities learned from the sweat and movement of our bodies, or in the words of Bruce T. Morril, a "practical knowledge borne by an 'anticipatory

---

25. Vanhoozer, *Drama of Doctrine*, 261; italics in the original.
26. Metz, "Courage to Pray," 28.

memory,"[27] a memory that anticipates the future and teaches our bodies to jump up and down, announcing the coming of the new time of justice and solidarity in Jesus Christ. Moreover, the spiritualities of the Eucharistic sacrament go beyond the strict dependence of time and space, that is, liturgies are not slaves of time, space, and objects but instead, time, space, and objects are at the service of whatever the people of God want to do, even if it is more than the one Sunday holy hour, even if we use different spaces for worship or move the baptismal font that costs so much money. What the Eucharistic sacrament does to us is to enhance our individual and collective spiritual lives. The noise of the world is counteracted by the sound of dancing bodies filled by the Holy Spirit around communal meals of renewal and healing. The spiritualities of the sacrament can become a more corporate spirituality, if we have more time to share our lives around the eucharistic table, by expanding borders of justice, of love, and of hospitality.

The ordo of the sacrament, so venerably kept by Reformed churches, is then "re-valued," "widened" into many possible orders. This multi-centric, multi-purposed, multi-performed and, multi-experienced (b)orders/(dis)orders, or in one word, these plural (b)orders, will help us not make everybody fit into what some people may define as one. No unity but learning to be together in and through our multiplicity, brokenness, and joys. Because to search for the oneness of God is often a way of learning how to live into another person's oneness. Instead, the ordos of the sacrament will expand the borders of commonalities and *non-commonalities*, mostly our differences, as we share the bread, the wine and a variety of food in a variety of gestures. Together, around many tables, food, gestures, sounds, prayers, and many orders, we can make sure that everyone is invited and that there will be enough food for everyone. All the beggars, those who fit and those who do not fit, will engage, say a thing or two, lead, and install a new egalitarian society.

27. Morrill beautifully uses Metz's notion of "anticipatory memory," which is Jesus' life and death bringing hopes and new values for a new political life, and connects this memory of Jesus with a spirituality that is born out of daily life. Morrill, *Anamnesis as Dangerous Memory*, 200.

THE BORDERS OF THE EUCHARIST IN UNITED STATES

The border between Mexico and United States is a powerful place to think about life in the Americas. The wall is a place of hatred and fear. As Trinh T. Minh-ha says:

> *Muros de odio*, as it is called in the U.S. southern borderlands, the border is the symbol of a new hatred which America is known to have effectively fueled. As Wole Soyinka says: "the wall that was dismantled in Berlin is being re-built brick by brick . . . The ideology might be different, but the desperation for dominance was the same." Or what we hear from cyberspace: "A border wall tells the world, we are a fearful nation"; "the high wall that keeps out is the same wall that keeps in"; "Call it a fence built to 'make good neighbors' but it is still a wall, and remember what the Berlin wall was called on the other side; it was a Anti-Fascist Protection Barrier."[28]

Before the brutal militarization of the borders, statistics suggested that every year three million people entered the United States without documents. Non-documented people hold twelve to fifteen million jobs in the United States, almost eight percent of the labor market. Moreover, "four to six million jobs have shifted to the underground market, as small businesses take advantage of the vulnerability of illegal residents."[29] It is not unfair to say that most of the food that Christians or any other US citizen eat in their homes, at church or religious potlucks, or at Eucharistic tables, was planted or picked, cleaned or transported by a mass of non-documented workers who are exploited, underpaid, and often called criminals.

However, the presence of these non-documented immigrants is good business in the United States. A great number of these *aliens*,[30] in any kind of business, receive their payments in checks, with income taxes deducted. However, since the immigrants fake Social Security numbers, this money will never come back to them, but is kept by the government to use for its own purposes. Bryan Welch, publisher and editorial director of Ogden

28. Trinh, *Elsewhere, Within Here*, 3–4.

29. Justich, "The Underground Labor Force is Rising to the Surface," cited in Welch, "Putting a Stop to Slave Labor, A Moral Solution to Illegal Immigrants," *UTNE Reader*, March-April, 2007, 43.

30. In the words of Guillermo Gómez-Peña, alien is "a term used by opportunistic politicians and sleazy reporters to describe any legal or illegal immigrant, people with heavy accents or exotic clothes, and people who exhibit eccentric social, sexual, or aesthetic behavior" (Gómez-Pena, *New World Border*, 240).

Publications adds, "if we shut down illegal immigration, a program to legalize our 'guest workers' would be a matter of necessity to save American agriculture . . . and because nothing meaningful is going to happen in the foreseeable future—illegal immigration endures as a testament to our hypocrisy."[31] If these illegal workers were to be legalized, their salary wage would have to be higher and the increase would be felt broadly.

> . . . jobs that offer a fair wage and humane working conditions cost money—and that cost would be passed on to consumers, who, for starters, might see an additional 10 percent added to their rent or mortgage payment and pay 15 percent more for groceries. That's not a change the average consumer would welcome, of course.[32]

Perhaps without knowing it, our familiar church and eucharistic tables are also a testament to the disconnection between our faith and acts of justice. When our religious tables are prepared, they already come *tainted* by a system of oppression that exploits a mass of poor people, who are indeed around the table with us but rendered invisible. Any bread, however small it might be, and any wine, whatever small a sip we take from the cup, is already marked by oppression. Agricultural fields in the United States are filled with undocumented immigrants working for slave wages. Thus, eucharistic tables, which promise freedom, redemption and an encounter with God can only be prepared by means of the "indirect" exploitation of non-documented immigrants.[33]

What happens here at our eucharistic tables has repercussions throughout the world. The agriculture subsidy provided by the United States and European governments has had a negative impact on small farm communities in Latin America since their costs of production are too high to be competitive.

> Fourteen-year-old Sixto Mendez Goyazo, from Chiapas, has never attended school. He is illiterate. He does not know the United States and does not know where he is going to be taken to work after crossing the border at Sasabe. Sixto travels with his thirty-two-year-old uncle Felipe Goyazo, a peasant who has no job in Chiapas because imports of subsidized American corn

---

31. Welch, "Putting a Stop to Slave Labor," 44.

32. Ibid.

33. One does not need to talk about our clothing, which is also marked by shameless wage paid to exploited workers in Asia and Central or Latin America.

have driven the price so low that local farmers can't make a living. Sixto wants to work in the U.S. to support his parents.[34]

How then can we make sense of Sixto's life when we celebrate Eucharist? How should we celebrate the sacrament if we knew he was about to arrive at the doors of our church? Somebody might say: we would need to recognize Sixto as our brother so we would welcome him in or midst. However, if the question here is one of recognition, what does recognition mean? In order to recognize Sixto in our midst we would need to make him go through a process of re-cognition, that is, to turn Sixto into the structures of our own cognition, to our understanding, and appropriate to our senses. This re-cognition process is the placement of borders before him so Sixto would need to pass through them until we let him get closer to us. Documents, class status, language, names, history, proper beliefs, religion, behavior, etc. are the things that help us re-cognize him, so we can understand/re-cognize/control him. Before that process, Sixto is marked by our inability to be aware of him, and he is deeply marked by the signs of our fears.

Thus, recognition or even the idea of tolerance for that matter is not what we need, since recognition and tolerance are concepts organized around those who control the fences and decide what or how to re-cognize or tolerate the other. Instead of that, we should work from another horizon

34. Chacón, "Mexico, Caught in the Web of U.S. Empire," 88.

of possibilities. We must engage with the fluidity of definitions/practices of the *cognito*, of knowledge, of understandings, of ways of beings, of languages, etc. This means that we will never know who is at the table, who we clearly are, and who God might be. We will need to share power, governance and authority. The task to know is a communal one, always unfinished, always dreadful, but always leaning on each other to know a little more.

Baptismal language, either before, during, or after the Eucharistic rite also has to have the markers of the global instances, the ethnic complications, the racial underpinnings, the economic disparities we are mentioning here. Michael L. Budde calls for an "ecclesial solidarity," i.e., "the conviction that 'being a Christian' is one's primary and formative loyalty, the one that contextualizes and defines the legitimacy of other claimants on allegiance and conscience—those of class, nationality and state, for example." [35] Baptismal language and practices thus create a language that crosses the borders of our denominations, of our belonging, of our citizenship, and heightens in us our allegiance to God's glory through our allegiance and commitment with the poor, among them, the immigrants.

The eucharistic table is this place for multiple cognitions and practices and unknowns, a fluid place where we can experience God's love with people who are not like us, mostly those who are disfranchised from our world. How does the incarnation of Christ around the Eucharistic table relate to the traditions of prayers, songs, theologies, ecclesiologies, polidoxy, ethnicities, globalization, empire, injustice, and economics? How does our faith influence the ways that the exercise of political power and money interests regulate the political sphere, our very lives and where the common wealth goes? Becoming the body of Christ and enacting the kingdom of God in justice, peace, and solidarity is our task so that we can create a society where the common wealth belongs to all and not just to some, where the private is put into question when it excludes others.

Thus, offering prayers and collecting money for the poor are not enough! Praying for the peace of the world is not enough! The very structures of our being the body of Christ forging the kin-dom of God made of equality must reflect and be reflected in, through and from our liturgies/mission. As the Brazilian liturgist Jaci C. Maraschin said: "Liturgy

---

35. Budde, *Borders of Baptism*, 3. In this book Budde wrestles with the understandings, allegiances, and loyalties of a Christian from a baptismal perspective. A great book that points to the invisible markers around our baptismal fonts and calls us to wrestle with God's call to us.

and mission dance together towards the kingdom of God."[36] The unjust distribution of wealth is not only a symbol, but it is visibly present when we eat and drink together at the table of God. The Insurgent Subcomandante Marcos, the famous spokesman from the "Zapatista Army For The National Liberation in Mexico" has said that the power of capitalism, "in a strict sense, is a new conquering war . . . it is everywhere, all the time and in every form, being the most global of the wars." He adds:

> United States has 53 companies that alone, in the past seven years, have made 40 percent of the world's money. These companies, along with other companies from Japan, Germany, France, England, Italy, Netherland, Switzerland, and South Korea, have earned more than 90 percent of the world's wealth.[37]

Marcos calls people to resist the force of neo-capitalism spread throughout the world.[38] Eucharist has to do with economics and resistance. Andrea Bieler and Luise Schottroff wrote a wonderful book where they weave together liturgical, biblical, and theological analysis of the economic impact of the sacrament.[39] They engage the ways in which our theologies, biblical interpretations, and bodies are marked at the Eucharistic sacrament by regulations of the world economic market. The bread of life and the cup of salvation at the table cannot be interpreted, understood, and/or taken, without the awareness of *homo-economicus* and the global market.[40] By being very aware of the forces of the global economic market, they offer us new ways to interpret some biblical texts used in Eucharistic prayers, help us see the ways in which we are shackled by the economy, and help us develop a powerful eschatological theology that expands our belief that God can indeed resurrect us every time we break and eat this bread together. In this way, by receiving new tools of understanding these connections with the Eucharist, we are better prepared to renegotiate our theologies and our practices around the Eucharistic table.

Yes, we are making ethical, political and economic choices when we prepare the table. However, it is important to say that these ways of dealing

36. Maraschin, "Culture, Spirit and Adoration," 47–63.

37. Subcomandante Marcos, "A IV Guerra Mundial e o Outro Mundo Possível. Conferência do Subcomandante Marcos," Instituto Humanitas Unisinos, March 28, 2007: http://www.ihu.unisinos.br/noticias/noticias-anteriores/6116-a-iv-guerra-mundial--e-o-outro-mundo-possivel-conferencia-do-subcomandante-marcos.

38. Ibid.

39. Bieler and Schottroff, *Eucharist*.

40. See Carvalhaes, Review of *The Eucharist*.

with the Eucharistic sacrament are not an act of only one political party. We do not go to church to do partisan politics in the sense of a political party. No, we go to church to pray and thank God, to praise, ask for mercy, to listen to God's word, and to enact a new word. In all of these practices, we do politics, in the sense of the polis, of what kind of life we decide to live together. In that sense we are making choices,[41] and in the midst of them we need to take political parties or any other organizational channel that is responsible for the ways in which society gears and structures our lives. As citizens of the world we must create the world we hope for and as Christians, we must reflect Jesus politics and exercise our ability to influence the creation of this world.

A table grounded in the ethics of justice will honor God and strive to honor every human being in their very daily lives and the ability to live with means for a dignified life. The Eucharist table challenges us to ask ourselves as individuals and communities: what are we to do with this sacrament? This table is deeply marked by the ethics of responsibility where the face of the other in/evolves every step of my liturgy before God. Taken from Miguel De La Torre's ethical proposal, we can say that the Eucharistic table must be marked by the "ethics de lo cotidiano (daily life), ethics of the nepantla (the in between places), ethics para la lucha (for the struggle), and ethics en conjunto (togetherness)."[42] The ethical Eucharistic table of the kin-don of God issues an unending call for people to meet Jesus Christ, a table that talks endlessly about Jesus and helps us encounter Christ. For the Eucharistic liturgy must be informed by Jesus Christ and Scripture, as Christ cannot not be present at the ethical/spiritual celebra-

41. Frei Betto, a Dominican monk in Brazil said the following: "I always affirm that we Christians are disciples of a political prisoner: Jesus did not die from sickness in bed, or by an accident with a camel in a corner of Jerusalem, but has been killed as many colleagues in Argentina and Brazil, has been imprisoned, tortured, taken to trial and sentenced to death on the cross. To say that Jesus did not get into politics is naïve, especially since at that time, the Cartesian division between religion and politics we have today, didn't exist, and those who had religious power had political power and vice versa. Now, you have to understand that religion is a different dimension of the political sphere, they are complementary in our lives and in social life. However, I will not say a mass for a program of a political party neither will I go to a political party meeting and say 'let's pray now.' Modern distinctions are necessary, but we must also be aware that there can be no neutrality. Religion has always implied a clear political position, either to legitimize the system of injustice and capitalist oppression or to accuse its abuse, denounce and fight for de-legitimization" (Betto, "La fe no es una ideología y el marxismo no es una fe").

42. De La Torre, Latina/o Social Ethics, 70. From page 70 on, he describes each of these necessary ethical markers for our theological work.

tion of the sacrament. But than, what Christ are we meeting there? As De La Torre says: "The theological question, who is Christ? Is inseparable from the ethical question, what are we to do?" and he answers by saying that this question cannot be separated from the praxis and the choice of what Christ we are to follow. Instead of the Eurocentric Christ, we bring here the Latino/a Christ who "is informed by the historical identification of Jesus with those who suffer under oppression," the Jesus Christ who "takes sides with the least among us against those who oppress them."[43] The Eucharistic celebration is always an exercise in incarnation, on Christ with the poor.

The eucharistic table challenges us to be together and foster our sense of struggle and who we are always becoming through these liturgies. To be together with a multiplicity of people does not mean to agree about things but to live together, not in spite of but because of our differences. The sacramental table is pressed by a multi-layered challenge, a very difficult task that demands all of us to figure out locally, within our communities, how to make sense of the multiple body of Christ and the message of Jesus Christ in our world today. I believe that the Mexican performer Guillermo Gómez-Pena captures the challenges of the eucharistic table when he talks about his vision of a "multicentric, hybrid American culture." Gómez-Pena makes a connection with art and present day living. If we shift the word "art" to "eucharist," we can sense how his challenge can relate to our liturgies around the Eucharist:

> What does it mean to be alive and to make art [*eucharist*] in an apocalyptic era framed/reframed by changing borders, ferocious racial violence, irrational fears of otherness and hybridity, spiritual emptiness, AIDS and other massively destructive diseases, ecological devastation, and, of course, lots of virtual space? How to function as a fluid border-crosser, intellectual "coyote," and intercultural diplomat in and around this abrupt landscape? And ultimately, how to understand the perils and advantages of living in a country that speaks at least ninety different languages and—unwillingly—hosts peoples from practically every nation, race, and religious creed on earth?[44]

Jesus' eucharistic table in this country is already marked by the elements he mentioned. How then, can Christian churches in this country answer these challenges and offer God the highest praise and offer God's love to each other through the celebration of the sacrament of the body of

43. Ibid., 81.
44. Gómez-Peña, *New World Border,* 1.

Christ? In what follows, I suggest some possible ways to start this relationship between the eucharistic table and the world "outside," in order to help those who gather around the eucharistic table to take responsibility for the world at large.

3. Performing Em-bodied Eucharists

> She had just crossed the border from Mexico and was being helped by a family she didn't know. The missionary went to see her and her daughter. Her other daughter had died on the way to the United States and her husband was killed in her country. As the missionary approached her, she didn't turn her face. She said "Hola" without looking at the missionary. As she prepared coffee, she invited the missionary to sit on the chair in the kitchen. Her 4 year old daughter would not stay on the ground at all. She looked so scared. After the coffee was done, she finally looked at the missionary who had no idea how to react to what she saw: that woman had her nose cut off by a violent gang in her country who killed her husband. She apologized. The missionary choked and also apologized. They had coffee and corn bread in front of them. Both of them cried in silence . . . until they could speak.

Even though the Presbyterian Church (U.S.A.)'s "Directory for Worship" is constantly reminding its churches "to do all things in an orderly way,"[45] it also reminds them that everything that is created by God can be brought to the worship service:

> The richness of color, texture, form, sound, and notion have been brought into the act of worship . . . The people of God have responded through creative expressions in architecture, furnishings, appointments, vestments, music, drama, language and movement. When these artistic creations awaken us to God's presence, they are appropriate for worship."[46]

In spite of this rich openness, many churches engage poorly with the other PCUSA liturgical book, the "Book of Common Worship" and due to a lack of better, more engaged appreciation, tend to dismiss or not use well the book with the argument that the Book of Common Worship

45. "Directory For Worship," W-1.4000.
46. Ibid., W-1.30.34.

offers only a repetition of words[47] that often takes away most of the creativity allowed and fostered by the Directory of Worship. As a consequence, usual liturgical orders of worship within these Reformed churches become liturgically poor, fixed, repetitive movements. Crammed into the one hour shackle, people are seated in unmovable pews, often stand to sing, and sit to say words and hear more words. Around the table, the movements are minimal and when the elements are distributed, there is often silence in order to maintain a sense of reverence. Hence, the body is taught to behave with measured gestures of order, decency, and quietness. The table is often furnished with meager food and everything else around the table is tight, tense, minimalist, and often somber. That should be one way not the only way to do it.

If we are to accept the challenges of recent New Testament scholarship and transform our single eucharistic table into many eucharistic tables; if we are to learn from a variety of experiences and movements from women in their liturgical performances; if we are to turn the eucharistic table to many directions and place it at the heart of the world as we learned with poor people in Latin America; if we are to offer that table to people of other faiths; and, if we are to trust the Holy Spirit as that which will make our celebration a sacrament, then, the result can be dazzling, powerful, and transformative. The Eucharist will become Eucharistic sacraments in various ways, forms, and kinds of meals, with enough food to feed everybody, with "excessive" movements of the body, and with the presence of poor, non-documented, excluded people. These will be the marks of these eucharistic liturgies.

What is marked, unarguably, is the body. The body is marked not only by personal events but also by social classes, political use of power, theological choices, and liturgical gestures. These piercing issues find their final location in the body of the believer where the link between the social and the private, and the dialectic between the universal and the local happen, stressing the ways that power relations are established. The body becomes a theological foci, a resource, a liturgical key element, marked by ecclesiastical borders where again, power relations happen. Foucault affirms: "Power relations have an immediate hold upon it. They invest it, mark it, train it, torture it, force it to carry out tasks, to perform ceremonies, to emit signs."[48]

---

47. The argument here serves as a critique to both the repetition of the same formula and to the bad use of it.

48. Foucault, *Discipline and Punish*, 25.

Hence, the embodiment of eucharistic rites is a way of gaining consciousness about the way power relations, both social and religious, mark, train, and force the body. The theological, liturgical/performative approach of the body evokes a certain awareness about the universal impositions of the one heavily theologized/ideologized/invented body, that of the Christ, both dead and resurrected, over the contingent, vague bodies of individuals in local communities. This very relation attests, rectifies, enforces, and/or prevents resistance to/from other oppressed bodies.

There is no simple way to fix unjust relations of power. However, struggles and resistance can promote better forms of power and lesser forms of oppression. When we relate that struggle to the eucharistic sacraments, we must expect the following: when bodies move beyond adjusted, expected, and almost mechanical gestures to get the bread and the wine in the eucharistic sacrament, when bodies become central to the rites, when people can have freedom to move their own knees and decide their movements, where their hands are free to move beyond the body, when people become aware that "hips don't lie,"[49] and our feet can dance, and our voices can speak, then Christ's incarnation can be expanded and noticed in the bodies/lives of those who are celebrating with us. Not only that, bodies in movement will pose questions regarding power relations and ways in which bodies are treated, moved, related, held back, or explored.

Also, when bodies are in movement, there are also movements of desire, of passion, known and unknown, and bodies can be connected to their sexualities in performative modes, all of which being engaged, as bodies move against the given heterosexual *essencialization* of the eucharistic rite, space, words, and movements. When all bodies are *queered*, we can all celebrate our joys and pains with our own stories and specificities without hierarchical modes of sexual choice as its source of authority.

Another bodily aspect of the eucharistic sacraments has to do with the bodies of those absent. They are remembered and connected through the body of Christ who is present/absent at the eucharistic meals, and whose anamnesis reminds us that his body was beaten up and murdered by an unjust system of oppression.[50] Our bodies at the table should be pierced by the memory of bodies who, like Jesus, are not there, and also

---

49. One of Shakira's hit songs is called "Hips Don't Lie," *Shakira's Deluxe Edition: Oral Fixation Vol. 1 and Vol. 2*, Sony ASIN B000EQH2QK, 2005, compact disc.

50. Tom Driver develops Richard Schechner's notion of performance as "showing of a doing" and helps us understand better the specifics, ambivalences and relation between doing and showing. See Driver, *Liberating Rites,* especially "Part II: Modalities of Performance."

like the body of Jesus, are still being brutally violated and killed; and unlike the body of Jesus, will never be remembered, honored, and, perhaps, never resurrected.

Doing the eucharist with a foreigner is to engage in what Julia Kristeva calls "polyphormic mutism."[51] Foreigners are stuck in this place where they "can instead of saying attempt doing . . ." something, which will always be an expenditure of what we know or are used to. The doing of the liturgy together might be this place where none of us speaks in our mother tongue, connecting to each other by the endless attempt to navigate through our bodily gestures. The doing of the liturgy together might be finding ways of remembering, honoring and paying attention to our common expenditures, rudeness, uncivilized manners, where the poor or the foreigner are *adiaphoras* (indifferent things) that help define the essentials to the praise of God.

Again, learning from (and definitely stretching) Calvin's pneumatology, from recent New Testament scholarship, from women, from the poor, and from people of other religions, Eucharistic rites are to be performed in expanded ways, with many bodily movements, improvised or not, created according to the problems and hopes of the local communities, making covenants with local groups, not only engaging in solidarity with others but resisting and challenging powers of oppression, breaking the circle that keeps communities enclosed in themselves, and bringing forth life anew. Thus, the widening of the possibilities for the Holy Spirit to move within each community can foster many forms to be challenged, healed, and transformed, strengthening the ways of empowerment to each community and individual, and calling us all into new ways of showing and doing thanksgiving.

One example: in a church where 95% of the congregation was undocumented, one day the pastor shares a story where she was violated in her rights during the week and robbed of her dignity. Her story created an outrage in the congregation and all of sudden congregants started to raise their hands wanting to share their own stories to comfort their pastor. The video that they used to record the services to give to people who could not come to church was turned off. The door was closed so they could feel comfortable. After the sharing of some stories, the whole congregation was weeping, feeling the weight of their status as third class non-citizens who gave their lives to this country only to be exploited, abused, and have their dignity stolen from them. Horror stories of sexual assault, violation

---

51. Kristeva, "Strangers to Ourselves," 276.

of the most primitive rights, threatening, abusive power use, and reports of the brutal force used by the police were shared by the community. That day the church had Eucharist and the pastor invited them to come around the table. At the table she invited people to pray for the Spirit to come and bring healing. After the prayer, she didn't have strength to say the words of institution or anything else. Everybody was exhausted by the stories told. Bread and wine was distributed. While eating and drinking, people started to regain their strength and slowly their bodies and heads started to rise up. Somebody went to the door and opened it again. Others turned on the video and the congregation started to sing. They sang for almost an hour. They circled the table with dancing and shouting. The kids were brought back and everybody danced and sang. The service was concluded without any prayer. They made a circle and looked at each other's eyes as if they were giving each other a blessing and a benediction. It was as if they were saying to each other: we are here together. We eat and drink together. We sing together. In the midst of pain and hurt we look at each other's eyes to remind ourselves that God is with us and we are not alone.

Ritualization/Ritualizing Eucharists

Under the work of the Holy Spirit, Reformed churches are called to expand their relationship around the eucharistic table. At the table, they are called to strengthen the community, turn the sacrament from one sole table to *many tables*, so they learn to welcome others in radical hospitality, from one shape to many forms, from hierarchical structures to churches in the round,[52] from building sanctuaries to other ecological sanctuaries, from tight gestures to ample movements, from its *useless* self-references to marked perspectives, from the safety of one form of ordered liturgy to many ordered/disordered/(b)order liturgies, from the struggling life of the middle class or the comfort of violence-proof upper-class zones to the unsafe and unprotected world of poor people. Grounded in the perspectives shown in previous chapters, we can affirm now that local churches can engage in a process of ritualizing or ritualization of liturgical orders and the Eucharistic sacraments. Within the realm of ritual studies, ritualizing and ritualization are terms that are related to practical ways of doing rituals.

Ritualization (Catherine Bell) and *ritualizing* (Ronald Grimes)[53] are ways of creating and cultivating ritual practices according to the needs of

52. Russell, *Church in the Round.*

53. For *ritualization*, see Bell, *Ritual Theory, Ritual Practice*, chapter 9. For

a chosen group. Both of these thinkers have greatly expanded these terms and shown both the advantages and problems inherent in creating rituals. For Catherine Bell, "[r]itualization is fundamentally a way of doing things to trigger the perception that these practices are distinct and the associations that they engender are special."[54] The ritualization of eucharistic tables is indeed a triggering of the series of perceptions considered around the relation between the table and the world. By creating a vast array of doings *with, in,* and *around* eucharistic tables, the perception that the ritualization of the eucharistic rites intends to foster is that new possibilities of actions, words, and worlds can be created. Moreover, the eucharistic tables can create free associations that can also engender a connection between the bread on the Reformed eucharistic tables and the crumbs eaten by poor people under the table.

As Bell says, ritualization triggers and enhances perceptions. Thus, well crafted creations of eucharists can foster good theology and practices, enhance the faith of people, and a better sense of koinonia by paying more attention to the use of space, the marks and gesturing of our bodies, the distribution of resources, and the forms of participation of people.[55] Then, the *giveness* of the gifts of God will be not only in the hands of those who have the means to name and create its meanings, but rather it will be in the very *relational* practical actions of our material and spiritual resources vis-à-vis one another.

The process of ritualization will help churches to find ways around their own and other different communities. How can a Reformed church in Boston, MA, or in Florida relate to a massive number of non-documented immigrants that live around these areas? Or how would a Reformed church in New York share its eucharistic table with the homeless, or a white church in Louisville share space with the larger black community, or an openly gay community pray together with a more conservative church?

---

ritualizing, see Grimes, *Reading, Writing, and Ritualizing,* chapters 1–3.

54. Bell, *Ritual Theory, Ritual Practice,* 220.

55. This claim is not to be linked necessarily with the emergent church movement, which sometimes forgets tradition entirely and turns itself into the desire of a few individuals. What is at stake here is the unwavering commitment to engage deeply and fundamentally with received traditions and its wealth of wisdom. The well crafted liturgies mentioned here are grounded in the work of the people from whatever church/community, a communal event done by Christian assemblies. Thus, this proposal is neither a sole work of the traditional churches nor does it belong to the emergent church movement. What I am proposing here does not try at any moment to align itself to any movement but to work with and between them. Perhaps, only perhaps, it is an attempt to create a third space.

Under the gospel demand of radical hospitality, these communities will have to find ritual actions that de-condition the conditions hidden in the lives of both communities' beliefs and practices that established their distance and fear of one another. The impossibility of these encounters can be engaged as we wrestle with the ways we engage, live and enact the table of Jesus Christ. Symbols, liturgical practices, food, gestures, songs, words, stories, food ethics, theatrical and liturgical inventions would have to be brought to the table in order to make these communities worship God together and read and listen to the Bible on a given Sunday morning. The ritualization of liturgical spaces is a way of working together so the Spirit of God will come and hover around us, naming these encounters sacraments, sacraments that at the same time "define, empower and constrain"[56] the lives of the believers. To mark the sacramental tables not necessarily with an official ritual of each denomination but with various ritual practices or ritualizing, is to try to avoid ritual universalization that only serves certain denominations and class understandings as well as creates spurious cultural generalizations and partial commonalities. Hence, the ritualizing of Eucharists can be the affirmation that, even though we are connected in many ways by globalization, each community has its own set of beliefs, meaningful structures, experiences and practices at and around the table. The globalization of the church is this: to learn and to share different resources and practices and not to establish one order over and above others. In our rituals of faith, we give incentives for transnationalization and trans-denominationalism of prayers, worship services and worship/hymn books; we transverse each other's cultural, theological, and liturgical practices by throwing ourselves in constant foreign liturgical territories where we become responsible to offer each other's food as well as a place to rest and be loved. Our liturgical practices will offer hospitality knowing that each worship service is a way of giving honor to God and to each other.

Along with Bell's definition of ritualization, Ronald Grimes offers his definition of *ritualizing*:

> The gerund form is to call attention to the activity of deliberately cultivating rites. Ritualizing is not often socially supported. Rather, it happens in the margins, on the threshold; so it is alternatively stigmatized and eulogized . . . The result of sustained ritualizing and revised theory of ritual to account for it is likely to be the bleeding of genres—the fuzzing of boundary lines that

56. Ibid., 221.

separate ritual from art, theater, politics, and therapy—but this bleeding of boundaries may not be a loss. It might represent instead ritual's connection with some of its vital sources and tributaries.[57]

It is this *fuzzing* in the ritualizing process that opens up possibilities for the appearance of the other to come and become a guest/owner of the table. Expanding the borders of liturgical practices into the borders of artistic performance, we could say that ritualizing allows us to think of liturgical performances along with the art form known as *installation.* "To install," says Erika Suderburg, "is a process that must take place each time an exhibition is mounted; 'installation' is the art form that takes note of the perimeters of that space and reconfigures it. The ideological impossibility of the neutrality of any site contributes to the extension and application of installation."[58] Within the site of the liturgical performances, the codes of the objects, and the shapes and formats of things, the codes of the social conventions and the ways we are used to relating to them are reconsidered. By breaking the patterns of these codes, "dissembling"[59] the official ritual and the space, one might have her perceptions undone, redone and redirected to other forms and possibilities not only of objects but "notions of occupancy, material forms and the body's relationship to the space it occupies and incessantly reformulates," as well as perceptions of God and sacramental notions of the world.

The ritualizing of eucharists within Reformed churches within the Unites States is deeply marked by its relationship to border crossings. For example, the borders between the United States and Mexico are both a very concrete and symbolic element to be ritualized constantly at any eucharistic celebration. It is impossible to avoid, neglect, or forget this border. This border defines so many things in this country: it fences many forms of hospitality, spurs political feelings towards the stranger, blurs, contaminates, expands and defines not only the multi-centric identity of this country but its economic and religious zeal. In one word, this border is unavoidable and must be considered alongside the borders of our eucharistic tables. Not to engage with it is to agree with it. Guillermo Gómez-Peña, a performer from Mexico, calls himself "a border Sisyphus."[60] This

---

57. Grimes, *Reading, Writing, and Ritualizing*, 24, 22.

58. Suderburg, *Space, Site, Intervention*, 4.

59. Ibid., 13.

60. Gómez-Peña, *New World Border*, 1.

is how he defines his work as a border performer throughout the United States:

> For me performance art is a conceptual "territory" with fluctuating weather and borders; a place where contradiction, ambiguity, and paradox are not only tolerated, but also encouraged. Every territory a performance artist stakes, including this text, is slightly different from that of his/her neighbor. "Here," tradition weighs less, rules can be bent, laws and structures are constantly changing, and no one pays much attention to hierarchies and institutional power . . . "Here," there is no government or visible authority. We are interstitial creatures and border citizens by nature—insiders/outsiders at the same time—and we rejoice in this paradoxical condition. In the act of crossing a border, we find temporary emancipation . . . Unlike the enforced borders of a nation/state, those in our "performance country" are open to welcome nomads, migrants, hybrids, and outcasts. Our performance country is a temporary sanctuary for other rebel artists and theorists expelled from mono-disciplinary fields and separatist communities. It's also an internal place, a fernhah, invented by each of us, according to our own political aspirations and deepest spiritual needs; our darkest sexual desires and obsessions; our troubling memories and relentless quest for freedom. As I finish this paragraph I bite my romantic tongue. It bleeds. It's real blood. My audience is worried.[61]

Gómez-Peña makes the borders his uncanny home, where a country is envisioned, practiced and invented. "There," which for him is always "here," no matter where he performs, he carries the ambiguities, the nervous and tense and violent aspects of the hybridity of the borders, its "temporary emancipation," a place where every nomad, migrant, and outcast is welcome. For borders are places for the outcasts, excluded, hungry people searching for something, not for those inserted in the social system who do not even perceive that there is a huge border defining this country in dangerous ways.

How then can the eucharistic table become and perform this United States/Mexican border? How can the sacrament be performed as "temporary emancipation" to people? On which side of the border is the table with its eucharistic foods and words of welcome? Who is present? Placed in the midst of the borders, eucharistic tables perform an identity unsettling

---

61. Guillermo Gómez-Peña, "In Defense of Performance Art," Pocha Nostra, 2001: http://www.pochanostra.com/antes/jazz_pocha2/mainpages/in_defense.htm.

function. If performed with, in, and around the tables, eucharistic sacraments will remember (*anamnesis*) so many border crossers who have died in this journey. Hence, placing the table always at the border, the ritualizing process also locates the sacrament at the margins, as it tries to opt for the poor. As Dwight N. Hopkins states,

> [t]he sacred vocation is to empower the poor, to work with them on their own negative spirituality, and also to participate in releasing them from structures of oppression created by the small group of owners of the world's wealth. As a result, we, under the guidance of the divine, can aid in gradually recreating a new personality and new social relations which will liberate even the minority population of monopolizers . . . the anchor of our belief is the preferential option for the poor. Upon this rock, we judge postmodernity.[62]

The preferential option for the poor is not a choice in this ritualizing process, but it is its most marked aspect. Being at the borders and at the margins, there is no other claim to make but to affirm that eucharistic tables aim at some sort of efficacy. By ritualizing the eucharists, the participant and the community try to make changes in the heart of individuals, to transform the quotidian of the community and the world. In that sense, the ritualizing of Jesus' Communion/Lord's Supper/Eucharistic table plays with aspects of the rites of passage. To perform borderless borders is to create liturgical performances in local communities as rites of passage to help communities mark life's passages with a strong sense of urgency, worthiness, and power. As Ronald Grimes affirms:

> The fundamental metaphor of rites-of-passage theory (largely the legacy of Van Gennep and Turner) is that of crossing a threshold or national frontier. If one attends to the boundary itself, the emphasis becomes spatial, but if one attends to the person making the crossing, the emphasis becomes temporal and processual.[63]

Rites of passage entail movements from one place to another, even though these places might not always be clear.[64] In the same way, eucha-

62. Hopkins, "More Than Ever," 141.

63. Grimes, *Rite Out of Place*, 113.

64. It was Arnold van Gennep who first defined the rites of passage. Everybody's life is a succession of changes that mark the movements or stages of life from birth to death, including age change, social commitments, occupations, life events, religious transformations, and so on. In every ritual passage, there are at least three elements

rists are moments that entail some sense of separation, transition, organization, regeneration, and accomplishment. Perhaps not all of these aspects are always present there since the sacrament is also caught up in the very movements that interrupt life or in the midst of unsolved movements that linger for too long, in separation or brokenness, without any closure that might initiate a transition to some sort of regeneration. However, by the power of the Holy Spirit, through our eucharistic meals and their powerful message of Jesus Christ, life and death, memory, resurrection, we will always try to foster a new world to come, and find help from each other to better our lives. The Eucharistic ritual pushes people to pay attention to what is necessary, to gain strength to keep going, to believe that we must continue in the struggle, to rehearse by faith what is yet to be/come, to search for things to be completed, to remind ourselves always that our commitment is with the poor. Moreover, eating together also propels us into the constant announcement of the *parousia* of Jesus Christ in our midst and a new life of justice and hope; it pushes us to a place where people can be regenerated so as to be able to pass through processes of challenge and change.

However, the ritualization and ritualizing of the eucharists cannot survive under the rubric of pure inventiveness. This is not the purpose of the chapter or the book. We are not thrilled by the empire of the new and that is why we must engage with the resources of wisdom carried by the church through history. If the Eucharist rituals are marked only by sheer inventiveness, the ritual loses the potentialities marked by about 2,000 years of practices and as a consequence, the powerful Eucharistic possibilities of transformation run the risk of becoming shallow. Moreover, to live only on the inventiveness of ritualization without dialoguing with ancient and new practices can be just a kind of religious fast food with no strings attached, with no demands made, no commitments acquired to serve each other to create a new society. Eucharistic tables issue a call to condemn the cultural individualism and consumerism so rampant today in United States society, where churches are more than ever being seduced to offer only what the consumer wants. Eucharistic rituals counter this consumerism and demand much from us. Rituals are not only to serve people but to ask people to do things.

Thus, instead of sheer newness, the Eucharist as a rite of passage, must connect some way, somehow, sometimes this way, sometimes that way, to

---

that structure the rites: separation, transition, and regeneration or incorporation, which can also be called preliminal, luminal, or postliminal rites. See van Gennep, *The Rites of Passage*, 11.

the many traditional rites of the eucharist known in history, picking up on something that a piece of a certain tradition has made known. Moreover, we must be attentive to the cultural ways of eating that strengthen communities so we can enhance our life around the table. Since there is no one single tradition or culture to follow, as we tap into a variety of traditional/ cultural ritual possibilities, we will enhance and expand on our Christian symbols, and the local, cultural, global, historical resources of people, movements, prayers, songs, theologies, and practices, old and new, for our eating together.

For example, eating on the ground with Afro Brazilians, engaging the various practices around bread and wine of the early Christian churches, checking how the Waldensians celebrated their communion making oaths of life and death, the ways of sharing food under plastic tents at a Landless Movement occupation in Brazil, eating the mais/corn with the indigenous people of the Americas, paying attention to the traditional ways represented by the books of common worship of traditional Protestant churches, practicing the Eucharist with the African-American churches in the United States, all of these possibilities can become sources for the enhancement of our practices around the table

In a constant dialectical process, the table connects to the traditional rites not as a definite authoritative reference but as a relational point of engagement since this rite, in its multiple liturgical and theological forms and content, has established the most ingrained structures of our lives for too many years and we must be attentive to it. In this movement of the old and new, the practice of everyday eating with thanksgiving gains expanded possibilities when it accesses contours of difference around a privileged space, where foreigners get together to share a meal somewhat known by some and unknown by others.

The Eucharist's ritualization/ritualizing does not flatten cultural or religious diversity but celebrates and invites diversity as it tries to deal with the differences within the groups/communities who are worshiping together. As said before, one way to know how this can be done is to place two communities together and have them work out how to live together. Practically, eucharists calls us to be cross-cultural, trans-national, pluri-ethnic, and even inter-religious places where different people eat together. People and communities have to make intentional efforts to invite different people to eat with them, and share the gospel of Jesus, and be shaped by the gospel of the other, always reminding ourselves that we are not attempting to convert the other but trying to convert ourselves from individualism and isolationism. The conversion should be mutual. In this way, sacraments can mark the lives of people who eat together with the traces of the love of God as they try to deal with the *ab-surdus* (impossible to hear) of life.

A group of Brazilians who arrived a couple weeks earlier from the border between Mexico and United States, had come "molhado/wet," which means that they came to United States through the river. However, on the way here, they were caught by "a migra" (U.S. Citizenship and Immigration Services) and imprisoned for about a month. They finally got out and arrived in Boston where they had family. The service had just started and when I asked the guests that night to introduce themselves, a member of our church introduced his brother, his two sisters, and his mother. He told us briefly where they were coming from and what had happened to them. I asked the deacons to close the doors of the church and to turn off the video camera that recorded all of our services. I then asked the guests to tell their stories. A mother started to tell their terrible experiences of losing huge sums of money, being exploited by some of the coyotes, of being handcuffed and shamed by the immigration police. She told us how her sixty-eight-year-old mother was mistreated and how much they feared never getting out of prison. They could not speak a word of English and barely spoke Spanish. They were visibly tired, and in a post-traumatic moment. Their stories provoked a commotion and became the order of the worship service. Nothing that was in the bulletin was followed. One of the guests told about his shame at having to walk barefoot throughout a month in jail because he had lost his shoes when he was passing through the river. He started to cry and said: "I have always been poor but my mother never let me walk barefoot in my life . . ." Later he added, "I have good news, I am going to be a shoe shiner in a hotel in Boston . . ." After they told their stories, people from the church also asked to tell their stories too. A feeling of sadness and pain filled the sanctuary. We ended the service with special prayers for them. We placed them within a circle and their names and many others were remembered as the church tried to console them. There were all wounded people trying to heal other wounded people. After the service, they made contacts among themselves and the two sisters found jobs. The mother was going to see a therapist.

Eucharistic ritualizings are ways of undoing power, the sovereignty of the sacrament in favor of shared governance, shared power. Even though the sacrament, by being a ritual, "it is power, of acts and actuates,"[65] it should unmask our drive for power. Through the process of ritualization, power is negotiated. "Ritual practices," Bell says, "are themselves the very production and negotiation of power relations."[66] These ritual practices, or ritualization, are ways of negotiating symbols, rules, relations, worldviews, and so on. However, as Siobhan Garrigan points out, there are some things that cannot be negotiated: "A situation of domination or oppression by definition involves one party depriving the other of an equal right to negotiate."[67]

The idea of negotiation here does not bear the economic aspect of it in terms of commercial trade, business, or profit. Rather, to negotiate is to do the Nietzschean work of the "transvaluation of all values," that is, to constantly shift power dynamics based on mutual care, love, and solidarity. Transvaluation means, among other things, the ability of a community to change (negotiate) their judgments and reactions against people/practices considered as outsiders or scary. Negotiation here wants to de-value the symbols of might, power, greed, private possessions beyond limits, and consumerism in this culture and to re-value these symbolic principles by notions of sharing, giving up, living in solidarity in deep connection with the limits of the earth cycles. Thus, the negotiation around our Eucharistic borders are neither grounded in monetary negotiation nor marked by usury. Instead, they are marked by carefulness, prudence, sharing and simplicity. The earth belongs to God and is borrowed to us to share it. Thus, negotiations here are not a fight for power, but a desire to serve, to live not under the rubrics of the unregulated greedy market but around systems of cooperative and intentional communities. No endowments invested in the financial market but instead, money invested directly in people and small poor communities. No salary differences among the people of God. The Eucharistic table cannot accept that! These ways of living that will evidence this mode of living will perhaps see the idea of egalitarianism as naïve but this is what is proposed here. I borrow Wendell Berry's words to tell us how we should consider it:

> When I hear the stock market has fallen,
> I say, "Long live gravity! Long live

65. Bell, *Ritual Theory, Ritual Practice*, 195.

66. Ibid., 196.

67. Garrigan, *Beyond Ritual*, 61.

Stupidity, error, and greed in the palaces
of fantasy capitalism!" I think
an economy should be based on thrift,
on taking care of things, not on theft,
usury, seduction, waste, and ruin.[68]

What we learn from poor people in Latin America is that even though God is present in the sacrament of Eucharist at the church, they cannot do it without the stamp of the hierarchy who holds the power of the presence of God. If poor people do not have power to negotiate their welcoming and doing at the altar/table, they will establish their tables in the world, where they live and struggle, juxtaposing many tables that are offered with plenty of crumbs for everyone. By doing that, they negotiate where and what they can, turning the Eucharistic tables around by negotiating with the official altar/table at a distance, making the power of the church lose its grip upon their lives, and making their own tables an unknown sacrament, a place to negotiate their part, their space, their right.

To negotiate is to juxtapose things, to place or deal with old and also unprecedented things close together for contrasting effects, trying to break into new ways of living the gospel and life. At the table, immigrants call our attention to their "illegal" status, juxtaposing by exposing to the table, the systemic neo-colonial approaches that define the value of the other, policies around immigration, and NAFTA agreements. Their presence juxtaposed to the bread of heaven expose the kumbaya multicultural inter-exchange in Protestant white churches that does not lead anywhere besides an attempt to avoid a guilt trip. At the table, small farmers from around the globe will juxtapose their corn and call our attention by exposing how big agri-businesses are preventing people from planting, producing, and developing their family/small communities' plantation. At the table, women and their children will show how they have their lives interrupted by ways of patriarchy and brutal violence against them. Being exposed by their presence and hurts, and by juxtaposing their stories with the story of Jesus, we might be able to learn how to undo these systems of oppression.

At the table, the sacrificial death of Jesus Christ is always juxtaposed with the sacrificial death of the poor around the globe to expose the ways in which very few live expanded lives. Death is always around us and it is always juxtaposed over our celebrations. We neither shy away from death nor subsume to the cultural fear of death. Instead, we name death, we

68. Berry, "Some Further Words," 30.

say where it happens and we wrestle with it. We linger with it and with those who are marked by the powers of death. Then, and only then, we affirm the power of life and resurrection in Jesus Christ. Thus, the death and resurrection of Jesus Christ is always in, and through, and around the Eucharistic table. For Jesus' life, death, and resurrection is a transformative message of power, giving us hope that in spite of our death, we will be resurrected now and at the end of times. Thus, eucharists as ritualizations will press the social order and its systemic oppression with increasing modes of social violence, turning social blind spots of reality into consciousness as a way of perceiving what usually we don't see, and finding tools to empower people to fight for a better life.

The ritualizing of the sacraments entails juxtaposition, transvaluation, and negotiation of space, words, and body movements that come out of the creative lives of people, by the communities who are performing them from many traditions. It uses multi-centric structures to deal with the dysfunctional aspects of life in order to create spaces of solidarity. Shifting patterns of praying, singing, eating, drinking, dancing, crying, telling stories, reading, and listening to and from others, feasting, mourning, inviting, sharing, and so on, all of these movements performed around Eucharistic tables can entail passages from one place to another, even if these places might not be as easily distinguished.

The ritualizing of the sacraments is a way of bringing the Dionysian dreams into Apollonian structures so as to free our bodies, our imagination, our thinking, and our movements from the logocentric stiffness of our body/book of orders and what we badly name as tradition. As Jaci Maraschin wrote: "The revision or recreation of our liturgical practices must come from the light of the Spirit. Immanence and transcendence are related to contextualization and globalization, Apollonian, and Dionysian cultures in order to produce a new quality of spiritual order in our adoration."[69] We must learn to invite/juxtapose Dionysus, the god of grape harvest, of epiphany (how symptomatic), this foreign god into our Apollonian eucharists so we might learn to dance and add more sensuality, sexuality, desire, fire, and movement into our practices as to empower us. We need to restore the madness of this rite to face the madness of our world.

As ritualizing, installation, and rites of passage, Eucharists try to push, foster, enhance and move "what has been done and left undone in this world."[70] This endless coming back of the practitioner and the com-

---

69. Maraschin, "Culture, Spirit and Adoration."
70. Walton, "Eucharist," 92–93.

munity to eat together at the borders of the Eucharist tables will make each participant and each community a Eucharistic border Sisyphus.

5. Hospitable Eucharistic Liturgies. How Do We Do It?

What I am proposing here comes from the experience I lived out with communities that I worked with, one in a poor area in São Paulo, one in Massachusetts with immigrants and one with students at Louisville Presbyterian Theological Seminary. To relate these crossing border performances to Reformed churches, the question still is "how" are we to do these eucharists? In my understanding, there is no set of rules or seven steps, except by starting where we are, and seeing whether we can create connections and changes we hope for as we celebrate our faith in Christ. It is by doing that we can learn how borders work, what changes they might effect, and what kinds of hospitality they set forth. Deeply influenced by Dewey, Noam Chomsky said "You learn by doing." It is the belief that you learn by doing that is the crux of our enterprise here. Chomsky states:

> I think you learn by doing—I'm a Deweyite from way back. You learn by doing, and you figure out how to do things by watching other people do them. That's the way you learn to be a good carpenter, for example, and the way you learn to be a good physicist. Nobody can train you on how to do physics . . . You just watch people doing it and participate with them in doing it . . . The way you do it is by trying to do it yourself, and in particular trying to show, although it's not all that difficult, the chasm that separates standard versions of what goes on in the world from what the evidence and people's inquiries will show them.[71]

What is ritualizing/ritualization if not the careful cultivating and the doing of ritual actions? It is by doing that we learn what to do, what not to do and even who we might be. Smith and Taussig provide examples of communities who learned how to celebrate the eucharist away from the official table just by doing it. The women mentioned in the third chapter learned to invent the rituals they needed to celebrate. The poor people in Latin America start with whatever they have at hand to do their rituals. The inter-religious practices between Reformed churches and Candomblé people developed in chapter 6 talks about Paulo Freire's methodology: *to*

---

71. Chomsky, "Liberating the Mind from Orthodoxies," interview by David Barsamian, *Z Magazine*, May 2001: http://www.zcommunications.org/liberating-the-mind-from-orthodoxies-by-david-barsamian.

see, to judge and to act. And in this chapter, Bell and Grimes talk about ritualizing and ritualization. From all of these sources of wisdom and resistance, people are always inventing not only the ways they eat, but the very fabric of their lives every single day.

We start by paying attention to the world and to the gospel. We then create situations and observe responses. Moving some borders of the liturgical ordos is a way to create possibilities for life to be *liturgized*, developed, and preserved. Within these border movements, juxtaposing the known and the unknown, shifting the spaces, the order(s) of things, and "living with the world at heart" as Heidegger said, are ways of calling forth the Spirit to move in and around us perhaps in a different key, changing our lives in new ways. We learn hospitality by doing; we invent and create it by doing. In turn we are also invented and done by the things we do.

On the other hand, the question of *how* we create hospitable eucharistic practices can entail a set of delimitations and the establishing of borders. As we saw in the introduction, borders are necessary and vital for the survival, developing, and strengthening of individuals and communities. They offer structure and provide necessary limits within which people can expand their human possibilities. For some communities, it is the creation of borders more than the undoing of them that might need to be done. Within the liturgical space, being this space wherever we choose, borders offer safety and spur new possibilities for eucharistic events and hospitable practices. Thus, this book does not want to naively destroy liturgical borders or advocate a "Eucharistic or liturgical anything goes" but rather, to challenge the already and loved established borders to see how we can improve, develop, and adjust them within the context of global exploitation and injustice. It is to take a certain step towards expanding the circle of traditions. As communities challenge the liturgical borders of the eucharistic table, they must define new borders around which Christian Eucharists might happen.

What is it then that makes any table a *Christian* eucharistic table? We must start by saying that an answer to this questions is rather difficult to define since the Spirit is free to move anywhere and to make a sacrament out of anything the Spirit wants. Moreover, the Eucharist cannot master life in its unending possibilities and our theologies/liturgies cannot define precisely what the Spirit can turn into a sacrament. There are many "undecidables" along the way that make theological and liturgical definitions of eucharistic sacraments difficult. However, this undecidability does not, and must not, prevent either eucharistic sacraments from being lived as sacraments, or Christian communities from making ethical decisions, taking risks, creating necessary borders around their tables, and calling their celebrations Sacrament. As the philosopher of religion John Caputo says, "undecidability does not mean aesthetic indecision but supplies instead the condition of possibility of deciding, i.e., of taking a risk."[72]

One must therefore start by realizing that no definition of eucharist is *proper* and even possible, since none will do justice to the sacrament; each one will always leave something behind. That being acknowledged, one must still make theological assertions and provide liturgical boundaries to supply communities with measures and support for celebrating the sacrament of the Eucharist. Thus, we must take a risk and establish some provisional norms, definitions, and borders with which to start.

For a community already established preparation can be very important. Prayers and movements and symbols can and must be prepared in advance. Groups of people preparing to eat together. A cook, an artist, a lay person, a community leader, a foreigner, a person from another religion, whomever can be at the table to prepare the eucharist together, deciding on Bible texts, collecting artistic, theological, liturgical, and communal sources, as well as defining themes for the Eucharistic celebration. What injustices are we fighting together? What healing is needed? How can we engage the gifts of our people? Who should we invite? Some

72. Caputo, "Instants, Secrets and Singularities," 216.

elements of a Christian eucharistic table that could be used not necessarily in this order: (1) prayers for the movement of the Spirit; (2) an open invitation to whomever wants to participate in giving honor to God and as consequence, honoring one another, (3) checking ways of eating in other communities and providing space for the sharing of the food with those who want to eat together, having the world at heart, (4) paying attention to where people are hurting locally and globally and reaching out in solidarity to the poor/oppressed, (5) certain movements that can be done in and around the table and the use of the space inside and outside of the church; (6) making local/global connections; (7) a link to what is known as the "traditional" eucharistic rites, (8) raising questions about hospitality; (9) relationship to biblical references; and (10) remembrance of the historical Jesus, his life, death, and resurrection.

These basic points are only suggestions since our ritualization might take us from and to very different places. Nonetheless, we must transform our worshiping communities into mixed communities where members remind each other with many movements and words about our ongoing processes of recreating our identity, since we can only afford to know our (shifting) identities through the eyes of the other. More often than not, these communities should get together and talk about their own practices, about the ways they are worshiping God and making decisions about eucharistic words and practices. By checking on its liturgical connections and actions, the community continues not only to do its liturgical Sisyphean border crossing mission as a way of improving its hospitable liturgical practices but also to learn to see, listen, feel, touch, smell, and taste the presence of God through the power of the Holy Spirit. These liturgical practices intend to take people out of their comfort zones in order to spread the gospel of Jesus through incarnational liturgical practices. The world to change is not only "out there" waiting for us to leave our liturgical services to encounter it, but it is also "right here," inside and around our own Eucharistic tables. Moreover, these liturgical movements come from the assumption that reality is not sacred, or often desecrated, and the world is ours to be created.

When you ask any of the old-timers how new life came to Grace Presbyterian Church, they all point to the same starting place. It began the spring that there was a hole in the roof of the sanctuary. For years the congregation had been slowly declining. They had watched the neighborhood around the old church building change as well. Crime had increased and the old houses surrounding the church seemed to be decaying. Many of the members of the church moved out of the neighborhood to the suburbs and while some continued to drive i to the city for Sunday morning services, it looked to be only a matter of time until the church would close its doors for good. The congregation had tried adding new services and offering programs. They might work for a while, but they never seemed to last. As the congregation grew smaller and smaller, all they could do was to gather for the regular services. When torrential rain came that spring, a leak began in the sanctuary and threatened to change the place that they gathered for worship. So the congregation took the last of the church's endowment to pay a roofer to patch up the roof. The roofer told them that he would start working on the roof during Holy Week and that the sanctuary would be closed. When the session began to plan the Good Friday service, they looked for a different place to meet. Given the situation that they were facing, their young pastors encouraged them to try something new. They would walk through the neighborhood and have a service of readings from the passion story at places where violence in the neighborhood had taken place during the last year. Amidst darkened skies, a small group of about twenty people met outside the old sanctuary at noon. They looked up to the sky and saw the roofing crew pounding nails. Slowly they made their way [up] the street to the first gathering place. Late in December, a young boy had been killed by gunfire from a drive-by shooting while playing in his living room. The group from the church stopped in front of the house and began to sing, "Were you there when they crucified my Lord?" An elder read of Jesus praying [in] the Garden of Gethsemane. And then they moved on to the next stop. In front of a small grocery store, they gathered at the place where an older woman had been robbed. The force of the blow on her head had caused her to fall and she was injured so badly that she died several weeks later. Quietly the church group sang again, "Were you there when they crucified my Lord?" Tears filled their eyes as the Gospel was read. After two hours, of walking through the neighborhood they returned to the church. The group was tired, but they promised to meet for an Easter service on Sunday morning. When they gathered three days later, the pastor stood up and announced. This morning, I have asked a few of our members to speak about the service we held on Friday. One by one, they told about how deeply they were moved by what they had seen and felt as they walked around the neighborhood. Then the pastor spoke: "We cannot stay inside the walls of this church

> any longer. *This morning we are unlocking the doors of this church and we are committing ourselves to working for justice in this community. May the Spirit of God breathe new life into us as we go forth. Christ is risen indeed. Alleluia!" The change did not come about magically. Day after day, they gathered for a small meal and began to walk around the same streets of the neighborhood. On Fridays, they began serving a meal at the church for homeless people in the neighborhood. On Mondays, they worked in the community garden planting, watering, and weeding. On Wednesday afternoons, they volunteered as tutors in the elementary school. Every Saturday morning, they picked up the trash in the school yard down the street. Starting that season of Easter, each Sunday service included reports on the church's involvement in the neighborhood and an open invitation to bring friends and neighbors to help with the work. At the end of each Sunday service, they gathered around the baptismal font and prayed for God to strengthen them and bless the work that had begun. Slowly, but surely, Grace Presbyterian Church began to grow.*[73]

This liturgical and eucharistic process, I believe, can empower Christian churches, even perhaps beyond the Reformed grid, to develop a certain Christian plural identity from which it can go on and negotiate borders. Again, the plurality of liturgical actions and Eucharistic practices proposed here are not intended to do away with the Reformed or any other church tradition or to dismiss their wisdom. Instead, it wants to position these liturgical changes within the well known reformation maxim: "A church reformed and always being reformed." Thus, the negotiation of borderless borders intends to produce a stronger sense of continuity with the Reformed tradition and promote necessary connections with the realities of our day. In fact, it is a way of keeping traditions alive! By affirming that there is no single eucharistic ritual center/form that can hold God's presence or unambiguously say what is liturgically proper and correct, this project follows what the *Confession of* 1967 of the Presbyterian Church did with church doctrine. The Confession states that no one declaration of faith can univocally hold the richness of the Christian faith. "No one type of confession is exclusively valid, no one statement is irreformable,"[74] and substituted a Book of [nine] Confessions for a single confession [The Westminster Confession]. The result is that the church does not hold itself

73. Carvalhaes and Galbreath, "Season of Easter," 10.

74. *The Confession of 1967*, in *The Constitution of the Presbyterian Church (U.S.A.)*. 9.01.03.

entirely to any one rigid statement of faith, but rather aligns itself with a particular *confessional tradition* which gives it a particular Christian identity. The work then is to continue to pay attention to other confessions of faith, such as the *Belhar Confession*[75] but also, other confessions or theological/liturgical sources that other churches are using. There must be an intentional movement towards other churches' resources as to learn and enhance the Eucharistic sacrament in the Reformed churches.

The hope thus is that Reformed and other Christian communities move with and around poor communities and pay attention to their cries; that these communities together call upon the Spirit to create another world of justice, making lives, spaces, and things sacred, even if only for a moment. The hope and the trust is that the Spirit will come and create in the lives of individuals and our communities brief sacramental moments, saturated by the irreducible and yet fleeting presence of God. In this ways, our tables can become eucharistic events of different encounters with Christ. As we move, process, deal, and create the world through our ritualizings, interspersing them with readings of the Bible, remembrances of Jesus, the presence of an-other, the telling of our stories, of other words of God and other stories, we repeat and invent liturgical practices that will redraw the lines of eucharistic hospitality.

As we practice our liturgies, we do not only rehearse our lives, or position ourselves towards the other as we pray *come Holy Spirit come*! It will be the duty of each community, always in relationship with an-other community, to prevent exploitation, to access and judge the world, to interpret the Bible, to incarnate Christ, and to decide whether the Spirit (has) visited that community during any liturgical practice. Practical questions must be asked and answered as the community tries to search not just for their own interests and needs, which could clog the channels of the Spirit, but for the less fortunate, and the forgotten and excluded, that must be the criterion for the liturgical gathering around the eucharistic table.

75. "The Belhar Confession has its roots in the struggle against apartheid in Southern Africa. This 'outcry of faith' and 'call for faithfulness and repentance' was first drafted in 1982 by the Dutch Reformed Mission Church (DRMC) under the leadership of Allan Boesak. The DRMC took the lead in declaring that apartheid constituted a confession in which the truth of the gospel was at stake" (Reformed Church in America, "Belhar Confession": https://www.rca.org/sslpage.aspx?pid=304).

Between the North of Mexico and the South of United States, there is a wall. A wall of sin, a wall of shame, a wall of embarrassment, a wall of hatred and xenophobia, a wall that explicitly shows the stupidity and ignorance and fear of the human soul. Cut by this wall, there is Nogales, a city that has the same name in both sides. From both sides, Protestant churches join Catholic churches to celebrate the Eucharist right at the wall. It is Sunday morning and these churches bring their guitars, and chalices, and patens. They put a table/altar on both sides and they sing and pray for each other. They repent and they cry over the wall. Each side has something prepared to talk about immigration, injustice, faith, and struggle. Within their themes are: "The right to emigrate and the right not to emigrate; The nature of borders—whether political, spiritual, or personal; The liturgy as a sacrament of unity, reconciliation and transformation; The understanding of what it means to be one body in Christ; The ability of goods to cross borders more easily than human beings; The building up of the community into one body healed of all division; The role of the Church as an agent of welcome and hospitality—a sanctuary for life; The preferential option for the poor—caring and welcoming the most vulnerable; The dignity of work and rights of workers—seeking a better life for one's family; The nature of solidarity—recognizing we are one human family and love of neighbor." There they pray the Eucharistic prayer and they open up the table for the body of Christ to celebrate. Enough of brokenness, enough of divisions, they decide to be a sign of unity and justice, a sign of faith and practical love lived together. The broken bread of Christ grasps the broken bodies of immigrants. The blood of Christ shed for all heals the wounds of those whose blood was shed in the desert because of the police, coyotes, and drug dealers. They close with a prayer of thanksgiving and the blessing at the end of the service is their promise that they will continue to do this worship until the day this wall comes crumbling down becoming a bridge to each other's land and hearts.[76]

Liturgy as practice and assessment to reality then can be a first act. Innovative liturgical practices *in relation* to traditional eucharistic words and gesturing comes as a response to the community and the world's situation. The theologizing of these actions and the judging of our intentions comes afterwards. The designs of our liturgical practices have to identify

76. See "Eucharist Without Borders": http://www.claudiocarvalhaes.com/blog/eucharist-without-borders/. For more information, see the movie *One Border, One Body.*

ways to relate Christ and two thousand years of Christian tradition to the life of each community in our globalized world. The intention is that each border should challenge, bless, and disturb another border. In this way, we can break the sovereignty of our own theological power (meaning) and become constantly troubled by those who are not part of our own communities.

We move on by juxtaposing not only liturgical elements to liturgical elements, or liturgy to liturgy, or eucharist to church but rather, by juxtaposing foreign, global, unknown, "exterior" elements to liturgical elements. Then, perhaps unexpected and "unreliable" presences along with the presence of tradition, of immigrants with citizens, the in and the out of the altar/table, can strive together for the improvement of our faith, and of ourselves in spite of our sins, and fears, and arrogances.

Andrea Bieler and Luise Schottroff did that in their book: they juxtaposed the eucharist with economy, Bible, bread and the global market, eschatology, resurrection and concrete bodies pulsing at the table. Fascinating enough, atheist Alain de Botton is also doing that. He seems to have perceived Eucharist in deeper ways than many Christians. Drawing from the early church's meals experiences, Mr. Botton wants to do this juxtaposition, creating a restaurant that would mirror the Christian mass and that kind of friendship lived in the early churches. Recently he gave an interview saying the following: "In the early church, these were known as 'agape (from the Greek for 'love') feasts.' In the modern city, there are many places to eat well, but there's an almost universal lack of venues that help us to transform strangers into friends."[77] Eucharistic spaces can help strangers become friends without being charged for anything, or asking for proper beliefs to belong. His example of juxtaposition is somewhat doing the work of love proclaimed by Christ. If he didn't charge people to eat that could be a "real" Eucharistic meal!

Thus, we do it by getting together around many congregational Eucharistic tables around the globe, raising awareness of the global situation of exclusion and being bold enough to hold the tradition we are attached to as well as to embrace other traditions. The movement of loving and transgressing our tradition happens by engaging other traditions, other forms of hospitality, new liturgical gestures, words, and actions. The poem

77. Stoyan Zaimov, "Atheist Alain de Botton Envisions Restaurant Modeled After Christian Mass." Business, *Christian Post*, March 19, 2012: http://www.christianpost.com/news/atheist-alain-de-botton-envisions-restaurant-modeled-after-christian-mass-71682/.

"Love After Love" by poet and Nobel Laureate in literature Derek Walcott can be said to describe the Eucharistic tables.[78]

The *World Social Forum*, in an editorial in their 2005 newspaper, exclaimed: "The world can only be changed by those who practice change."[79] Liturgical ritualizing/installations are indeed local practices of changes, ways of moving borders,[80] a constant work on borderless borders, with the purpose of reshaping understandings of the way in which we practice hospitality. By working on hospitality, we will necessarily work on borders, on politics, on friendship, on Jesus, on the sacraments. In a sense, it is a naïve and impossible project. But as Brazilian scientist Miguel Nicodelius affirms, "the impossible is the fact that nobody gave enough energy to make it happen,"[81] and as theater and performance theoretician Herbert Blau states, "the impossible takes a little time,"[82] we just need to rehearse and practice it.

78. See Walcott, *Collected Poems, 1948–1984*, 328.

79. Editorial, *World Social Forum*, 2005, 5.

80. Moving borders means the constant shifting of borders, sometimes holding them, sometimes dismantling them. Borders are very necessary for our existence and we must account for that. What is proposed here is not that every border must be destroyed. Instead, every border must be open to be negotiated which does not mean that all of them must be negotiated. The revolving troubling of borders is a way of making sure the borders we structure are always on the search for justice and hospitality.

81. Miguel Nicolelis is a Brazilian scientist who keeps talking about the necessity of the impossible and that we don't need to fear the impossible. See his book *Muito Além do Nosso Eu*; and his inaugural lecture at Brasilia University in Brazil: http://www .youtube.com/watch?v=SgLepzpxXYI.

82. Blau, *Dubious Spectacle*, 36.

Conclusion

Onkotô?

My mother tongue is a foreign language.[1]

—EDMOND JABÈS

The crisis consists precisely in the fact that the old is dying and the new cannot be born; in this interregnum a great variety of morbid symptoms appear.[2]

—ANTONIO GRAMSCI

"ONKOTÔ?" WAS THE TITLE of a Brazilian dance group who gave their last performance at Brooklyn Academy of Music in the Fall of 2005. I did not understand this word. As I read the program of the evening's performance, I learned that it was a slang word, an abbreviation of the phrase "where am I?" used by Brazilian people in the state of Minas Gerais. Living in a foreign country, I am used to the fact that I live between two (or more) worlds. I can never get settled since I am perpetually trying to negotiate my ways, vocabularies, and feelings within and between worlds. When I go to Brazil, I am always reminded of how much I have changed and how much of a "gringo" I have become, something that brings desolation to my heart. I realize how far I am from the poor upbringings in which I was raised. When I am there, I don't remember Portuguese words; I can see my Portuguese increasingly getting worse, while my English does not necessarily improve. Then, when I am in the United States, I am constantly

1. Edmond Jabès, cited in Walsroy, *Lavish Absence*.
2. Gramsci, *Selections from the Prison Notebooks*, 276.

reminded that I do not belong here, that my ways—the way I speak, write, think, behave—are often strange to people wherever I go, be it in the academy, the church, or on the streets. I feel like I am *illiterate* in both Portuguese and English, as well as in both cultures.[3]

This (in)constant flux frequently makes me constantly ask, "Onkotô?" Where am I? It has sensitized me to the pressures of the borders around me and around the world. Having grown up as a poor kid doing shoe shining at the age of nine, having started to work at a full time job at thirteen to help my parents, having worked as a pastor with the poor who often did not have a place to stay or anything to eat, then having committed to a non-documented immigrant church in the U.S., finally having come all the way to where I am now, I cannot help but perceive the world marked with borders of all kinds. These borders not only taint my eyes but also my entire living, which seem to be in perpetual tension. My writing is not different and when I write it feels unsettled, unchecked, nervous, fast, mixed with feelings of all kinds, almost desperate, on the verge of becoming a manifesto, a scream, a revolutionary act; always pointing to an urgency, a desperation, to a borderless hospitality in an un-negotiable now. The *fronteira/frontera/border* of my body/writing/heart is always elsewhere. Onkotô?

In the introduction to this book, I developed Derrida's ideas of hospitality, which can be rightly divided into the "Law of hospitality" and the "law of hospitality." By the "Law of hospitality" with a capital letter, he meant an impossible hospitality, a hospitality with no borders, no limits, no conditions, where every guest, either expected or not, is always welcome. This hospitality is *haunted* by the arrival of somebody or something that comes without announcing what, who, when, or how. It frightens our settled ways. It is an unconditional hospitality offered to everyone—even to the enemy, who could be a friend, even if a mortal friend—without measure, without negotiations or law. *True* hospitality for Derrida happens when all the laws of hospitality are suspended.

However, Derrida argues that this Law of hospitality is impossible. No one can or should live without minimal laws of protection for an individual, a community, a country. It would be irresponsible to live such a Law of hospitality if this hospitality makes Lot offer his two daughters to the men from Sodom, or allows the rape and the slaughter of the

---

3. This feeling was beautifully described by Fernanda Montenegro, a famous Brazilian actress when she received the Globe Awards for her role in the movie Central Station. She said: "My English is poor but my heart is better."

concubine by her "master" in the Book of Judges. What Derrida might be saying, perhaps, is that every law of hospitality should be questioned, before deciding whether and where to place borders.

Moreover, Derrida's use of the word hospitality also includes other notions and perspectives. He says that hospitality is "a problem of economy, of appropriation, misappropriation, *hospitality is economy*."[4] Thus, to talk about hospitality is to talk about politics, about the trans-nationality of the world, the configurations of national borders, theological systems, constant appropriations and misappropriation of power as it shapes the ways that laws are created.

In the same way, both the Law and law of hospitality affect the sacrament of the Eucharists. Throughout this book I have shown how access to the table of the eucharistic sacrament is marked by an array of borders that control its celebration and interpretation. I argued that the Sacrament correlates itself to broader aspects of life, such as politics, the economy, social class, gender, racism, etc., but also helps to define, keep, or change all of these things. Hence, to speak of eucharists is also to talk about hospitality, what goes on in and around the meal, its negotiations, appropriation and misappropriation. Eucharists force us to consider how borders are created and placed around the tables as well as how every border has to be questioned by a hospitality without condition, under the conditions of a totally Other, exposed by the presence/limits of people, so that communities can challenge themselves to move toward, and beyond, their own borders of safety.

In this book, in order to find ways to get at the Law of hospitality as it relates to Reformed Eucharistic tables, I have worked with elements that are not part of Derrida's Law of hospitality, namely theological *calculations*, liturgical *negotiations*, and ecclesiological *conditions*. In some ways, this project represents a festival of appropriations and misappropriations, like any other theological/liturgical/ecclesiastical project. In each chapter I have identified ways in which the borders of hospitality were established and/or challenged. Through these measurements, appropriations, misappropriations, mis/calculations, conditions and negotiations, and shared grace, I have demonstrated that the borders of the eucharistic sacrament can become even more plural, multicentric, polidoxy liturgical/theological places, which offer a more expanded notion of hospitalities. Thus, the core of this book suggests that Eucharistic tables can reflect a borderless borders hospitality, which means, a constant, unending negotiation and

4. Derrida, "Politics and Friendship"; emphasis added.

renegotiation of any border around the tables, always from the perspective of the disfranchised, those who have no power, those who are on the side lines or at the fringes of society. By *borderless*, I mean unconditionality, that every border has to be checked, critiqued, and challenged by its intentionality, conventionalities, and historical underpinnings. As for the *borders* part of borderless borders, I recognize that we all have a need for boundaries and conditions that define our lives and surround us with necessary protection. These two words together, *borderless borders*, create the necessary tension between the borders that we need to live and then to challenge in order to expand them toward the other, thus offering hospitality in ways perhaps never considered and foreseen before.

> *She had already mourned her two sons and her husband in a lost missile that bombed a house next to hers. She was alone now, without a job and with her three year old boy and a five year old girl to feed. The country was devastated and this strange war was destroying masses of people. Resistance forces were trying, with meager resources but intense ferocity, not to let enemy forces take over their country. Her family was in the countryside, but she had no idea what had happened to them. She had to feed her kids and didn't know how . . . All of a sudden she heard that a nearby supermarket was invaded and people were taking food. She left the kids alone in the remains of what was once her home and ran to get food. Before she left she said to them: Don't go anywhere and don't open the door to anybody. On the streets, she saw a crowd going inside the supermarket. She forced her way in and found a couple packets of flour on the floor. She held them as if she was holding her life. She ran out of the supermarket and when she was close to her house, a lost bullet hit her in the back and she fell on the ground . . .*

Borderless borders start with an option for the margins, a radical decision for those who have been forgotten, the crippled, the poor, the foreigner. Eucharists are closer to unconditional hospitality when they enact and reflect an effort to re-figure and re-shape borders in churches that have set them against the people whom they often exclude. However, hospitality cannot be practiced without some "violence" to the group that decides to open their doors wider. In the ritualization process, proper arrangements, careful preoccupation with the guests, together with proper concerns for the limits of the believers within the congregation, will not be safe or easy. Practicing borderless border hospitality is an ongoing disruptive event, sometimes improper, sometimes indecent according to the accepted rules of order and decency. In the process, someone will always be offended, hurt, misrepresented, frustrated, and we must find ways to deal with that.

Let us imagine that a Presbyterian church in Arizona reaches out and visits undocumented immigrant families working in the tomato fields about twenty miles away from the church and invites them to come and eat together.[5] How might they receive these families also in the sanctuary around a big table for a eucharistic meal? What does this movement entail? What needs to move and be moved? The congregation gathers together to think about these questions. They invite other people or organizations that work with illegal immigrants and ask for help. After these assessments are made, they think about the liturgy. What to do and what not to do? How should this liturgical space resemble a place where everyone is a foreigner searching to make it home, a temporary home for all who are there? What should be offered to the adults and children? A Spanish course is prepared to help the church people to connect to the guests. They visit the farm worker families to get to know them better. They share breakfast; they let their kids play together. These farm workers eventually accept the invitation and they gather together with the church people. The hosting church provides the welcoming, at first: food, liturgy, and interpreters to make all the connections. Now, what should they do? How do they tell these families they are welcome and in what ways? They gather together once, twice, and decide that they will do that for six months. They try everything they think is possible to mix the two communities. The farm workers' families are invited to the planning team and they decide together what to do next: songs, food, gestures, stories, experiences that challenge both communities. Perhaps the church people on some days will help these families pick up tomatoes at 6:00 am. Perhaps they will contact lawyers to help with their documentation. The immigrant community will also say what they need and what they have to offer. They will share each others' lives, share power, until both communities become able to recognize themselves as foreigners and strangers.[6] We must recognize that we serve and worship a God who can never be totally recognized, thus always a stranger to us.

5. See the description of undocumented families in the tomato fields in Arizona in ed. Cull and Carrasco, *Alambrista and the U.S. Mexico Border*.

6. "But it is perhaps on the basis of that contemporary individualism's subversion, beginning with that moment when the citizen-individual ceases to consider himself as unitary and glorious but discovers his incoherences and abysses, in short his

What comes out of this experience can became a way into new experiences between these two communities, and then with other communities. Eventually, everyone will ask: onkotô? And they will need the help of others to figure out together where and what this liturgical space might perform and become. There are borders there but the task, the Sisyphus task, is to constantly push and re-negotiate them.

Ritualizing eucharists is risky, difficult, messy, and, at times, uncomfortable. Reaching for agreements is not easy. Those involved must practice living with dissent, disagreement, and some level of anger/frustration. Onkotô? When I remember my mother's family arriving at home, I dissented, I was angry. I disagreed with my mother. I didn't want them there. They were smelly; they took away what was mine; but there was no way out. If my mother had to offer hospitality without condition, it had to be done without too much concern for what I was feeling. She knew I was safe and that was enough for her.

As a pastor of an undocumented church hosted by a local Presbyterian church in Massachusetts, we had to deal with each other. It was hard. There were accusations from both sides. Every week there were talks about insensibilities and lack of proper behavior in their House of the Lord. One day, one of our kids broke one of the stained glass windows and the situation became unsustainable. We paid for the window, but we could not stay anymore. What do we do to stay together when we break each other's sacred objects? I would not have liked to have any annoying people taking over my place of worship, messing up things that were very expensive and carried a sense of history. So, after a few years, we had to move. The guest is often a parasite who is always on the verge of being thrown away. They don't have the keys to the house. To invite another into our spaces/lives is always to invite someone who can undo, break, deviate, or annoy our own ways of being. It is to offer them the keys to our houses. And yet, this immigrant congregation was not open either. They would be biased against new immigrants and very protective about their own community. They were afraid to offer the keys of their own house to the new foreigners. And the movement went on . . .

We are "strangers to ourselves," says Julia Kristeva:

> Strangely, the foreigner lives within us: he is the hidden face of
> our identity, the space that wrecks our abode, the time in which

'strangeness'—that the questiona rises again: no longer that of welcoming the foreigner within a system that obliterates him but of promoting the togetherness of those foreigners that we all recognize ourselves to be" (Kristeva, "Strangers to Ourselves," 265).

understanding and affinity founder. By recognizing him within ourselves, we are spared detesting him to himself. A symptom that precisely turns "we" into a problem, perhaps makes it impossible. The foreigner comes in when the consciousness of my difference arises, and he disappears when we all acknowledge ourselves as foreigners, unamenable to bonds and communities.[7]

What Kristeva is saying is that there isn't and there never has been the idea of "they" in our history but only "we." We are in this web of relations that makes us responsible for each other and we cannot escape that anymore. Moreover, if we have a *we* to deal with, people from other religions are not excluded from our daunting task of offering hospitality. Candomblé people are also *we* and *we* move along in life together, for they might be holding the keys to our happiness!

Our Eucharistic prayers are temporary signs, perpetual moves in transient areas, places to eat and drink, to tap into the subversive memory of Jesus Christ and gain strength to keep going on the journey, carrying our tabernacles and temporary structures along. Onkotô? Our liturgies are fundamentally a foreign place, a temporary structure, a burning bush that is indeed consumed, burnt briefly into an offering to God, a cultural memorial of ages past into a society yet to exist, sketches of a nation without a state, a country without a "nationality code," made with nomadic people on the move toward a new heaven and new earth. Kristeva helps us think in that way:

> Let us not seek to solidify, to turn the otherness of the foreigner into a thing. Let us merely touch it, brush by it, without giving it a permanent structure. Simply sketching out its perpetual motion through some of its former, changing representations scattered throughout history. Let us escape its hatred, its burden, fleeing them not through leveling and forgetting, but through the harmonious repetition of the differences it implies and spreads.[8]

In order to move beyond self-absorbed and self-enclosed communities that are worried primarily about our local history and safety, liturgical borderless borders are tools to challenge local churches to expand their borders of hospitality to others. Eucharists entail *a constant call* for social transformation through performative-border-crossing/installation/rites of passage movements within the communities as a challenge to enhance

7. Ibid., 264.
8. Ibid., 265.

the perceptions of the community about the other. Moreover, eucharists carry a *charge* and a *demand* that we move our tables to places of disorder, injustice, fear and oppression. It is when we move toward the other, the other of ourselves, the other that gives me the sense of myself, of my limits, of my identity, that I have an encounter with God, who is always approaching in unexpected ways, with disguised angels and coyotes.

Within these encounters, the "Law of hospitality" and the "laws of hospitality" will be held in tension. For churches that want to share the love of God, the Law of hospitality is an imperative. In order to offer hospitality, churches must liturgize with other communities within their own liturgical spaces. Thus, they will continue to change themselves to move beyond their comfort zone to *zones of invisibility*, such as the tomato fields, private prisons, streets, and dumpsters where people live, shadowy zones of our societies where immigrant people are not heard, counted, or cared about. Or, they will search for countries that politically and economically "do not exist" on the map, and will try to find ways to engage with them and their lives also out of liturgical performances. Or, they will walk toward inter-religious places, or find out about ethnic communities that are isolated in this country but close to the church building. Or open the doors of the church during the winter for the poor to actually sleep in and have late meals/eucharists with homeless people. Hence, communities that celebrate Eucharists will make a choice to extend their tables to poor people, to create bridges from liturgical zones of safety in risky places where lawlessness is the *law*, as this lawlessness creates places where they form "states of exception."[9]

As "Sisyphus border"[10] crossers, ritualizing Eucharists, we move outside of the borders of the prescribed liturgical settings, and make new forms of sacraments happen at tables shared with poor people. Eucharistic movements of hospitality create a space in-between, where everyone can be both lost and found. In the meantime, the poor do not and will not wait for the goodwill of plentiful eucharistic tables. They create their own sacraments, feasting around their own tables, multiplying their crumbs, fishes, and loaves, and making changes as they can, offering and receiving the food of life. Many of them find some sacraments of justice and hospitality not through kindness or offered love, but through resistance, through appropriation of lands not given to them, through revolution. Happiness

9. Agamben, *State of Exception.*
10. Gómez-Pena, *New World Border,* i.

is their "prove dos nove,"[11] the final proof of what they live and perform. Brazilian singer Chico Buarque sings: "My people were bitterly sad, but created a drumbeat to stop suffering; Blessed is the pleasure. Blessed is the pleasure. In this immodest party, let's honor anyone who lends us this joy."[12] Julia Kristeva also mentions happiness to foreigners. She says:

> [T]he feeling that there is a special, somewhat insolent happiness in the foreigner. Happiness seems to prevail, *in spite of everything*, because something has definitely been exceeded: it is the happiness of tearing away, of racing, the space of a promised infinite. Such happiness is, however, constrained, apprehensively discreet, in spite of its piercing intrusion, since the foreigner keeps feeling threatened by his former territory, caught up in the memory of a happiness or a disaster—both always excessive. Can one be a foreigner and happy? The foreigner calls forth a new idea of happiness. Between the fugue and the origin: a fragile limit, a temporary homeostasis. Posited, present, sometimes certain, that happiness knows nevertheless that it is passing, like fire that shines only because it consumes. The strange happiness of the foreigner consists in maintaining that fleeing eternity or that perpetual transience.[13]

The movement of people around the globe continues to happen. Onkotô, Onkotô? Where is our house? Where is God's house? The worship space performs a territory without citizenship, without state borders. We are all nomads wandering in God's world, which is nobody's land. Worship places are resting areas for pilgrims, those who are not from this world and who are walking without proper theological/liturgical maps toward a new earth and a new heaven. Worship places are places for unexpected encounters, customs areas without anybody asking for proper liturgical documents, saying hi and goodbye and peace of Christ all the time. Worship places as borderless border places invite the body and the mind and the soul and the spirit, concrete situations of those who happen to inhabit that land during that time. The Eucharistic meal will go beyond measures and make sure everyone is welcomed, fed, and properly cared for. Commensality, prayers, health insurance for all, songs, food for the hungry, the word of God, sharing resources to pay each other's bills, school for every

---

11. Andrade, *Utopia Antropofágica*, 27.

12. Chico Buarque, "Festa Imodesta," in *Sinal Fechado*, Distrito Federal, 1974, CD.

13. Kristeva, "Strangers to Ourselves," 267.

kid, Babel/Pentecost languages, prophetic voices, transnational liturgies, more prayers and open grace are all intertwined around this table.

Our worship places/houses are neither in Jerusalem nor on Mt. Gerizim, but in the *shalom* of God.[14] At every worship place / rest area / foreign country, when we ask onkotô we will respond to each other: We are at the shalom of God, a temporary *oikos* of God for everybody to live in. These nomadic places are places where we, the Sisyphus people of our time, do our best to bring the stone all the way up, never giving up. Never! Mobility, woundedness, thinking, praying, and happiness are at the heart of these worshiping gatherings, Eucharistic celebrations for the sole glory of God.

Worship places as nomadic places do not subscribe but are closely related to what Rosi Braidotti calls the Nomadic Subjects/Nomadic Theory. She says that nomadic thought

> [m]akes all thinking into affirmative activity that aims at the production of concepts, precepts and effects in the relational motion of approaching multiple others. Thinking is about tracing lines of flight and zigzagging patters that undo dominant representations. Dynamic and outward bound, nomadic thought undoes the static authority of the past and redefines memory as the faculty that decodes residual traces of half-effaced presences; it retrieves leftover sensations and accesses afterthoughts . . . each nomadic connection offers at least the possibility of an ethical relation of opening out toward an empowering connection to others. Each relation is therefore an ethical project indexed on affirmation and mutual specification, not the dialectics of recognition and lack . . . (Nomadic thought) critiques the self interest, the repressive tolerance, and the deeply seated conservatism of the institutions that are officially in charge of the knowledge production.[15]

Instead of owning the worship spaces, people share these places that are foreign for everyone. For worship spaces are always a foreign land we call home. Thus, as those at eucharistic tables and in this work, Reformed churches are called to share a common ground with poor people offering not only almsgiving, but their tables and resources to the poor as ways of discovering new eucharistic ways of celebrating God's presence among us, new ways of being Christians and new ways of being human.

---

14. Elwood, "Death in Egypt."

15. Bradotti. *Nomadic Theory*, 2–3.

Eucharist and Globalization

Those who gather around Reformed tables within the United States can make expanded efforts to share their tables with the neighbors they fear, those who, awkwardly enough, make their lives better. Then, we might come to realize that the fear we have has nothing to do with *them*, but with the ways we have learned to relate to one another. Onkotô? Ritualizing eucharists challenges us to move our tables of sacraments toward places of oppression and injustice where other religious sacraments are also created and experienced. Ritualizing eucharists pushes our tables toward inter-religious communities to make them our friends.

> *A local church in the U.S. partners with a local church in Mexico and they join their efforts to hear about the disappeared women in Juarez. They collect information and bring names of disappeared women and families. They learn about this disaster and they join other organizations. They create prayers, they bring songs to be sung around the Eucharistic table. They speak in English and Spanish. At the table, along with bread and wine they have pictures of women who disappeared. They weep and they hold hands around the table. The subversive memory of Jesus is called upon the elements and they raise their voices and hopes and renew their hopes and strength. They pray out loud as a Pentecostal people and they beg for God's mercy. They leave torn out by the facts of pain. They leave renewed in their faith in Jesus Christ and their love for those whom they have never met.*

If we move, and move constantly, the incarnation of Christ will become fuzzy; we will lose ourselves in the midst of the poor, not knowing what word/world is ours, what language we speak and what people is ours. Onkotô? This moving process entails a constant change of liturgies and theologies that are negotiated between the conditions and the unconditionality of hospitality. Thus, Eucharists are a work to be done together since, as mentioned in the third chapter, there is no community that "emits the right signs."[16] We can learn this with Riobaldo, one of the most fascinating characters in Brazilian literature, who said:

16. Bhabha, *Location of Culture*, 303.

Life invents! We start things, without knowing why, and from there we lose the power to continue—because life is a work of everybody, mixed and seasoned by everyone.[17]

Onkotô? Where am I? We will ask it every time we meet. Where am I eating today? Who are these people? And God will ask us: Where are you? Why are you hiding? Why are you weeping? Where is your brother and sister? The world is always unfolding in us and to us through liturgical actions around many eucharistic tables. At every table, we belong to many worlds, with many sacraments and with many and diverse people of God. Moreover, around this table that is indeed ours, but always belonging to somebody else as well, we practice a Sysiphus borderless border Eucharist, and speak a "mother tongue [that] is a foreign language." There, around the table, which is always a here and an elsewhere, among strangers, nomads, poor, and strange people, we can have life-changing encounters with God, even with a stranger God, so we might learn to worship God, pray, eat, live, and finally love each other. As the Brazilian writer Clarice Lispector once said, "[B]read is love among strangers."[18]

Onkotô?

17. "A vida inventa! A gente principia as coisas, no não saber por que, e desde aí perde o poder de continuação—porque a vida é mutirão de todos, por todos remexida e temperada" (Rosa, *Grande Sertão*).

18. Lispector, "Repartição dos Pães," 29.

Bibliography

Adam, Júlio Cézar. *Liturgia com os Pés, Estudo sobre a função social do culto cristão*. São Leopoldo, RS: Editora Sinodal, 2012.

Agamben, Giorgio. *State of Exception*. Translated by Kevin Attell. Chicago: University of Chicago Press, 2005.

Althaus-Reid, Marcella. *Indecent Theology: Theological Perversions in Sex, Gender and Politics*. London: Routledge, 2000.

Althaus-Reid, Marcella, editor. *Liberation Theology and Sexuality*. Aldershot, UK: Ashgate, 2006.

Anderson, Benedict. *Imagined Communities*. London: Verso, 1983.

Anderson, E. Byron, and Bruce T. Morrill, editors. *Liturgy and the Moral Self: Humanity at Full Stretch Before God*. Collegeville, MN: Liturgical, 1998.

Andrade, Oswald de. *A Utopia Antropofágica: A Antropofagia ao alcance de todos*. Vol. 6 of *Obras completas de Oswald de Andrade*. São Paulo: Globo & Secretaria de Estado da Cultura, 1990.

Anidjar, Gil. "Notes on Hospitality." In *Acts of Religion*, by Jacques Derrida, translated and edited by Gil Anidjar, 356–57. New York: Routledge, 2002.

Anzaldua, Gloria E. *Borderlands: La Frontera: The New Mestiza*. San Francisco: Aunt Lute, 1987.

Aponte, Edwin David, and Miguel De La Torre, editors. *Handbook of Latina/o Theologies*. St. Louis: Chalice, 2006.

Appiah, Kwame Anthony. *Cosmopolitanism: Ethics in a World of Strangers*. New York: Norton, 2006.

Aquino, María Pilar. *Our Cry for Life: Feminist Theology from Latin America*. Maryknoll, NY: Orbis, 1993.

Aquino, María Pilar, and Roberto S. Goizueta, editors. *Theology: Expanding the Borders*. South Bend, IN: Twenty-Third, 1998.

Aquino, María Pilar, et al., editors. *A Reader in Latina Feminist Theology*. Religion and Justice. Austin: University of Texas Press, 2002.

Aschcroft, Bill, et al. *Post-Colonial Studies: the Key Concepts*. London: Routledge, 2000.

Azevedo, Marcello de C. *Basic Ecclesial Communities in Brazil: The Challenge of a New Way of Being Church*. Washington, DC: Georgetown University Press, 1987.

Baker-Fletcher, Karen. *Sisters of Dust, Sisters of Spirit: Womanist Wordings on God and Creation*. Minneapolis: Fortress, 1998.

Barros, Marcelo. "Multipla Pertença, o Pluralismo Religioso." In *Teologia Pluralista Libertadora Intercontinental*, edited by José M. Vigil, Luiza E. Tomita, Marcelo Barros, 41–60. ASETT, EATWOT. São Paulo: Edições Paulinas, 2008.

Barth, Markus. *Rediscovering the Lord's Supper*. Atlanta: Knox, 1988.

Bastide, Roger. *O Candomblé da Bahia*. São Paulo: Companhia das Letras, 2009.

Bauer, Walter. *Orthodoxy and Heresy in Earlier Christianity*. Edited by Robert A. Kraft and Gerhard Krodel. Translated by a team from the Philadelphia Seminar on Christian Origins. Philadelphia: Fortress, 1971.

Bauman, Zygmunt. *Wasted Lives: Modernity and its Outcasts*. Cambridge: Polity, 2004.

Bebblethwaite, Margaret. *Base Communities: An Introduction*. London: Chapman, 1993.

Bell, Catherine. *Ritual: Perspectives and Dimensions*. New York: Oxford University Press. 1997.

———. *Ritual Theory, Ritual Practice*. New York: Oxford University Press, 1992.

Berger, Teresa. *Fragments of Real Presence: Liturgical Tradition in the Hands of Women* New York: Crossroad, 2005.

———. *Women's Ways of Worship: Gender Analysis and Liturgical History*. Collegeville, MN: Liturgical. 1999.

Berger, Teresa, editor. *Dissident Daughters: Feminist Liturgies in Global Context*. Louisville: Westminster John Knox, 2001.

Berry, Wendell. "It All Turns on Affection." 41st Jefferson Lecture in the Humanities, June, 23, 2012.

———. "Some Further Words." In *Given: Poems*, 28–33. Berkeley: Counterpoint, 2006.

Betcher, Sharon V. "Take My Yoga upon You: A Spiritual Pli for the Global City." In *Polydoxy: Theology of Multiplicity and Relation*, edited by Catherine Keller and Laurel Schneider, 57–80. New York: Routledge, 2011.

Betto, Frei. *BECs, Rumo À Nova Sociedade, O 5º Encontro Intereclesial das Communidade Eclesiais de Base*. São Paulo: Edições Paulinas, 1983.

———. "La fe no es una ideología y el marxismo no es una fe." Interviewed by Paulo Margaria, *Nuevo Mundo, Mundos Nuevos*, Sao Paulo, October 2011. Online: http://nuevomundo.revues.org/62990?lang=es#ftn4.

Bhabha, Homi K. *The Location of Culture*. London, New York: Routledge, 1994.

———. "The Third Space." In *Identity, Community, Culture, Difference*, edited by Jonathan Rutherford, 207–21. London: Lawrence & Wishart, 1990.

Bial, Henry. *The Performance Studies Reader*. London, New York: Routledge, 2004.

Bieler, Andrea, and Luise Schottroff. *The Eucharist: Bodies, Bread & Resurrection*. Minneapolis: Fortress, 2007.

Blau, Herbert. *The Dubious Spectacle: Extremities of Theater, 1976–2000*. Minneapolis: University of Minnesota Press, 2002.

Blount, Brian K., and Leonora Tubbs Tisdale, editors. *Making Room at the Table: An Invitation to Multicultural Worship*. Louisville: Westminster John Knox, 2001.

Boff, Clodovis. *Theologia e Prática: Teologia do Político e suas Mediações*. Rio de Janeiro: Editora Vozes, 1978.

Boff, Leonardo. *A Águia e a Galinha: Uma Metáfora da Condição Humana*. Rio de Janeiro: Editora Vozes, 2006.

———. *Church, Charism and Power: Liberation Theology and the Institutional Church*. Translated by John W. Diercksmeier. New York: Crossroad, 1986.

———. *Ecclesiogenesis: The Base Communities Reinvent the Church*. Translated by Robert R. Barr. Maryknoll, NY: Orbis, 1986.

———. *Igreja, Charisma e Poder: Ensaios de Ecclesiologia Militante*. Rio de Janeiro: Editora Vozes, 1990.

———. *Jesus Christ Liberator: A Critical Christology for Our Times*. Translated by Patrick Hughes. Maryknoll, NY: Orbis, 1978.

———. *Sacraments of Life, Life of the Sacraments*. Translated by John Drury. Portland: Pastoral, 1987.

Bois, Yve-Alain, and Rosalind E. Krauss. *Formless: A User's Guide*. New York: Zone, 1997.

Bonhoeffer, Dietrich. *The Cost of Discipleship*. Translated by R. H. Fuller. New York: Touchstone, 1995.

Book of Common Worship. Prepared by the Theology and Worship Ministry Unit for the Presbyterian Church (U.S.A.) and the Cumberland Presbyterian Church. Louisville: Westminster John Knox, 1993.

Book of Confession. The Constitution of the Presbyterian Church (U.S.A.): Part I. Louisville: Office of the General Assembly, 1999.

Book of Order 2013–2015. The Constitution of the Presbyterian Church (U.S.A.): Part II. Louisville: Office of the General Assembly, 2013.

Bower, Peter C., editor. *The Companion to the Book of Common Worship*. Louisville: Geneva and Office of Theology and Worship, Presbyterian Church (U.S.A.), 2003.

Bradotti, Rosi. *Nomadic Theory: The Portable Rosi Bradotti*. New York: Columbia University Press, 2011.

Bradshaw, Paul. *Early Christian Worship: A Basic Introduction to Ideas and Practice*. Collegeville, MN: Liturgical, 1996.

————. *The Search for the Origins of Christian Worship: Sources and Methods for the Study of Early Liturgy*. New York: Oxford University Press, 1992.

Bradshaw, Paul, editor. *The New Westminster Dictionary of Liturgy and Worship*. Louisville: Westminster John Knox, 2003.

Bradshaw, Paul, and Lawrence A. Hoffman, editors. *The Making of Jewish and Christian Worship*. Notre Dame, IN: University of Notre Dame Press, 1991.

Breton, André. *Mad Love*. Lincoln, NE: University of Nebraska Press, 1987.

Bria, Ion. "The Liturgy after the Liturgy." Round Table "Education for Change and diaconia." Online: http://www.rondtb.msk.ru/info/en/Bria_en.htm.

Brook, Peter. *The Empty Space. A Book About the Theatre: Deadly, Holy, Rough, Immediate*. New York: Touchstone, 1996.

Buarque de Holanda, Sérgio. *Raízes do Brasil*. Rio de Janeiro: José Olympo, 1991.

Budde, Michael L. *The Borders of Baptism: Identities, Allegiances, and the Church*. Eugene, OR: Cascade, 2011.

Burki, Bruno. "The Reformed Tradition in Continental Europe: Switzerland, France and Germany." In *The Oxford History of Christian Worship*, edited by Geoffrey Wainwright and Karen B. Westerfield Tucker, 436–62. Oxford: Oxford University Press, 2006.

Butler, Judith. "Bodily Inscriptions, Performative Subversions." In *The Judith Butler Reader,* edited by Sara Salih with Judith Butler, 90–118. Malden, MA: Blackwell, 2004.

————. *Precarious Life: The Powers of Mourning and Violence*. London, New York: Verso, 2004.

Calvin, John. *Calvin's Institutes: A New Compend*. Edited by Hugh T. Kerr. Louisville: Westminster John Knox, 1989.

————. *Institutes of the Christian Religion*. 2 vols. Edited by John T. McNeill. Translated by Ford Lewis Battles. Library of Christian Classics 20–21. Philadelphia: Westminster, 1960.

————. *Institutes of the Christian Religion*. Translated by Henry Beveridge. Grand Rapids: Eerdmans, 1989.

————. *Treatises Against the Anabaptists and Against the Libertines*. Translation, introduction, and notes by Benjamin Wirt Farley. Grand Rapids: Baker, 1982.

———. *A Warning Against Judiciary Astrology and Other Prevalent Curiosities.* Translated by Mary Potter. *Calvin Theological Journal* 18 (1983) 157–89.

Caputo, John D. "Instants, Secrets and Singularities: Dealing Death in Kierkegaard and Derrida." In *Kierkegaard in Post/Modernity,* edited by Martin J. Matustik and Merold Westphal, 216–238. Bloomington: Indiana University Press, 1995.

———. *The Weakness of God: A Theology of the Event.* Bloomington: Indiana University Press, 2006.

Caputo, John D., editor. *Deconstruction in a Nutshell: A Conversation with a Commentary by John D. Caputo.* New York: Fordham University Press, 1997.

Caputo, John D., and Michael J. Scanlon, editors. *God, The Gift, and Postmodernism.* Bloomington: Indiana University Press, 1999.

Carneiro, Edison. *O Quilombo dos Palmares.* São Paulo: Civilização Brasileira, 1966.

Carvalhaes, Cláudio. Review of *The Eucharist: Bodies, Bread, and Resurrection,* by Andrea Bieler and Andrea Schottroff. *Interpretation* 63/3 (2009) 320.

Carvalhaes, Cláudio, and Paul Galbreath. "The Season of Easter: Imaginative Figurings for the Body of Christ." *Interpretation* 65 (2011) 5–16.

Castles, Stephen. *The Age of Migration: International Population Movements in the Modern World.* Basingstoke, UK: Macmillan, 1998.

Cavanaugh, William T. *Torture and Eucharist.* Challenges in Contemporary Theology. Malden, MA: Blackwell, 1998.

Certeau, Michel de. *The Practice of Everyday Life.* Translated by Steven Rendall. Berkeley: University of California Press, 1984.

Chacón, Justin Akers. "Mexico, Caught in the Web of U.S. Empire." In *No One Is Illegal: Fighting Racism and Violence on the U.S.-Mexico Border,* edited by Justin Akers Chacón and Mike Davis, 89–214. Chicago: Haymarket, 2006.

Chauvet, Louis-Marie. *Symbol and Sacrament.* Translated by Patrick Madigan and Madeleine Beaumont. Collegeville, MN: Liturgical, 1995.

Chomsky, Noam. "Liberating the Mind from Orthodoxies." Interview by David Barsamian. *Z Magazine,* May 2001. Online: http://www.zcommunications.org/liberating-the-mind-from-orthodoxies-by-david-barsamian.

Chow, Rey. *The Protestant Ethnic and the Spirit of Capitalism.* New York: Columbia University Press, 2002.

Chupungco, Anscar, editor. *Sacraments and Sacramentals.* Vol. 4 of *Handbook of Liturgical Studies.* Collegeville, MN: Liturgical, 2000.

———. *The Eucharist.* Vol. 3 of *Handbook of Liturgical Studies.* Collegeville, MN: Liturgical, 1999.

Cixous, Hélène, and Jacques Derrida. *Veils.* Translated by Geoffrey Bennington. Stanford: Stanford University Press, 2001.

Collins, Mary. "Principles of Feminist Liturgy." In *Women at Worship: Interpretations of North American Diversity,* edited by Marjorie Procter-Smith and Janet R. Walton, 9–28. Louisville: Westminster John Knox, 1993.

———. *Worship: Renewal to Practice.* Washington, DC: Pastoral, 1987.

Conferência Nacional dos Bispos do Brasil. *Comunidades Eclesiais de Base no Brasil, Experiências e Perspectivas.* São Paulo: Edições Paulinas, 1981.

Corley, Kathleen E. *Private Women, Public Meals.* Peabody, MA: Hendrickson, 1993.

Cossard, Gisele Omindarewá. *Awó, O Mistério dos Orixás.* Rio de Janeiro: Pallas, 2006.

Coutin, Susan Bibler. *The Culture of Protest: Religious Activism and the U.S. Sanctuary Movement.* Conflict and Social Change. Boulder, CO: Westview, 1993.

Crockett, William R. *Eucharist: Symbol of Transformation.* New York: Pueblo, 1989.

Crossan, John Dominic. *The Birth of Christianity: Discovering What Happened in the Years Immediately After the Execution of Jesus*. New York: HarperCollins, 1998.

———. *The Historical Jesus: The Life of a Mediterranean Jewish Peasant*. New York: HarperCollins, 1991.

Cull, Nicholas J., and David Carrasco. *Alambrista and the U.S.-Mexico Border: Film, Music and Stories of Undocumented Immigrants*. Albuquerque: University of New Mexico Press, 2004.

Debord, Guy. *The Society of the Spectacle*. New York: Zone, 1995.

De La Torre, Miguel A. *Latina/o Social Ethics: Moving Beyond Eurocentric Moral Thinking*. Waco: Baylor University Press, 2010.

Deleuze, Gilles. *The Fold. Leibniz and the Baroque*. Translated by Tom Conley. Minneapolis: University of Minnesota Press, 1993.

Derrida, Jacques. *Adieu to Emmanuel Levinas*. Translated by Pascalle-Anne Brault and Michael Naas. Stanford: Stanford University Press, 1999.

———. *Aporias*. Translated by Thomas Dutoit. Stanford: Stanford University Press, 1993.

———. *Dissemination*. Translated by Barbara Johnson. Chicago: University of Chicago Press, 1981.

———. "Epoché and Faith." In *Derrida and Religion: Other Testaments*, edited by Yvonne Sherwood & Kevin Hart, 27–52. New York: Routledge, 2005.

———. *The Gift of Death*. Translated by David Wills. Chicago: University of Chicago Press, 1995.

———. "Hostipitality." In *Acts of Religion*, translated and edited by Gil Anidjar, 358–420. New York: Routledge, 2002.

———. *Of Grammatology*. Translated by Gayatri Chakravorty Spivak. Baltimore: John Hopkins University Press, 1976.

———. *Of Hospitality: Anne Dufourmantelle Invites Jacques Derrida to Respond*. Stanford: Stanford University Press, 2000.

———. *On Cosmopolitanism and Forgiveness*. Translated by Mark Dooley. London: Routledge, 2001.

———. *Points, Interviews 1974–1994*. Edited by Elisabeth Weber. Translated by Peggy Kamuf, et al. Stanford: Stanford University Press, 1992.

———. "Politics and Friendship: A Discussion with Jacques Derrida." Centre for Modern French Thought, University of Sussex, 1 December 1997. Online: http://www.livingphilosophy.org/Derrida-politics-friendship.htm.

———. *The Politics of Friendship*. Translated by by George Collins. London: Verso, 1997.

———. *Sovereignties in Question: The Poetics of Paul Celan*. Edited by Thomas Dutoit and Outi Pasanen. New York: Fordham University Press, 2005.

———. *Specters of Marx: The State of the Debt, the Work of Mourning, and the New International*. Translated by Peggy Kamuf. London: Routledge, 1994.

———. *Writing and Difference*. Translated by Alan Bass. London: Routledge, 1978.

Deutsche, Rosalyn. *Evictions. Art and Spatial Politics*. Cambridge, MA: MIT Press, 1996.

Dix, Dom Gregory. *The Shape of the Liturgy*. London: Continuum, 2001.

Doty, Roxanne Lynn. Review of *Challenging Boundaries: Global Flows, Territorial Identities*, edited by Michael J. Shapiro and Hayward Alker. *American Political Science Review* 91/2 (1997) 510–11.

Bibliography

Douglas, Mary. "Deciphering a Meal." In *Implicit Meanings: Essays in Anthropology*, 231–52. London: Routledge, 1978.

Dowey, Edward A., Jr. *The Knowledge of God in Calvin's Theology*. Grand Rapids: Eerdmans, 1994.

Downey, Michael. *Worship at the Margins: Spirituality and Liturgy*. Washington DC: Pastoral, 1994

Driver, Tom F. *Liberating Rites: Understanding the Transformative Power of Ritual*. Boulder, CO: Westview, 1998.

Dussel, Enrique D. *1942, O Encubrimento do Outro: A Origem do Mito da Modernidade*. Translated by Jaime A. Clasen. Conferencias de Frankfurt. Rio de Janeiro: Editora Vozes,1993.

———. "Hipóteses para uma história da teologia na America Latina." In *Historia da Teologia na America Latina*, 165–196. São Paulo: Edições Paulinas, 1981.

Dussel, Enrique D., et al. *Historia da Teologia na America Latina*. São Paulo: Edições Paulinas, 1981.

Edel, Abraham. *Aristotle and his Philosophy*. Chapel Hill: University of North Carolina Press, 1982.

Elwood, Christopher. *The Body Broken: The Calvinist Doctrine of the Eucharist and the Symbolization of Power in Sixteenth-Century France*. New York: Oxford University Press, 1999.

———. "A Death in Egypt." Sermon delivered at Louisville Presbyterian Theological Seminary, February 9, 2007. Online: http://caldwellchapel.blogspot .com/2007/02/death-in-egypt.html.

Farelli, Maria Helena. *Comida de Santo*. Rio de Janeiro: Pallas Editora, 2009.

Fenwick, John, and Bryan Spinks. *Worship in Transition: The Liturgical Movement in the Twentieth Century*. New York: Continuum, 1995.

Foucault, Michel. *Discipline and Punish: The Birth of Prison*. Translated by Alan Sheridan. New York: Vintage, 1979.

Freidenreich, David M. *Foreigners and Their Food: Constructing Otherness in Jewish, Christian and Islamic Law*. Berkeley: University of California Press, 2011.

Freire, Paulo. *Education for Critical Consciousness*. Translated by Myra B. Ramos. New York: Continuum, 2005.

———. *Pedagogy of the Oppressed*. Translated by Myra B. Ramos. New York: Continuum, 2000.

Galbreath, Paul. *Leading from the Table*. Herndon, VA: Alban Institute, 2008.

———. *Doxology and Theology*. New York: Lang, 2008.

Gamble, Richard C. "Calvin's Controversies." In *The Cambridge Companion to John Calvin*, edited by Donald K. Mckim, 188–206. Cambridge Companions to Religion. Cambridge: Cambridge University Press, 2004.

Ganoczy, Alexandre. "Calvin's Life." In *The Cambridge Companion to John Calvin*, edited by Donald K. McKim, 3–24. Cambridge Companions to Religion. Cambridge: Cambridge University Press, 2004.

Garrigan, Siobhán. *Beyond Ritual: Sacramental Theology After Habermas*. Aldershot, UK: Ashgate, 2004.

Gebara, Ivone. "Pluralismo Religioso, Uma Perspectiva Feminista." In *Teologia Latino-Americana Pluralista da Libertação*, edited by Luiza E. Tomita, José M. Vigil, and Marcelo Barros, 277–98. ASETT, EATWOT. São Paulo: Editora Paulus, 2006.

————. *Out Of Depths: Women's Experience of Evil and Salvation.* Translated by Ann Patrick Ware. Minneapolis: Fortress, 2002.

————. *Longing for Running Water: Ecofeminism and Liberation.* Translated by David Molineaux. Minneapolis: Fortress, 1999.

Gerrish, B. A. *Grace and Gratitude: The Eucharistic Theology of John Calvin.* Minneapolis: Fortress, 1993.

Gomes, Flávio. *Palmares.* São Paulo: Contexto, 2005.

Gómez-Pena, Guilhermo. *Dangerous Border Crossers.* New York: Routledge, 2000.

————. *The New World Border: Prophecies, Poems & Loqueras For the End of the Century.* San Francisco: City Lights, 1996.

Gramsci, Antonio. *Selections From The Prison Notebooks Of Antonio Gramsci.* New York: International, 1971.

Grimes, Ronald L. *Rite Out of Place.* Oxford: Oxford University Press, 2006.

————. *Deeply Into the Bones: Re-Inventing Rites of Passage.* Berkeley: University of California Press, 2000.

————. *Readings in Ritual Studies.* New Jersey: Prentice-Hall, 1996.

————. *Reading, Writing, and Ritualizing: Ritual in Fictive, Liturgical, and Public Places.* Washington, DC: Pastoral, 1993.

————. *Ritual Criticism: Case Studies in Its Practice, Essays on Its Theory.* Columbia: University of South Carolina Press, 1990.

Guimarães, Frei Almir Ribeiro. *Communidades de Base no Brasil: Uma Nova Maneira de Ser em Igreja.* Rio de Janeiro: Vozes, 1998.

Gutiérrez, Gustavo. *A Theology of Liberation: History, Politics, and Salvation.* Translated and edited by Sister Caridad Inda and John Eagleson. Rev. ed. Maryknoll, NY: Orbis, 1988.

Haas, Guenther M. "Calvin Ethics." In *The Cambridge Companion to John Calvin,* edited by Donald K. McKim, 93–105. Cambridge: Cambridge University Press, 2004.

Hageman, Howard G. *Pulpit and Table: Some Chapters in the History of Worship in the Reformed Churches.* Richmond, VA: Knox, 1962.

Haight, Roger. *Christian Community in History.* Vol. 2, *Comparative Ecclesiology.* New York: Continuum, 2005.

————. *Christian Community in History.* Vol. 1, *Historical Ecclesiology.* New York, London: Continuum, 2004.

Harding, Rachel E. *A Refuge In Thunder: Candomblé and Alternative Spaces of Blackness.* Bloomington: Indiana University Press, 2000.

Hardt, Michael, and Paolo Virno, editors. *Radical Thought in Italy: A Potential Politics.* Minneapolis: University of Minnesota Press, 1996.

Hewitt, W. E. *Base Christian Communities and Social Change in Brazil.* Lincoln, NE: University of Nebraska Press, 1991.

Hopkins, Dwight N. "More Than Ever: The Preferential Option for poor people." In *Opting for the Margins. Postmodernity and Liberation in Christian Theology,* edited by Joerg Rieger, 127–42. Oxford: Oxford University Press, 2003.

Irarrázaval, Diego. "Salvação Indígena e Afro-Americana." In *Teologia Pluralista Libertadora Intercontinental,* edited by José M. Vigil, Luiza E. Tomita, Marcelo Barros, 61–88. ASETT, EATWOT. São Paulo: Edições Paulinas, 2008.

Irwin, K. *Liturgical Theology: A Primer.* Collegeville, MN: Liturgical, 1990.

Isasi-Diaz, Ada Maria. *Mujerista Theology: A Theology for the Twenty-First Century.* Maryknoll, NY: Orbis, 1996.

Bibliography

Jameson, Fredric, and Masao Miyoshi, editors. *The Cultures of Globalization*. Durham, NC: Duke University Press, 1998.

Jameson, Michael. "Private Space and the Greek City." In *Domestic Architecture and the Use of Space*, edited by Susan Kent, 92–113. Cambridge: Cambridge University Press, 1978.

Jelinek, Estelle C. *The Tradition of Women's Autobiography: From Antiquity to the Present*. Boston: Twayne, 1986.

Jiménez, Roberto. *La Iglesia Popular en America Latina*. Bogotá: Universidad Católica del Táchira, 1987.

Kantorowicz, Ernst. *The King's Two Bodies: A Study in Mediaeval Political Theology*. Princeton: Princeton University Press, 1997.

Kavanagh, Aidan. *On Liturgical Theology*. New York: Pueblo, 1984.

Kearney, Richard. *Strangers, Gods, and Monsters: Interpreting Otherness*. London: Routledge, 2003.

Keller, Catherine, et al., editors. *Postcolonial Theologies. Divinity and Empire*. St Louis: Chalice, 2004.

Keller, Catherine, and Laurel Schneider, editors. *Polydoxy: Theology of Multiplicity and Relation*. New York: Routledge, 2010.

Kelly, George A., editor. *The Sacrament of the Eucharist in Our Time*. Boston: St Paul Editions, 1978.

Kent, Susan, editor. *Domestic Architecture and the Use of Space*. Cambridge: Cambridge University Press, 1978.

Kilmartin, Edward J. *The Eucharist in the West: History and Theology*. Collegeville, MN: Liturgical, 1998.

Klinghardt, Matthias. *Gemeinschaftsmahl und Mahlgemeinschaft: Soziologie und Liturgie frunchchristlich Mahlfeiern*. Tubingen: Francke, 1996.

Knitter, Paul F. *Introducing Theologies of Religions*. Maryknoll, NY: Orbis, 2002

Kostelanetz, Richard. *The Theatre of Mixed-Means*. New York: RK, 1980.

Kristeva, Julia. "Strangers to Ourselves." In *The Portable Kristeva*, edited by Kelly Oliver, 264–94. New York: Columbia University Press, 1997.

Lathrop, Gordon W. *Holy People: A Liturgical Ecclesiology*. Minneapolis: Fortress, 1999.

———. *Holy Things: A Liturgical Theology*. Minneapolis: Fortress, 1993.

———. "Ordo and Coyote: Further Reflections on Order, Disorder and Meaning in Christian Worship." *Worship* 80/3 (2006) 194–212.

Lazarus, Neil, editor. *Postcolonial Literary Studies*. Cambridge: Cambridge University Press, 2004.

Lee, Jae Won. "Paul and the Politics of Difference: A Contextual Study of the Jewish-Gentile Difference in Galatians and Romans." PhD diss., Union Theological Seminary, 2001.

Lefebvre, Henri. *The Production of Space*. Translated by Donald Nicholson-Smith. Malden, MA: Blackwell, 1991.

Leon-Dufour, Xavier. *Sharing the Eucharistic Bread: The Witness of the New Testament*. Mahwah, NJ: Paulist, 1987.

Léry, Jean de. *History of a Voyage to the Land of Brazil*. Translation and introduction by Janet Whatley. Berkeley: University of California Press, 1992.

Levinas, Emmanuel. *Difficult Freedom: Essays on Judaism*. Translated by Sean Hand. Baltimore: John Hopkins University Press, 1990.

———. *In the Time of the Nations*. Translated by Michael B. Smith. Bloomington: Indiana University Press, 1994.

————. *Totality and Infinity: An Essay on Exteriority.* Translated by Alphonso Lingus. Pittsburgh: Duquesne University Press, 1969.

Lieu, Judith M. *Christian Identity in the Jewish and Graeco-Roman World.* Oxford: Oxford University Press, 2004.

Lingus, Alphonso. *The Community of Those Who Have Nothing in Common.* Bloomington: Indiana University Press, 1994.

Lispector, Clarice. "A Repartição dos Pães." In *Legião Estrangeira,* 29–32. Rio de Janeiro: Rocco, 1999.

Lorentzen, Robin. *Women in the Sanctuary Movement.* Philadelphia: Temple University Press, 1991.

Lubac, Henri de. *Corpus Mysticum: The Eucharist and the Church in the Middle Ages.* Translated by Gemma Simmonds. Notre Dame, IN: University of Notre Dame Press, 2007.

Machado, Daisy. "Women and Religion in the Borderlands." *Union Seminary Quarterly Seminary* 57/3–4 (2003) 146–58.

Mack, Burton L. *Who Wrote the New Testament? The Making of the Christian Myth: Origins, Logic, and Legacy.* New York: Continuum, 2001.

Maraschin, Jaci. *A Beleza da Santidade, Ensaios de Liturgia.* São Paulo: ASTE, 1996.

————. "Culture, Spirit and Adoration." *Anglican Theological Review* 82/1 (2000) 47–63.

————. "The Transient Body: Sensibility and Spirituality." Paper presented at "Liturgy and the Body," Union Theological Seminary, New York, October 20, 2003.

Marciniak, Katarzyna. *Alienhood: Citizenship, Exile, and the Logic of Difference.* Minneapolis: University of Minnesota Press, 2006.

Marion, Jean-Luc. *God Without Being: Hors-Texte.* Translated by Thomas A. Carlson. Chicago: University Of Chicago Press. 1995.

————. "On the Gift." In *God, The Gift, and Postmodernism,* edited by John D. Caputo and Michael J. Scanlon, 54–78. Bloomington: Indiana University Press, 1999.

McDonnell, Killian. *John Calvin, the Church, and the Eucharist.* Princeton: Princeton University Press, 1967.

McGowan, Andrew. *Ascetic Eucharist: Food and Drink in Early Christian Ritual Meals.* Oxford: Clarendon, 1999.

McKenna, Megan. *Rites of Justice.* Maryknoll, NY: Orbis, 1997.

McKim, Donald K., editor. *Major Themes in the Reformed Tradition.* Grand Rapids: Eerdmans. 1992.

————. *Readings in Calvin's Theology.* Grand Rapids: Baker, 1984.

Metz, Johannes. "The Courage to Pray." In *The Courage to Pray* by Johannes Metz and Karl Rahner, 1–28. Translated by Sarah O'Brien Twohig. New York: Crossroad, 1981.

Michaelsen, Scott, and David E. Johnson, editors. *Border Theory: The Limits of Cultural Politics.* Minneapolis: University of Minnesota Press, 1997.

Miller, J. Hillis. "Critic as Host." In *Deconstruction and Criticism,* edited by Harold Bloom et al., 177–207. London: Continuum, 2005.

Mitchell, Nathan D. *Eucharist as Sacrament of Initiation.* Forum Essay 2. Chicago: Liturgy Training, 2007.

————. *Meeting Mystery, Liturgy, Worship and Sacrament.* Maryknoll, NY: Orbis, 2009.

Moore-Keish, Martha L. *Do This in Remembrance of Me: A Ritual Approach to Reformed Eucharistic Theology.* Grand Rapids: Eerdmans, 2008.

Bibliography

Morrill, Bruce T. *Anamnesis as Dangerous Memory: Political and Liturgical Theology in Dialogue*. Collegeville, MN: Liturgical, 2000.

Motta, Luiz Gonzaga. *Estratégias e culturas da comunicação*. Compós: Associação Nacional dos Programas de Pós-Graduação em Comunicação, 2002.

Nancy, Jean-Luc. *Being Singular Plural*. Translated by Robert D. Richardson and Anne E. O'Byrne. Stanford: Stanford University Press, 2000.

———. *The Creation of the World or Globalization*. Translated by Francois Raffoul and David Pettigrew. New York: State University of New York Press, 2007.

———. *The Inoperative Community*. Edited by Peter Connor. Translated by Peter Connor et al. Minneapolis: University of Minnesota Press, 1991.

Naphy, William G. "Calvin's Geneva." In *The Cambridge Companion to John Calvin*, edited by Donald K. McKim, 25–40. Cambridge: Cambridge University Press, 2004.

Nausner, Michael. "Homeland as Borderland: Territories of Christian Subjectivity." In *Postcolonial Theologies: Divinity and Empire*, edited by Catherine Keller et al., 118–132. St. Louis: Chalice, 2004.

Neu, Diann L. *Women's Rites: Feminist Liturgies for Life's Journeys: Women's Alliance for Theology, Ethics and Ritual*. Cleveland: Pilgrim, 2003.

Nicolelis, Miguel. *Muito Além do Nosso Eu: A nova neurociência que une cérebro e máquinas e como ela pode mudar nossas vidas*. São Paulo: Companhia das Letras, 2011.

Nóbrega, Lígia de Moura P. *BECs e Educação Popular*. Rio de Janeiro: Vozes, 1998.

Novaes, Adauto, editor. *Muito Além do Espetáculo*. São Paulo: Editora Senac, 2004.

Nunes, Benedito. "Anthropophagic Utopia: Barbarian Metaphysics." In *Inverted Utopias: Avant-Garde Art in Latin America*, edited by Mari Carmen Ramirez and Hector Olea, 57–62. New Haven: Yale University Press, 2004.

O'Donovan, Oliver. *The Desire of the Nations: Rediscovering the Roots of Political Theology*. Cambridge: Cambridge University Press, 1996.

Oliveira, Rafael Soares de, editor. *Diálogos Fraternos Contra a Intolerância Religiosa*. Rio de Janeiro: DP&A, 2003.

Parsons, Susan Frank, editor. *The Cambridge Companion to Feminist Theology*. Cambridge: Cambridge University Press, 2002.

Pauw, Amy Plantinga, and Serene Jones, editors. *Feminist and Womanist Essays in Reformed Dogmatics*. Louisville: Westminster John Knox, 2006.

Penn, Michael Philip. *Kissing Christians: Ritual and Community in the Late Ancient Church*. Philadelphia: University of Pennsylvania Press, 2005.

Pereira, Nancy Cardoso. "Des-Evangelização dos Joelhos: Epistemologia, Sexualidade e Osteoporose." In *Epistemologia, Violência, Sexualidade*, edited by Elaine Neuenfeldt, Karen Bergesch, and Mara Parlow, 161–68. São Leopoldo, Brazil: Editora Sinodal, 2008.

Prandi, Reginaldo. *Os Candomblés de São Paulo*. São Palo: Hucitec-EDUSP, 1991.

Presbyterian Church (USA). *Invitation to Christ: A Guide to Sacramental Principles*. Louisville: Presbyterian Church (USA), 2006. Online: http://www.pcusa.org/media/uploads/sacraments/pdfs/invitationtochrist.pdf.

Procter-Smith, Marjorie. *In Her Own Rite: Constructing Feminist Liturgical Tradition*. Akron, OH: OSL, 2000.

———. *Praying With our Eyes Open: Engendering Feminist Liturgical Prayer*. Nashville: Abingdon, 1995.

Procter-Smith, Marjorie, and Janet W. Walton, editors. *Women at Worship: Interpretations of North American Diversity.* Louisville: Westminster John Knox, 1993.

Ramshaw, Gail. *God Beyond Gender: Feminist Christian God-Language.* Minneapolis: Fortress, 1995.

Reinelt, Janelle G., and Joseph R. Roach, editors. *Critical Theory and Performance.* Ann Arbor: University of Michigan Press, 1992.

Rice, Howard L., and James C. Huffstutler. *Reformed Worship.* Louisville: Geneva, 2001.

Ricoeur, Paul. *The Rule of Metaphor.* Translated by R. Czerny. Toronto: Toronto University Press, 1997.

Robinson, James M., and Helmut Koester, editors. *Trajectories through Early Christianity.* Philadelphia: Fortress, 1971.

Rogoff, Irit. *Terra Infirma: Geography's Visual Culture.* London: Routledge, 2000.

Romero, Oscar. *The Church Is All of You: Thoughts of Archbishop Oscar A. Romero.* Edited by James R. Brockman. Minneapolis: Winston, 1984.

Rosa, João Guimarães. *Grande Sertão: Veredas.* Edição Comemorativa. São Paulo: Editora Nova Fronteira, 2006.

Ross, Susan A. "Body." In *Dictionary of Feminist Theologies,* edited by Letty M. Russell and J. Shannon Clarkson, 32. Louisville: Westminster John Knox, 1996.

———. *Extravagant Affections: a Feminist Sacramental Theology.* New York: Continuum, 1998.

———. "Then Honor God in your Body (1 Cor. 6:20): Feminist and Sacramental Theology on the Body." *Horizons* 16/1 (1989) 7–27.

Rubin, Miri. *Corpus Christi: The Eucharist in Late Medieval Culture.* Cambridge: Cambridge University Press, 1991.

Ruether, Rosemary Radford. *Women-Church: Theology and Practice of Feminist Liturgical Communities.* San Francisco: Harper & Row, 1985.

Russell, Letty M. *Church in the Round: Feminist Interpretation of the Church.* Louisville: Westminster John Knox, 1993.

Russell, Letty M., and J. Shannon Clarkson, editors. *Dictionary of Feminist Theologies.* Louisville: Westminster John Knox, 1996.

Saliers, Don E. "Afterword: Liturgy and Ethics Revised." In *Liturgy and the Moral Self: Humanity at Full Stretch Before God,* edited by E. Byron Anderson and Bruce T. Morrill, 209–24. Collegeville, MN: Liturgical, 1998.

———. "Liturgy and Ethics: Some New Beginnings" in *Liturgy and the Moral Self: Humanity at Full Stretch Before God,* edited by E. Byron Anderson and Bruce T. Morrill, 15–38. Collegeville, MN: Liturgical, 1998.

———. *Worship as Theology: Foretaste of Glory Divine.* Nashville: Abingdon, 1996.

———. *Worship Comes To Its Senses.* Nashville: Abingdon, 1996.

Sassen, Saskia. *Territory, Authority, Rights: From Medieval to Global Assemblages.* Princeton: Princeton University Press, 2006.

Schechner, Richard, and Willa Appel, editors. *By Means of Performance: Intercultural Studies of Theater and Ritual.* Cambridge: Cambridge University Press, 1990.

Schmemann, Alexander. *Introduction to Liturgical Theology.* Crestwood, NY: St. Vladimir's Seminary Press, 1966.

Schüssler-Fiorenza, Elizabeth. *In Memory of Her: A Feminist Theological Reconstruction of Christian Origins.* New York: Crossroad, 1983.

Schwarz, Henry, and Ray Sangeeta, editors. *A Companion to Postcolonial Studies.* Oxford: Blackwell, 2000.

Searle, Mark. *Liturgy and Social Justice.* Collegeville, MN: Liturgical, 1980.

Seasoltz, R. Kevin, editor. *Living Bread, Saving Cup: Readings on the Eucharist.* Collegeville, MN: Liturgical, 1982.

Serres, Michel. *The Parasite.* Baltimore: John Hopkins University Press, 1982.

Shapiro, Michael J., and Hayward R. Alker, editors. *Challenging Boundaries: Global Flows, Territorial Identities.* Borderlines 2. Minneapolis: University of Minnesota Press, 1996.

Silveira, Flavio Leonel Abreu da, and Manuel Ferreira Lima Filho. "Por Uma Antropologia do Objeto Documental: Entre a 'alma nas coisas' e a coisificação do Objeto." *Horizontes Antropológicos* 11/23 (2005). Online: http://www.scielo.br/scielo.php?pid=S0104-71832005000100003&script=sci_arttext.

Smith, Dennis E. *From Symposium to Eucharist: The Banquet in the Early Christian World.* Minneapolis: Fortress, 2003.

Smith, Dennis Edward, and Hal E. Taussig. *Many Tables: The Eucharist in the New Testament and Liturgy Today.* Eugene,OR: Wipf & Stock, 2001.

Smith, Jonathan Z. *To Take Place: Toward Theory in Ritual.* Chicago: University of Chicago Press, 1987.

Sobrino, J., and I. Ellacuría, editors. *Mysterium Liberationis: Fundamental Concepts of Liberation Theology.* Maryknoll, NY: Orbis, 1993.

Spivak, Gayatri Chakravorty. "Can the Subaltern Speak?" In *Marxism and the Interpretation of Culture,* edited by Cary Nelson and Lawrence Grossberg, 271–316. Champaign: University of Illinois Press, 1988.

———. "Diasporas Old and New: Women in the Transnational World." In *Class Issues, Pedagogy, Cultural Studies, and the Public Sphere,* edited by Amitava Kumar, 87–116. New York: New York University Press, 1997.

Steger, Manfred, *Globalization: A Very Short Introduction.* New York: Oxford University Press, 2009.

Steinmetz, David C. "The Theology of John Calvin." In *The Cambridge Companion to Reformation Theology,* edited by David Bagchi and David C. Steinmetz, 113–129. Cambridge: Cambridge University Press, 2004.

Stroher, Marga J. "É Preciso que Haja Pão! Ecologias da Partilha e Cuidado com as Sobras: Um Estudo a Partir de Jo 6:1–15." *Estudos Teológicos* 46/1 (2006). Online: http://www3.est.edu.br/publicacoes/estudos_teologicos/vol4601_2006/et2006-1h_mstroher.pdf.

Suderburg, Erika, editor. *Space, Site, Intervention: Situating Installation Art.* Minneapolis: University of Minnesota Press, 2000.

Taft, Robert F. , S.J. "Mass Instruction: Fr. Robert Taft on liturgical reform," interview by Bryan Cones, *U.S. Catholic* (November 4, 2009): http://www.uscatholic.org/church/prayer-and-sacraments/2009/11/mass-instruction-fr-robert-taft-liturgical-reform.

———. "Mass without the Consecration? The Historic Agreement on the Eucharist Between the Catholic Church and the Assyrian Church of the East." *American Catholic Press* (October 26, 2001): http://www.americancatholicpress.org/Father_Taft_Mass_Without_the_Consecration.html.

Tanner, Norman O., editor. *Decrees of the Ecumenical Councils.* Vol. 1, *Nicaea I to Lateran V.* London: Sheed & Ward, 1990.

Taussig, Hal E. "Dealing Under the Table: Ritual Negotiation of Women's Power in the Syro-Phoenician Woman Pericope." In *Reimaging Christian Origins: A Colloquium*

Honoring Burton L. Mack, edited by Elizabeth A. Castelli and Hal Taussig, 264–79. Valley Forge, PA: Trinity, 1996.

———. *In The Beginning Was the Meal: Social Experimentation and Early Christian Identity.* Philadelphia: Fortress, 2009.

Taussig, Michael. *Defacement, Public Secrecy and the Labor of the Negative.* Stanford: Stanford University Press, 1999.

———. *Walter Benjamin's Grave: A Profane Illumination.* Chicago: University of Chicago Press, 2006.

Taylor, Barbara Brown. *The Preaching Life.* Cambridge, MA: Cowley, 1993.

Taylor, Mark C. *After God.* Chicago: University Of Chicago Press, 2009.

———. *Altarity.* Chicago: The University of Chicago Press 1998.

———. *Confidence Games: Money and Market in a World Without Redemption.* Chicago: University Of Chicago Press, 2005.

Taylor, Mark C., editor. *Critical Terms for Religious Studies.* Chicago: University of Chicago Press, 1998.

Thompson, Bard. *Liturgies of the Western Church.* Cleveland: World, 1961.

Tillard, J.-M. R. *Carne de la Iglesia, Carne de Cristo.* Translated by Alfonso Ortiz Garcia. Salamanca: Ediciones Sígueme, 1994.

Tomsho, Robert. *The American Sanctuary Movement.* Austin: Texas Monthly, 1987.

Torres, Sergio, and John Eagleson, editors. *The Challenge of Basic Christian Communities.* Maryknoll, NY: Orbis, 1981.

Townes, Emilie. *Womanist Ethics and the Cultural Production of Evil.* New York: Palgrave Macmillan, 2006.

Trinh, T. Minh-Ha. *Elsewhere, Within Here. Immigration, Refugeeism and the Boundary Event.* New York: Routledge, 2011.

Van Dyk, Leanne, editor. *A More Profound Alleluia: Theology and Worship in Harmony.* Grand Rapids: Eerdmans, 2005.

Van Gennep, Arnold. *The Rites of Passage.* Chicago: University of Chicago Press, 1960.

Vigil, José M. *Teologia do Pluralismo Religioso, para uma releitura pluralista do Cristianismo.* São Paulo: Paulus, 2006.

———. *Teologia Pluralista Libertadora Intercontinental.* ASETT, EATWOT. São Paulo: Edições Paulinas, 2008.

Vischer, Lukas. "Worship as Christian Witness to Society." In *Christian Worship in Reformed Churches Past and Present,* edited by Lukas Vischer, 415–26. Grand Rapids: Eerdmans, 2003.

Vischer, Lukas, editor. *Christian Worship in Reformed Churches Past and Present.* Grand Rapids: Eerdmans, 2003.

Volf, Miroslav, and Dorothy C. Bass, editor. *Practicing Theology: Beliefs and Practices in Christian Life.* Grand Rapids: Eerdmans, 2002.

Vosko, Richard S. *God's House is Our House: Re-Imagining the Environment for Worship.* Collegeville, MN: Liturgical, 2006.

Vries, Henri de, and Samuel Weber, editors. *Religion and Media.* Stanford: Stanford University Press, 20001.

Wainwright, Geoffrey, et al., editors. *The Oxford History of Christian Worship.* Oxford: Oxford University Press, 2006.

———. *Doxology.* New York: Oxford University Press, 1980.

Walcott, Derek. *Collected Poems, 1948–1984.* New York: Farrar, Straus & Giroux, 1987.

Wallace, Ronald S. *Calvin's Doctrine of the Word and Sacrament.* Tyler, TX: Geneva Divinity School Press, 1982.

Wallis, Brian. *If You Lived Here: The City in Art, Theory, and Social Activism. A Project by Martha Rosler.* Dia Art Foundation. New York: New, 1991.

Walsroy, Rosmarie. *Lavish Absence: Recalling and Rereading Edmond Jabès* Middletown, CT: Wesleyan University Press, 2005.

Walton, Janet R. *Feminist Liturgy: A Matter of Justice.* Collegeville, MN: Liturgical, 2000.

———. "Eucharist." In *Dictionary of Feminist Theologies,* edited by Letty M. Russell and J. Shannon Clarkson, 92–93. Louisville: Westminster John Knox, 1996.

Wandel, Lee Palmer. *The Eucharist in the Reformation: Incarnation and Liturgy.* Cambridge: Cambridge University Press, 2006.

Wannenwetsch, Bernd. *Political Worship: Ethics for Christian Citizens.* Oxford: Oxford University Press, 2004.

Weaver, Jace. "Indigenousness and Indigeneity." In *A Companion to Postcolonial Studies,* edited by Henry Schwarz and Sangeeta Ray, 221–35. Oxford: Blackwell, 2000.

Weber, Max. *The Protestant Ethic and the Spirit of Capitalism.* London, New York: Routledge, 2001.

Welch, Bryan. "Putting a Stop to Slave Labor, A Moral Solution to Illegal Immigrants." *UTNE Reader,* March-April, 2007. Online: http://www.utne.com/2007-03-01/PuttingaStoptoSlaveLabor.aspx.

Wendel, François. *Calvin: The Origins and Development of His Religious Thought.* New York: Harper & Row, 1963.

Whatley, Janet. "Introduction." In *History of a Voyage to the Land of Brazil,* by Jean de Léry. Translated by Janet Whatley. Berkeley: University of California Press, 1990.

Wheeler, Geraldine. "Revisiting the Question of the Use of Visual Art, Imagery, and Symbol in Reformed Places of Worship." In *Christian Worship in Reformed Churches Past and Present,* edited by Lukas Vischer, 348–70. Grand Rapids: Eerdmans, 2003.

White, James F. *Documents of Christian Worship: Descriptive and Interpretative Sources.* Louisville: Westminster John Knox, 1992.

———. *Introduction to Christian Worship.* Nashville: Abingdon, 2000.

———. *Protestant Worship: Traditions in Transition.* Louisville: Westminster John Knox, 1998.

———. *The Sacraments in Protestant Practice and Faith.* Nashville: Abingdon, 1999.

White, Susan J. *A History of Women in Christian Worship.* Cleveland: Pilgrim, 2003.

Willimon, William H. *The Service of God: How Worship and Ethics are Related.* Nashville: Abingdon, 1983.

Wyschogrod, Edith. "Autochthony and Welcome: Discourse of Exile in Levinas and Derrida." In *Derrida and Religion: Other Testaments,* edited by Yvonne Sherwood and Kevin Hart, 52–62. New York, London: Routledge, 2005.

Zimmerman, Joyce Ann. *Liturgy and Hermeneutics.* Collegeville, MN: Liturgical, 1999.

Index

African American, 140, 221, 232, 27

African Brazilian, 14, 204, 215

Africans, 221–22, 231

Altar, 1–3, 7–8, 24, 31, 52, 61, 67, 72, 90, 96–98, 112, 154, 163, 168, 187–88, 198, 201, 233, 246–47, 282, 291–92, 319

Alterity, 167–68, 177, 184, 188, 218, 221, 226

Althaus-Reid, Marcella, 175, 177, 307

Anamnesis, 172, 223, 259–60, 270, 277, 316

Ancestors / Ancestry, 211, 213, 215–16, 224, 232, 234, 239

Anzaldua, Gloria, 19, 141, 307

Aporia, 28, 311

Arrival / Arrivant, 15, 20, 24, 30, 44, 50, 73, 85, 135, 168, 191, 295

Authentic / Authenticity / Authenticates, 6, 19, 22, 93, 142, 145, 149–50, 157–58, 169, 188, 201, 221, 253, 256

Authority, 58, 62, 84, 91, 97, 99–100, 138, 144, 146, 149, 159, 186, 229, 245, 249, 253, 259, 264, 270, 276, 303, 317

Axé, 212, 215–16, 220, 224–27, 235, 238, 261

Babalorixá / Yalorixá, 205, 210–13, 215–16, 228–29, 231, 233

Banquet(s), 20, 35–59, 67–70, 129, 182, 248, 257, 318

Baptism, 85, 112, 126–29, 186, 227, 254–55, 260, 264, 289, 309

Basic Ecclesial Communities / BEC, 173, 175–78, 180, 184–89, 307–8

Bastide, Roger, 210, 214, 216–17, 307

Being-with, 32–33

Bell, Catherine, 33, 200, 215, 240, 272–74, 281, 285, 306

Belong / Belonging, 4, 6, 17, 32, 34, 36, 42, 51, 71, 73–74, 92–94, 96, 103–4, 131, 164, 183, 196, 205, 214, 217, 221–22, 233, 235–37, 243–44, 247, 259, 264, 281, 292, 295, 305

Berger, Teresa, 143, 154, 308

Berry, Wendell, 5, 281–82, 308

Beto, Frei, 178, 180, 186, 203, 266, 308

Bhabha, Homi, 162, 304, 308

Bible / Biblical, 1, 13–14, 51, 63, 107, 112, 116, 118, 123, 135, 138, 173, 183, 186–87, 224, 233, 245, 250–54, 258–59, 265, 274, 286–87, 290, 292

Body / Bodies, 12–13, 25, 29, 31, 35, 43, 50, 63–64, 66, 75, 87–117, 129, 133–34, 139, 141–42, 145–46, 150–56, 158–59, 162, 176, 189, 192, 198, 200–201, 214, 218, 220, 222, 224, 226–27, 235–37,

Body / Bodies (*cont.*)
239, 250, 254–56, 260, 267,
269–73, 275, 283, 291–93,
295, 302, 308, 310, 312,
314–15, 317

Boff, Leonardo, 171, 174, 176,
178–89, 195, 197, 219, 249,
308

Book of Common Worship, 84,
121, 123–24,131, 135,
254–55, 268, 309

Border(s) / Border–Crossing, 3–4,
7–36, 45, 47–48, 50, 52,
56–58, 63, 66–68, 71, 73, 77,
79, 92, 94–96, 119, 125–26,
129, 131–32, 135, 137–42,
144–46, 148–49, 152, 154,
158, 160–63, 166, 170, 172,
189, 192, 199, 207, 229,
242–50, 254, 257, 260–64,
267–69, 275–77, 280–81,
284–87, 289, 291–93,
295–305, 307, 309–11, 313,
315–16

Borderless Borders, 12–15, 29–34,
36, 50, 77, 199, 242–97, 300

Boundaries, 3, 6, 21–22, 26, 36–37,
39, 41, 43, 47, 53, 56, 61, 65,
83, 95, 127, 140–42, 148,
159–60, 162–64, 188, 204–5,
207, 228, 234–35, 238, 275,
286, 297, 311, 318

Brazil / Brazilian, 4, 6, 7, 12, 23, 34,
93, 138, 160, 167, 175–93,
195, 199, 201, 204–9, 212,
215, 219, 221, 223, 227–29,
235–36, 238–40, 249–50,
264, 266, 279–80, 293–95,
302, 304–5, 307, 313–14,
316, 320

Bread, 1, 2, 6–7, 9, 23, 34–35, 39,
53, 55, 57, 60–61, 63–64,
68–69, 72–73, 82, 90, 93–94,
96–98, 101–4, 107, 109–12,
116, 124, 126–27, 130, 132,

139, 161, 187–88, 191, 196–
99, 201, 230–33, 245, 254,
257, 260, 262, 265, 268, 270,
272–73, 279, 282, 291–92,
304, 308, 310, 314, 318

Calvin, John, 14, 23, 50, 71, 78–91,
94–96, 99–122, 125, 128–30,
134, 136–39, 190, 236,
247–48, 251–53, 255, 271,
309–10

Candomblé, 204–17, 219, 221,
223–24, 226–33, 236,
238–40, 249, 284, 300

Cardoso, Nancy Pereira, ix, 194,
219, 316

Celebration, 2, 4, 10, 12, 30–31, 40,
62, 64, 71, 77, 97, 116, 123,
124–25, 127, 136, 138, 141,
143, 146, 148–50, 158–59,
178, 186–87, 199, 206, 217,
222, 230, 233, 238, 250,
254–57, 259, 267, 269, 275,
282, 286, 296, 303

Certain Step, 22–23, 32, 160, 286

Charismatic / Charisma / Charism,
179, 181–84, 187, 224, 230,
308

Chauvet, Louis-Marie, 31, 310

Chomsky, Noam, 284, 310

Citizenship, 6, 11–12, 18, 70, 80,
86, 161, 264, 280, 302, 315

Class / Social Class, 2, 4, 7, 9, 11,
17, 25, 31, 43–45, 48–51,
65, 68, 73, 80, 100–101, 110,
129, 131, 141, 159–60, 161,
173–74, 178, 186, 234, 259,
263–64, 269, 271–72, 274,
296, 318

Collins, Mary, 147, 155, 310

Colonialism / Colonization, 163,
170, 204, 282, 307, 314, 316,
318, 320

Commensality, 52, 55–56, 65,
216–17, 231–33, 239, 302

Common / Commonality, 1, 5–6, 16, 21, 31–32, 36–37, 39–42, 44, 49, 53, 59, 63, 67, 109, 113, 123, 128, 133, 139, 150, 164, 169, 172, 198, 203, 206, 220, 222–27, 229–30, 232–34, 238–40, 260, 264, 271, 274, 279, 303

Communion, 3, 7, 9, 31, 42, 72, 74, 77, 85, 109–10, 115, 117, 119, 124–28, 132, 153, 198, 217, 222, 231–32, 277, 279

Community, 5, 9, 16–18, 23, 31, 33, 36–38, 40–43, 46, 51–57, 63–64, 67, 72–74, 81, 85, 87–88, 92–94, 96, 99, 103, 105, 110, 113, 115, 118, 120–22, 124–25, 128, 130–32, 134, 136, 138, 146–47, 150–52, 154, 162, 169, 172–73, 180–83, 185–87, 194, 196, 198–99, 207, 210–11, 213, 215, 217, 222, 224, 226, 227–34, 237, 239, 250, 257, 271–74, 277, 281, 284, 286–87, 289–92, 295, 298–99, 301, 304, 308, 313, 315–16

Condition, ix, 2, 4, 13–14, 21, 23–29, 31–32, 55, 93, 101, 116, 118, 130, 133, 138, 160, 163, 167, 180, 201, 213, 218, 233, 237, 248, 262, 274, 276, 286, 295–97, 299, 304

Corley, Kathleen E , 36, 41, 47, 49, 56, 68, 310

Cossard, Gisele Ormindarewa, 210, 215, 310

Crossan, John Dominic, 7, 35–36, 54–56, 59–61, 65–66, 68, 311

Crumbs, 188–89, 194, 197–201, 249, 273, 282, 301

De La Torre, Miguel, 266–67, 288, 307, 311

Deconstruction, 22, 29, 36, 179, 310, 315

Derrida, Jacques, 1, 15, 20–29, 32, 138, 160, 166, 247, 295–96, 307, 310–11, 320

Diaspora, 11, 164, 318

Didache, 55, 61

Directory of Worship PCUSA, 125–27, 254, 269

Dislocation, 225

Disruption/disruptive, 16, 69, 87, 168, 175, 198, 298

Driver, Tom, 270, 312

Eat / Eating, 7, 13, 20–21, 25, 27, 34, 36, 39–41, 53, 55, 57–58, 63, 66–67, 70–74, 79, 93–95, 109–10, 113, 127, 129–30, 134–35, 137–38, 164, 189–93, 197–200, 205–6, 212, 216–17, 220, 223–24, 228–30, 233–34, 236, 238–40, 244–45, 249, 254, 258–59, 261, 265, 272, 278–80, 283–87, 292, 295, 298, 300, 305

Economy / Economic, 2–7, 11–13, 17, 19, 31, 35, 47, 49, 55, 58–59, 66–68, 73, 82, 85–86, 88–90, 109, 118, 125, 130, 132, 152, 163, 173, 175, 178–79, 183, 190, 200, 207, 219, 264–65, 275, 281–82, 292, 296, 301

Ecumenic / Ecumenism, 23, 73, 218, 253, 318

Elwood, Christopher, 82–83, 89–91, 94, 99, 101–3, 107, 118, 120, 303, 312

Ethics / Ethical, 3, 5, 7, 23, 28–29, 31–32, 40–43, 46, 51, 64, 67, 82, 109, 120–21, 125, 130–31, 134, 142, 146,

Ethics / Ethical (*cont.*)
148–49, 155, 160–61, 164,
198, 220, 265–67, 274, 286,
303, 307, 311, 313, 316–17,
319–320

Event, 11, 14, 26, 28–30, 35–36, 39,
41, 44, 47–49, 51, 55, 57–58,
61–62, 64, 67, 70–71, 86,
90, 92, 99, 114, 117–18, 120,
123, 130–31, 133–36, 147,
150, 152, 156, 161, 181–84,
186, 193, 195–96, 208,
213–14, 228, 230, 232–33,
235, 243, 248, 250–51, 255,
269–70, 273, 277, 282,
285–86, 290, 298–99, 310,
319

Experience, 2, 8, 15, 26, 29, 33, 38,
42, 46, 69, 80, 82, 95–96, 99,
101–2, 106–7, 114–15, 118–
19, 122, 124, 127, 132–33,
135, 137, 140–41, 145–47,
149–53, 155, 157–59, 170,
174, 182, 193, 195–96,
212–13, 215, 217, 224–25,
233, 239, 247, 250, 257–58,
260, 264, 269, 274, 280, 284,
298–99, 304, 313

Feast, 2, 8, 30, 48, 110, 124, 129,
136, 214–15, 233, 254, 283,
292, 301

Feminist Liturgies, 141–65

Feminist Theologies, 153, 158, 317,
319

Fence(s), 6, 7, 11, 70–72, 87, 89,
94–95, 118–20, 126, 128,
130, 134, 139–40, 142, 152,
161, 243, 254, 261, 263, 275

Food / Food Offering, 1, 6, 14–16,
20, 26–27, 30–31, 35–37,
39–43, 48–49, 54, 58–59,
61, 65–67, 69–70, 72–73,
79, 103, 110–11, 124–26,
128–29, 132–34, 136,

157, 190–93, 199, 201–7,
214–17, 223–25, 227–33,
236, 238–39, 241–42, 244,
249, 258–61, 269, 274, 276,
278–79, 287, 297–98, 301–2,
312, 315

Foreign / Foreigner, 6, 14, 26, 27,
32–33, 47, 80, 93, 135, 141,
155–56, 167, 170, 192, 223,
228, 236, 252, 271, 274, 283,
286, 292, 294, 297–99, 300,
302–3, 305, 312

Forgive / Forgiven / Forgiveness,
32, 101, 121, 128, 224,
228–29, 233, 235, 237, 249,
311

Fourth Lateran Council, 96–97,
318

Freire, Paulo, 174, 186, 220, 284,
312

Friends / Friendship, ix, x, 37–40,
42–43, 46–47, 67, 69, 72,
100–101, 131, 176, 190–92,
201, 206, 227, 241, 244, 245,
252, 257–58, 289, 292–93,
295–96, 304, 311

Frontera / Fronteira, 19, 154, 295,
307, 317

Galbreath, Paul, ix, 73, 109, 245,
252–53, 289, 310, 312

Garrigan, Siobhán, ix, 9, 142, 144,
149–50, 281, 312

Gate, 15, 50, 87, 98, 117–19, 135,
149, 167, 177, 221, 239, 249,
271, 307, 312

Gebara, Ivone, 219, 241, 312

Gestures, 14, 17, 32–34, 38, 43,
57–58, 61, 63, 67, 69–70,
73–74, 77, 101–2, 112, 120,
124–25, 127–28, 131–34,
138, 156–57, 164, 169, 172,
193–94, 200–201, 214, 220,
225–226, 234–236, 245, 251,
256, 258, 260, 269–72, 274,
292, 298

Global / Globalization / Globalized, 3–5, 8–9, 12, 14–34, 61, 161, 179, 204, 225, 245, 247, 250, 264–65, 274, 279, 283, 286–87, 292, 308, 311, 314, 316–18

Gomez-Pena, Guillermo, 22, 261, 267, 275–76, 313

Grace 78, 81–82, 89, 100–101, 102–7, 116–17, 120–22, 128, 136–37, 200, 224, 236, 287, 289, 296, 303, 313

Greco-Roman, 13, 35–77, 124, 234, 248

Grimes, Ronald, 272–75, 277, 285, 313

Guests, 8, 15–16, 18–19, 23–24, 26–27, 38–39, 42–45, 48, 50, 53–55, 58, 66–67, 70, 73, 93, 95, 124, 133–34, 138, 152, 154, 191–93, 216–17, 224, 226, 242, 257, 259, 262, 275, 280, 295, 297–99

Gutierrez, Gustavo, 174, 176, 199, 313

Haight, Roger, ix, 85, 87, 110, 113, 313

Heal / Healing, 5–6, 11, 31, 53–54, 82, 125, 131, 157, 161, 172, 175, 206, 211, 213–14, 216, 223–24, 237–39, 245, 260, 271–72, 280, 286, 291, 302

Hierarchy, 23, 36, 49, 141, 146, 149, 156, 167, 176–78, 181–82, 184–85, 188, 210–11, 233, 270, 272, 276, 282

Holanda, Sérgio Buarque de, 192–93, 208, 309

Holy Kiss, 234–36

Holy Spirit, 1, 8, 12, 29, 90, 101–4, 107, 118, 120–22, 129, 132, 134–37, 139, 181, 184–185, 222–27, 232, 235, 245, 251–53, 256–57, 259–60, 269, 271–72, 278, 287, 290

Host / Hostility / Hostage, 2, 23–24, 26–27, 39, 43–45, 47–48, 52–55, 58, 67, 70, 82, 94, 97, 99, 102–3, 112, 124, 129, 133–34, 152, 167, 190, 192–93, 267, 298–99, 311, 315

House, 5, 11, 15–16, 18, 24–25, 27, 39, 45, 48, 52, 55, 67, 79, 130, 139–40, 143, 155, 181, 190, 196–97, 205, 210, 212, 215–16, 224, 231, 252, 288, 297, 299, 302–3, 319

Identity, 7, 17, 19, 22, 26, 31–32, 37, 40–42, 47, 51, 67, 74–76, 92, 119, 121, 133, 143, 149, 168, 189, 207, 213, 225, 228, 241, 275–76, 287, 289–90, 299, 301, 308–9, 311, 313, 318

Imagination / Reimagination, 2, 5, 19, 26–27, 48, 52, 68, 74–77, 110, 112, 114, 116, 133–34, 140, 146–49, 155–58, 173, 238, 241, 259, 283, 296, 307, 310, 318–19

Immigrant / Immigration, ix, 3, 6, 11 12, 16–18, 23–24, 29, 92, 100, 129, 131, 138, 155, 161, 163, 168–69, 189–90, 225, 245–47, 250, 258, 261–62, 264, 273, 280, 282, 284, 291–92, 295, 298–99, 301, 309, 319–20

Impossible / Impossibility, 3, 7, 26, 28–30, 32, 69, 74, 113, 137, 159–60, 237, 240–41, 248, 274–75, 280, 293, 295, 300

Incarnation, 7, 12, 18, 24, 66, 89, 91–92, 95, 102, 115–16, 118, 122, 126, 133–34, 159, 172, 199, 224, 264, 267, 270, 287, 304, 318

Inter-religious, 14, 202, 204–6,
  218–20, 234, 236, 240, 249,
  279, 284, 301, 304
Interrupts / Interrupting /
  Interrupted, 44, 134, 206,
  224, 276, 282
Irarrázaval, Diego, 220, 313
Itinerary, 236–38, 241

Joy / Happiness, 37–40, 42–43, 46,
  67, 94, 129, 134, 136–38,
  146, 151, 170–71, 175,
  188–89, 192, 196–97, 199,
  202, 206–7, 213, 217, 233,
  249, 260, 270, 302, 320
Just / Justice, 1, 2, 5–8, 11, 14–15,
  17, 20, 23, 26, 29–30, 35,
  37, 43, 48–49, 55, 58, 61,
  65, 75–76, 80, 91–92, 125,
  129–32, 134, 138, 143, 148,
  150, 157–64, 174, 177–80,
  182, 184, 188, 193, 197,
  199, 201, 203–5, 211, 219,
  222, 224–25, 228, 234, 243,
  245–47, 256–57, 260–62,
  264–66, 268, 270, 278, 280,
  284, 286, 289–91, 293, 301,
  304, 307, 310, 315, 318–19
Juxtaposition, 142, 150, 155–58,
  164, 283, 292

Kavanagh, Aidan, 143–44, 314
King, Jr., Martin Luther, 160
Kitchen, 72, 132, 135, 214, 216, 268
Klinghardt, Matthias, 37, 44, 314
Koinonia, 37–38, 40, 42, 47, 67, 69,
  72, 258, 273
Kristeva, Julia, 271, 299–300, 302,
  314

Labor, 90, 128, 143–44, 151, 163,
  171, 179, 225, 261–62, 318,
  320

Land, 1, 4–5, 19, 80, 135, 164, 166,
  191, 221, 243–45, 291, 301–3
Landless Movement, 4, 23, 160,
  202, 219, 279
Language, 17, 20–21, 26, 28, 63,
  80, 105, 122–23, 126, 131,
  133–34, 155, 157, 160, 163,
  169, 191, 254–55, 263–64,
  267–68, 294, 303–5, 315
Latin America, 2, 14, 64, 166–202,
  218–22, 249, 262, 269, 282,
  284, 307, 316
Law, 3, 5, 17, 24–32, 35, 45, 53,
  82, 92, 94, 96, 113, 119,
  124, 134, 142–44, 147, 155,
  160–61, 163, 177–78, 181,
  190, 206, 209, 211, 220, 276,
  295–96, 298, 301, 308–9,
  312, 318
Lex Orandi/Credendi/Agendi,
  142–45, 155, 220
Liberation, 13–14, 170, 187
Liberation Theology/Theologians,
  10, 14, 64, 153, 166–67,
  171–76, 178, 180–81, 189,
  199, 218–20, 222, 307–8,
  313, 316, 318
Limits, 4–5, 9, 15–17, 21, 24,
  27–28, 30, 40, 45, 52, 58, 70,
  73–75, 80, 83–84, 86, 94–96,
  116–17, 122, 128, 137, 142,
  146, 149, 153, 162–63, 169,
  179, 182, 195, 207, 221, 228,
  238, 247, 281, 285, 295–97,
  301, 303, 315
Lispector, Clarice, 199, 305, 315
Liturgical actions, 11, 28, 52, 59,
  68–70, 171, 250, 257, 289,
  303
Location, 14, 39–40, 50, 52, 62,
  107, 137, 160, 162, 197, 201,
  212, 225, 246, 269, 304, 308
Love, ix, 1, 2, 12, 16, 25, 31–32, 44,
  66–67, 104, 109, 113,

Love (*cont.*)
    117, 120, 129–32, 134–36,
    138, 155, 157, 170, 182–83,
    190, 199, 218–21, 223–24,
    227, 229, 234–35, 237–38,
    240–41, 245, 249, 253, 258,
    260, 264, 267, 274, 280, 286,
    291–93, 301, 304–5, 309
Luther, Martin, 96, 109

Map / Unmapped, 12, 33, 80,
    135–36, 170–71, 301–2
Maraschin, Jaci C., ix, 227, 264–65,
    283, 315
Marx/Marxist, 173–74, 179,
    182–84, 266, 308, 311, 318
Material/materiality, 33, 35–36,
    55, 65–66, 91, 95, 97, 101,
    103–4, 107, 110–12, 115–16,
    124–25, 133, 145, 157, 173,
    175, 179, 186, 195, 199, 209,
    211, 213, 246, 251, 258, 273,
    275
Memory, 27, 53, 80, 146, 158, 163,
    195, 208, 211–12, 216–17,
    223, 229, 232, 239, 245, 259,
    260, 270, 278, 300, 302, 304,
    316–17
Moore-Keish, Martha L., ix, 105,
    116, 248, 315
Multiple / Multiplicity /
    Multicentric, 6, 12, 13, 33,
    53, 62, 72, 95, 112, 147, 151,
    154, 156, 158, 162, 212,
    217–19, 222, 241, 251, 254,
    256–58, 260, 264, 267, 275,
    279, 282–83, 296, 301, 303,
    307–8, 314

Nancy, Jean Luc, 14, 223
Negotiation/Negotiating, 6, 8, 12–
    13, 17, 32, 34, 45, 47–48, 50,
    54–58, 65, 68, 75–77, 89, 99,
    140, 142, 145, 156, 159–65,
    193, 199, 229, 233–234, 245,
    248–50, 265, 281–83, 289,
    293–97, 299, 304, 318
Neighbor, 5, 8, 16, 29, 31, 43, 54,
    104, 120, 125, 128–31, 172,
    225, 227, 229, 259, 261, 274,
    287–89, 291, 304
Nomads/nomadic, 276, 300, 302–3,
    305, 309
Non-documented /
    Undocumented, ix, 6, 12,
    16, 18, 92, 163, 250, 261–62,
    269, 271, 273, 295, 298–99,
    311

Oikos, 5–6, 8, 303
Onkotô, 34, 294–95, 299–305
Oppression, 1, 2, 32, 152–53, 157,
    164, 174, 180, 194, 212, 245,
    262, 266–67, 270–71, 277,
    281–83, 301, 304
Ordo, 12, 59, 123–24, 127, 130–31,
    148, 163, 169, 250–51, 260,
    185, 314
Orixás, 203–41

Pentecostal, 8, 87, 100, 175, 193,
    226, 230, 304
Performance / Performing /
    Performative, 6, 17, 32–34,
    37, 58, 61, 65, 67, 75–76,
    112, 115, 117, 126, 131, 134,
    146, 149, 151–52, 157, 167,
    170–71, 186–88, 191, 214,
    220, 240, 242, 247, 259–60,
    267–71, 275–77, 283–84,
    293–94, 299–302, 308–9,
    317
Phagocytosis, 240
Pluralism, 206, 218–20, 222, 241,
    307, 312, 319
Polidoxy, 13, 156, 162, 264, 296
Possibility, 21, 29, 57, 73, 81, 91,
    102, 113, 123, 136–37, 159,
    167, 195, 204, 210, 221, 225,

Possibility (*cont.*)
229–30, 248–49, 256–57,
259, 286, 303
Praxis, 14, 143–44, 149–50, 152,
173–74, 204, 206, 217–19,
221, 223, 234, 236, 240, 245,
249, 267
Prayer, 1, 4, 14, 21, 30, 38, 52,
60–61, 73, 79, 87, 94, 107,
109–10, 122, 137–38, 144,
150, 154–55, 202, 204,
216, 220, 224, 226–27, 234,
238–39, 244, 246, 254–56,
258–60, 264–65, 272, 274,
279–80, 286–87, 291, 300,
302–4, 317
Presbyterian Church(es), 7, 12, 65,
79, 92–94, 100, 120–21, 123,
125, 128–29, 132, 134, 163,
224, 237, 247–48, 250, 253,
268, 287, 289, 298–99, 309,
316
Proper, 6, 11, 17, 23, 27, 29–30, 40,
45–49, 53, 59, 63, 65, 69–70,
72–75, 80, 82–84, 88, 92–93,
96, 101, 104–6, 113–14,
119–23, 130, 135–39, 143,
146, 149, 153, 155, 158,
167–70, 199–201, 210, 214,
216, 231–32, 241, 248–49,
254–56, 258, 263, 286, 289,
292, 297–99, 302

Racism, 64, 145, 157, 175, 200,
205–6, 208, 229, 239–40,
249, 296, 310
Radical Hospitality, 6, 27, 34, 65,
132, 134, 192, 199, 219, 223,
240, 247, 272, 274
Real Presence, ix, 66, 74, 96, 98,
102, 116, 154, 258, 308
Reformed Church(es), 68, 70–71,
73, 76, 84, 154, 247, 253,
256, 260, 269, 272–73, 275,
284, 290, 303, 313, 319–20

Reformed Tradition, 36, 78, 87,
120, 122, 134, 232, 237, 247,
255–56, 289, 309, 315
Remembrance, 101, 105, 116, 172,
187, 230, 248, 255, 287, 290,
315
Resistance, 1–2, 4, 29, 33, 75–76,
116, 152, 157, 172, 180, 208,
212, 217, 232, 239, 265, 270,
285, 297, 301
Rhizomic, 162
Ritualization, 41, 43, 61, 82, 98,
116, 225, 236, 240, 250,
272–74, 278–79, 281,
283–85, 287, 297
Ritualizing, 76, 225, 240, 250, 272–
75, 277–79, 281, 283–85,
290, 299, 301, 304, 313
Romero, Oscar, 1, 2, 30, 317
Ross, Susan, 147, 153, 158, 163, 317

Saliers, Don, 7, 13, 317
Salvation, 14, 32, 82, 98–99, 105,
107, 130, 196, 220–21, 265,
313
Sanctuary Movement, 24, 161, 310,
315, 319
Sex / Sexuality(ies), 4, 6, 29, 38,
49–50, 67–70, 75, 145, 157,
163, 172, 175, 200–201, 216,
261, 270–71, 276, 283, 307,
311, 316
Share / Sharing, 4, 8, 21–22,
30–31, 39, 41–43, 46, 48,
55, 57–58, 63, 66, 72–73,
88, 100, 111–13, 116–17,
122, 124, 127–28, 132, 146,
148, 150–51, 153, 157, 159,
161, 169, 181–82, 186–87,
196, 198, 206, 213, 216–19,
223–24, 227, 229–30, 232–
36, 238–41, 245, 249–50,
254, 259–60, 264, 271–74,
279, 281, 283, 287, 296, 298,
301–304, 308, 314

Sisyphus / Sisyphean, 31, 33, 245, 275, 284, 287, 299, 301, 303

Slave / Slavery, 45, 49, 163, 204, 206–8, 212–13, 215, 224, 260–62, 320

Smith, Dennis E., 36–37, 61, 318

Solidarity, 1, 2, 8, 14, 32, 64, 85, 128, 131, 146, 154, 157, 163–64, 182, 199, 212, 217, 247, 260, 264, 271, 281, 283, 287, 291

Spivak, Gayatry Chakravorty, 163–64, 311, 318

Stories, 11–14, 21, 31, 34, 51, 57, 67, 72–73, 133, 141, 145–46, 148, 151–52, 156, 187, 189, 201, 210–11, 230, 233, 250, 258–59, 270–72, 274, 280, 282–83, 290, 298, 311

Stranger, 16, 21–22, 25–28, 32, 34, 47–48, 53, 70–71, 73, 119, 125, 131–32, 140, 161, 191, 199, 204, 223–24, 271, 275, 292, 298–99, 305, 307, 314

Struggle, 1, 2, 5, 29, 58, 75, 82, 84, 161, 164, 172–75, 178–79, 182–85, 208–9, 211, 221, 225–26, 240, 266–67, 270, 278, 282, 290–91

Sursum Corda, 94, 103

Symbiosis, 221, 240

Symbol / Symbolic, 5, 17, 19, 31, 40–41, 45–46, 53, 57, 59, 61, 66–67, 82–83, 87, 89, 91–92, 102–3, 109, 111–12, 118, 122, 126, 130, 138, 147, 150, 155–57, 171, 183, 186, 194, 197–99, 201, 220–21, 224, 231, 246, 261, 265, 274–75, 279, 281, 286, 310–12

Taft, Robert, 255–58

Taussig, Hal, 35, 37, 39–41, 49, 51–52, 55–57, 59–62, 64, 66–68, 70, 74–76, 164, 171, 198, 251, 256–57, 284, 318

Taylor, Mark C., 80–81, 83, 89, 91, 99, 120, 169, 319

Terreiro(s), 87–88, 205–6, 209, 212–16, 222–23, 231, 237

Territory, 138, 171, 276, 302, 317

Thanksgiving, ix, x, 9, 97, 131, 239, 254, 259, 271, 279, 291

Theologies of religious pluralism, 206, 219–20

Transformation, 3–4, 18, 68, 75, 82–83, 103, 120, 162, 175, 180, 184, 208, 224, 227, 233, 245, 248, 277–78, 291, 300, 310

Transgression, 32

Trinh, T. Minh-Ha, 161–62, 164–65, 261, 319

Unconditional/ unconditionality, 13, 23–29, 31–32, 130, 295, 297, 304

Unexpected, 8, 15, 22, 26–28, 39, 44–45, 50, 55, 70, 73, 139, 156, 196, 226, 246, 257, 292, 301–2

Values, 37, 40–42, 46, 58, 69, 149, 168, 251, 260, 281

Verger, Pierre, 210

Vigil, José M., 190, 218, 220, 307, 312, 319

Vocabulary, 9, 74, 97, 133, 204

Wall, 18, 21, 75, 95–96, 132, 148–49, 161–62, 175, 224, 238, 246, 261, 288, 291, 319

Walton, Janet R., 141, 145, 147–49, 155–60, 225, 283, 310, 317

Wandel, Lee Palmer, 78, 80, 98, 101, 112, 115, 119, 320

Welcome, 192, 204, 208, 212, 219, 224, 226, 229, 238, 240–41,

Welcome (*cont.*)
  262–63, 272, 276, 291, 295,
  298, 302, 320
Widening, 145, 158, 271
Wine, 1, 2, 7, 9–10, 39, 42, 45–46,
  49, 57, 60–61, 63–64, 68–70,
  72–73, 82, 93–94, 96–98,
  101, 104, 109–12, 116, 124,
  126–27, 130, 132, 139, 187,
  196, 231, 233, 239, 244–45,
  257, 260, 262, 270, 272, 279,
  203, 304

Womanist, 154, 307, 316, 319
Words of Institution, 71, 73, 93, 97,
  135–37, 139, 227, 250–56,
  259, 272
Worship practices, 36, 51, 57,
  142–43, 146

Yorubá, 203–4, 209–10, 219–22,
  225–26, 233, 238–41

Lightning Source UK Ltd.
Milton Keynes UK
UKHW020737060322
399626UK00005B/454